The Post-Modern Reader

Ron Arad, *Distressed Concrete Record Player and Speakers*, 1983. © Charles Jencks.

READER

The Post-Modern Reader

Edited by Charles Jencks
with Eva Branscome and Léa-Catherine Szacka

(Second Edition)

WILEY

A John Wiley and Sons Ltd, Publication

Dedicated to the Loyal Opposition Everywhere

Executive Commissioning Editor: Helen Castle
Project Editor: Miriam Swift
Assistant Editor: Calver Lezama

ISBN   978-0-470-74867-1 (hb)
       978-0-470-74866-4 (pb)

Designed by Artmedia, London
Printed and bound in Great Britain by TJ International, Ltd, Padstow, Cornwall, an ISO14001 Environmental Management System Accredited Company, using vegetable-based ink and FSC paper

Front cover image © Charles Jencks

Editorial Note on Presentation and Editing of Texts

This anthology aims to be inclusive, therefore some texts must appear in abbreviated form in the course of presenting others in their entirety. Some texts have been edited to shorten them, to exclude references that require more space for a full explanation and to preserve the flow of argument. Information for the sources of edited and complete texts is given in the copyright line after each text. The term 'From' preceding a copyright line signifies that a specific extract or extracts has been taken from a longer text. Otherwise texts are given in their entirety or edited to indicate the argument of the whole.

Texts have been clearly marked to show where they have been edited. The following conventions have been used throughout: Suspended points '…' are used to denote the omission of words or phrases within a sentence. Suspended points within a square bracket […] are used to denote omissions extending from a complete sentence to a paragraph. Three asterisks * * * mark omissions of more than one paragraph, and may denote exclusion of a complete subdivision of the original text. A paragraph may end […] if the last sentences of that paragraph are omitted or if the following paragraph is omitted. A paragraph may also start with […] if one or more sentences at the beginning of that paragraph have been omitted or if a previous paragraph has been omitted. Typographical errors and errors of transcription have been corrected when discovered in the anthologised texts. Otherwise idiosyncrasies of spelling or punctuation remain unchanged. For titles and text, each author's choice of spelling for the word Post-Modern has been respected.

Notes and references have been included only where judged to be necessary to the text as printed. In some cases text notes have been renumbered for this edition, in which case a note to this effect is given after the copyright.

Contents

Preface
Post-Modernism – the Ism that Returns

Charles Jencks

Most Isms become Wasms and, it is the argument of this anthology, Post-Modernism is one of the few that did not. During the late 1970s it spread throughout culture and the arts with such self-styled movements as Post-Modern Dance, or disciplines such as Post-Modern geography. The usual age of a movement in the arts and thought is from two to 10 years; Vorticism two, Surrealism (as a creative movement) 10. The general temper of an age, Romanticism, can continue longer and become a transhistorical concept, or what is sometimes called the colouration of a period. So it is with post-modernism.

The height of fashion by 1980, Po-Mo suffered the fate of all fashions by the 1990s when a generalised neo-modernism struck back, at least in architecture. Fashion, consumer culture and today the web devour movements and those few Isms that live longer, such as Modernism, spread as deeply as they do widely. They become conditions of society (such as modernity), ideas underpinning the economy (such as Adam Smith's hidden hand) and technological change (such as Henry Ford's version of mass-production). Equally, post-modernism is part of the deep sea change of post-industrialisation and a future that Marshall McLuhan predicted in the 1960s, the global village, instantly tied together by electronic communication.

'Sea change' is an ancient metaphor tied to the idea that historical movements flow over time, and used as often to describe transformation as other images of flow: tidal waves and oceanic currents. According to this model, Modernism is the deepest and widest Nile flowing strongly, if intermittently, since at least the Renaissance. At that point the nation state emerged, and with it a host of new institutions and positive phrases such as *moderna*. Post-Modernism, in this picture, becomes part of the long Modern watercourse, an important stream which also meanders and cuts deeply but is still a branch of the larger river. Maybe it is a tributary or a significant part of the recent delta, along with Late-Modernism. In any case, considered as waves of time, and they both are time-obsessed words; Modernism is a long wave (500 years) and Post-Modernism a medium wave (50 years).

Why has post-modernism spread into every field from religion to science, from literature to music, to define its transhistorical identity? That is a question which many of the contributors to this volume address, and provide a clue. One linguistic answer turns on the paradox that the phrase chose us; it spoke us rather than was imposed from above by some universal academy in charge of language. The word has a hidden logic that competing terms lack. Its great strength and why it may be around for another hundred years – as long as modernism rules – is that it is both precise and suggestive. It clearly marks the port we have left, the inadequate worldview of modernism, but only hints at where we are going. This curious mixture explains why most people will spontaneously adopt it, as if for the first time, to overcome the era and worldview they wish to transcend. As a richly evocative phrase about the present tense plus the next move it is hard to beat.

Today I would prefer the designation Critical Modernism, because this captures one of its most dynamic tendencies. Other writers, including Nicolas Borriaud, and the Tate in Britain have proffered Altermodern. In a three-month Tate Triennial of 2009 dedicated to that alternative polemic, while 'the death of postmodernism' was announced the argument was made quite convincingly for an identifiable global movement. The problem, however, was that most of the displays took post-modern themes only an inch or two forward ('creolisation' after 'multiculturalism'), and the term was just as easily assimilated into its progenitor. Words are cannibalistic; they eat up competitors and conserve meanings in a kind of linguistic Darwinism. Since Post-Modernism effectively has taken out the patent on movements that are post-the-present it will not be easily supplanted. Those who want an umbrella term with which to challenge the reigning Modernism can cycle through the synonyms, but whether these will take hold is another thing.

The preservative nature of language partly explains today's return of post-modern into contemporary usage, a restoration after being unfashionable in the 1990s. Another explanation is the new generation who are again asking questions about the hegemony of modernism and what comes next. In architecture, the young are returning to a different kind of post-modernism, a new version of ornament created by computer production, another type of complexity and a radical form of communication. This discernible movement has gone on since at least the year 2000, and the flowering of the iconic building and Digital Baroque. Similar movements in the other arts, and a general appreciation of the medium wave of post-modernism are leading to some large surveys, among them the one at the Victoria and Albert Museum in London, 2011.

But in one way the situation is less clear today than 30 years ago. Now with post-modernism disseminated so widely as a set of ideas and practices, and with the de-definition of modernism into mass culture, distinctions have become blurred. Indeed, crossover is the rule. The resultant anomaly can be that some of today's best post-modernism is produced by modernists discovering, for the first time, how enjoyable it is to breed outside the parent stock. The hybrid Post-, with its hyphen, is what I have termed in my essay below a deepening of both traditions. The rivers, to revert to metaphor, are together cutting deeper.

The book to hand is itself a mixture of past and present essays, among the latter those by Felipe Fernández-Armesto, John Gray and Anatole Kaletsky. Also new to this anthology are essays by Jane Jacobs, Robert Venturi, Ihab Hassan, Zygmunt Bauman and myself. Some of the other writings were published in a collection, *The Post-Modern*

Reader, which I edited in 1992. As before I am indebted to many collaborators and writers in the field of post-modernism, first among them the friends and colleagues who took part in the many Portrack Seminars we held in Scotland, Los Angeles and London since the late 1980s. Charlene Spretnak, David Ray Griffin and Richard Falk helped organise these three day meetings where we hammered out a shared type of Restructive Post-Modernism. Even before our meeting we had long considered this, not Deconstruction, the way forward.

I am also beholden to Helen Castle for suggesting and overseeing this volume as well as Calver Lezama and Miriam Swift at John Wiley & Sons for their work producing this book. Particularly enjoyable to work with have been my co-selectors, Eva Branscome and Léa-Catherine Szacka. Both scholars investigating the late 1970s and early 1980s, and the 1980 Venice Biennale of Architecture, they are revealing post-modern threads that have received too little attention, among which is the primary motive of increased communication. Eva and Léa-Catherine have re-edited the selections and written the concise summaries that precede them. These introductions point out the relevance of the essays, and highlight and cross-reference common themes. For the most part this anthology favours my view that Post-Modernism is a continuation of Modernism and its transcendence, neither a deconstructive nor anti-modern tradition. Hence its hybrid nature, its double-coding, its deepening of Modernism.

Like most anthologies, *The Post-Modern Reader* is a radical selection from a voluminous literature and can be read in various ways, or simply dipped into, since each article is semi-autonomous. However, the three parts follow a logic. Part 1, Defining the Post-Modern, sets up the historical context and debate with Modernism. Since most of the early discussion occurred within two disciplines, literature and architecture, these become the major subjects of Part 2. As I have mentioned, post-modernism has spread as a concept and practice into every field and a small selection of these areas occupies Part 3: sociology, economics, feminism and science. It would be tendentious to argue that these areas exist as neatly defined categories. For instance, while it makes sense to say that ecological Post-Modernism is an important part of the widespread movement, and that modernist economic success has brought on the several crises facing the globe, it is also true that there are some ecological movements that are traditionally oriented and, by contrast, modernist. An obvious case of these types is the movement around Prince Charles, and that concerned with geo-engineering: the former is urban and traditional while the latter imagines the way to cope is by sending up gigantic reflectors, or by creating artificial volcanoes that manipulate the atmosphere. Neither is post-modern. Ecology, like any growing and vital discipline, has more than one head.

A warning about the various spellings of Post-Modern. All the authors have their preference respected but I have followed a general pattern that is often adopted. The capital-lettered and hyphenated phrase is used to refer to the conscious cultural movement; the lower case to the general social condition of post-modernity. The hyphenated usage also suggests the hybrid nature of the movement which is why I prefer it to the streamlined or elided postmodernism. To avoid nomenclature fatigue, a real possibility in a book of this type, several shorthands are used – PM or pm for the movement versus the condition, and Po-Mo for the pastiche or commercial version. Probably in a modern era, when the word pastiche is used as a synonym for degraded or kitsch, it is necessary to say that, like the Shakespearean and Mozartian variety, when adopted with skill pastiche can be a superior genre.

The Victoria and Albert exhibit on Postmodernism, curated by Jane Pavitt and running from October 2011 to January 2012, focuses on a limited time span and space, as exhibitions must: mostly the 1980s. This was the decade of its popularity and then the reaction against it. But it is also true to say that the themes and styles that characterised the larger movement, since the 1960s, are being transformed today whether or not they get the PM label. Like Modernism, and the proverbial king, it is a question of being both dead and, at the same time, very much long-lived.

Charles Jencks, October 2009. © 2010 John Wiley & Sons Ltd.

PART 1 Defining the Post-Modern

What Then Is Post-Modernism?

Charles Jencks

How ironic to ask this question after so many years, as if there were a clear answer. And the quandary has only deepened in the meantime, since a generation has grown up, untrained in the old doctrines. The young now double the question –'Well then old man, what was Modernism?' How could you possibly explain these terms to someone who had no knowledge of recent global history, an infant or a digital surfer of the depthless present?

Responding to this challenge near the outset of debate in 1982, the exasperated French philosopher Jean-François Lyotard wrote *The Postmodern Explained to Children*, but far from settling the matter the children only increased the dispute. The classification of an age is always controversial. Imagine telling a young British architect just starting out that he is going to live in the Age of King Charles (which is probably the case, but trivial). In the anthology to hand you will find many attempts to crack the big conundrum of our time – how should our period be classified? Or who are we? Or where are we going? Before we address these portentous but pressing questions, in conclusion, and pull out the threads that tie Modernism and Post-Modernism together in a significant way, let us pause to survey the riotous scene with detachment, defining both monikers together as is usually done, and with irony. After all, anything as serious as identity must be taken lightly.

Contrasting the Modern and Post-Modern

Consider various walks of life. For contemporary historians, such as the diplomat Robert Cooper, the strong American state in its policeman role is very modern, whereas the conglomerate EU, which acts through the soft power of law, is post-modern.[1] Economists usually see the most successful modern corporation as General Motors, especially now that it is failing; while consumers are finding Amazon to be typically post-modern.[2] Or, the customary opposition that Robin Murray makes between Fordism and Post-Fordism: the sluggish leviathan and the fast-changing, computerised company of less than 50 people that interacts with it (see Part 3). Indeed, the huge sprawling factory was where most modern production took place, and because office work characterised the post-industrial nation by the 1960s, sociologists often put the post-modern shift at this point.

Today, with the information world and Google, this post-modernisation has gone into an extended network in everyone's PC, an ill-defined area. That digital no-place of electronic heaven is rather a pm virtual space, one to be contrasted with its very material predecessors of the factory and the bank. Moreover, if materialism was *the* major philosophy of Modernism this leads to a curious observation. It means that the very pm Madonna famously mis-sung herself in 1985, as 'I'm a Material Girl'. Yes, of course, she is materialistic but her constant change of persona, her use of multiple media and even her name brand her as quintessential Po-Mo.

Consider those new-old words defining the major economic system of the recent past. The neologisms 'capitalism and socialism' were modern when they were first used in 1810, but today the hybrid 'socitalism' of the advanced economies could be called post-modern. Even with their regulation-lite, the G20 governments control about 40 per cent of their economies, and their deficit spending on armaments amounts to a kind of guaranteed social expenditure. Today's socitalism is not quite the goal that the Modernist Karl Marx had in mind for his utopia, and its unsavoury mixture needs to be consumed with a strong dose of PM sarcasm.

Let us follow this last point into hybrid foods. If the pure Camembert cheese is modern, then the mixed Cambozola is post-modern and the recent crossbreed Camelbert (like Brie but from camel milk) is very pm. Or, switch to the horrors of the political landscape, return to the philosopher Jean-François Lyotard and his fundamental definition.[3] This turns on the archetypal killing factory of Modernism, Auschwitz. That death camp was so successful in its rationalisation and mass-production that, Lyotard argues, it ushered in its opposite, postmodernism (he writes it streamlined). But then, if there is a recent media counterpart of this catastrophe, it might be George Bush's bombing of Baghdad on night-time TV, 'Shock & Awe'. Branded terrorism could be considered a post-modern form of pre-announced murder.

Shift to everyday attitudes and behaviour. It is no doubt a cliché to say so, but straightforwardness, transparency and honest simplicity have been valued among the modern virtues, from the boy scouts to the Bauhaus; while irony and ambiguity characterise Post-Modern architecture and literature. Umberto Eco gave one of the most famous definitions of the latter in his *Postscript to the Name of the Rose*, excerpted below. Because it is canonical, and brings up in a striking way a general truth about our age, I quote it at some length:

> I think of the postmodern attitude as that of a man who loves a very cultivated woman and knows he cannot say to her, 'I love you madly', because he knows that she knows (and that she knows that he knows) that these words have already been written by Barbara Cartland. Still there is a solution. He can say, 'As Barbara Cartland would put it, I love you madly'. At this point, having avoided false innocence, having said clearly that it is no longer possible to speak innocently, he will nevertheless have said what he wanted to say to the woman: that he loves her; but he loves her in an age of lost innocence.[4]

The Age of Lost Innocence is a pertinent classifier for our time especially because it speaks to the age of branding where politicians and media routinely spin the truth. More importantly, it stems from an insight into the most dominating of all discourses, that is, language. Since language – speech and writing – is the slowest changing and most imperial of all sign systems, even more conservative than architecture, it has to confront the problem of lost innocence every day, the perplexity of how to handle 'the already said'. How can one speak anew and with authenticity using old words and hackneyed expressions? One solution is Eco's advice to his sophisticated lovers. Irony, with quotation marks that bring it to consciousness, thus surround pm love letters, or literature, or what Linda Hutcheon and others call 'metafiction', (see Part 2). Post-modern literature and architecture confront a truth which many of the more abstract arts joyfully disregard: the way understanding and meaning must depend on a negotiation between the past, present and future. Like DNA, which has an almost four billion year history, this post-modernism is about time-binding, a theme to which I will return.

After this breathless survey let us take stock of the post-modern landscape, so far. The first ambiguity is the spelling of the label. It varies from the cultural *movement* (capitalised) to the social and economic *condition* (lower case), from the abbreviated PM to the sarcastic even dismissive Po-Mo (usually applied to pastiche works), from the hyphenated (meaning hybrid pluralism) to the streamlined (meaning integrated). Second, the list of contrasts suggests my argument. Post-Modernism is not a total break with Modernism, but rather its *combination with other things*, a slide away from its parent rather than an act of patricide, a sometime loyal opposition rather than an anti-modern movement. Above all, it is a deepening of Modernism. Thus, to typify the present age one could put an 'and' between the two terms of the following list because, I am claiming, they are interdependent and today mutually defining:

Modern	And	Post-Modern
American nation hard power		EU conglomerate soft power
General Motors Corp		Amazon and Post-Fordism
Factory production		Tertiary + production
Materialism		Information world
Holocaust		Shock & Awe
Capitalism/socialism		Socitalism
Straightforwardness		Ironic self-referencing
Innocence		Lost innocence
Present tense		Time-binding

From this beginning list another thing is clear: to support or condemn either movement or condition *en bloc* is not helpful. When both are here to stay we need to hack out a critical path through their respective snags.

Let us continue the *tour d'horizon* into the arts, considering some epigones from each movement. No one disputes that Piet Mondrian, Mies van der Rohe and Minimalism were the epitome of the modern movement; but, less clearly, in a sort of muddy pm way, Mark Tansay, Frank Gehry and Radical Eclecticism are Post-Modern.

One trouble with such clear distinctions is that, for instance, early Mondrian and Mies were steeped in a kind of Expressionism. Before they reduced art and architecture to abstraction, to their virtuous 'almost nothing', their work was brooding with a dark spirituality, a harbinger of the post-modern cosmic. This brings us to another truth of changing paradigms. There are some figures in the arts, such as Picasso and Le Corbusier,

Frank Gehry, Chiat/Day Building, Main Street, Santa Monica, 1985–91. An eclectic collage of styles to facilitate and communicate different functions of this ad agency. The binoculars relate to the Pop tradition of Los Angeles roadside architecture. Their curves also signal elegantly how one negotiates a car into the parking garage and the overall function of the agency: market research. A white boat shape, left, and the copper trees, right, also support other office and administration functions, and relate to the seaside and hillside nature nearby. This is an *architecture parlante*. © Charles Jencks.

who were clearly part of both movements. That is, like the protean creator Michelangelo who strode triumphantly from early to high Renaissance and then from Mannerism to Baroque completely oblivious to the terms, they straddle epochs and classifiers. Such creators laugh at human categories, as they skate on by.

Labels and period classifiers should never be taken too seriously it would appear; yet, our ironic historian answers, they often are. Reputations and careers hang by the thread of a prefix such as post-, whether it is Impressionism or another 'postie', and the minute historians decide to banish all talk of Roman or Gothic or, in politics, Whig and Tory, these terms are smuggled back in a series of disguised synonyms. Language, with its 'already said', again plays its conservative trick. Unconscious Modernist and Post-Modernist theories are just as powerful and insidious after their labels have been forgotten. Generals, without reflecting on received ideas, usually fight the last war; governments, following Keynes, bail out banks too big to fail; and parents, unaware they are carrying on the theories of Dr Spock, fail to be good disciplinarians.

Thus theories and practices of our time can be divided fruitfully into Modern and Post-Modern as long as the labels are taken with a pinch of irony. This is particularly true of the sciences. The modern sciences of simplicity are based on reduction, on analysing reality into atoms, molecules and the units of social organisation like neighbourhoods, functions and classes. By contrast, the post-modern sciences of complexity are based on emergence and feedback, synthesising parts into their interacting wholes, like weather patterns, the stock market and the human personality. The former sciences gave us atomic theory and determinism, the latter are bringing us nonlinear dynamics and a creative universe. Newton versus Prigogine, Adam Smith versus George Soros, mechanism versus organicism and materialism versus self-organising systems. So far so clear and helpful.

The amusing problem arises when we examine such things as the space between these theories, as in classical versus nuclear physics. The former are deterministic and the latter indeterministic. Since both theories work to a great degree of accuracy, in their realms of large and small size, physicists used to explain their schizophrenia with a joke. They use the classical theory on Monday, Wednesday and Friday reserving the other three workdays to quantum mechanics, and fuzziness.

Indeed, Fuzzy Logic is, with its 'sort-ofs' and kind-ofs', typically post-modern. Is a half-eaten apple still an apple? When does a sweater with holes become holes with fabric attached? Or, the notorious pm query of the philosopher Bruno Latour: what defines the pulsating, wobbling hole in the ozone layer; how big does the old hole have to get to become a real hole? Reality comes with *many more* states of 'more or less' than 'either/or' and so, the argument goes, reality is mostly post-modern. The same goes for Mother Nature (which many people take for reality).

Consider this contrast of views. Modern geometry is clearly defined, based on the classical solids and self-same in its repetitions; while the geometry of nature, or *most* of it, is fractal, crinkly, irregular, grainy and self-similar in pattern. The pm scientist and mathematician Benoît Mandelbrot wrote *The Fractal Geometry of Nature* in 1977 applying it successfully to clouds, coastlines, rocks, lightning and the stock market. Ever

Charles Jencks, *Fractal Terrace*. Two views of ultimate nature. To the left the Platonic notion, that the ultimate forms are regular solids; to the right, the recent fractal view of nature by Benoît Mandelbrot. The terrace metamorphoses from primary forms – the Cézanne and Le Corbusier view – to the more prevalent idea that nature is *mostly* made from self-similar elements. But since the underlying geometry seems to be both types the rectangles turn to squares and then morph to rhomboids, irregular forms and then scale down to fractals. Garden of Cosmic Speculation, Scotland 2001. © Charles Jencks.

since these convincing demonstrations and his dramatic contrasts between the past and present views of nature – the Platonic and the fractal view – I have been pondering this very fuzzy pm word 'most'. Could they be presented together as a continuum? I wondered, and then forced a marriage of the competing theories into a landscape called the Fractal Terrace. It morphs, from the clear rectangles and squares of Cézanne and Le Corbusier on one side, into the irregular rhomboids and fractals on the other. From self-sameness to self-similarity, from repetition to scaling, from Modern to Post-Modern, it shows a continuous meld. It also brings up some historical ambiguities.

The Battle of the Labels and the Demon of Time

Go way back in time since time is the great constructor. The word *modernus* was apparently coined sometime in the 3rd century by the Christians, to show their superiority over the pagans, and the term has carried a progressive impulse ever since, both technical and moral. 'I am cleaner than thou and, while your soul may be immortalised in stone in Rome, mine will be eternal in heaven.' Such one-upmanship we may doubt was ever put like this though, because of the meaning of *modernus*, it was possible. The modern, coming from the Latin *modo* signifying 'just now', had the major patent on the present tense.

It was logical that the Renaissance thereafter used it to contrast with the previous age of the Gothic. Hence the subsequent Battles of the Ancients and the Moderns, from the 1600s to the 1850s, when such terms were employed by philosophers, architects and Shakespeare, for insult or for praise.[5] Then, upping the ante, from 1875 to 1975 the many 'posties' arrived, from post-Impressionism to post-industrial to post-modern, and they all had 'posteriority' built into their logic. If one stops to think about this paradox – being 'post-present', that is being 'just now plus in the future' – one can tease out the devastating strength of the phrase, the way it captured the Zeitgeist. It suddenly rendered the up-to-dateness of the Modern obsolete, just as Modernists had lampooned the Ancients for three centuries. Oscar Wilde conveyed the ironies of time in the succession of modern-isms: 'Nothing is so dangerous as being too modern,' he pronounced in a famous epigram, 'one is apt to grow old-fashioned quite suddenly.' Or, another wit added later, after many art movements were killed off in the 1920s: 'all the Isms have become Wasms.' A melancholic truth of the Zeitgeist, 'the spirit of the time', the way fashion makes movements prematurely grey. Sometimes liberating, mostly fashion-time is a killer. The time-binding of Post-Modern culture tries to arrest this commercial obsolescing, the ideal is to slow it down by turning it into complex time.

The first use of 'post-modern' was as a throwaway challenge in 1875, and then a minor description of departures from within Modernism of Spanish poetry in 1934. Arnold Toynbee, in his 1947 *A Study of History*, used the term as an encompassing category to describe a new historical cycle starting in 1875.[6] This formulated the end of Western dominance, the decline of individualism, capitalism and Christianity, and the rise to power of non-Western cultures. In addition it referred in a positive way to a pluralism and world culture, meanings which are still essential to its definition today – part of the cumulative argument which is so important. But Toynbee was, on the whole, sceptical of the decline implicit in the prefix 'post' and it is interesting that this scepticism was shared by the literary critics Irving Howe and Harold Levine, who first used the term polemically. Their essentially *negative* description has stayed to haunt and, paradoxically, help the movement because of its paranoiac overtones, its suggestion of decline, of having arrived on the scene too late.[7] However, like many negative labels – Gothic, Baroque, Rococo, Impressionism and Fauve among many others – it soon became a badge of courage, a tactical insult to turn against the Modernists. And then their anger amplified PM into a media event and kept it in the public eye for 20 years. Just as 'Roundhead and Cavalier' flipped from derisory to praiseworthy, just as 'Whig and Tory' reversed their negative meaning and were taken into battle to create the two-party system, so the abusive slur became the empowering tribute.

Virtually the first *positive use* of the prefix 'post' was by the writer Leslie Fiedler in 1965, when he repeated it like an incantation and tied it to current radical trends which made up the counterculture: 'post-humanist, post-male, post-white, post-heroic … post-Jewish.' These anarchic and creative departures from orthodox liberalism represent the first stirrings of the cumulative tradition, although Fiedler and others in the 1960s were never to put the argument as the overarching concept of Post-Modernism.[8] One of their goals was to challenge the monoculture of Western dominance and reach a large and diverse audience, without becoming populist.

Yet, an explicit defence had to wait until the 1970s and the writings of Ihab Hassan, by which time the radical movements which Fiedler celebrated were somewhat out of fashion, the post-Isms turned to Wasms. Also, a problem of definition arose as Hassan tied the postmodern (he again streamlines the term) to the ideas of ultra-experimentalism in the arts and ultra-technology in architecture. His list of exemplars included William Burroughs and Buckminster Fuller and such key terms as 'Anarchy, Exhaustion/Silence … Decreation/Deconstruction/Antithesis … Inter-text …'[9] In effect, his canon defined the origins of *Deconstructive* Postmodernism, and that created a double movement with two heads. His departures were Modernist trends taken to an extreme by the agonistic wing of the avant-garde, and that is why I, with others such as the writer John Barth, would characterise them as *Late*-Modern, or *Ultra*-Modern, or *Most*-Modern – Mo-Mo not Po-Mo. John Cage was Hassan's exemplary postmodernist, a musician who took the 'almost nothing' of the minimalists to the next step of 'absolutely nothing' – total silence.

Post-Modernism as Double-Coding

Given such extremes it was predictable that a different Post-Modern culture emerged. As I've mentioned, it is written hyphenated to show its pluralism not streamlined like a rocket, and capitalised to signify a *cultural* movement and not a *condition* of the economy and society. The culture could be positive and reconstructive, the condition was a global economy not open to control. Architecture was the field that led the way in defining this reconstruction for several compelling reasons. Architects have to deal with pluralism, directly and widely differing taste-cultures, in the words of the sociologist Herbert Gans and his important analysis. Architects also have to deal with fast- and slow-changing technologies, with the virtues and vices of modernisation. Think of the Modernist injunction against ornament, and in favour of mass-production. Or, put the positive contrast the other way and contemplate how, by the 1970s, Post-Modernists criticised the boring repetition of mass-production and prophesied the coming variable computer production.

Such oppositions are *not* at work in art, music or poetry in any compelling way, and that is why I defined post-modern architecture, in 1975 and subsequently in many books, as essentially involved with pluralism and double-coding.[10]

Socially and semantically architecture has to mediate between the ephemeral tastes of fashion and, like language and genetics, the slow-moving codes of the past. In the 1970s the typical double-codes of hyphenated Post-Modernism were new/old, high art/low art, professional/common, elite/populist, abstract/iconic and Non-Modern/Modern. In a nutshell, PM was the contrast of Modernism *and* its Other.

This double-coding naturally produced the characteristic style which caught on, the juxtaposition of codes that underscored these oppositions, as they did with Umberto Eco's lovers. Since the rich, middle class and poor (to use Modernist class terms) have varying speeds of change, a single style or code will not be effective for complex, urban situations. These have to mediate different speeds, they have to bind various times together and, as sociologists began to show, urban villagers have a different time-frame from itinerant cosmopolites. Double-coding, or really multiple coding, is the necessity of much architecture. Modern projects that failed to perform within the various codes of the users were often blown up by dynamite, as they were in St Louis in 1972. This famous detonation led to my framing the Death of Modern Architecture (see Part 2), a surprise to many who did not realise that the Modern was not as the early Christians hoped, the Eternal. For many, including the historian John Summerson, this death was liberating. They could see, in the phrase of the Vatican cardinals longing for a new pope, 'where there's death there's hope'; or, the physicists' similar remark in 1900 against the stranglehold of tenure, 'physics proceeds death by death'. The 1970s was the decade of civic-minded explosions around the world, and they refuted Modern urbanism and architecture in a way that Modern music was never blown up, nor Modern poetry.

My own work, *The Language of Post-Modern Architecture* (1977), was the first book to thematise a post-modern movement and use the phrase in the title. Putting the disputatious moniker on the cover of a tome, coupled with the fact that the architectural movement had direction and a visible coherence, led people to say that I invented the term and concept, a claim that is true only in the sense that I theorised, popularised and made it the name of a book. But it was the architectural style, the clear double-coding, and the moral arguments of Jane Jacobs, Robert Venturi and a host of others fighting for a more just and complex urbanism who carried the day. The imperative for the hybrid language existed in architecture as it did not in most of the other arts. Inevitably it continues to today, with the iconic building and the various mixed languages that characterise some architecture, particularly the urban fragment. Time-binding, eclecticism and the impurity of signs are more natural to the public arts that must communicate to a wide audience, while abstraction can dominate large movements of painting, music and tone poetry.

above: James Stirling and Michael Wilford, Neue Staatsgalerie, Stuttgart, 1977–84. Multiple language games, mixture of new and old codes, pluralism – many post-modern values are realised here including much signalled irony. Stirling liked the comparison with Umberto Eco's definition of post-modernism saying it well represented his intentions. *left:* James Stirling surrounded by young admirers at Stuttgart State Gallery, 1984. I witnessed various groups interpreting the building throughout one day – travellers, amateur painters, lovers, scholars, businessmen, the young and old – and, in spite of their quite opposite readings, they were all positive. An interesting vindication of multiple-coding. © Charles Jencks.

9/15 – Default Modernism Explodes Again

In this sense, Post-Modernism is a social style of the arts and Modernism an elite style, although the latter can be very popular. Ponder the ironies of populist abstraction. Everybody in New York City comes to wonder at the abstract, steel monoliths of Richard Serra, celebrated at the Museum of Modern Art in 2007, but nobody knows what they mean. Or rather, they do know very well. Like much Modern abstraction, it comes down to one strong meaning, the aesthetic charge of 'wow', how did they squeeze these 1,000-ton torqued ellipses into the low-ceilinged second floor? MoMA, on its website, animates these installations for populist consumption, showing the pure rusted abstractions descending on the museum garden as if from a heavenly crane, off camera. God, as Plato averred, loves abstract primary forms, He's a mathematician, using Corten steel that's pre-rusted. These magical associations then flow directly into the body of the perceiver as he makes a tiny pilgrimage of 60 feet through the leaning tilt of the industrial age, the 1850s. Is this really *Pre*-Modernism?

No. It is really *Late*-Modernism because it is so exclusively aesthetic and because abstraction is also well suited to an age that is fragmented into many taste-cultures, and confused about issues of content. This compounds the ironies. The Marxist theorist, Fredric Jameson, argues angrily and thoroughly against PM, in *Postmodernism, or the Cultural Logic of Late Capitalism*. That is what he called the logic in 1984 for *The New Left Review*, and an influential book of that title in 1991. The problem with his connection of global capitalism and consumer culture is not in their loving relationship, but in his prefix of *Post*. If he had examined the number of abstract, middle-class buildings filling up the town centres of middle America; if he had taken a statistical view of corporate monoliths all over the world and set them against other styles; if he had weighed the reigning styles of Minimalism in the arts, he would have found the dominance of the aesthetic sign over other signification, and pragmatic cost-saving over meaning. The cultural logic of Late Capitalism is the hegemony of impersonal abstraction, of corporate good taste, of Late-Modernism. Most architecture created by global corporations (80 per cent?) stays away from questions of meaning and is abstract for the very good reason that a global culture does not know what to signify much beyond the power of capital.

Thus we reach a paradox with which I have been playing. As the reader will have realised there is a telling contradiction in the argument about taste and popularity. Architecture, *the* public art, often leads in local situations towards Post-Modern double-coding; but the majority of *large* commissions result in the aesthetic coding of Late-Modernism. These two departures from Modernism have to be seen together and in relationship to the parent.

The only problem for this truth is one of overtones. No one wants to adopt the prefix 'Late-', except on one occasion the architect Peter Eisenman, because it implies they were born dead on arrival.[11] Call them Still Modernists, they still want to act, build and speak as if it were 1920. In architecture, and much painting and sculpture, a Neo-Minimalism came to dominate these arts since the 1990s. Generalising this style across the spectrum of the arts one could speak of a Default Modernism, the preferred mode that dare not speak its

Late-Modernism squeezed into a London piazza. Richard Serra's *Fulcrum*, Liverpool Street, London 1987, Corten steel tilts into the Barbican. © Charles Jencks.

Default Modernism. When they were finished in 2007, the Four Towers of Madrid became the ultimate expression of the top of the market. They vary in height from 223 to 250 metres (731 to 820 feet), an extraordinary concentration of offices on a parallel Madrid in an open plain. The smooth beauty of debt packaging finds its apotheosis as abstraction, abstract financial instruments that only the chosen few will understand; if them. © Charles Jencks.

name. Aesthetically safe, it became the default mode when a young designer wanted the job but had no idea of what to signify – and so clearly signified it: nullity. Conservative and easy on the brain, it has been the corporate assumption of the globe for 20 years.

When faced with social contradictions politicians such as Tony Blair, during these same years, adopted the mantra 'modernise', as if it had a clear meaning and unchallengeable mandate. Yes, modernise the economy by all means, create abstract banking rules, aesthetic financial derivatives, instruments that are high-sounding, so very high-tech. In the 1990s many such beautiful tools were created by the modernisers, called 'collateralised debt obligations' (CDOs) and 'collateralised mortgage obligations' (CMOs). Abstract? Hard to fathom? Meaning almost anything, like an enigmatic minimalist box? Some pointed out the 'toxicity', even then. Also created to sound more objective and impersonal were the CDSs, the 'credit *default* swaps', the most radioactive of all modern innovations. These also structured debt, so that computers could model what was supposed to lie inside the box. As they were sold on, from one speculator to the next, the credit bubble was amplified many times. Soon the financiers were passing each other IOUs with complex derivatives that, as a whole, no one could understand. This spreading of debts was called 'securitisation' and was supposed to lessen risk if everybody took it on. A misnomer. Because this actually multiplied risk, beyond that which caused the 1930s depression, it should have been called 'insecuritisation'.

The world's biggest stock investors, George Soros and Warren Buffet (for a while the richest men in the world) understood what was inside the dumb box perfectly well. In 2003, the latter called derivatives WMD, 'weapons of mass destruction'.

The authorities paid little heed to these warnings, the US and UK governments kept dancing to the tune of their CDSs and CDOs and while they waltzed Gordon Brown, the Iron Chancellor, followed the American lead into 'regulation-lite', that is, no regulation. After all, in the abstract those using derivatives were doing rather well, and achieving Triple-A ratings, in the circular manner of Late-Modern Abstraction (being successful, like Enron, for being successful). The music built to a crescendo in the summer of 2007 and then started to sound discordant. One by one banks dropped from the dance and, following Northern Rock, had to be (virtually) nationalised. And then on 9/15 came the Big One, the crunch in credit that would be heard throughout the world. It was the moment when beautiful abstraction stopped, when too many credit default swaps could not be swapped, and blew up. On 15 September 2008, the giant bank, Lehman Brothers – 'too big to fail' – was *allowed* to fail.

This was a mistake in government policy, because Modernist theory said there was no choice but to support Lehman's. In the connected global system you have to prop up the giants or the machine stops. So, the next giants in trouble, AIG and companies, were rescued in the biggest state finance of private banks in American and British history. In part, this flip-flop from no rescue to saving any Leviathan led to the final irony. Public government came to the rescue of private greed, the poor taxpayers supported the rich stockholders. An American joke summarised the inversion of Late-Capitalist logic: 'too big to fail' had become 'socialism for the rich and capitalism for the poor'.

Was this a Late-Capitalist *and* Late-Modernist collapse? A financial version of the blowing up of Pruitt-Igoe; or the meltdown of Chernobyl; or the collapse of the Soviet Union? Or, just one more of the many Deaths of Modernism that ushered in the postmodern (in Lyotard's phrase about Auschwitz)? Even though it is contentious to assert, and aided by the post-modern information world, the greatest global financial crisis in history is a clear product of modernity in its late phase. Indeed, the response to the crunch is also textbook modernisation action, with its reliance on big government propping up only the biggest players, such as AIG and General Motors. In a word, political modernism is Bigness Inc, or the way the Leviathan of Hobbes still, after 300 years, dominates the grand game of politics and power. Post-Modern critics are lined up against this monster, which does not mean that they win very often.

My Ideal Post-Modernist

So, the Modernist reality is often grim and its economic practice rather dismal, to use the standard phrase about its non-science (see Anatole Kaletsky on economics, Part 3). However, Modern culture, stemming from this reality is sometimes very different from its background, and also critical of modernisation. This critical strand is precisely the one that leads into Post-Modernism, a golden thread of continuity. To be brief, it includes such works as Giorgio de Chirico's metaphysical paintings, Picasso's *Guernica*, Stravinsky's *Sacre de Printemps*, Le Corbusier's buildings at Ronchamp and Chandigarh, TS Eliot's *The Waste Land* and James Joyce's *Ulysses*. All these monuments of Modernism are fundamentally concerned with time-binding and responding to the myths embedded in contemporary life. Cathy Gere's recent *Knossos and the Prophets of Modernism* even shows how most of these great works are involved with a single past myth: that of ancient Crete and the Minoan myth of the Minotaur. These creations are complex mixtures of many discourses and, in the terms I have been stressing, typically double-coded between past and present, high art and low, etc. They eschew the reductive impulse of most Modernist work and while abstract at moments they resist the eliminative strain of the Modern. In a word, they are proto-Post-Modern, the strand that continues to run unbroken through the 20th century – albeit as the thin thread of a minority.

The writer John Barth, like Umberto Eco, calls attention to this strand in *The Literature of Replenishment* (republished in full, Part 2), as he emphasises the inclusive nature of PM:

> My ideal postmodernist author neither merely repudiates nor merely imitates either his twentieth-century Modernist parents or his nineteenth-century premodernist grandparents. He has the first half of our century under his belt, but not on his back. Without lapsing into moral or artistic simplism, shoddy craftsmanship, Madison Avenue venality, or either false or real naiveté, he nevertheless aspires to a fiction more democratic in its appeal than such late-modernist marvels (by my definition and in my judgement) as Beckett's *Stories and Texts for Nothing* or Nabokov's *Pale Fire*. He may not hope to reach and move the devotees of James Michener and Irving Wallace – not to mention the lobotomized mass-media illiterates. But he

THE LEVIATHAN SUNK BY THE CRITICS

and $ crashes?

Arendt
Jane Jacobs
ng San Suu Kyi
Anna Politkovskaya
Rachel Carson

Jeremy Paxman
Naom Chomsky
Simon Jenkins

CHARLES JENCKS GILLIAN INNES

The Critic Laughs. Bush sinks, the Leviathan shakes the biggest skyscraper in the world, the Burj Dubai. Petrodollars fall from the sky, the Furies Smile, the Hydra of Truth shows the follies of Bigness, while Cerberus critiques the follies of Power. But hold on, is Bush sinking or rising? The crash in the $$$$$$ is the quickest way to pay off the trillions in debt. The US-of-Oil now has five large military bases in Iraq set around the pumps. It has control of the $30 trillion in black gold reserves. Who has won, who has failed? (And who has lost a nation, and who are the 655,000 dead?) © Charles Jencks.

should hope to reach and delight, at least part of the time, beyond the circle of what Mann used to call the Early Christians: professional devotees of high art.[12]

Here again Post-Modernism gains by being contrasted with Late-Modernism and enhanced by relating to previous Modernisms, not being a rupture or an anti-modernism. Also, Barth's formulation of an ideal post-modernist is helpful. This is particularly true when there is such widespread confusion in the public's mind between the social condition and the high culture that relates to it; or because of Fredric Jameson's confusion between Late-Capitalism and the cultural movement that critiques it. Most bewilderment stems from the muddle between a global consumer system and a high culture. Indeed, many Still Modernists do not grant this distinction and, like the writer Arthur Kroker, see the whole movement *en bloc* as 'excremental culture'.[13] Such oversimplification misses the point, especially the threads that lead out of Modernism, those of TS Eliot, Le Corbusier *et al.*

The exemplary post-modernist, as Barth avers, acknowledges the realities of Ford, Marx, Freud and Darwin, but has these ideas and realities 'under his belt, but not on his back'. As the reader will find, for every Fordism there is now a Post-Fordism, and for every Darwinian there is a follower who has understood how Darwin was half-right. This does not mean, as the recent cover issue of the *New Scientist* put it, that 'Darwin was Wrong'.[14] Many Post-Darwinists have pointed out, over the last 30 years, that in describing evolution many other factors beside the environment have to be taken into account. They include internal factors within the organism, Hox genes, ecological interactions and recently horizontal gene transfer (HGT). Elsewhere I have written on this Post-Darwinism and it is especially important in design and architecture, for framing questions of the responsibility of the designer versus chance. If the Darwinian paradigm underlay Modernism through its reductivism, Haeckel, Nietzsche and social Darwinists like John D Rockefeller, then a Post-Darwinism is also essential to the growing PM paradigm. This is discussed in Part 3 by Charles Birch and Edward Goldsmith, a Darwinism that is 'under the belt, but not on our back'.

My ideal post-modernist, like Barth's, is fundamentally concerned with time-binding, with making clear the connection of past, present and future. One of the chronic problems of the dominant Modernism today, especially in its late phase, is its loss of memory and continuity, the way it is infantilised by the marketplace. Gore Vidal chides the USA as 'the United States of Amnesia', and his sometime enemy Norman Mailer at least agreed on this point, saying that US architects had created in their Late-Modern developments 'empty landscapes of psychosis'. The fast-changing economy and the imperatives of work and consumption create the depthless present where cultural continuity is lost, if it exists at all. So, if I have to point to an ideal post-modern artist I would mention Anselm Kiefer who binds various epochs together in his contemporary constructions. The recent past, and for him this would include the Nazi catastrophe, ancient myth, future hope, archetypal drama are realised in a new grammar. Many discourses cross on his large canvases and constructions. His work is the PM equivalent of *The Waste Land* and *Guernica*, and on occasion so was that of Ron Kitaj.

Anselm Kiefer, *Mohn und Gedächtnis* (Poppy and Memory), 1989. Kiefer often turns the elements of destruction into a poetics of melancholy that refers both to recent history and the promise of the future. *Mohn und Gedächtnis*, with its droopy lead airplane that cannot fly, relates to Second World War war machines, a burnt landscape, toxic pollution, the lead books that are stacked on its wings and the growth of wheat. A paradoxical but potent mixture, these constructions are often completed with handwritten messages. The mixed palette is a dramatic synthesis of past, present and future codes. Hamburger Bahnof, Museum für Gegenwartf, Berlin. Photo © Charles Jencks.

Yet there is another essential aspect of an ideal post-modernism that eludes contemporary artists and that concerns contemporary metaphysics. Any great period of culture well expresses the fundamental insights of the reigning scientific paradigm and, if that has morphed ahead from Modernism, it still awaits a Michelangelo to transform it into art. Let me reiterate the shifts: from Newton to Einstein, from linear to nonlinear dynamics, from determinism to self-organising systems, or from simple to complex systems. So the slides and developments go, each one *not* a refutation of its modernist counterpart but a deeper insight into the universe. The last section of this book, Part 3, is devoted to them, in particular Tito Arecchi's short article 'Chaos and Complexity'.

These collective post-modern sciences of complexity, that are named as such in the 1980s, actually grow out of those that were mooted in the 1960s, the latter a period I would therefore call Complexity 1. As the reader will also find in Part 2, Jane Jacobs in 1961 and Robert Venturi in 1966 sounded the first bell of post-modernism with their respective theories of complex urbanism and architecture. Complexity in the city and complexity and contradiction in architecture were explicitly formulated as the shift in these two fields and they had a profound effect, deepening their professional orientations. But 20 years later, as the film puts it in *The Postman Always Rings Twice*, by this time round we could actually say that the universe itself is a complex, self-organising system; we could understand a deeper complexity theory. The Santa Fe Institute was the place where these 'sciences of the 21st century' were explicitly formulated, and Complexity II became the metaphysics of our Post-man. At the time however, I found it was hard to persuade the earlier theorists, such as Venturi, that this was true. Perhaps architects are more conservative than urbanists, because Jane Jacobs certainly appreciated Mark 2 and the economists at Santa Fe.

By the late 1990s at least 30 different attempts were made by scientists and philosophers to capture what was at stake, and several best-selling books on the subject had appeared.[15] In an issue of *Architectural Design* in 1997, 'New Science = New Architecture', I also tried to summarise this new paradigm, with several definitions of a nonlinear architecture, and above all of complexity itself. Defining complexity adequately was like trying to pin down sudden creation on the wing:

Complexity is the theory of how emergent organisation may be achieved by interacting components pushed far from equilibrium (by increasing energy, matter or information) to the threshold between order and chaos. This important border or threshold is where the system often jumps, bifurcates or creatively interacts in a new nonlinear, unpredictable way (the Eureka moment) and where the new organisation may be sustained through feedback and the continuous input of energy.

In this process quality emerges spontaneously as self-organisation, meaning, value, openness, fractal patterns, attractor formations and (often) increasing complexity (a greater degree of freedom).[16]

The new complexity paradigm in architecture was then emerging, an identifiable, second stage of Post-Modernism, led now not by Robert Venturi but by Peter Eisenman, Daniel Libeskind, Cecil Balmond, Frank Gehry and ARM. It has continued to thrive ever since although, as with many movements that become global, it bloomed as both a commercial and academic fashion. And so once again fashion-time played its game of asset-strip, and reduced complexity to computer software and, in architecture, to funny shapes.

In any case, no architect, artist or creator has yet expressed the canonic version of contemporary metaphysics. In terms of searching for the ideal post-modernism, a masterpiece summarising the complexity view of the universe does not exist. But, there are many interesting attempts visible on the horizon, and it must be a matter of time, and willpower.

Long Wave, Medium Wave: Deepening Modernism

Where does this quick, and selective, survey lead in the answer to the big question posed at the outset, where and what is our time? If one took an informal poll among experts, and concerned participants in the debate, it would probably lead to some agnostic results, some of which are unexceptional. Obviously, there are at least two somewhat opposed Post-Modernisms, a deconstructive version that I and others would call Late-Modernism, and a reconstructive version offered here. What unites these two PMs is a shared concern for pluralism, and a critique of monolithic culture, what Lyotard called 'a war on totality'. This essential definition would mean that post-modernists of all shades would deny that a single label could be adequate to the multispeed times of global reality. They are all cultural relativists in this sense though not in others.

However, stepping back and looking at the larger picture of global development gives a more nuanced answer. With the growth of modernisms since at least the Renaissance, when *moderna* came in vogue, when the nation state became dominant and capitalism started in Italy and elsewhere, it does make sense to talk about the Modern World as historians do. At the same time one insists on the legitimacy of the 5,000 languages, and cultures, which cut it into many parts. The hegemony of modernism starts about 1500, and there are many holocausts to go with it, most of them brought to consciousness, named and debated only in the last 30 years (like the 'American Holocaust').[17] Placing the various modernisms within this overarching long wave, one could say that there are at least two historical medium waves that develop roughly since the 1960s, the Late- and Post- ones that agitate the waters. Wave theory is, of course, just another branch of physics and a metaphor for historians, but it helps to illuminate the question.

If the big wave is made up from the three aspects – modernity, modernisation and Modernism – and I believe it is, then the globe is still very much in a modern period. It rules, not OK as far as minorities and ecologists are concerned, but it still dominates most cultures. Nevertheless, its critics and creators have moved elsewhere, to adopt a spatial metaphor, both forward and back and to the side, creating these medium waves as they do so. So, while it is true that Post-Modernism is really a part of the bigger wave and has not yet fundamentally changed its force or direction, the cultural movement has, I would argue, deepened its quality and thought. That is to say, the PM ecological agenda has little to show against the juggernaut of the global economy except many high-sounding pronouncements and one or two ameliorations such as lessening that indeterminate hole in the ozone layer; while pm science has many accomplishments to its credit.

To get a picture of how the contemporary world views reality, it is more convincing to concentrate on these sciences of complexity and see the way they combine with the sciences of simplicity. It is a picture of both/and, not either/or. Thus the fractal geometry of nature, that appears to cover most of reality, still has to defer to Euclidean geometry in the case of spherical planets, hexagonal beehives, and so much architecture in the right-angled city. But fractal geometry is the more general science and they are both useful. In like manner, Einsteinian relativity theory is a better description of the cosmos than Newton's theory of gravity. In particular, we know it is much better at framing the universe at high speeds, over great distances and in supergravity. But since we live *mostly* in the slow-moving, Newtonian world, our everyday experience denies this deeper truth. The point is also that neither Einsteinian nor quantum physics disproved Newtonian mechanics – the keystone of modern science. They were just deeper and more general explanations of reality.

This analogy of a dual and hybrid view is largely true for the other sciences of complexity: thermodynamics, nonlinearity, the chaos sciences, biology and cosmology, to name but a few. They have merged with and deepened their modern progenitors. Again, like post-industrialisation these complexity sciences take off in a big way during the 1960s. Weather prediction, the chaos science accidentally discovered by Edward Lorenz, is the standard example. And these formulations are wider, deeper, more general than their forebears. In a sense, they include the sciences of simplicity, the linear ones, as limiting cases.

I think we can follow this parallel from the sciences into the relationship between the Modern and Post-Modern. The two different orientations complement each other and are often synthesised or else hybridised together. This is certainly true in art and architecture, where the styles and ideas are merged in such profusion that classification becomes difficult, even pedantic. Pluralism now reigns in the arts with maybe 100 or so global styles extant, and at any large art fair it is this PM variety that is most evident, not an integrated Modernism. True, it is a market pluralism, without deep conviction, but an important differentiation nonetheless.

What characterises the sciences and the arts is recognisable in other areas of culture and civilisation. Modern orientations have been synthesised by post-modern ones, or exist in tension with them, or they are melded and hybridised. Dual, paired, merged or one swallowing the other? Probably every discipline and discourse should be examined separately. But, following the contrasts I mentioned at the outset, I present a very modernist diagram, a list of the father and the daughter. The argument would be that in nearly every case, to get an idea of what kind of world we are in, we should put a big 'and' between the two sides of this bloodline. Maybe that explains the irony of today asking, what period are we in?

MODERN either hybridised or paired with POST-MODERN

In politics
1	nation states	regional bodies (EU)
2	totalitarian	democratic
3	consensus	dissensus
4	class friction	new agenda issues, green

In economics
5	Fordism	Post-Fordism (networking)
6	Capitalism/socialism	regulated socitalism
7	centralised	decentralised
8	rational choice	reflexivity
9	hidden hand	behavioural

In society
10	industrial	post-industrial
11	class-structured	many clustered
12	proletariat	cognitariat

In culture
13	Purism	double-coding
14	elitist	multiple taste-cultures
15	objectivism	values in nature

In aesthetics
16	simple harmonies	disharmonious harmony
17	formal flatness	content-driven
18	top-down integrated	conflicted semiosis
19	abstract/ahistorical	time-binding

In philosophy
20	monism	pluralism
21	materialism	semiotic view
22	utopian	heterotopian
23	reductivist	holistic

In science
24	mechanistic	self-organising
25	simple/linear	complex/nonlinear
26	deterministic	indeterministic
27	Newtonian	relativity

In spirituality
28	atheism	panentheism
29	patriarchical	post-patriarchical
30	disenchantment	re-enchantment

In media
31	world of print	electronic
32	fast-changing	instant changing
33	spatialised	globalised WWW

In worldview
34	mechanical	ecological
35	hierarchical	heterarchical
36	accidental universe	anthropic principle
37	existentialist/alienated	embedded
38	innocent/straightforward	lost innocence/ironic

These 38 contrasts reveal a pattern and of course do not fully define either side of the equation. I have only discussed a few of them, while some others are treated by contributors to this anthology. Obvious lacunae in my sketch are feminism, multiculturalism, the decline of religion and rise of a pm spirituality. But the general argument I think can be sustained that, as usual, an individual and culture are both mixtures of different epochs, sedimentations of various orientations. The pattern of our time is the post-modern sublating the modern, but the economy and society of the globe is still based on modernisation. Now, at the time of writing (August 2009), that the global system seems to have been momentarily saved from meltdown by a huge effort of reflation, no one can doubt that Modernist theory and practice still dominate. Bigness and massification and the Leviathan still rule, but not OK. One can conceive of an ideal post-modernism as the loyal opposition to its father, or the continuation of modernism and its transcendence, and those who do not conceive of movements in terms of their ideals are doomed to misunderstanding.

Notes

1 See Robert Cooper, *The Breaking of Nations*, Atlantic Books (London), 2003, pp 26–37 for these political distinctions.
2 See John Kay, 'Lessons from the rise and fall of a carmaker', *Financial Times*, 3 June 2009: 'The history of modern business is the history of GM and vice versa. Adam Smith saw that the division of labour was the key to prosperity ...' Here Kay discusses the decline of the ultimate modern corporation, General Motors, under globalisation as consumers became more discriminating and the market more focused on niches. In conversation, we discussed what would be the typical post-modern corporation and I believe he thought maybe it would not be a corporation at all, but something like the Web. Anyway, Amazon is the archetypal information-based corporation.
3 Jean-François Lyotard, *The Postmodern Explained to Children, Correspondence 1982–1985*, Turnaround (London), 1992, pp 30–1.
4 Umberto Eco, *Postscript to the Name of the Rose*, Harcourt Brace Jovanovitch (New York and London), pp 67–8.
5 For a brief overview of 10 versions of Modernism since the 3rd century see my *Critical Modernism: where is post-modernism going?* John Wiley (London and New York), 2007, pp 8–11.
6 Arnold Toynbee, *A Study of History*, ed DC Somervell, Oxford University Press (New York), 1947–57, 1: 39.
7 Irving Howe, 'Mass Society and Postmodern Fiction' (1963), in *The Decline of the New*, Harcourt Brace and World (New York), 1970. For Harold Levine, see 'What was Modernism?', in *Refractions: Essays in Comparative Literature*, Oxford University Press (New York), 1966.
8 Like many writers formulating a negative or positive version of the post-modern Fiedler does not see the movement across all the arts and as a new episteme, nor does he attempt a whole book on the subject. See his 'The New Mutants' (1965), in *The Collected Essays of Leslie Fiedler*, vol. 2, Stein and Day (New York), 1970.
9 Ihab Hassan has somewhat shifted his definitions of postmodernism over the years to be more inclusive and pluralist, and less Late-Modern (in my terms). His oppositions between the Modern versus Post-Modern can be found in his entry on Wikipedia, where 33 are given. They include the following contrasts: Romanticism/Symbolism-Pataphysics-Dadaism; Form (conjunctive, closed)/ Antiform: (disjunctive, open); Purpose/Play; Design/Chance; Hierarchy/Anarchy, and so on. As I will argue it seems to me absurd to argue that Post-Modernism isn't fundamentally romantic, symbolic, formal, purposeful, designed, hierarchical in parts, and so on. Post-Modernism is as Robert Venturi wrote, involved with 'both/and' not 'either/or'. The full list of Hassan's terms defines his concept as mostly Late- or Deconstructive Modernism, and is more coherent and applicable as such, but the reader can judge his position more fully in the text in this Reader.
10 My first lectures on Post-Modern architecture occurred in early 1975, and I organised an RIBA

Conference on it that year; the nascent pluralist movement was described in 'The Rise of Post-Modern Architecture', *AAQ*, London, 1975. Thereafter I wrote many books on aspects of PM, and published seven editions of *The Language of Post-Modern Architecture* (1977, 1978, 1981, 1984, 1986, 1991, 2002); it was translated into at least 11 foreign languages. The contrasts made with its double were published in *Late-Modern Architecture*, Academy Editions (London), 1980, and since then I have understood that at least these two major movements have contested the departures from their common parent. Double-coding as a definer was introduced in the 1978 edition of *LPMA*.

11   Since approximately 2006, Peter Eisenman, reading Edward Saïd on the idea of the Late Work of artists, has talked about his own work as 'late' in these terms. I heard him talk about this version, contrasting it with Modernism and Post-Modernism, at the RIBA, November 2008. Strangely he denied that he understood the 'new paradigm' of science, and its implications; strangely, because we have discussed it on many occasions, and his work often shows such an understanding. But then, Peter is always clear and never simple in his categorisations, especially about himself. He is certainly not what I am characterising as a Still Modernist.

12   John Barth, 'The Literature of Replenishment, Postmodernist fiction,' *The Atlantic*, January 1980, pp 65–71.

13   Arthur Kroker, *The Postmodern Scene: Excremental Culture and Hyperaesthetics*, St Martin's Press (New York), 1986. Perhaps there are a few Post-Modernists who would embrace this epithet, such as the artists Gilbert and George and Jeff Koons.

14   'Darwin was Wrong', *New Scientist*, 24 January 2009, pp 34–9. The issue is concerned mostly with horizontal gene transfer.

15   Among the popular books on complexity theory there was M Mitchell Waldrop, *Complexity: The Emerging Science at the Edge of Order and Chaos*, Simon and Schuster (New York), 1992; Roger Lewin, *Complexity: Life at the Edge of Chaos*, JM Dent (London), 1992; more specialised books were Brian Goodwin, *How the Leopard Changed Its Spots*, Weidenfeld and Nicolson (London) 1994, and my own, *The Architecture of the Jumping Universe*, Academy-Wiley (London), 1995. The writings of Stuart Kauffmann, Ian Stewart, Frijof Capra and Paul Davies also were important in this developing paradigm not to mention Ilya Prigogine and his co-workers. His epochal *Order out of Chaos*, though not so explicitly concerned with complexity, had appeared in the 1980s.

16   Charles Jencks, Guest Editor, 'New Science = New Architecture', *Architectural Design*, July 1997, p 8.

17   See David E Stannard, *American Holocaust, Columbus and the Conquest of the New World*, Oxford University Press (New York), 1992. Stannard put the number of those killed within 50 years of Columbus's 'discovery' at between 60 million and 80 million. The figure is contentious for two reasons: the difficulty of measurement and the question of how many were killed intentionally, or by disease and germ warfare. For a more general discussion of the way modernisation could itself be lethal and violent, see Theodore H Von Laue, *The World Revolution of Westernization*, Oxford University Press (New York), 1987. Whether the genocides of recent years in various countries deserve the epithet holocaust is equally debated. Without wishing to address the subject here, I would only claim that there is a big question for modernists of all persuasions to answer and a good book with which to start reflecting is Zygmunt Bauman's *Modernity and the Holocaust*, Polity Press (Cambridge, UK), 1989.

Charles Jencks, October 2009. © 2010 John Wiley & Sons Ltd.

Answering the Question: What Is Postmodernism?

Jean-François Lyotard

This text, originally commissioned by the Quebec government, was published in French as a sociological report on the condition of knowledge in 1979 and translated into English in 1984. Lyotard's main observation is the incredulity towards metanarratives in the postmodern age, a scepticism partly due to science but from which it, like all organising ideas, does not escape. In a later book, *The Postmodern Explained to Children*, Lyotard summarised his position on the project of modernity: 'I would argue that the project of modernity (the realisation of universality) has not been forsaken or forgotten but destroyed, "liquidated". There are several modes of destruction, several names, which are symbols for them. "Auschwitz" can be taken as a paradigmatic name for the tragic "incompletion" of modernity.'[i] For Lyotard, the incredulity towards metanarratives is not only an effect of science but an essential condition for progress.

A French philosopher and literary theorist associated with poststructuralism, Lyotard (1924–98) is known for his conceptual framing of the notion of the postmodern. As a member of the group Socialisme ou barbarie, Lyotard engaged in a struggle against the state capitalism of communist Europe, Marxism, Freudian psychoanalysis and the Algerian war. Lyotard pursued a career as an activist and an academic in many universities around the world, proclaiming the end of metanarratives as well as the explosion and incompatibility of the different fields of knowledge. *LCS*

Introduction

The object of this study is the condition of knowledge in the most highly developed societies. I have decided to use the word *postmodern* to describe that condition. The word is in current use on the American continent among sociologists and critics; it designates the state of our culture following the transformations which, since the end of the 19th century, have altered the game rules for science, literature and the arts. The present study will place these transformations in the context of the crisis of narratives.

Science has always been in conflict with narratives. Judged by the yardstick of science, the majority of them prove to be fables. But to the extent that science does not restrict itself to stating useful regularities and seeks the truth, it is obliged to legitimate the rules of its own game. It then produces a discourse of legitimation with respect to its

---

i Jean-François Lyotard, *Le Postmoderne expliqué aux enfants: correspondance 1982–1985*, Éditions Galilée, Paris, 1986, trans Julian Pefanis and Morgan Thomas, *The Postmodern Explained to Children: Correspondence 1982–1985*, Turnaround (London), 1992, p 30.

own status, a discourse called philosophy. I will use the term *modern* to designate any science that legitimates itself with reference to a metadiscourse of this kind making an explicit appeal to some grand narrative, such as the dialectics of spirit, the hermeneutics of meaning, the emancipation of the rational or working subject, or the creation of wealth. For example, the rule of consensus between the sender and addressee of a statement with truth-value is deemed acceptable if it is cast in terms of a possible unanimity between rational minds: this is the Enlightenment narrative, in which the hero of knowledge works towards a good ethico-political end – universal peace. As can be seen from this example, if a metanarrative implying a philosophy of history is used to legitimate knowledge, questions are raised concerning the validity of the institutions governing the social bond: these must be legitimated as well. Thus justice is consigned to the grand narrative in the same way as truth.

Simplifying to the extreme, I define postmodern as incredulity towards metanarratives. This incredulity is undoubtedly a product of progress in the sciences; but that progress in turn presupposes it. To the obsolescence of the metanarrative apparatus of legitimation corresponds, most notably, the crisis of metaphysical philosophy and of the university institution which in the past relied on it. The narrative function is losing its functors, its great hero, its great danger, its great goal. It is being dispersed in clouds of narrative language elements – narrative, but also denotative, prescriptive, descriptive and so on. Conveyed within each cloud are pragmatic valencies specific to its kind. Each of us lives at the intersection of many of these. However, we do not necessarily establish stable language combinations, and the properties of the ones we do establish are not necessarily communicable.

The decision makers, however, attempt to manage these clouds of sociality according to their input/output matrices, following a logic which implies that their elements are commensurable and that the whole is determinable. They allocate our lives for the growth of power. In matters of social justice and of scientific truth alike, the legitimation of the power is based on its optimising the system's performance – efficiency. The application of this criterion to all of our games necessarily entails a certain level of terror, whether soft or hard: be operational (that is, commensurable) or disappear.

The logic of maximum performance is no doubt inconsistent in many ways, particularly with respect to contradiction in the socio-economic field: it demands both less work (to lower production costs) and more (to lessen the social burden of the idle population). But our incredulity is now such that we no longer expect salvation to rise from these inconsistencies, as did Marx.

Still, the postmodern condition is as much a stranger to disenchantment as it is to the blind positivity of delegitimation. Where, after the metanarratives, can legitimacy reside? The operativity criterion is technological; it has no relevance for judging what is true or just. Is legitimacy to be found in consensus obtained through discussion, as Jürgen Habermas thinks? Such consensus does violence to the heterogeneity of language games. And invention is always born of dissension. Postmodern knowledge is not simply a tool of the authorities; it refines our sensitivity to differences and reinforces our ability to tolerate the incommensurable. Its principle is not the expert's homology, but the inventor's paralogy.

Here is the question: is a legitimation of the social bond, a just society, feasible in terms of a paradox analogous to that of scientific activity? What would such a paradox be?

The text that follows is an occasional one. It is a report on knowledge in the most highly developed societies and was presented to the Conseil des Universités of the government of Quebec at the request of its president. I would like to thank him for his kindness in allowing its publication.

It remains to be said that the author of the report is a philosopher, not an expert. The latter knows what he knows and what he does not know: the former does not. One concludes, the other questions – two very different language games. I combine them here with the result that neither quite succeeds.

The philosopher at least can console himself with the thought that the formal and pragmatic analysis of certain philosophical and ethico-political discourses of legitimation, which underlines the report, will subsequently see the light of day. The report will have served to introduce that analysis from a somewhat sociologising slant, one that truncates but at the same times situates it.

Such as it is, I dedicate this report to the Institut Polytechnique de Philosophie of the Université de Paris VIII (Vincennes) – at this very postmodern moment that finds the university nearing what may be its end, while the institute may just be beginning.

The Field: Knowledge in Computerised Societies
Our working hypothesis is that the status of knowledge is altered as societies enter what is known as the post-industrial age and cultures enter what is known as the postmodern age.[1] This transition has been under way since at least the end of the 1950s, which for Europe marks the completion of reconstruction. The pace is faster or slower depending on the country, and within countries it varies according to the sector of activity: the general situation is one of temporal disjunction which makes sketching an overview difficult.[2] A portion of the description would necessarily be conjectural. At any rate, we know that it is unwise to put too much faith in futurology.[3]

Rather than painting a picture that would inevitably remain incomplete, I will take as my point of departure a single feature, one that immediately defines our object of study. Scientific knowledge is a kind of discourse. And it is fair to say that for the last 40 years the 'leading' sciences and technologies have had to do with language: phonology and theories of linguistics,[4] problems of communication and cybernetics,[5] modern theories of algebra and informatics,[6] computers and their languages,[7] problems of translation and the search for areas of compatibility among computer languages,[8] problems of information storage and data banks,[9] telematics and the perfection of intelligent terminals,[10] paradoxology.[11] The facts speak for themselves (and this list is not exhaustive).

These technological transformations can be expected to have a considerable impact on knowledge. Its two principal functions – research and the transmission of acquired learning – are already feeling the effect, or will in future. With respect to the first function, genetics provides an example that is accessible to the layman: it owes its theoretical paradigm to cybernetics. Many other examples could be cited. As for the second function, it is common knowledge that the miniaturisation and commercialisation of machines is already changing the way in which learning is acquired, classified, made available and exploited.[12] It is reasonable to suppose that the proliferation of information-processing machines is having, and will continue to have, as much of an effect on the circulation of learning as did advancements in human circulation (transportation systems) and later, in the circulation of sounds and visual images (the media).[13]

The nature of knowledge cannot survive unchanged within this context of general transformation. It can fit into the new channels, and become operational, only if learning is translated into quantities of information.[14] We can predict that anything in the constituted body of knowledge that is not translatable in this way will be abandoned and that the direction of new research will be dictated by the possibility of its eventual results being translatable into computer language. The 'producers' and users of knowledge must now, and will have to, possess the means of translating into these languages whatever they want to invent and learn. Research on translating machines is already well advanced.[15] Along with the hegemony of computers comes a certain logic, and therefore a certain set of prescriptions determining which statements are accepted as 'knowledge' statements.

We may thus expect a thorough exteriorisation of knowledge with respect to the 'knower', at whatever point he or she may occupy in the knowledge process. The old principle that the acquisition of knowledge is indissociable from the training (*Bildung*) of minds, or even of individuals, is becoming obsolete and will become ever more so. The relationship of the suppliers and users of knowledge to the knowledge they supply and use is now tending, and will increasingly tend, to assume the form already taken by the relationship of commodity producers and consumers to the commodities they produce and consume – that is, the form of value. Knowledge is and will be produced in order to be sold, it is and will be consumed in order to be valorised in a new production: in both cases, the goal is exchange. Knowledge ceases to be an end in itself, it loses its 'use-value'.[16]

It is widely accepted that knowledge has become the principal force of production over the last few decades;[17] this has already had a noticeable effect on the composition of the work force of the most highly developed countries[18] and constitutes that major bottleneck for the developing countries. In the post-industrial and postmodern age, science will maintain and no doubt strengthen its pre-eminence in the arsenal of productive capacities of the nation states. Indeed, this situation is one of the reasons leading to the conclusion that the gap between developed and developing countries will grow ever wider in the future.[19]

But this aspect of the problem should not be allowed to overshadow the other, which is complementary to it. Knowledge in the form of an informational commodity indispensable to productive power is already, and will continue to be, a major – perhaps *the* major – stake in the worldwide competition for power. It is conceivable that the nation states will one day fight for control of information, just as they battled in the past for control over territory, and afterwards for control of access to and exploitation of raw materials and cheap labour. A new field is opened for industrial and commercial strategies on the one hand, and political and military strategies on the other.[20]

However, the perspective I have outlined above is not as simple as I have made it appear. For the mercantilisation of knowledge is bound to affect the privilege the nation states have enjoyed, and still enjoy, with respect to the production and distribution of learning. The notion that learning falls within the purview of the state, as the brain or mind of society, will become more and more outdated with the increasing strength of the opposing principle, according to which society exists and progresses only if the messages circulating within it are rich in information and easy to decode. The ideology of communicational 'transparency', which goes hand in hand with the commercialisation of knowledge, will begin to perceive the state as a factor of opacity and 'noise'. It is from this point of view that the problem of the relationship between economic and state powers threatens to arise with a new urgency.

Already in the last few decades, economic powers have reached the point of imperilling the stability of the state through new forms of the circulation of capital that go by the generic name of *multinational corporations*. These new forms of circulation imply that investment decisions have, at least in part, passed beyond the control of the nation states.[21] The question threatens to become even more thorny with the development of computer technology and telematics. Suppose, for example, that a firm such as IBM is authorised to occupy a belt in the earth's orbital field and launch communications satellites or satellites housing data banks. Who will have access to them? Who will determine which channels or data are forbidden? The state? Or will the state simply be one user among others? New legal issues will be raised, and with them the question: 'who will know?'

Transformation in the nature of knowledge, then, could well have repercussions on the existing public powers, forcing them to reconsider their relations (both de jure and de facto) with the large corporations and, more generally, with civil society. The reopening of the world market, a return to vigorous economic competition, the breakdown of the hegemony of American capitalism, the decline of the socialist alternative, a probable opening of the Chinese market – these and many other factors are already, at the end of the 1970s, preparing states for a serious reappraisal of the role they have been accustomed to playing since the 1930s: that of gilding, or even directing investments.[22] In this light, the new technologies can only increase the urgency of such a re-examination, since they make the information used in decision making (and therefore the means of control) even more mobile and subject to piracy.

It is not hard to visualise learning circulating along the same lines as money, instead of for its 'educational' value or political (administrative, diplomatic, military) importance; the pertinent distinction would no longer be between knowledge and ignorance, but rather, as is the case with money, between 'payment knowledge' and 'investment knowledge' – in other words, between units of knowledge exchanged in a daily maintenance framework (the reconstitution of the work force, 'survival') versus funds of knowledge dedicated to optimising the performance of a project.

If this were the case, communicational transparency would be similar to liberalism. Liberalism does not preclude an organisation of the flow of money in which some channels are used in decision making while others are only good for the payment of debts. One could similarly imagine flows of knowledge travelling along identical channels of identical nature, some of which would be reserved for the 'decision makers', while the others would be used to repay each person's perpetual debt with respect to the social bond …

Answering the Question: What Is Postmodernism?

A Demand

This is a period of slackening – I refer to the colour of the times. From every direction we are being urged to put an end to experimentation, in the arts and elsewhere. I have read an art historian who extols realism and is militant for the advent of a new subjectivity. I have read an art critic who packages and sells 'Transavantgardism' in the marketplace of painting. I have read that under the name postmodernism, architects are getting rid of the Bauhaus project, throwing out the baby of experimentation with the bath water of functionalism. I have read that a new philosopher is discovering what he drolly calls Judaeo-Christianism, and intends by it to put an end to the impiety which we are supposed to have spread. I have read in a French weekly that some are displeased with *Mille Plateaux* (by Deleuze and Guattari) because they expect, especially when reading a work of philosophy, to be gratified with a little sense. I have read from the pen of a reputable historian that writers and thinkers of the 1960s and 1970s avant-gardes spread a reign of terror in the use of language, and that the conditions for a fruitful exchange must be restored by imposing on the intellectuals a common way of speaking, that of the historians. I have been reading a young philosopher of language who complains that Continental thinking, under the challenge of speaking machines, has surrendered to the machines the concern for reality, that it has substituted for the referential paradigm that of 'adlinguisticity' (one who speaks about speech, writes about writing, intertextuality), and who thinks that the time has now come to restore a solid anchorage of language in the referent. I have read a talented theatrologist for whom postmodernism, with its games and fantasies, carries very little weight in front of political authority, especially when a worried public opinion encourages authority to a politics of totalitarian surveillance in the face of nuclear warfare threats.

I have read a thinker of repute who defends modernity against those he calls the neoconservatives. Under the banner of postmodernism, the latter would like, he believes, to get rid of the uncompleted project of modernism, that of the Enlightenment. Even the last advocates of *Aufklärung*, such as Popper and Adorno, were only able, according to him, to defend the project in a few particular spheres of life – that of politics for the author of *The Open Society*, and that of art for the author of *Ästhetische Theorie*. Jürgen Habermas (everyone has recognised him) thinks that if modernity has failed, it is allowing the totality of life to be splintered into independent specialities which are left to the narrow competence of experts, while the concrete individual experiences 'desublimated meaning' and 'destructured form', not as a liberation but in the mode of that immense *ennui* which Baudelaire described over a century ago.

Following a prescription of Albrecht Wellmer, Habermas considers that the remedy for this splintering of culture and its separation from life can only come from 'changing the status of aesthetic experience when it is no longer primarily expressed in judgements of taste', but when it is 'used to explore a living historical situation', that is, when 'it is put in relation with problems of existence'. For this experience then 'becomes a part of a language game which is no longer that of aesthetic criticism'; it takes part 'in cognitive processes and normative expectations'; 'it alters the manner in which those different moments *refer* to one another'. What Habermas requires from the arts and the experiences they provide is, in short, to bridge the gap between cognitive, ethical and political discourses, thus opening the way to unity of experience.

My question is to determine what sort of unity Habermas has in mind. Is the aim of the project of modernity the constitution of sociocultural unity within which all the elements of daily life and of thought would take their places as in an organic whole? Or does the passage that had to be charted between heterogeneous language games – those of cognition, of ethics, of politics – belong to a different order from that? And if so, would it be capable of effecting synthesis between them?

The first hypothesis, of a Hegelian inspiration, does not challenge the notion of a dialectically totalising *experience*, the second is closer to the spirit of Kant's *Critique of Judgment*; but must be submitted, like the *Critique*, to that severe re-examination which postmodernity imposes on the thought of the Enlightenment, on the idea of a unitary end of history and of a subject. It is this critique not only Wittgenstein and Adorno have initiated, but also a few other thinkers (French or other) who do not have the honour to be read by Professor Habermas – which at least saves them from getting a poor grade for their neoconservatism.

Realism

The demands I began by citing are not all equivalent. They can even be contradictory. Some are made in the name of postmodernism, others in order to combat it. It is not necessarily the same thing to formulate a demand for some referent (and objective reality), for some sense (and credible transcendence), for an addressee (and audience), or an addressor (and subjective expressiveness) or for some communicational consensus (and a general code of exchanges such as the genre of historical discourse). But in the diverse invitations to suspend artistic experimentation, there is an identical call for order, a desire for unity, for identity, for security, or popularity (in the sense of *Öffentlichkeit*, of 'finding a public'). Artists and writers must be brought back into the bosom of the community, or at least, if the latter is considered to be ill, they must be assigned the task of healing it.

There is an irrefutable sign of this common disposition: it is that for all those writers nothing is more urgent than to liquidate the heritage of the avant-gardes. Such is the case, in particular, of the so-called transavantgardism. The answers given by Achille Bonito Oliva to the questions asked by Bernard Lamarche-Vadel and Michel Enric leave no room for doubt about this. By putting the avant-gardes through a mixing process, the artist and critic feel more confident that they can suppress them than by launching a frontal attack. For they can pass off the most cynical eclecticism as a way of going beyond the fragmentary character of the preceding experiments; whereas if they openly turned their backs on them, they would run the risk of appearing ridiculously neoacademic. The *Salons* and the *Académies*, at the time when the bourgeoisie was establishing itself in history, were able to function as purgation and to grant awards for good plastic and literary conduct under the cover of realism. But the capitalism inherently possesses the power to derealise familiar objects, social roles and institutions to such a degree that the so-called realistic representations can no longer evoke reality except as nostalgia or mockery, as an occasion for suffering rather than for satisfaction. Classicism seems to be ruled out in a world in which reality is so destabilised that it offers no occasion for experience but one for ratings and experimentation.

This theme is familiar to all readers of Walter Benjamin. But it is necessary to assess its exact reach. Photography did not appear as a challenge to painting from the outside, any more than industrial cinema did to narrative literature. The former was only putting the final touch to the programme of ordering the visible elaborated by the quattrocento; while the latter was the last step in rounding off diachronies as organic wholes, which had been the ideal of the great novels of education since the 18th century. That the mechanical and the industrial should appear as substitutes for hand or craft was not in itself a disaster – except if one believes that art is in its essence the expression of an individuality of genius assisted by an elite craftsmanship.

The challenge lay essentially in that photographic and cinematographic processes can accomplish better, faster, and with a circulation a hundred thousand times larger than narrative or pictorial realism, the task which academicism had assigned to realism: to preserve various consciousnesses from doubt. Industrial photography and cinema will be superior to painting and the novel whenever the objective is to stabilise the referent, to arrange it according to a point of view which endows it with a recognisable meaning, to reproduce the syntax and vocabulary which enable the addressee to decipher images and sequences quickly, and so to arrive easily at the consciousness of his own identity as well as the approval which he thereby receives from others – since such structures of images and sequences constitute a communication code among all of them. This is the way the effects of reality, or if one prefers, the fantasies of realism, multiply.

If they too do not wish to become supporters (of minor importance at that) of what exists, the painter and novelist must refuse to lend themselves to such therapeutic uses. They must question the rules of the art of painting or of narrative as they have learned and received them from their predecessors. Soon those rules must appear to them as a means to deceive, to seduce and to reassure, which makes it impossible for them to be 'true'. Under the common name of painting and literature, an unprecedented split is taking place. Those who refuse to re-examine the rules of art pursue successful careers in mass conformism by communicating, by means of the 'correct rules', the endemic desire for reality with objects and situations capable of gratifying it. Pornography is the use of photography and film to such an end. It is becoming a general model for the visual or narrative arts which have not met the challenge of the mass media.

As for the artists and writers who question the rules of plastic and narrative arts and possibly share their suspicions by circulating their work, they are destined to have little credibility in the eyes of those concerned with 'reality' and 'identity'; they have no guarantee of an audience. Thus it is possible to ascribe the dialectics of the avant-gardes to the challenge posed by the realisms of industry and mass communication to painting and the narrative arts. Duchamp's 'ready made' does nothing but actively and parodistically signify this constant process of dispossession of the craft of painting or even of being an artist. As Thierry de Duve penetratingly observes, the modern aesthetic question is not 'What is beautiful?' but 'What can be said to be art (and literature)?'

Realism, whose only definition is that it intends to avoid the question of reality implicated in that of art, always stands somewhere between academicism and kitsch. When power assumes the name of a party, realism and its neoclassical complement triumph over the experimental avant-garde by slandering and banning it – that is, provided the 'correct' images, the 'correct' narratives, the 'correct' forms which the party requests, selects and propagates can find a public to desire them as the appropriate remedy for the anxiety and depression that the public experiences. The demand for reality – that is, for unity, simplicity, communicability, etc – did not have the same intensity nor the same continuity in German society between the two world wars and in Russian society after the revolution: this provides a basis for a distinction between Nazi and Stalinist realism.

What is clear, however, is that when it is launched by the political apparatus, the attack on artistic experimentation is specifically reactionary: aesthetic judgement would only be required to decide whether such or such a work is in conformity with the established rules of the beautiful. Instead of the work of art having to investigate what makes it an art object and whether it will be able to find an audience, political academicism possesses and imposes a priori criteria of the beautiful, which designate some works and a public at a stroke and for ever. The use of categories in aesthetic judgement would thus be of the same nature as in cognitive judgement. To speak like Kant, both would be determining judgements: the expression is 'well formed' first in the understanding, then the only cases retained in experience are those which can be subsumed under this expression.

When power is that of capital and not that of a party, the 'transavantgardist' or 'postmodern' (in Jencks's sense) solution proves to be better adapted than the anti-modern solution. Eclecticism is the degree zero of contemporary general culture: one listens to reggae, watches a Western, eats McDonald's food for lunch and local cuisine for dinner, wears Paris perfume in Tokyo and 'retro' clothes in Hong Kong; knowledge is a matter for TV games. It is easy to find a public for eclectic works. By becoming kitsch, art panders to the confusion which reigns in the 'taste' of the patrons. Artists, gallery owners, critics and public wallow together in the 'anything goes', and the epoch is one of slackening. But this realism of the 'anything goes' is in fact that of money; in the absence of aesthetic criteria, it remains possible and useful to assess the value of works of art according to the profits they yield. Such realism accommodates all tendencies, just as capital accommodates all 'needs', providing that the tendencies and needs have purchasing power. As for taste, there is no need to be delicate when one speculates or entertains oneself.

Artistic and literary research is doubly threatened, once by the 'cultural policy' and once by the art and book market. What is advised, sometimes through one channel, sometimes through the other, is to offer works which, first, are relative to subjects which exist in the eyes of the public they address, and second, works so made ('well made') that the public will recognise what they are about, will understand what is signified, will be able to give or refuse its approval knowingly, and if possible, even to derive from such work a certain amount of comfort.

The interpretation which has just been given of the contact between the industrial and mechanical arts, and literature and the fine arts is correct in its outline, but it remains narrowly sociologising and historicising – in other words, one-sided. Stepping over Benjamin's and Adorno's reticences, it must be recalled that science and industry are no more free of the suspicion which concerns reality than are art and writing. To believe otherwise would be to entertain an excessively humanistic notion of the Mephistophelian functionalism of sciences and technologies. There is no denying the dominant existence today of techno-science, that is, the massive subordination of cognitive statements to the finality of the best possible performance, which is the technological criterion. But the mechanical and the industrial, especially when they enter fields traditionally reserved for artists, are carrying with them much more than power effects. The objects and the thoughts which originate in scientific knowledge and the capitalist economy convey with them one of the rules which supports their possibility: the rule that there is no reality unless testified by a census between partners over a certain knowledge and certain commitments.

This rule is of no little consequence. It is the imprint left on the politics of the scientist and the trustee of capital by a kind of flight of reality out of the metaphysical, religious and political certainties that the mind believed it held. This withdrawal is absolutely necessary to the emergence of science and capitalism. No industry is possible without a suspicion of the Aristotelian theory of motion, no industry without a refutation of corporatism, of mercantilism and of physiocracy. Modernity, in whatever age it appears, cannot exist without a shattering of belief and without discovery of the 'lack of reality' of reality, together with the invention of other realities.

What does this 'lack of reality' signify if one tries to free it from a narrowly historicised interpretation? The phrase is of course akin to what Nietzsche calls nihilism. But I see a much earlier modulation of Nietzschean perspectivism in the Kantian theme of the sublime. I think in particular that it is in the aesthetic of the sublime that modern art (including literature) finds its impetus and the theology of the avant-gardes finds it axioms.

The sublime sentiment, which is also the sentiment of the sublime, is according to Kant a strong and equivocal emotion: it carries with it both pleasure and pain. Better still, in it pleasure derives from pain. Within the tradition of the subject, which comes from Augustine and Descartes and which Kant does not radically challenge, this contradiction, which some would call neurosis or masochism, develops as a conflict between the faculties of a subject, the faculty to conceive of something and the faculty to 'present' something.

Knowledge exists if, first, the statement is intelligible, and second, if 'cases' can be derived from the experience which 'corresponds' to it. Beauty exists if a certain 'case' (the work of art), given first, by the sensibility without any conceptual determination, the sentiment of pleasure independent of any interest the work may elicit, appeals to the principle of a universal consensus (which may never be attained).

Taste, therefore, testifies that between the capacity to conceive and the capacity to present an object corresponding to the concept, an undetermined agreement, without rules, giving rise to a judgement which Kant calls reflective, may be experienced as pleasure. The sublime is a different sentiment. It takes place, on the contrary, when the imagination fails to present an object which might, if only in principle, come to match a concept. We have the idea of the world (the totality of what is), but we do not have the capacity to show an example of it. We have the idea of the simple (that which cannot be broken down, decomposed), but we cannot illustrate it with a sensible object which would be a 'case' of it. We can conceive the infinitely great, the infinitely powerful, but every presentation of an object destined to 'make visible' this absolute greatness or power appears to be painfully inadequate. Those are ideas of which no presentation is possible. Therefore, they impart no knowledge about reality (experience); they also prevent the free union of the faculties which gives rise to the sentiment of the beautiful; and they prevent the formation and the stabilisation of taste. They can be said to be unpresentable.

I shall call modern the art which devotes its 'little technical expertise' (son 'petit technique'), as Diderot used to say, to present the fact that the unpresentable exists. To make visible that there is something which can be conceived and which can neither be seen nor made visible: this is what is at stake in modern painting. But how to make visible that there is something which cannot be seen? Kant himself shows the way when he names 'formlessness, the absence of form' as a possible index to the unpresentable. He also says of the empty 'abstraction' which the imagination experiences when in search of a presentation of the infinite (another unpresentable): this abstraction itself is like a presentation of the infinite, its 'negative presentation'. He cites the commandment, 'Thou shalt not make graven images' (Exodus), as the most sublime passage in the Bible in that it forbids all presentation of the Absolute. Little needs to be added to those observations to outline an aesthetic of sublime painting. As painting, it will of course 'present' something though negatively; it will therefore avoid figuration or representation. It will be 'white' like one of Malevitch's squares; it will enable us to see only by making it impossible to see; it will please only by causing pain. One recognises in those instructions the axioms of avant-gardes in painting, inasmuch as they devote themselves to making an allusion to the unpresentable by means of visible presentations. The systems in the name of which, or with which, this task has been able to support or to justify itself deserve the greatest attention; but they can originate only in the vocation of the sublime in order to legitimise it, that is, to conceal it. They remain inexplicable without the incommensurability of reality to concept which is implied in Kantian philosophy of the sublime.

It is not my intention to analyse here in detail the manner in which the various avant-gardes have, so to speak, humbled and disqualified reality by examining the pictorial techniques which are so many devices to make us believe in it. Local tone, drawing, the mixing of colours, linear perspective, the nature of support and that of the instrument, the treatment, the display, the museum: the avant-gardes are perpetually flushing out artifices of presentation which make it possible to subordinate thought to the gaze and to turn it away from the unpresentable. If Habermas, like Marcuse, understands this task of derealisation as an aspect of the (repressive) 'desublimation' which characterises the avant-garde, it is because he confuses the Kantian sublime with Freudian sublimation, and because aesthetics has remained for him that of the beautiful.

The Postmodern

What, then, is the postmodern? What place does it or does it not occupy in the vertiginous work of the questions hurled at the rules of image and narration? It is undoubtedly a part of the modern. All that has been received, if only yesterday (*modo, modo*, Petronius used to say), must be suspected. What space does Cézanne challenge? The Impressionists's. What object do Picasso and Braque attack? Cézanne's. What presupposition does Duchamp break with in 1912? That which says one must make a painting, be it Cubist. And Buren questions that other presupposition which he believes had survived untouched by the work of Duchamp: the place of presentation of the work. In an amazing acceleration, the generations precipitate themselves. A work can become modern only if it is first postmodern. Postmodernism thus understood is not modernism at its end but in the nascent state, and this state is constant.

Yet I would like not to remain with this slightly mechanistic meaning of the word. If it is true that modernity takes place in the withdrawal of the real and according to the sublime relation between the presentable and the conceivable, it is possible, within this relation, to distinguish two modes (to use the musician's language). The emphasis can be placed on the powerlessness of the faculty of presentation, on the nostalgia for presence felt by the human subject, on the obscure and futile will which inhabits him in spite of everything. The emphasis can be placed, rather, on the power of the faculty to conceive, on its 'inhumanity' so to speak (it was the quality Apollinaire demanded of modern artists), since it is not the business of our understanding whether or not human sensibility or imagination can match what it conceives. The emphasis can also be placed on the increase of being and the jubilation which result from the invention of new rules of the game, be it pictorial, artistic or any other. What I have in mind will become clear if we dispose very schematically a few names on the chessboard of the history of avant-gardes: on the side of melancholia, the German Expressionists, and on the side of *novatio*, Braque and Picasso, on the former Malevitch and on the latter Lissitsky, on the one Chirico and on the other Duchamp. The nuance which distinguishes these two modes may be infinitesimal; they often coexist in the same piece, are almost indistinguishable; and yet they testify to a difference (*un différend*) on which the fate of thought depends and will depend for a long time, between regret and assay.

The work of Proust and that of Joyce both allude to something which does not allow itself to be made present. Allusion, to which Paolo Fabbri recently called my attention, is perhaps a form of expression indispensable to the works which belong to an aesthetic of the sublime. In Proust, what is being eluded as the price to pay for this allusion is the identity of consciousness, a victim to the excess of time (*au trop de temps*). But in Joyce, it is the identity of writing which is the victim of an excess of the book (*au trop de livre*) or of literature.

Proust calls forth the unpresentable by means of a language unaltered in its syntax and vocabulary and of a writing which in many of its operators still belongs to the genre of novelistic narration. The literary institution, as Proust inherits it from Balzac and Flaubert, is admittedly subverted in that the hero is no longer a character but the inner consciousness of time and in that the diegetic diachrony, already damaged by Flaubert is here put in question because of the narrative voice. Nevertheless, the unity of the book, the odyssey of that consciousness, even if it is deferred from chapter to chapter, is not seriously challenged: the identity of the writing with itself throughout the labyrinth of the interminable narration is enough to connote such unity, which has been compared to that of *The Phenomenology of Mind*.

Joyce allows the unpresentable to become perceptible in his writing itself, in the signifier. The whole range of available narrative and even stylistic operators is put into play without concern for the unity of the whole, and new operators are tried. The grammar and vocabulary of literary language are no longer accepted as given; rather, they appear as academic forms, as rituals originating in piety (as Nietzsche said) which prevent the unpresentable from being put forward.

Here, then, lies the difference: modern aesthetics is an aesthetic of the sublime, though a nostalgic one. It allows the unpresentable to be put forward only as the missing contents; but the form, because of its recognisable consistency, continues to offer to the reader or viewer matter for solace and pleasure. Yet these sentiments do not constitute the real sublime sentiment, which is in an intrinsic combination of pleasure and pain: the pleasure that reason should exceed all presentation, the pain that imagination or sensibility should not be equal to the concept.

The postmodern would be that which, in the modern, puts forward the unpresentable in presentation itself; that which denies itself the solace of good forms, the consensus of a taste which would make it possible to share collectively the nostalgia for the unattainable; that which searches for new presentations, not in order to enjoy them but in order to impart a stronger sense of the unpresentable. A postmodern artist or writer is in the position of a philosopher: the text he writes, the work he produces are not in principle governed by pre-established rules, and they cannot be judged according to a determining judgement, by applying familiar categories to the text or to the work. Those rules and categories are what the work of art itself is looking for. The artist and the writer, then, are working without rules in order to formulate the rules of what *will have been done*. Hence the fact that work and text have the characters of an *event*; hence also, they always come too late for their author, or, what amounts to the same thing, their being put into work, their realisation (*mise en oeuvre*) always begins too soon. Post modern would have to be understood according to the paradox of the future (*post*) anterior (*modo*).

It seems to me that the essay (Montaigne) is postmodern, while the fragment (*The Athaeneum*) is modern.

Finally, it must be clear that it is our business not to supply reality but to invent allusions to the conceivable which cannot be presented. And it is not to be expected that this task will effect the last reconciliation between language games (which, under the name of faculties, Kant knew to be separated by a chasm), and that only the transcendental illusion (that of Hegel) can hope to totalise them into a real unity. But Kant also knew that the price to pay for such an illusion is terror. The 19th and 20th centuries have given us as much terror as we can take. We have paid a high enough price for the nostalgia of the whole and the one, for the reconciliation of the concept and the sensible, of the transparent and the communicable experience. Under the general demand for slackening and for appeasement, we can hear the mutterings of the desire for a return of terror for the realisation of the fantasy to seize reality. The answer is: Let us wage a war on totality; let us be witnesses to the unpresentable; let us activate the differences and save the honour of the name.

Notes

1   Alain Touraine, *La Société postindutrielle*, Denoël (Paris), 1969; Eng trans Leonard Mayhew, *The Post-Industrial Society*, Wildwood House (London), 1974; Daniel Bell, *The Coming of the Post-Industrial Society*, Basic Books (New York), 1973; Ihab Hassan, *The Dismemberment of Orpheus: Towards a Post Modern Literature*, Oxford University Press (New York), 1971; Michel Benamou and Charles Caramello (eds), *Performance in Postmodern Culture*, Center for Twentieth Century Studies & Coda Press (Wisconsin), 1977; M Köhler 'Postmodernismus: ein begriffgeschichtlicher Überblick', *Amerikastudien* 22, 1, 1977.

2   An already classic literary expression of this is provided in Michel Butor, *Mobile: Etude pour une représentation des Etats-Unis*, Gallimard (Paris), 1962.

3   Jib Fowles (ed), *Handbook of Futures Research*, Greenwood Press (Westport, CT), 1978.

4   Nikolai S Trubetskoi, *Grunszüge der Phonologie*, Travaux du cercle linguistique de Prague, vol 7, 1939; Eng trans Christiane Bultaxe, *Principles of Phonology*, University of California Press, (Berkeley, CA), 1969.

5   Norbert Wiener, *Cybernetics and Society: The Human Use of Human Beings*, Houghton Miflin (Boston), 1949; William Ross Ashby, *An Introduction to Cybernetics*, Chapman & Hall (London), 1956.

6   See the work of Johannes von Neumann, 1903–57.

7   S Bellert, 'La Formalisation des systèmes cybernétiques', *Le Concept d'information dans la science contemporaine*, Editions de Minuit (Paris), 1965.

8   Georges Mounin, *Les Problèmes théoriques de la traduction*, Gallimard (Paris), 1963. The computer revolution dates from 1965, with the new generation of IBM 360s: R Moch, '*Le Tournant informatique*', Documents contributifs, Annexe 4, *l'Information de la société*, La Documentation française (Paris), 1978; RM Ashby, 'La Seconde Génération de la micro-électronique', *La Recherche* 2, June 1970, pp 127 ff.

9   CL Gaudfernan and A Taib, 'Glossaire', in P Nora and A Mine, *L'Information de la société*, La Documentation française (Paris), 1978; R Béca, 'Les Banques de donnés', *Nouvelle informatique et nouvelle croissance*, Annexe 1, *L'Informatisation de la société*.

10 L Joyeux, 'Les Applications avancées de l'informatique', Documents contributifs. Home terminals (Integrated Video Terminals) will be commercialised before 1984 and will cost about $1,400, according to a report of the International Resource Development: *The Home Terminal*, IRD Press, (Conn), 1979.

11 Paul Watzlawick, Janet Helmick-Beavin, Don D Jackson, *Pragmatics of Human Communication: A Study of Interactional Patterns, Pathologies, and Paradoxes*, Norton (New York), 1967.

12 JM Treille, of the Groupe d'analyse et de prospective des systèmes économiques et technologiques (GAPSET), states that, 'Not enough has been said about the new possibilities for

disseminating stored information, in particular using semiconductor and laser technology … Soon everyone will be able to store information cheaply wherever he wishes, and, further, will be able to process it autonomously' (*La Semaine media* 16, 16 February 1979). According to a study by the National Science Foundation, more than one high school student in two has ready access to the services of a computer, and all schools will have one in the early 1980s (*La Semaine media* 13, 25 January 1979).

13 L Brunel, *Des Machines et des hommes*, Québec Science (Montréal), 1978: Jean-Louis Missika and Dominique Wolton, *Les Réseaux pensants, Librairie technique et documentaire*, 1978. The use of video conferences between the province of Quebec and France is becoming routine: in November and December 1978 the fourth series of video conferences (relayed by the satellite 'Symphonie') took place between Quebec and Montreal on the one hand, and Paris (Université Paris Nord and the Beaubourg Centre) on the other (*La Semaine media* 5, 30 November 1978). Another example is provided by electronic journalism. The three big American networks (ABC, NBC and CBS) have increased the number of production studios around the world to the extent that almost all the events that occur can now be processed electronically and transmitted to the United States by satellite. Only the Moscow offices still work on film, which is sent to Frankfurt for satellite transmission. London has become the great 'packing point' (*La Semaine media* 20, 15 March 1979).

14 The unit of information is the bit. For this definition see Gaudefernan and Taïb, 'Glossaire'. This is discussed in René Thom, 'Un Protée de la sémantique: l'information' (1973), *Modèles mathématique de la morphogenèse*, Union Générale d'Edition (Paris), 1974. In particular, the transcription of messages into code allows ambiguities to be eliminated: see Watzlawick et al, *Pragmatics of Human Communication*, p 98.

15 The firms Craig and Lexicon have announced the commercial production of pocket translators: four modules for four different languages with simultaneous reception, each containing 1,500 words with memory. Weidner Communication Systems Inc produces a Multilingual Word Processor that allows the capacity of an average translator to be increased from 600 to 2,400 words per hour. It includes a triple memory: bilingual dictionary, dictionary of synonyms, grammatical index (*La Semaine media* 6, 6 December 1978, p 5).

16 Jürgen Habermas, *Erkenntnis und Interesse*, Suhrkamp (Frankfurt), 1968; trans Jeremy Shapiro, *Knowledge and Human Interests*, Beacon (Boston), 1971.

17 'Man's understanding of nature and his mastery over it by virtue of his presence as a social body … appears as the great foundation-stone [*Grundpfeiler*] of production and of wealth', so that 'general social knowledge becomes a *direct force of production*', writes Marx in the *Grundrisse* (1857–8), Dierz Verlag (Berlin), 1953, p 593; trans Martin Nicolaus, Vintage (New York), 1973, p 705. However, Marx concedes that it is not 'only in the form of knowledge, but also as immediate organs of social practice that learning becomes force', in other words, as machines: machines are '*organs of the human brain created by the human hand*; the power of knowledge, objectified' (p 706). See Paul Mattick, Marx and Keynes, *The Limits of the Mixed Economy*, Extending Horizons Books (Boston), 1969. This point is discussed in Lyotard, 'La Place de l'alienation dans le retournement marxist' (1969), *Dérive à partir de Marx et Freud*, Union Générale d'Edition (Paris), 1973, pp 78–166.

18 The composition of the labour force in the United States changed as follows over a 20-year period (1950–71):

	1950	1971
Factory, services sector, or agricultural workers	62.5%	51.4%
Professionals and technicians	7.5	14.2
White-collar	30.0	34.0
	(Statistical Abstracts, 1971)	

19 Because of the time required for the 'fabrication' of a high-level technician or the average scientist in comparison to the time needed to extract raw materials and transfer money-capital. At the end of the 1960s, Mattick estimated the net rate of investments in underdeveloped countries at 3–5% of the GNP and at 10–15% in the developed countries (*Marx and Keynes*, p 248).

20 Nora and Mine, *L'Informatisation de la société*, especially pt 1, 'Les défis', Y Stourdzé, 'Les Etats-Unis et la guerre des communications', *Le Monde*, 13–15 December 1978. In 1979, the value of the world market of telecommunications devices was $30 billion; it is estimated that in 10 years it will reach $68 billion (*La Semaine media* 19, 8 March 1979).

21 F De Combret, 'Le redéploiement industriel', *Le Monde*, April 1978; M Lepage, *Demain le capitalisme*, Le Livre de Poche (Paris), 1979; Alain Cotta, *La France et l'impératif mondial*, Presses Universitaires de France (Paris), 1978.

22 It is a matter of 'weakening the administration', of reaching the 'minimal state'. This is the decline of the Welfare State, which is accompanying the 'crisis' that began in 1974.

From Jean-François Lyotard, 'Answering the Question: What is Postmodernism?' translated by Régis Durand, from Ihab Hassan and Sally Hassan (eds), *Innovation/Renovation*, The University of Wisconsin Press, 1983. © by permission of The University of Wisconsin Press. 'Réponse à la question: qu'est-ce que le postmodernisme?' was first published in *Critique* 419, April 1982.

Mapping the Postmodern

Andreas Huyssen

This article is a thorough investigation into the relationships of modernism, postmodernism and poststructuralism. Huyssen charts the development across the disciplines of American and western European art, architecture, literature, sociology and politics starting as early as the 1950s. He acknowledges the difficulty of defining postmodernism as a separate movement. Key to his understanding is the new acceptance of an extended understanding of culture that includes both mass and minority culture, and he concludes by advocating postmodernism as a culture of resistance that posits new opportunities for investigation.

Born in Germany in 1942, Andreas Huyssen is a founding editor of the academic journal *New German Critique* and Professor of German and Comparative Literature at Columbia University. This is the place where the Frankfurt School found refuge during the Second World War, but as a purely research-oriented institution. Huyssen has taught a course on the Frankfurt School since taking up his post in 1986. *EB*

* * *

Habermas and the Question of Neo-Conservatism

Both in Europe and the US, the waning of the 1960s was accompanied by the rise of neo-conservatism, and soon enough there emerged a new constellation characterised by the terms postmodernism and neo-conservatism. Even though their relationship was never fully elaborated, the left took them to be compatible with each other or even identical, arguing that postmodernism was the kind of affirmative art that could happily coexist with political and cultural neo-conservatism. Until very recently, the question of the postmodern was simply not taken seriously on the left,[1] not to speak of those traditionalists in the academy or the museum for whom there is still nothing new and worthwhile under the sun since the advent of modernism. The left's ridiculing of postmodernism was of a piece with its often haughty and dogmatic critique of the countercultural impulses of the 1960s. During much of the 1970s, after all, the thrashing of the 1960s was as much a pastime of the left as it was the gospel according to Daniel Bell.

Now, there is no doubt that much of what went under the label of postmodernism in the 1970s is indeed affirmative, not critical, in nature, and often, especially in literature, remarkably similar to tendencies of modernism which it so vocally repudiates. But not all of it is simply affirmative, and the wholesale writing off of postmodernism as a symptom of capitalist culture in decline is reductive, unhistorical and all too reminiscent of Lukács's attacks on modernism in the 1930s. Can one really make such clear-cut distinctions as to uphold modernism, today, as the only valid form of 20th-century 'realism',[2] an art that is adequate to the *condition moderne*, while simultaneously reserving all the old epitheta – inferior, decadent, pathological – to postmodernism? And isn't it ironic that many of the same critics who will insist on this distinction are the first ones to declare emphatically that modernism already had it all and that there is really nothing new in postmodernism ...

[...] It was, of course, Jürgen Habermas's intervention which, for the first time, raised the question of postmodernism's relationship to neo-conservatism in a theoretically and historically complex way. Ironically, however, the effect of Habermas's argument, which identified the postmodern with various forms of conservatism, was to reinforce leftist cultural stereotypes rather than challenge them. In his 1980 Adorno prize lecture,[3] which has become a focal point for the debate, Habermas criticised both conservatism (old, neo and young) and postmodernism for not coming to terms either with the exigencies of culture in late capitalism or with the successes and failures of modernism itself. Significantly, Habermas's notion of modernity – the modernity he wishes to see continued and completed – is purged of modernism's nihilistic and anarchic strain just as his opponents', eg Lyotard's,[4] notion of an aesthetic (post)modernism is determined to liquidate any trace of the enlightened modernity inherited from the 18th century which provides the basis for Habermas's notion of modern culture. [...]

During the 1970s, Habermas could observe how German art and literature abandoned the explicit political commitments of the 1960s, a decade often described in Germany as a 'second enlightenment'; how autobiography and *Erfahrungstexte* replaced the documentary experiments in prose and drama of the preceding decade; how political poetry and art made way for a new subjectivity, a new romanticism, a new mythology; how a new generation of students and young intellectuals became increasingly weary of theory, left politics and social science, preferring instead to flock toward the revelations of ethnology and myth. [...]

His questions were these: How does postmodernism relate to modernism? How are political conservatism, cultural eclecticism or pluralism, tradition, modernity and anti-modernity interrelated in contemporary Western culture? To what extent can the cultural and social formation of the 1970s be characterised as postmodern? And, further, to what extent is postmodernism a revolt against reason and enlightenment, and at what point do such revolts become reactionary – a question heavily loaded with the weight of recent German history? In comparison, the standard American accounts of postmodernism too often remain entirely tied to questions of aesthetic style or poetics; the occasional nod toward theories of a post-industrial society is usually intended as a reminder that any form of Marxist or neo-Marxist thought is simply obsolete. In the American debate, three positions can be schematically outlined. Postmodernism is dismissed outright as a fraud and modernism held up as the universal truth, a view which reflects the thinking of the 1950s. Or modernism is condemned as elitist and postmodernism praised as populist, a view which reflects the thinking of the 1960s. Or there is the truly 1970s proposition that 'anything goes', which is consumer capitalism's cynical version of 'nothing works', but which at least recognises that the older dichotomies no longer work. Inevitably, none of these positions ever reached the level of Habermas's interrogation.

However, there were problems not so much with the questions Habermas raised, as with some of the answers he suggested. Thus his attack on Foucault and Derrida as young conservatives drew immediate fire from poststructuralist quarters, where the reproach was turned around and Habermas himself was labelled a conservative. At this point, the debate was quickly reduced to the silly question: 'Mirror, mirror on the wall, who is the least conservative of us all?' [...]

In the uproar over Habermas's attack on the French poststructuralists, the American and European neo-conservatives were all but forgotten, but I think we should at least take cognisance of what cultural neo-conservatives actually say about postmodernism. The answer is fairly simple and straightforward: they reject it and they think it is dangerous. [...]

The only place where Habermas could rest assured of neo-conservative applause is in his attack on Foucault and Derrida. Any such applause, however, would carry the proviso that neither Foucault nor Derrida be associated with conservatism. And yet, Habermas was right, in a sense, to connect the postmodernism problematic with poststructuralism. [...]

What, then, can one conclude from these ideological skirmishes for a mapping of postmodernism in the 1970s and 1980s? Firstly, Habermas was both right and wrong about the collusion of conservative political vision of a post-modern society freed from all aesthetic, ie, hedonistic, modernist and postmodernist subversions, or whether the issue is aesthetic postmodernism. Secondly, Habermas and the neo-conservatives are right in insisting that postmodernism is not so much a question of style as it is a question of politics and culture at large. The neo-conservative lament about the politicisation of culture since the 1960s is only ironic in this context since they themselves have a thoroughly political notion of culture. Thirdly, the neo-conservatives are also right in suggesting that there are continuities between the oppositional culture of the 1960s and that of the 1970s. But their obsessive fixation on the 1960s, which they try to purge from the history books, blinds them to what is different and new in the cultural developments of the 1970s. And, fourthly, the attack on poststructuralism by Habermas and the American neo-conservatives raises the question of what to make of that fascinating interweaving and intersecting of poststructuralism with postmodernism, a phenomenon that is much more relevant in the US than in France. It is to this question that I will now turn in my discussion of the critical discourse of American postmodernism in the 1970s and 1980s.

Poststructuralism: Modern or Postmodern?

The neo-conservative hostility towards both is not really enough to establish a substantive link between postmodernism and poststructuralism; and it may indeed be more difficult to establish such a link than it would seem at first. Certainly, since the late 1970s we have seen a consensus emerge in the US that if postmodernism represents the contemporary 'avant-garde' in the arts, poststructuralism must be its equivalent in 'critical theory'.[5] [...] Mere simultaneity of critical and artistic discourse formations does not per se mean that they have to overlap, unless, of course, the boundaries between them are intentionally dismantled, as they are in modernist and postmodernist literature as well as in poststructuralist discourse.

And yet, however much postmodernism and poststructuralism in the US may overlap and mesh, they are far from identical or even homologous. I do not question that the theoretical discourse of the 1970s has had a profound impact on the work of a considerable number of artists both in Europe and in the US. What I do question, however, is the way in which this impact is automatically evaluated in the US as postmodern and thus sucked into the orbit of the kind of critical discourse that emphasises radical rupture and discontinuity. Actually, both in France and in the US, poststructuralism is much closer to modernism than is usually assumed by the advocates of postmodernism. The distance that does exist between the critical discourses of the New Criticism and poststructuralism (a constellation which is only pertinent in the US, not in France) is not identical with the differences between modernism and postmodernism. I will argue that poststructuralism is primarily a discourse of and about modernism,[6] and that if we are to locate the postmodern in poststructuralism it will have to be found in the ways various forms of poststructuralism have opened up new problematics in modernism and have reinscribed modernism into the discourse formations of our own time.

Let me elaborate my view that poststructuralism can be perceived, to a significant degree, as a theory of modernism. I will limit myself here to certain points that relate back to my discussion of the modernism/postmodernism constellation in the 1960s and 1970s: the questions of aestheticism and mass culture, subjectivity and gender. [...]

Much recent writing has challenged the American domestication of French poststructuralism.[7] But it is not enough to claim that in the transfer to the US, French theory lost the political edge it has in France. The fact is that even in France the political implications of certain forms of poststructuralism are hotly debated and in doubt.[8] It is not just the institutional pressures of American literary criticism which have depoliticised French theory; the aestheticist trend *within* poststructuralism itself has facilitated the peculiar American reception. Thus it is no coincidence that the politically weakest body of French writing (Derrida and the late Barthes) has been privileged in American literature departments over the more politically intended projects of Foucault and Baudrillard, Kristeva and Lyotard. But even in the more politically conscious and self-conscious theoretical writing in France, the tradition of modernist aestheticism – mediated through an extremely selective reading of Nietzsche – is so powerful a presence that the notion of a radical rupture between the modern and the postmodern cannot possibly make much sense. It is furthermore striking that despite the considerable differences between the various poststructuralist projects, none of them seems informed in any substantial way by postmodernist works of art. Rarely, if ever, do they even address postmodernist works. In itself, this does not vitiate the power of the theory. But it does make for a kind of dubbing where the poststructuralist language is not in sync with the lips and movements of the postmodern body. There is no doubt that centre stage in critical theory is held by the classical modernists: Flaubert, Proust and Bataille in Barthes; Nietzsche and Heidegger, Mallarmé and Artaud in Derrida; Nietzsche, Magritte and Bataille in Foucault; Mallarmé and Lautréamont, Joyce and Artaud in Kristeva; Freud in Lacan; Brecht in Althusser and Macherey, and so on ad infinitum. The enemies still are realism and representation, mass culture and standardisation, grammar, communication and the presumably all-powerful homogenising pressures of the modern state.

I think we must begin to entertain the notion that rather than offering a *theory of postmodernity* and developing an analysis of contemporary culture, French theory provides us primarily with an *archaeology of modernity*, a theory of modernism at the stage of its exhaustion. It is as if the creative powers of modernism had migrated into theory and come to full self-consciousness in the poststructuralist text – the owl of Minerva spreading its wings at the fall of dusk. Poststructuralism offers a theory of modernism characterised by *Nachträglichkeit*, both in the psychoanalytic and the historical sense. Despite its ties to the tradition of modernist aestheticism, it offers a reading of modernism which differs substantially from those offered by the New Critics, by Adorno or by Greenberg. It is no longer the modernism of 'the age of anxiety', the ascetic and tortured modernism of a Kafka, a modernism of negativity and alienation, ambiguity and abstraction, the modernism of the closed and finished work of art. Rather, it is a modernism of playful transgression, of an unlimited weaving of textuality, a modernism all confident in its rejection of representation and reality, in its denial of the subject, of history, and of the subject of history; a modernism quite dogmatic in its rejection of presence and in its unending praise of lacks and absences, deferrals and traces which produce, presumably, not anxiety but, in Roland Barthes's terms, *jouissance*, bliss.[9]

But if poststructuralism can be seen as the *revenant* of modernism in the guise of theory, then that would also be precisely what makes it postmodern. It is a postmodernism that works itself out not as a rejection of modernism, but rather as a retrospective reading which, in some cases, is fully aware of modernism's limitations and failed political ambitions. The dilemma of modernism had been its inability, despite the best intentions, to mount an effective critique of bourgeois modernity and modernisation. The fate of the historical avant-garde especially had proven how modern art, even where it ventured beyond art for art's sake, was ultimately forced back into the aesthetic realm. Thus the gesture of poststructuralism, to the extent that it abandons all pretence to a critique that would go beyond language games, beyond epistemology and the aesthetic, seems at least plausible and logical. It certainly frees art and literature from that overload of responsibilities – to change life, change society, change the world – on which the historical avant-garde was shipwrecked, and which lived on in France through the 1950s and 1960s embodied in the figure of Jean Paul Sartre. Seen in this light, poststructuralism seems to seal the fate of the modernist project which, even where it limited itself to the aesthetic sphere, always upheld a vision of a redemption of modern life through culture. That such visions are no longer possible to sustain may be at the heart of the postmodern condition, and it may ultimately vitiate the poststructuralist attempt to salvage aesthetic modernism for the late 20th century. At any rate, it all begins to ring false when poststructuralism presents itself, as it frequently does in American writings, as the latest 'avant-garde' in criticism, thus ironically assuming, in its institutional *Selbstverständnis*, the kind of teleological posturing which poststructuralism itself has done so much to criticise

* * *

[...] We face the paradox that a body of theories of modernism and modernity, developed in France since the 1960s, has come to be viewed, in the US, as the embodiment of the postmodern theory. In a certain sense, this development is perfectly logical. Poststructuralism's readings of modernism are new and exciting enough to be considered somehow beyond modernism as it has been perceived before; in this way poststructuralist criticism in the US yields to the very real pressures of the postmodern. But against any facile conflation of poststructuralism with the postmodern, we must insist on the fundamental non-identity of the two phenomena. In America, too, poststructuralism offers a theory of modernism, not a theory of the postmodern.

As to the French theorists themselves, they rarely speak of the postmodern. Lyotard's *La Condition postmoderne*, we must remember, is the exception, not the rule.[10] What the French explicitly analyse and reflect upon is *le texte moderne and la modernité*. Where they talk about the postmodern at all, as in the cases of Lyotard and Kristeva,[11] the question seems to have been prompted by American friends, and the discussion almost immediately and invariably turns back to problems of the modernist aesthetic. For Kristeva, the question of postmodernism is the question of how anything can be written in the 20th century and how we can talk about this writing. She goes on to say that postmodernism is 'that literature which writes itself with the more or less conscious intention of expanding the signifiable and thus the human realm'.[12] With the Bataillean formulation of writing-as-experience of limits, she sees the major writing since Mallarmé and Joyce, Artaud and Burroughs as the 'exploration of the typical imaginary relationship, that to the mother, through the most radical and problematic aspect of this relationship, language.'[13] Kristeva's is a fascinating and novel approach to the question of modernist literature, and one that understands itself as a political intervention. But it does not yield much for an exploration of the differences between modernity and postmodernity. Thus it cannot surprise that Kristeva still shares with Barthes and the classical theorists of modernism an aversion to the media whose function, she claims, is to collectivise all systems of signs thus enforcing contemporary society's general tendency towards uniformity.

Lyotard, who like Kristeva and unlike the Deconstructionists is a political thinker, defines the postmodern, in his essay, 'Answering the Question: What is Postmodernism?', as a recurring stage within the modern itself. He turns to the Kantian sublime for a theory of the nonrepresentable essential to modern art and literature. Paramount are his interest in rejecting representation, which is linked to terror and totalitarianism, and his demand for radical experimentation in the arts. At first sight, the turn to Kant seems plausible in the sense that Kant's autonomy aesthetic and notion of 'disinterested pleasure' stands at the threshold of a modernist aesthetic, at a crucial juncture of that differentiation of spheres which has been so important in social thought from Weber to Habermas. And yet, the turn to Kant's sublime forgets that the 18th-century fascination with the sublime of the universe, the cosmos, expresses precisely that very desire of totality and representation which Lyotard so abhors and persistently criticises in Habermas's work.[14] Perhaps Lyotard's text says more here than it means to. If historically the notion of the sublime harbours a secret desire for totality, then perhaps Lyotard's sublime can be read as an attempt to totalise the aesthetic realm by fusing it with all other spheres of life, thus wiping out the differentiations between the aesthetic realm and the life-world on which Kant did after all insist. At any rate, it is no coincidence that the first moderns in Germany, the Jena romantics, built their aesthetic strategies of the fragment precisely on a rejection of the sublime which to them had become a sign of the falseness of bourgeois accommodation to absolutist culture. Even today, the sublime has not lost its link with terror which, in Lyotard's reading, it opposes. For what would be more sublime and unrepresentable than the nuclear holocaust, the bomb being the signifier of an ultimate sublime. But apart from the question whether or not the sublime is an adequate aesthetic category to theorise contemporary art and literature, it is clear that in Lyotard's essay the postmodern as aesthetic phenomenon is not seen as distinct from modernism. The crucial historical distinction which Lyotard offers in *La Condition postmoderne* is that between the *métarécits* of liberation (the French tradition of enlightened modernity) and of totality (the German Hegelian/Marxist tradition) on the one hand, and the modernist experimental discourse of language games on the other. Enlightened modernity and its presumable consequences are pitted against aesthetic modernism. The irony in all of this, as Fred Jameson has remarked,[15] is that Lyotard's commitment to radical experimentation is politically 'very closely related to the conception of the revolutionary nature of high modernism that Habermas faithfully inherited from the Frankfurt School'.

No doubt, there are historically and intellectually specific reasons for the French resistance to acknowledging the problem of the postmodern as a historical problem of the 20th century. At the same time, the force of the French rereading of modernism proper is itself shaped by the pressures of the 1960s and 1970s, and it has thus raised many of the questions pertinent to the culture of our own time. But it has done very little towards illuminating an emerging postmodern culture, and it has largely remained blind to or uninterested in many of the most promising artistic endeavours today. French theory of the 1960s and 1970s has offered us exhilarating fireworks which illuminate a crucial segment of the trajectory of modernism, but, as appropriate with fireworks, after dusk has fallen. This view is borne out by none less than Michel Foucault who, in the late 1970s, criticised his own earlier fascination with language and epistemology as a limited project of an earlier decade: 'The whole relentless theorisation of writing which we saw in the 1960s was doubtless only a swansong.'[16] Swansong of modernism indeed; but as such already a moment of the postmodern. Foucault's view of the intellectual movement of the 1960s as a swansong, it seems to me, is closer to the truth than its American rewriting, during the 1970s, as the latest avant-garde.

Whither Postmodernism?

The cultural history of the 1970s still has to be written, and the various postmodernisms in art, literature, dance, theatre, architecture, film, video and music will have to be discussed separately and in detail. All I want to do now is to offer a framework for relating some recent cultural and political changes to postmodernism, changes which already lie outside the conceptual network of 'modernism/avant-gardism' and have so far rarely been included in the postmodernism debate.[17]

I would argue that the contemporary arts – in the widest possible sense, whether they call themselves postmodernist or reject that label – can no longer be regarded as just another phase in the sequence of modernist *and* avant-gardist movements which began in Paris in the 1850s and 1860s and which maintained an ethos of cultural progress and vanguardism through the 1960s. On this level, postmodernism cannot be regarded simply as a sequel to modernism, as the latest step in the never ending revolt of modernism against itself. The postmodern sensibility of our time is different from both modernism and avant-gardism precisely in that it raises the question of cultural tradition and conservation in the most fundamental way as an aesthetic and a political issue. It doesn't always do it successfully, and often does it exploitatively. And yet, my main point about contemporary postmodernism is that it operates in a field of tension between tradition and innovation, conservation and renewal, mass culture and high art, in which the second terms are no longer automatically privileged over the first; a field of tension which can no longer be grasped in categories such as progress vs reaction, left vs right, present vs past, modernism vs realism, abstraction vs representation, avant-garde vs. kitsch. The fact that such dichotomies, which after all are central to the classical accounts of modernism, have broken down is part of the shift I have been trying to describe. I could also state the shift in the following terms: modernism and the avant-garde were always closely related to social and industrial modernisation. They were related to it as an adversary culture, yes, but they drew their energies, not unlike Poe's *Man of the Crown*, from their proximity to the crises brought about by modernisation and progress. Modernisation – such was the widely held belief, even when the word was not around – had to be traversed. There was a vision of emerging on the other side. The modern was a world-scale drama played out on the European and American stage, with mythic modern man as its hero and with modern art as a driving force, just as Saint-Simon had envisioned it already in 1825. Such heroic visions of modernity and of art as a force of social change (or, for that matter, resistance to undesired change) are a thing of the past, admirable for sure, but no longer in tune with current sensibilities, except perhaps with an emerging apocalyptic sensibility as the flip side of modernist heroism.

Seen in this light, postmodernism at its deepest level represents not just another crisis within the perpetual cycle of boom and bust, exhaustion and renewal, which has characterised the trajectory of modernist culture. It rather represents a new type of crisis *of* that modernist culture itself. [...]

But modernism's running feud with mass society and mass culture as well as the avant-garde's attack on high art as a support system of cultural hegemony always took place on the pedestal of high art itself. And certainly that is where the avant-garde has been installed after its failure, in the 1920s, to create a more encompassing space for art in social life. To continue to demand today that high art leave the pedestal and relocate elsewhere (wherever that might be) is to pose the problem in obsolete terms. The pedestal of high art and high culture no longer occupies the privileged space it used to, just as the cohesion of the class which erected its monuments on that pedestal is a thing of the past; recent conservative attempts in a number of Western countries to restore the dignity of the classics of Western civilisation, from Plato via Adam Smith to the high modernists, and to send students back to the basics, prove the point. I am not saying here that the pedestal of high art does not exist any more. Of course it does, but it is not what it used to be. Since the 1960s, artistic activities have become much more diffuse and harder to contain in safe categories or stable institutions such as the academy, the museum or even the established gallery network. To some, this dispersal of cultural and artistic practices and activities will involve a sense of loss and disorientation; others will experience it as a new freedom, a cultural liberation. Neither may be entirely wrong, but we should recognise that it was not only recent theory or criticism that deprived the univalent, exclusive and totalising accounts of modernism of their hegemonic role. It was the activities of artists, writers, film makers, architects and performers that have propelled us beyond a narrow vision of modernism and given us a new lease on modernism itself.

In political terms, the erosion of the triple dogma modernism/modernity/avant-gardism can be contextually related to the emergence of the problematic of 'otherness', which has asserted itself in the sociopolitical sphere as much as in the cultural sphere. I cannot discuss here the various and multiple forms of otherness as they emerge from differences in subjectivity, gender and sexuality, race and class, temporal *Ungleichzeitigkeiten* and spatial geographic locations and dislocations. But I want to mention at least four recent phenomena which, in my mind, are and will remain constitutive of postmodern culture for some time to come.

Despite all its noble aspirations and achievements, we have come to recognise that the culture of enlightened modernity has also always (though by no means exclusively) been a culture of inner and outer imperialism, a reading already offered by Adorno and Horkheimer in the 1940s and an insight not unfamiliar to those of our ancestors involved in the multitude of struggles against rampant modernisation. Such imperialism, which works inside and outside, on the micro and macro levels, no longer goes unchallenged either politically, economically or culturally. Whether these challenges will usher in a more habitable, less violent and more democratic world remains to be seen, and it is easy to be sceptical. But enlightened cynicism is as insufficient an answer as blue-eyed enthusiasm for peace and nature.

The women's movement has led to some significant changes in social structure and cultural attitudes which must be sustained even in the face of the recent grotesque revival of American machismo. Directly and indirectly, the women's movement has nourished the emergence of women as a self-confident and creative force in the arts, in literature, film and criticism. The ways in which we now raise questions of gender and sexuality, reading and writing, subjectivity and enunciation, voice and performance are unthinkable without the impact of feminism, even though many of these activities may take place on the margin or even outside the movement proper. Feminist critics have also contributed substantially to revisions of the history of modernism, not just by unearthing forgotten artists, but also by approaching the male modernists in novel ways.

This is true also of the 'new French feminists' and their theorisation of the feminine in modernist writing, even though they often insist on maintaining a polemical distance from an American-type feminism.[18]

During the 1970s, questions of ecology and environment have deepened from single-issue politics to a broad critique of modernity and modernisation, a trend which is politically and culturally much stronger in West Germany than in the US. A new ecological sensibility manifests itself not only in political and regional subcultures, in alternative lifestyles and the new social movements in Europe, but it also affects art and literature in a variety of ways: the work of Joseph Beuys, certain land art projects, Christo's California running fence, the new nature poetry, the return to local traditions, dialects and so on. It was especially due to the growing ecological sensibility that the link between certain forms of modernism and technological modernisation has come under critical scrutiny.

There is a growing awareness that other cultures, non-European, non-Western cultures must be met by means other than conquest or domination, as Paul Ricoeur put it more than 20 years ago, and that the erotic and aesthetic fascination with 'the Orient' – so prominent in Western culture, including modernism – is deeply problematic. This awareness will have to translate into a type of intellectual work very different from that of the modernist intellectual who typically spoke with the confidence of standing at the cutting edge of time and of being able to speak for others. Foucault's notion of the local and specific intellectual as opposed to the 'universal' intellectual of modernity may provide a way out of the dilemma of being locked into our own culture and traditions while simultaneously recognising their limitations.

In conclusion, it is easy to see that a postmodernist culture emerging from these political, social and cultural constellations will have to be a postmodernism of resistance, including resistance to that easy postmodernism of the 'anything goes' variety. Resistance will always have to be specific and contingent upon the cultural field within which it operates. It cannot be defined simply in terms of negativity or non-identity à la Adorno, nor will the litanies of a totalising, collective project suffice. At the same time, the very notion of resistance may itself be problematic in its simple opposition to affirmation. After all, there are affirmative forms of resistance and resisting forms of affirmation. But this may be more a semantic problem than a problem of practice. And it should not keep us from making judgements. How such resistance can be articulated in artworks in ways that would satisfy the needs of the political and those of the aesthetic, of the producers and of the recipients, cannot be prescribed, and it will remain open to trial, error and debate. But it is time to abandon that dead-end dichotomy of politics and aesthetics which for too long has dominated accounts of modernism, including the aestheticist trend within poststructuralism. The point is not to eliminate the productive tension between the political *and* the aesthetic, between history and the text, between engagement and the mission of art. The point is to heighten that tension, even to rediscover it and to bring it back into focus in the arts as well as in criticism. No matter how troubling it may be, the landscape of the postmodern surrounds us. It simultaneously delimits and opens our horizons. It's our problem and our hope.

Notes

1 It is with the recent publication by Fred Jameson and Hal Foster of *The Anti-Aesthetic* that things have begun to change.

2 Of course, those who hold this view will not utter the word 'realism' as it is tarnished by its traditionally close association with the notion of 'reflection', 'representation' and a transparent reality; but the persuasive power of the modernist doctrine owes much to the underlying idea that only modernist art and literature are somehow adequate to our time.

3 Jürgen Habermas, 'Modernity versus Postmodernity', *NGC* 22, Winter, 1981, pp 3–14. Reprinted in *The Anti-Aesthetic*, ed Hal Foster, Bay Press (Port Townsend), 1984.

4 Jean-François Lyotard, 'Answering the Question: What is Postmodernism?' *The Postmodern Condition*, University of Minnesota Press (Minneapolis), 1984, pp 71–82.

5 I follow the current usage in which the term 'critical theory' refers to a multitude of recent theoretical and interdisciplinary endeavours in the humanities. Originally, critical theory was a much more focused term that referred to the theory developed by the Frankfurt School since the 1930s. Today, however, the critical theory of the Frankfurt School is itself only a part of an expanded field of critical theories, and this may ultimately benefit its reinscription in contemporary critical discourse.

6 This part of the argument draws on the work of Foucault by John Rajchman, 'Foucault, or the Ends of Modernism', *October* 24, Spring 1983, pp 37–62, and on the discussion of Derrida as theorist of modernism in Jochen Schilte-Sasse's introduction to Peter Bürger, *Theory of the Avantgarde*, University of Minnesota Press (Minneapolis), 1984.

7 Jonathan Arac, Wlad Godzich, Wallace Martin (eds), *The Yale Critics: Deconstruction in America*, University of Minnesota Press (Minneapolis), 1983.

8 See Nancy Fraser's article in *NGC* 33, Fall, 1984.

9 'Bliss' is an inadequate rendering of *jouissance* as the English term lacks the crucial bodily and hedonistic connotations of the French word.

10 Jean-François Lyotard, *La Condition postmoderne*, Editions de Minuit (Paris), 1979. English translation, *The Postmodern Condition*, University of Minnesota Press (Minneapolis), 1984.

11 The English translation of *La Condition postmoderne* includes the essay, important for the aesthetic debate, 'Answering the Question: What is Postmodernism?' For Kristeva's statement on the postmodern see 'Postmodernism?', *Buckwell Review* 25:11, 1980, pp 136–41.

12 Kristeva, 'Postmodernism?', *Buckwell Review* 25:11, 1980, p 137.

13 Ibid, p 139 f.

14 In fact *The Postmodern Condition* is a sustained attack on the intellectual and political traditions of the Enlightenment embodied for Lyotard in the work of Jürgen Habermas.

15 Fredric Jameson, 'Foreword', Lyotard, *The Postmodern Condition*, p xvi.

16 Michel Foucault, 'Truth and Power', *Power/Knowledge*, Pantheon (New York), 1980, p 127.

17 The major exception is Craig Owens, 'The Discourse of Others', *Anti-Aesthetic*, ed Foster, pp 65–98.

18 Cf Elaine Marks and Isabelle de Courtivron (eds), *New French Feminisms*, University of Massachusetts Press (Amherst), 1980. For a critical view of French theories of the feminine cf the work by Alice Jardine: 'Theories of the Feminine', *Enclitic* 4:2, Fall 1980, pp 5–15; 'Pre-texts for the Transatlantic Feminist', Yale French Studies 62, 1981, pp 220–36; and her essay 'Gynesis', *Diacritics* 12: 2, Summer, 1982, pp 54–65.

Originally appeared in Andreas Huyssen, *After the Great Divide*, Macmillan (London), 1988, after having first been published in *New German Critique* 33, Fall 1984. Earlier versions of this article were presented at the XVIIth World Congress of Philosophy in Montreal, August 1983, and at a conference on 'The Question of the Postmodern: Criticism/Literature/Culture' organised at Cornell University by Michael Hays, April 1984. © Reproduced with permission of Palgrave Macmillan and Indiana University Press. For this edition notes have been renumbered.

Defining the Post-Modern

Margaret A Rose

Margaret Rose contends that the term post-modernism had lost its meaning by 1991 when it started to refer to almost anything; in this extract, she traces its origins. Travelling across time, from Arnold J Toynbee (1939), Joseph Hudnut (1945), C Wright Mills (1959), Leslie Fiedler (1965), Frank Kermode (1966), Nikolaus Pevsner (1966) and Philip Johnson (1979), she explains how the term postmodern has taken on different spellings and different significations. Indeed, Rose admirably explains how postmodern was associated with the ultramodern, the rise of the industrial urban working class, the 'after modern age' – the new style successor to the international modern style – the double-coding and the reaction against modernism, to finally become a historical modern period – a new era.

Margaret A Rose (1947–) is originally from Melbourne, Australia. She lectured in the history of ideas at Deakin University, Geelong, Australia for a number of years, and then taught briefly at the University of Melbourne. *LCS*

Dick Hebdige opens the section on post-modernism in his *Hiding in the Light: On Images and Things* of 1988 with the statement that 'The success of the term postmodernism … has generated its own problems', and that:

> It becomes more and more difficult as the 1980s wear on to specify exactly what it is that 'postmodernism' is supposed to refer to as the term gets stretched in all directions across different debates, different disciplinary and discursive boundaries, as difficult factions seek to make it their own, using it to designate a plethora of incommensurable objects, tendencies, emergencies.[1]

Despite this and other similar complaints,[2] there is, however, no necessary reason why some of the 'factional' or other differences behind the variety of definitions of post-modernism and the post-modern in general which we now have may not be defined as such, and the different meanings which have been given the term be categorised more succinctly. One major source for the idea that post-modernism is a movement in which 'anything goes' is, in fact, to be found in an attack by the French theorist Lyotard on a rival concept of post-modernism, which, in addition, cannot be said to describe its target accurately.[3]

Many (although certainly not all) recent discussions of post-modernism have also followed Lyotard's writings on the subject in some regard. Hebdige himself, for example, goes on after summarising a variety of uses of the term 'postmodernism' to use it, without specifically saying so, in the Lyotardian sense of a critique of metanarratives,[4] when he claims that his following overview of the term will entail his 'going against the spirit of postmodernism', understood as being 'founded in the renunciation of claims to mastery and dominant specularity'.[5]

While the 'renunciation of claims to mastery' evokes Lyotard's deconstruction of the 'metanarratives' of modernity, the positing of a 'dominant specularity' as yet another target of the post-modernist also recalls the terminology of works such as Guy Debord's *Society of the Spectacle* of 1967, and the use of it by Jean Baudrillard in his contribution to Hal Foster's *Postmodern Culture* [6] or his 'The Orders of Simulacra' of 1975. In this latter text Baudrillard had not only spoken of the 'burlesque spectacle' of the political class,[7] but had also divided history into three dominant 'orders of appearance' since the Renaissance: of *Counterfeit* for the period from the Renaissance to the Industrial Revolution; *Production* for the industrial era; and *Simulation* for the current phase, in which reality is said to be continuously overtaken by its images and to be ruled by indeterminacy.[8] While Baudrillard had been speaking here, as elsewhere, largely of the modern world, rather than something termed the post-modern (or 'postmodern'), one theorist of post-modernism writing prior to both Hebdige and Lyotard, Ihab Hassan, will be seen to have taken the post-modern age to be an age of 'indeterminacy', while others, such as Fredric Jameson, will be seen to have echoed Baudrillard in viewing the present age as a 'neo-capitalist cybernetic order' which aims at total control.[9]

Hebdige's commentary on post-modernism also continues in a Baudrillardian vein when he claims that 'postmodernity is modernity without the hopes and dreams which made modernity bearable'[10] and adds that 'it is a hydra-headed, decentred condition in which we get dragged along from pillar to post across a succession of reflecting surfaces, drawn by the call of the wild signifier'.[11] Further to this we shall see later that Hebdige's description of post-modernism as 'bricolage, pastiche, allegory, and the hyperspace of the new architecture'[12] echoes a 'Baudrillardian' characterisation of post-modernism by Fredric Jameson which has projected characteristics onto post-modernism[13] which others, such as Charles Jencks, have preferred to describe as 'Late-Modern' rather than as 'Post-Modern'.[14]

Although it gives a somewhat broader account of the concept of the post-modern than Hebdige's survey, and those like it,[15] the *Oxford English Dictionary*'s (*OED*) *Supplement* of 1982 was of necessity also too restricted in its coverage of the use of the term to give all the details required for an accurate history of it or of the sometimes related term 'post-modernism'.[16]

The *OED Supplement*'s entry begins:

post-mo.dern, *a*. Also **post-Modern**. (POST-B. lb.) Subsequent to, or later than, what is 'modern'; *spec*. in the arts, esp. *Archit.*, applied to a movement in reaction against that designated 'modern' (cf. MODERN a. 2h.)[17] Hence **post-mo.dernism**, **post-mo.dernist**, *a*. and *sb*.

Despite the generally scientific appearance of the above entry, it contains a number of problems which the reader aware of the possible variety of definitions of the post-modern may already have been able to discern. Firstly, the word 'post-modern' is not always thought to be subsequent to or later than the 'modern', but may both be contemporary with it, or, as in the writings of Lyotard, 'prior' to the modern. Secondly, although one other theorist of post-modernism, Charles Jencks, has questioned the sense of Lyotard's claims, he himself has not seen the post-modern in architecture as simply a reaction against the 'modern', but has described it as a 'double-coding' of the modern style with some other style or 'code'.[18]

Further to the above, the *OED Supplement*'s cross-reference to its '2h' definition of the 'modern' in its characterisation of the 'post-modern' as, 'with reference to the arts and architecture', a 'movement in reaction against that designated 'modern', creates some problems not only on account of its conflation of the terms 'modern' and 'modernism' in its application of the former to the arts, where the two terms might not always be able to describe the same phenomena, but also because its 2h definition of the modern has described the 'modern' in terms of its 'departure from or ... repudiation of accepted or traditional styles and values'.[19] Hence we have a definition of the post-modern which not only describes it negatively as a reaction against the modern, but which also relates it to a description of the modern which sees it too in negative terms as a reaction against other traditions. Although the latter may be true for some modernisms it is not the only aspect of the modern, or of modernism, which has been addressed by post-modernists who have reacted specifically to modernist alternatives to other traditions as well as to modernist rejections of the past.

Other problems abound in giving a history of today's usage of the term post-modern. The *OED Supplement*'s reference to Joseph Hudnut's use of the term post-modernism in relation to architecture (which the dictionary's entry goes on to date as being from 1949 and as the earliest use of the term 'post-modern', whereas it is in fact used by Hudnut from at least 1945 on, and by others prior to that)[20] is, for example, to a concept of 'post-modern' architecture as mass-produced prefabricated building which would today be rejected by many post-modernist architects as describing an 'ultra-modern' rather than a 'post-modern' form of architecture.[21] Further to this, the quotation given by the dictionary entry from Hudnut gives little idea of the application of the term to the prefabricated house in his article: 'He shall be a modern owner, a post-modern owner, if such a thing is conceivable. Free from all sentimentality or fantasy or caprice.'[22]

Hudnut had published these words in an article of 1945 entitled 'the post-modern house' as well as in a 1949 collection of essays entitled *Architecture and the Spirit of Man*.[23] The passage from which they are taken reads in full:

> I shall not imagine for my future house a romantic owner, nor shall I defend my client's preferences as those foibles and aberrations usually referred to as 'human nature'. No, he shall be a modern owner, a post-modern owner, if such a thing is conceivable. Free from all sentimentality or fantasy or caprice, his vision, his tastes, his habits of thought shall be those most necessary to a collective-industrial scheme of life; the world shall, if it pleases him, appear as a system of casual sequences transformed each day by the cumulative miracles of science.

Even so he will claim for himself some inner experiences, free from outward control, unprofaned by the collective conscience. That opportunity, when the universe is socialised, mechanised and standardised, will yet be discoverable in the home. Though his house is the most precise product of modern processes there will be entrenched within it this ancient loyalty invulnerable against the siege of our machines. It will be the architect's task, as it is today, to comprehend that loyalty – to comprehend it more firmly than anyone else – and, undefeated by all the armaments of industry, to bring it out in its true and beautiful character.[24]

I have quoted this passage at length because there are several points made in it which are of interest for understanding Hudnut's concept of the post-modern. Firstly, the concept of the post-modern is clearly used to describe what could also be denoted in Hudnut's own terms a modern or ultra-modern owner. Secondly, Hudnut had spoken in the opening of his 1945 article on the 'post-modern house' of the 'prefabricated' hut or house as the house of the future,[25] and had also suggested in his 1949 text that his vision had been produced by 'thinking about those factory-built houses, pure products of technological research and manufacture, which are promised us as soon as a few remaining details of finance and distribution are worked out'.[26] As Hudnut envisaged these houses in 1949 they were to be 'pressed by giant machines out of plastics or chromium steel, pouring out of assembly lines by the tens of thousands, delivered anywhere in response to a telephone call, and upon delivery made ready for occupancy by the simple process of tightening a screw'.[27] After flying over a parking lot beside a baseball stadium, Hudnut had also been inspired to see the thousands of automobiles parked there in herringbone patterns as a foreshadowing of those future suburbs in which 'every family will have each its standardised mass-produced and movable shell, indistinguishable from those of its thousand neighbours except by a choice of paint and the (relative) ambitions of their owners to be housed in the latest model'.[28]

In addition to this, Hudnut's post-modern owner's house is described in his conclusion as the epitome of the results of 'the cumulative miracles of science', which might even be termed the forces of 'modernisation', given that Hudnut had also spoken in his article of the coming of a 'collective-industrial scheme of life' which now appears to have looked back to the relations of modern industrial society rather than forward to any new 'post-industrial' scheme of things similar to those spoken of by Jencks in his writings on the post-modern in architecture.[29] For this reason too Hudnut's vision could be said to be 'ultra' rather than 'post'-modern. Only when Hudnut goes on to speak of the architect as providing an antidote to the machine, by providing the way of bringing out the 'true and beautiful character' of the post-modern house, might we in fact find something which looks forward to at least some of the post-modern architectural theory of the 1970s.

Charles Jencks has even written of Hudnut in his *What is Post-Modernism?* of 1986 that he had 'introduced the term "Post-Modernism" into the "architectural subconscious"', and, in being at Harvard with Walter Gropius, 'may have wished to give this pioneer of the Modern Movement a few sleepless nights'.[30] Although Jencks does not refer specifically to the passage, Hudnut's 1945 article had also contained the statement that while the author would not advise a return to 'that harlequinade of Colonial, Regency, French Provincial, Tudor and Small Italian Villa which adds such dreary variety to our suburban landscapes', he sometimes thought 'that the eclectic soul of these suburbs is, by intuition if not by understanding, nearer the heart of architecture than those rigid minds which understand nothing but the economics of shelter and the arid technicalities of construction'.[31] In that the Modern Movement had not yet achieved all it should achieve for Hudnut, who also wrote that 'we have not yet learned to give them [ie the modern techniques and motives] any persuasive meaning',[32] he may well have placed the concept of the post-modern into the 'architectural subconscious', as suggested by Jencks.[33] At the same time it has also to be noted that Hudnut was writing in the 1940s largely within the debates of his time, and that, while critical of the distortion of modernism into pure functionalism still saw many of the ideals of the Modern Movement as being basically sound.[34] Added to this it must again be recalled that Hudnut has used the term post-modern itself not to describe a better alternative to the modern, but to describe an ultra-functionalist version of the modern house. If Hudnut is to be understood to have sought to give his modernist colleagues 'a scare' with his vision of the 'post-modern house' of the coming years it was therefore with what might now be seen as a dystopian vision of what their modernism could degenerate into, rather than with a utopian insight into any of the post-modern alternatives recommended by post-modernist architects of today.

Although Arnold J Toynbee had used the term post-modern in several volumes of his *A Study of History* of 1939 and1954, and it had also been used in the 1946 DC Somervell abridgement of the early volumes of 1939 written prior to Hudnut's articles, it is only to his *Historian's Approach to Religion* of 1956 to which the *OED* entry next makes reference, and again without giving an explanation of the specific meaning of the term there.[35] In addition to using the term post-modern in his 1956 text to describe the changes experienced by Western civilisation since the end of the 19th century, Toynbee had used it in volume V of his *A Study of History* of 1939 to describe the age inaugurated by the war of 1914–18.[36] Only after the end of the Second World War had Toynbee gone on to apply it, as indicated by DC Somervell's abridgement of the first six volumes of that work of 1946,[37] to the period of Western civilisation from 1875 on.[38] While this is the period to which the term 'post-modern' is attached by Toynbee in the post-Second World War volumes of his *A Study of History* of 1954,[39] it should be noted that when that period is mentioned in volume I of 1934, at the place related to that in which the term 'Post-Modern' appears in Somervell's abridgement of 1946, the term 'Post-Modern' is not used.[40]

Further to being used in the post-war volumes of Toynbee's *A Study of History* to describe the period from the end of the 19th century, the term post-modern (now written 'post-Modern') had been used by Toynbee in those volumes to describe the rise of an industrial urban working class, and after the term 'Modern' had been used by him to describe the 'middle classes' of Western civilisation. Toynbee wrote, for example, in volume VIII of his *A Study of History*:

The most significant of the conclusions that suggest themselves is that the word 'modern' in the term 'Modern Western Civilisation', can, without inaccuracy, be given a more precise and concrete connotation by being translated 'middle class'. Western communities became 'modern' in the accepted Modern Western meaning of the word, just as soon as they had succeeded in producing a bourgeoisie that was both numerous enough and competent enough to become the predominant element in Society. We think of the new chapter of Western history that opened at the turn of the fifteenth and sixteenth centuries as being 'modern' *par excellence* because, for the next four centuries and more, until the opening of a 'post-Modern Age' at the turn of the nineteenth and twentieth centuries, the middle class was in the saddle in the larger and more prominent part of the Western World as a whole.

Toynbee added:

This definition of the Modern Western culture as being a phase of Western cultural development that is distinguished by the ascendancy of the middle class throws light on the conditions under which, before the advent in the West of a post-Modern Age marked by the rise of an industrial urban working class, any alien recipients of this Modern Western culture would be likely to be successful in making it their own. During the currency of the Modern Age of Western history the ability of aliens to become Westerners would be proportionate to their capacity for entering into the middle-class Western way of life.[41]

As later notes will show, to Toynbee the 'post-Modern Age' was also to be marked not only by the rise of a new industrial urban working class in the West, but by both the rise of other nations and their proletariats and the rise of a variety of 'post-Christian' religious cults as well as sciences.

While Charles Jencks has written in his *Post-Modernism: The New Classicism in Art and Architecture* of 1987 that the term post-modern had also acquired an element of Spenglerian doom in Toynbee's *A Study of History* in being used there to refer to 'the end of Western dominance, Christian culture and individualism',[42] it should also be noted that Toynbee had used the term in post-Second World War (1954) volumes of his *History* which he himself saw as optimistic rather than pessimistic. Toynbee wrote, for instance, in the opening of the chapter on 'Law and Freedom in History' of volume IX of his *A Study of History* that when he was planning his study in the summer of 1927 he had seen that he would have to 'grapple with the problem of the respective roles of Law and Freedom in human history before he could attempt to win a Pisgah sight of the prospects of the Western Civilisation'. It was, however, only in June 1950 when, after a seven-years-long interruption extending over the years 1939 to 1946, he at last reached this point in the writing of the book, that he found himself working in a new atmosphere that was 'decidedly more congenial to his theme'.

Toynbee's discussion of the 'post-Modern' age is also carried out largely in this post-war work, where he dates the post-modern period from the end of the 19th century.[43] Further to this, these postwar volumes by Toynbee had also criticised those who had taken the end of their own period to be the end of history as such.[44] [...]

Further examples of the use of the term 'post-modern' given by the *OED* include C Wright Mills's use of it in his *The Sociological Imagination* of 1959 to describe a new 'Fourth Epoch' after the 'Modern Age';[45] Leslie Fiedler's 1965 reference to post-modernist literature (again the quotation given by the dictionary is not very explanatory, being Fiedler's sentence: 'I am not now interested in analysing ... the diction and imagery which have passed from Science Fiction into post-Modernist literature');[46] Frank Kermode's 1966 remarks that Pop Fiction demonstrates 'a growing sense of the irrelevance of the past', and that 'post-Modernists are catching on';[47] Nikolaus Pevsner's reference in *The Listener* of 29 December 1966, to a 'new style', a 'successor' to his 'International Modern' of the 1930s which he 'was tempted to call ... a post-modern style';[48] a reference in the *New York Review of Books* of 28 April 1977 to 'the post-modernist demand for the abolition of art and its assimilation to "reality"';[49] two somewhat different remarks in the *Journal of the Royal Society of Arts* of November 1979 to 'Post-Modern architects [who] use motifs ... in questionable taste', and to 'Post-Modernists who have substituted the body metaphor for the machine metaphor'; a reference in *Time* of January 1979 to Philip Johnson as 'the nearest Post-Modernism has to a senior partner'; and another, finally, to *The Times Higher Education Supplement* of 7 March 1980 in which 'Postmodernism, structuralism, and neo-dada' are all said to represent 'a reaction against modernism'.

Several of these uses of the term post-modernism will be discussed at greater length, or referred to again in either text or notes, presently. Other early uses of the term not listed by the *OED* have included several given by Michael Koehler in his article entitled '"Postmodernismus": ein begriffsgeschichtlicher Ueberblick', which was completed in November 1976 and published in 1977.[50] Here Koehler drew attention to the use made of the term and its variants by the professor Federico de Onis in 1934, the anthologist Dudley Fitts in 1942 (although the use ascribed to Fitts is attributed by Fitts himself to his assistant HR Hays), Arnold J Toynbee (whose usage of the term post-modern Koehler dates only from 1947), Charles Olson (in the years between 1950 and 1958), Irving Howe (1959), Harry Levin (1960), Leslie Fiedler (1965) and John Perreault,[51] as well as Amitai Etzioni in his *The Active Society* of 1968,[52] Ihab Hassan in his *The Dismemberment of Orpheus* and 'POSTmodernISM' essay of 1971,[53] and Ralph Cohen in his autumn 1971 edition of *New Literary History* in which Hassan's 'POSTmodernISM' essay was published.[54]

* * *

Michael Koehler concludes his survey of the term 'post-modernism' with the statement that it not only shows that there is still no agreement over that which may be counted as 'post-modern', but that one of the reasons for this is the double meaning of the concept of the 'modern' period. This, Koehler writes, can be used as a synonym for 'die Neuzeit' (literally, 'the new age', although it is usually translated as 'the modern period' or 'modern times'), which for Koehler refers to the time since the European Renaissance, from around

1500,[55] or it can be used to designate the most recent historical period from around 1900 and is then concurrent with the cultural concept of modernism. As has just been seen from our comparison of the uses of the term postmodernism by de Onis and Hudnut, this 'cultural concept of modernism' can itself be divided into several different periods and movements – from, for instance, Symbolism to Abstractionism, Expressionism, Surrealism or any other such modern 'ism' selected by the theorist. Further to this, several other meanings of the term modern could be added to those given by Koehler, such as, for instance, those given it in the phrase describing 'the battle of the ancients and the moderns' from the late 17th century on.[56]

Koehler himself continues to argue from his set of alternatives that while Toynbee and Olson may be said to have used the word 'modern' in the first sense given by him (to refer, that is, to a modern period dating from around 1500),[57] they have produced confusion by using the word post-modern to cover a period in which modernism was also born and developed.[58] Koehler adds that this use of the term post-modern is therefore comparable with all those theories which contest the view that the most recent art has broken with the paradigm of modernism. Whether this is either an accurate or a helpful view of Arnold Toynbee's position may, however, be questioned, especially as although Toynbee had used the term 'post-Modern' to refer to a new 'post-Middle class' age, he had continued to see the middle class as the force behind the production of 'Modern' art of both archaic and futurist kinds and to criticise both those types of art.[59] While it is clear that the question of whether a new 'post-Modernist' art might still arise from the 'post-Modern Age' and its proletariats was one left unanswered by Toynbee, it is also clear that he believed that there was much in existing modernist art which needed to be changed.[60]

One other point which needs to be made here, and which Koehler himself suggests in a footnote,[61] is also that a comparison of Toynbee's views on the 'post-Modern' with more recent views on post-modernism and its relationship to modernism is problematic in that the 'post-modernist' art spoken of in the last two decades was not only unknown to Toynbee, but is inclusive of a great many reactions to, and extensions of, a variety of modernisms.

From the subject described above, Koehler goes on to speak of those theories which have equated the modern with modernism[62] and to detail those by, for example, Irving Howe and Harry Levin which date the end of the modern period from the end of the Second World War. According to Koehler the years of the 1950s then see a reaction to the extremes of modernist Formalism and a return to Realism which is not so evident in the more 'avant-garde' 1960s, which, Koehler suggests (in an echo of de Onis's terminology), might rather be seen as 'ultra-modern' if the 1950s are to be described as postmodern.

One other hypothesis – which Koehler sees as having been put by Leslie Fiedler and Ihab Hassan – views, by contrast, the 1960s as representative of a 'postmodern sensibility'. (In fact, Hassan will be seen to have taken his 'postmodernism' back much further than this.) According to this view, continues Koehler, the 1950s are seen as being only an early phase of 'postmodernity'.[63]

For Koehler this approach also revolts against the canonisation of a classical modernism which suppresses the 'aesthetic praxis' of 'alternative' modern 'traditions' such as Dadaism and Surrealism. Koehler adds, however, that 'insofar as the "post" in "postmodern" does not just imply a temporal relation, but also designates a break with the preceding style', this approach leads to an 'internal contradiction', for here 'the postmodernism in question breaks only with the conventions of the (so-called) classical Modern, but not with its "alternative" tradition'. Although it could be argued (as others have since Koehler) that the term post-modern need not necessarily designate a total break with the modern (or 'post-modernism' with 'modernism') in the first place,[64] Koehler goes on to conclude from the above that the 1960s should be seen as 'late modern' rather than as 'postmodern'.[65]

The argument over whether a movement is 'late' or 'post'-modern is also one around which several post-modernist debates have circled since Koehler wrote his article. As we shall see, they include the contributions made by Charles Jencks that the 'Post-Modern' in both art and architecture involves a 'double-coding' of the 'Modern' with other 'codes' where the 'Late-Modern' does not, and that theories of the post-modern which do not see it as aiming to double-code the modern with another code, but as simply 'deconstructing' the modern, should themselves only be seen as being 'late modern'.[66]

Koehler's last alternative, and preferred, view of the post-modern is that of a 'model' which would cover the last two decades from the point of view of two 'sometimes intersecting developments'. During the 1950s, Koehler claims, a 'traditionalism' born of the 'modern classics' was dominant, but at the same time a 'Neo-Avantgardism' developed from the premises of Dadaism and Surrealism which finally 'wore itself out' in the 1960s.[67] In the second half of that period a new sensibility was evident which was, however, no longer in harmony with either of the modernisms previously mentioned. Koehler adds that this 'tentative postmodernism' only begins to take form in the 1970s, but is still not easy to define. For Koehler the 'postmodern' thus begins only after 1970, and the period from 1945 to 1970 must therefore he called 'late modern'.

Despite the above vagueness over the nature of the 'postmodern', as well as some lack of clarity in Koehler's text over the boundaries between the words 'postmodern', 'postmodernity' and 'postmodernism',[68] and some minor errors,[69] it must still be seen as one of the earliest systematic attempts to give a history of the term post-modernism, although it may also now seem ironic, given the growth of post-modernist architecture in recent years and the use of the term post-modern in theoretical writings on the subject of architecture from at least 1945 on, that the one field omitted from its survey was that of architecture.[70]

Amongst the other early uses of the term post-modernism not listed by either the *OED Supplement* of 1982 or by Koehler in his 1977 essay[71] is, moreover, one by the Australian art historian Bernard Smith which may well be one of the first 20th-century applications of the term to the visual arts.[72] Smith (who had been reading Toynbee's *A Study of History* through the war years[73]) had used the word 'post-Modernist' in the Conclusion of his *Place, Taste and Tradition* of 1945 (the text of which was completed in February 1944) with reference to the emergence of a new social and political realism in the Australian work of the artists Noel Counihan, Josl Bergner and Victor O'Connor. This 'new' form of Realism (in which elements from Expressionism and other 20th-century styles mixed with the realistic depiction of the subject matter of poverty and labour) represented for Smith a move away from modernist abstract art, as well as a reaction to what he saw to be the '*l'art pour l'art*' mentality of many of the modernists of the 20th century,'[74] and was described by him as having arisen in the 'post-Modernist world' of the 1940s.[75] [...]

Further to referring us to the theories of Bell and Sorokin, Smith's use of the term 'Post-Byzantine' again recalls the work of Arnold J Toynbee in that the latter had both described the contemporary world as a 'machine age' in the pre-Second World War volumes of his *A Study of History* and used the word 'Byzantine' in his fifth volume of 1939 to describe the 'archaism' of movements such as that of the 'Pre-Raphaelites' and 'Neo-Gothicists'.[76] Following Toynbee's use of the term 'Byzantine' to describe those forms of modernism which he thought to be 'archaic', Smith had used the term 'Post-Byzantine' to designate the reaction of modernist abstractionist against the 'Byzantine'. While de Onis's and Fitts/Hays's post-modernisms could be said to share some characteristics with that which Smith has termed 'Post-Byzantine' art, of, for instance, a reaction against earlier modernist Symbolist art, Smith's chosen category of 'post-Modernist' art is understood as standing in contrast to the cold abstractions of the 'Post-Byzantine'. Put in summary this could read:

> *Toynbee (1939)*: Post-First World War = *Post-Modern Age; Modern Art* = either Byzantine Archaism (Neo-Gothic or Pre-Raphaelite) or Futurism;
> *De Onis (1934) and Fitts/Hays (1942)*: 'postmodernismo' poetry = a reaction to earlier modernist decorativeness;
> *Hudnut (1945)*: the '*post-modern* house' = (1) extension of Modern Movement functionalism and lack of decorativeness, and (2) in need of architect's sensibility;
> *Smith (1945)*: modern '*Post-Byzantine*' Art = a reaction to decorativeness and a move towards greater action; 'Post-Modernist' art (of the 1940s) = a reaction against modernist abstraction.[77]

Here the modernism to which de Onis and Fitts/Hays's 'postmodernismo' was an alternative may be aligned (though not equated) with the Byzantine Archaism condemned by Toynbee[78] and their 'postmodernist' alternatives compared with the 'post-Byzantinism' to which Smith's 'post-Modernism' was seen by him to have acted as an alternative.[79] Although the Realism described by Smith as 'post-Modernist' in 1944 might now be described as a modern form of 19th-century Social Realism, and, hence, as also carrying on a tradition of modernism which existed prior to abstract modernism,[80] the use made by Smith of the term 'post-Modernism' in 1944/5 to describe a reaction to abstract modernism has also been echoed, despite Smith's own more recent condemnation of contemporary post-modernism,[81] in some contemporary uses of the term postmodernism and its concomitants in the fields of both art and architecture to denote a turning-away from the modernist obsession with abstraction.[82] [...]

Many of the early uses of the terms post-modern and post-modernism discussed here have also become outdated now because that which was for them post-modern has come to be seen in more recent years as a part of a now historical modern period. Whether current uses of the term will prove to have a better foothold in history remains to be seen, but they do at least seem at this point of time to have a wider distribution than that enjoyed by those of the 1930s and 1940s in their time.

Notes

1 See Dick Hebdige, *Hiding in the Light: On Images and Things*, Comedia (London and New York), 1988, pp 181 ff.

2 See, for example, Ihab Hassan, 'The Question of Postmodernism', *Romanticism, Modernism, Postmodernism*, ed Harry R Garvin, *Bucknell Review* 25, 2 (London and Toronto), 1980, p 120; Wallace Martin, 'Postmodernism: Ultima Thule or Seim Anew?', *Romanticism, Modernism, Postmodernism*, ed Garvin, p 145.

3 Ironically, the term 'anything goes' may more accurately describe Lyotard's relativistic stance, although even here a close analysis of his position will show that not everything 'does go', and especially when he is speaking of targets of his post-modernism which he has described as modernist 'metanarratives'.

4 The spelling of the term post-modernism without its hyphen is often an indication that the user is following Deconstructionist post-modernist theories, although some editorial intervention may also be responsible. (And see also note 18 on other reasons for the form 'postmodernism'.) Other 'tracers' (to use a term suggested to me by Charles Jencks to refer to words or concepts from which origins or theoretical underpinnings may be traced) include the designation, following Jameson, of the Portman Bonaventure Hotel as post-modern rather than late-modern, the use of concepts such as 'hyperreality' or 'normless pastiche', and the use, following Hassan, of the concept of indeterminacy. As with all tracings of ideas, other factors involved in the use of similar ideas, such as chance or misunderstanding, will also have to be taken into account, although in most cases there will be other factors involved, such as a direct reference to an author or to his or her other ideas, which may support the use of a 'tracer' in the above manner.

5 Hebdige, *Hiding in the Light*, p 183.

6 See Jean Baudrillard, 'The Ecstasy of Communication', *The Anti-Aesthetic*, ed Hal Foster, Bay Press (Port Townsend), 1983.

7 Jean Baudrillard. 'The Orders of Simulacra', trans Philip Beitchmann, *Simulations* (New York), 1983, p 128.

8 Baudrillard, *Simulations*, p 83, pp 103 ff.

9 Ibid, p 111.

10 Hebdige, *Hiding in the Light*, p 195.

11 Ibid.

12 Ibid.

13 Hebdige is not altogether uncritical of Baudrillard's attitudes to contemporary society and its culture (see, for example, Hebdige, *Hiding in the Light*, pp 176, 253, note 6), but does take over many of Baudrillard's characterisations of the latter for his depiction of the post-modern and from either Baudrillard himself (see Hebdige p 253 for examples of his reading of Baudrillard) or from other readers of Baudrillard such as Fredric Jameson. (See for example, Hebdige, *Hiding in the Light*, p 254.)

14 Hebdige's discussion of the theories of post-modernism also revolves in general around the figures of Lyotard, Baudrillard, Habermas and Richard Rorty, rather than theorists of post-modern architecture such as Charles Jencks.

15 Mike Featherstone's introductory essay to the special issue of *Theory, Culture & Society* on post-modernism of June 1988 (vol 5, nos 2–3, pp 195–215), 'In Pursuit of the Postmodern: an Introduction', also provides a list of 'definers' of post-modernism on p 203, which brings together several different schools of thought about the subject without always making their separate identities clear.

16 See the *Oxford English Dictionary Supplement* (Oxford, 1982), vol III, p 698, or the *Oxford English Dictionary*, second edition (Oxford, 1989), vol XII, p 201. The dictionary's coverage of the history of the term is not only limited by the space allotted it, but by its omission of texts such as those by Charles Jencks on post-modern architecture.

17 Here the dictionary refers to its previous definition of the term modern (in col II of the supplement to the first edition, p 993; or the second edition, vol IX, p 948) as being 'of a movement in art or architecture, or the works produced by such a movement: characterised by a departure from or a repudiation of accepted or traditional styles and values'. As noted earlier, the derivation of the word modern from the Latin for 'today' or 'just now', is given in vol VI of the *OED*, first edition, p 573, and may also be found in the new, second, edition in vol IX, pp 947–8.

18 The term 'double-coding' is used by Jencks at least from 1978 on (in the second edition of his *The Language of Post-Modern Architecture*), and refers to how the post-modern building may use both a 'Modern' code (described as a code because it, like other architectural styles, is understood as sending out messages to its users in a similar way to other codes or speech acts) and at least one other style or code (such as, for example, the classical codes used in Stirling, Wilford and Associates' new Stuttgart State Gallery). While Jencks uses the hyphenated term 'Post-Modern' from at least 1977 on, and then together with the term 'Post-Modernism', Hassan, Lyotard, Jameson and other recent critics will be seen to have spoken of 'postmodernism'. One other form of the word 'post-Modernism' has also been used by Leslie Fiedler (in 1965) and by Bernard Smith (in 1945), while Arnold J Toynbee had used the spelling 'post-Modern' from at least 1954 on. Sometimes the particular form taken by the word has also been influenced by the form taken by it in the language from which it has been translated (such as, for example, Spanish, French or German) in which hyphens are not used, although, as pointed out in the preceding note 4, it may also follow, in other instances, from the particular canon of post-modernist theory being supported by the user in question. Except where quoting from a particular usage, this text will use the form given in the *OED* of the hyphenation 'post-modern' as being the most correct form for usage in English.

19 See note 17.

20 Hudnut had used the term in 1945 in an article entitled 'the post-modern house' in the *Architectural Record* 97, May 1945, pp 70–5. The article was also published in the *Royal Architectural Institute of Canada Journal* 22, pp 135–40. (See also note 23.)

21 To my knowledge, no self-professed post-modern architect of recent times has described the prefabricated houses as post-modern on that basis alone. When Charles Jencks illustrates his partly prefabricated Garagia Rotunda of 1977 in the fifth edition of his *The Language of Post-Modern Architecture*, p 120, he describes it as 'Architecture as prefabrication plus cosmetics'. And see also Lucien Kroll's condemnation of the prefabricated house as a product of modernism in his *The Architecture of Complexity* of 1983, trans Peter Blundell Jones (London), 1986, p 10.

22 The *OED* is quoting p 119 of Joseph Hudnut's *Architecture and the Spirit of Man* (Harvard), 1949. The misleading nature of the *OED*'s entry on Hudnut's usage of the word post-modern may also be reflected in Frank Kermode's interpretation of its 1949 usage in his *History and Value* (Oxford), 1988, p 129, to refer to 'a kind of architecture that came later than, and reacted against, the Modern Movement in that field'.

23 See note 20 for details of Hudnut's 1945 article. It was a slightly different version of that article that was published by Hudnut in his *Architecture and the Spirit of Man*, pp 108–19, under the same title of 'the post-modern house'.

24 Hudnut, 'the post-modern house', 1945, p 75; and 1949, p 119.

25 Hudnut had begun his 1945 article with the words: 'I have been thinking about that cloud burst of new houses which as soon as the war is ended is going to cover the hills and valleys of New England with so many square miles of prefabricated happiness' (see Hudnut, 'the post-modern house', 1945, p 70).

26 Hudnut, 'the post-modern house', 1949, p 108.

27 Ibid.

28 Ibid.

29 Toynbee's descriptions of the 'post-Modern Age' in the postwar (1954) volumes of his *A Study of History* also characterise it as 'collective industrial' in a way which makes it seem fixed in a stage prior to the post-industrial as described by Bell and others in more recent years.

30 See Charles Jencks, *What is Post-Modernism?* (London), 1986, p 14. Jencks also refers to Hudnut in a 'Foot-Note' to the introductions of the 1978 and following revised editions of his *The Language of Post-Modern Architecture* of 1977 as having made 'what appears to be' the 'first use of Post-Modern in an architectural context'. See Jencks, *Language of Post-Modern Architecture*, fourth revised enlarged edition (London), 1984, p 8.

31 See Hudnut, 'the post-modern house', 1945, pp 72–3. Hudnut had, however, also added on p 73 with regard to the 'harlequinade' of styles used in the suburbs that he thought 'that that adventure is at an end'.

32 Ibid, p 73. One of the criteria for post-modernism suggested by Jencks is that it give meaning to its techniques and motives.

33 Jencks has also criticised modern architecture's belief in the 'myth of the machine aesthetic'. See, for example, his 1975 article 'The Rise of Post Modern Architecture' in the *Architectural Association Quarterly* 7, no 4, p 6: 'What is modern architecture based on? Why … the myth of the machine aesthetic, an abstract language, geometry and good taste.'

34 Although Gropius had also experimented with prefabricated housing in America, Hudnut had defended him and other founders of the Modern Movement in architecture for their ideals, while also criticising those who had 'distorted' the latter into a 'cold and uncompromising functionalism' in his 1945 article, 'the post-modern house', pp 73–4. In addition to such statements, Hudnut's 1949 collection of essays also contains passages where he defends the 'modernist dictum' that 'form follows function'. (See Hudnut, 'the post-modern house', pp 113, 13.)

35 Toynbee's use of the term post-modern will be discussed more fully presently. In being used as early as 1939 it predates Hudnut's usage rather than the other way around as suggested by the *OED*. Even earlier uses of the term will, however, also be dealt with in this essay in following pages.

36 See Arnold J Toynbee, *A Study of History*, vol V (London), 1939, p 43.

37 *A Study of History* by Arnold J Toynbee, abridged by DC Somervell, Oxford, 1946, p 39.

38 As suggested in the text, the first use of the term 'post-Modern' to denote the period from 1875 on in Toynbee's own *A Study of History* is only to be found in the postwar volumes published in 1954. When used in Somervell's abridgement to describe the period from 1875 on the term 'Post-Modern' is also followed by a question mark.

39 See note 37.

40 Somervell's abridgement was completed in 1946 and approved by Toynbee. The use of the term 'Post-Modern' in the abridgement with a question mark may mean that Somervell thought that this was the direction which Toynbee's work was taking in the postwar years.

41 Toynbee, *A Study of History*, vol VIII, p 338. Toynbee also makes some references to Western architecture on pp 374–5 of vol VIII, and describes the 'sky-scrapers' of the 20th century as 'Modern Neo-Gothic'. Previously (see, for example, Somervell, *A Study of History*, pp 446–7 or Toynbee, *A Study of History*, vol V, 1939, pp 60–1), Toynbee had also attacked both the 'Gothic revival' in 'modern' architecture as a decadent archaism, and (Somervell, *A Study of History*, pp 446–7 or Toynbee, *A Study of History*, vol V, 1939, p 482) the modern commercialisation of art. Both were signs of decay for Toynbee, who also went on to condemn the 'Futurist' destruction of the heritage of the past as equally damaging. (See, for example, Somervell, *A Study of History*, p 519, or Toynbee, *A Study of History*, vol VI, pp 115 ff.)

42 See Charles Jencks, *Post-Modernism: the New Classicism in Art and Architecture* (London), 1987, p 13, and also Jencks's foreword to his *What is Post-Modernism?*, 1986, p 3.

43 See also Toynbee, *A Study of History*, vol IX, p 235.

44 Ibid, p 421.

45 See C Wright Mills, *The Sociological Imagination* (Harmondsworth), 1983, pp 184 ff. Mills characterises the 'Fourth Epoch' as one in which the liberalism and socialism 'born of the Enlightenment' have both 'virtually collapsed as adequate explanations of the world'; 'the ideas of freedom and reason have become moot'; and 'increased rationality may not be assumed to make for increased reason'.

46 See Leslie Fiedler, 'The New Mutants', *Partisan Review*, 1965, p 508, or in *Collected Essays of Leslie Fiedler*, vol II (New York), 1971, pp 379–400. Just prior to this passage Fiedler had been referring to the influence of science fiction on Wilhelm Reich, Buckminster Fuller, Marshal McLuhan and ('perhaps') Norman O Brown as well as on writers such as William Golding, Anthony Burgess, William Burroughs, Kurt Vonnegut Jr, Harry Matthews and John Barth. The passage quoted by the *OED* had continued: 'but rather in coming to terms with the prophetic content common to both; with the myth rather than the modes of Science Fiction'. Fiedler had then proceeded (*Collected Essays*, p 382) to describe that myth as 'quite simply the myth of the end of man', and, more specifically, as the idea of turning humans into newly irrational, and even 'barbaric' beings, or, that is, 'the new mutants', and had then also gone on to speak at length of the new 'post-modernist' irrationality, cultism and antipathy to the precepts of the Protestant work ethic which he found to be

already evident in the 1960s. Later, in an article published in *Playboy* in December 1969 entitled 'Cross the Border – Close the Gap', Fiedler also spoke of 'Post-Modernist' literature as closing the gap between 'High' and Pop literature to align itself with the latter and its subservient (parodistic and other) forms as the culture of the present, and of the need created thereby for a new 'Post-Modernist criticism', able to make judgements 'about the "goodness" and "badness" of art quite separated from distinctions between "high" and "low" with their concealed class bias'.

47 In *Encounter*, vol 26, no 4, April 1966, p 73. Here Kermode was referring, however, largely to Fiedler's use of the term, and did not agree with Fiedler's assessment that something so new was happening in literature.

48 Nikolaus Pevsner's December 1966 remarks were in *The Listener*, 29 December 1966, p 955, following a discussion of the buildings of Churchill College, Cambridge, and referred to architecture of the 1950s and 1960s which Jencks and others have since described as 'late-modern'. Pevsner's second article in *The Listener*, 5 January 1967, pp 7–9, was, however, to include some buildings in his new category which Jencks will at least classify as both late-modern and post-modern, such as Eero Saarinen's TWA Terminal and Joorn Utzon's Sydney Opera House. (See, for example, the entries on Saarinen and Utzon in Charles Jencks, *The Language of Post-Modern Architecture*, and his *Architecture Today*, London, 1988, as well as the latter's 'evolutionary trees' of 'Late-Modernism' and 'Post-Modernism' on pp 20, 110.)

49 Although clearer than some of the other quotations, it should be noted that this is again a reference to a particular view of post-modernism, and not one which can be generalised to cover all forms of post-modernism.

50 Michael Koehler's '"Postmodernismus": ein begriffsgeschichtlicher Uerberblick' is published in *Amerikastudien* 22, 1, 1977, pp 8–18. An editorial note to Koehler's article on p 8 also refers the reader to the next article in the journal by Gerhard Hoffmann, Alfred Hornung and Ruediger Kunow, '"Modern", "Postmodern" and "Contemporary" as Criteria for the Analysis of 20th-Century Literature', in *Amerikastudien* 22, 1, 1997, pp 19–46, for further bibliographic information.

51 Hoffmann, Hornung and Kunow, '"Modern", "Postmodern" and "Contemporary"', p 45, list the following papers by Olson: 'The Act of Writing in the Context of Post-Modern Man' of 1952; 'The Present is Prologue' of 1955; 'Definitions by Undoings' of 1956; and 'Equal, That Is, To Real Itself of 1958'. Koehler, '"Postmodernismus", p 11, also sees Olson as following Toynbee in dating the post-modern from the last quarter of the 19th century. (See also the following notes on Toynbee in this chapter.) The reference given by Koehler for Harry Levin's usage is his 'What is Modernism?' in the *Massachusetts Review* of 1960, for Howe his 'Mass Society and Postmodern Fiction' in the *Partisan Review* of 1959, and for Fiedler his 'The New Mutants' in the *Partisan Review* of 1965. While Howe's essay is summarised as describing the new mass society as eliminating many of the moral and aesthetic bases on which classical modernism has been based, Levin's text is described as contrasting the ('postmodern') fiction which he saw to be popularising the achievements of the more experimental modernists of earlier times with the more innovatory nature of the latter. Both are thus seen by Koehler to have used the term post-modern in a negative manner to mourn the demise of modernism. (Further reference to Perreault, whose use of the term occurred in articles in the *Village Voice*, New York, will be made presently.)

52 Amitai Etzioni's *The Active Society: a Theory of Societal and Political Processes* (London and New York), 1968 describes the modern period as having 'ended with the radical transformation of the technologies of communication, knowledge and energy that followed World War Two', and dates the onset of the 'post-modern period' at 1945. Later Etzioni also goes on to claim that the post-modern is similar to the 'late-modern' in some important respects, but still gives some differences, such as that just quoted, by which other theorists will also come to classify the 'post-industrial' society as different from the 'industrial' society.

53 This article has recently been republished in Hassan's *The Postmodern Turn*, 1987.

54 The issue of the journal was entitled 'Modernism and Postmodernism: Inquiries, Reflections and Speculations' and was vol 3, no 1, Autumn 1971. Cohen is quoted by Koehler, '"Post-modernismus", p 14, as saying that 'The issue was planned as an attempt to deal with contemporary avantgarde movements' and that Cohen had decided on the term 'post-modern' 'as the best way to distinguish them from past movements of the avant-garde'. Other journals mentioned by Koehler as having used the term 'post-modern' include *Boundary* 2 of 1972, *Triquarterly* of autumn 1973 and spring 1975, the *Journal of Modern Literature* of July 1974, the *New York Drama Review* of March 1975 and the *Hudson Review* of autumn 1973.

55   See Koehler, "Postmodernismus", pp 16 f, and also the earlier discussion of the use of the term modern to cover this period in the Introduction and its first note.

56   Jencks writes of this quarrel in his 'The New Classicism and its Emergent Rules', *Architectural Design* 58, nos 1/2, 1988, Profile 70, p 24, that it may also be said to have led to the 'struggle between Modernists of all brands that is still with us today'; and see also on this and other issues relating to the definition of modernity and modernism, Matei Calinescu's *Five Faces of Modernity*, Durham, NC, 1987. This work, which I saw only after completing the body of this manuscript, also has an interesting discussion of de Onis on modernism and post-modernism, as well as of the avant-garde. Calinescu's final (1986) chapter on postmodernism is, however, rather more problematical in its apparent conflation (following Linda Hutcheon) on p 285, of the double-coding which I described as a characteristic of literary parody in my *Parody/Metafiction*, London, 1979 (a book used by Hutcheon, together with several other works, for her work on both parody and post-modernism, though not referred to by Calinescu) and the double-coding of which Charles Jencks speaks with reference to post-modern architecture.

57   But see also the earlier discussion of Toynbee's usage of the term post-modern to describe the post-1914 years in 1939, and the post-1875 period in his later texts.

58   Koehler, "Postmodernismus", p 16 'diese "Postmoderne" schliesst den Modernismus schon in seiner ganzen Dauer ein'. As noted previously, Koehler, however, has only made mention of Toynbee's post-Second World War dating of the 'Post-Modern Age' as being from 1875 on, and has made no mention of Toynbee's earlier 1939 dating of it as being from 1914 onwards.

59   See the previous pages on Toynbee for further discussion of his view, as well as both the discussion of Toynbee's view on modernist art in the pages on Bernard Smith's use of the term 'post-Modernism' at the end of this chapter and the following note 60.

60   In addition to condemning both 'futurist' and 'archaic' types of art of the modern and 'post-modern' (that is, for him, post-1975) periods in his *A Study of History*, Toynbee was also to put Frank Lloyd Wright's 'Mayan-style' Imperial Hotel in Tokyo in the same class of archaic art as 19th-century Pre-Raphaelite painting in his later article 'Art: Communicative or Esoteric?', in the collection *On the Future of Art*, introduced by Edward F Fry (New York) 1970, p 18. While Toynbee condemned such historicising art as esoteric in a way which suggests that he might also have been antipathetic to much of the post-modernist architecture of recent years, he had also both criticised the role played by modern specialisation in the creation of such esotericism and argued for an increased valuation of communication in much the same way as some 'historicising' (and other) post-modernist architects and architectural theorists have done, and in a way which suggests that even if he were not to agree with the solutions provided by the latter, he had agreed with their analyses of the problems of both modernity and modernism. (And see also chapter 2 on Arthur J Penty's criticisms of modernist specialisation and chapter 4 on the writings of Charles Jencks on post-modernist architecture.)

61   See Koehler, "Postmodernismus", p 16, note 17.

62   Ibid, p 17.

63   Koehler sometimes shifts from speaking of 'postmodernism' to speak of either the 'postmodern' or 'postmodernity' without fully defining the differences between these terms.

64   See, for example, the pages on Jencks in this chapter.

65   See Koehler, "Postmodernismus", p 17–18.

66   Jencks is, however, unlike Koehler in seeing the late-modern and post-modern as running concurrently from the 1960s on, where Koehler, as explained in the following paragraphs of the text, sees the latter as developing largely from the time when the other has worn itself out. As suggested elsewhere, it may also be because others have assumed the post-modern architecture of which Jencks has spoken to have followed the late-modern from the 1960s on, rather than to have run concurrently with it, that they have accepted Jameson's designation of Portman's 1970s Bonaventure Hotel as post-modern.

67   Like several other German critics (including Habermas) Koehler also appears to have taken up some of the ideas put forward by Peter Bürger in his *Theory of the Avant-Garde* (Manchester and Minneapolis), 1984. Like Bürger (and Habermas after him) Koehler chooses, for instance, the Surrealists and Dadaists as representative of the modern avant-garde (instead of, say, the Russian Constructivists of the 1920s), and then goes on to speak somewhat arbitrarily of these chosen groups. For further discussion of the concept of the avant-garde, and a critique of the restrictiveness of the Bürger view on it, see also the following chapters 3 and 4.

68 See note 63.
69 Namely the attribution to Fitts rather than to Hays of the use of the term 'postmodernism' in Fitts's 1942 anthology; the dating of Toynbee's usage of the term 'post-Modern' at 1947; and the interpretation of Hassan's periodisation of 'postmodernism'.
70 Although Charles Jencks's influential book *The Language of Post-Modern Architecture* only appeared first in 1977, the year in which Koehler's article was published, he had used the word post-modern in an architectural essay of 1975 (see note 33), while other uses of the term had, as noted previously, also been applied to architecture in earlier years by both Joseph Hudnut (in 1945) and by Nikolaus Pevsner (in the 1960s). Like Koehler, several other commentators on the concept of the post-modern have also continued to ignore or avoid architectural uses of the term, especially when writing of either literature or French literary theory, although it has also been suggested by others that architecture is the area where the term has been most clearly defined and used, and especially when applied to architecture of the 1960s and after, which has consciously shared some of the precepts of the concepts in question.
71 Apart from the missing architectural references mentioned in the note above, Koehler's survey has been seen by Hans Bertens in his essay 'The Postmodern Weltanschauung and its Relation to Modernism: an Introductory Survey', (*Approaching Postmodernism*, eds Douwe Fokkema and Hans Bertens, John Benjamins (Amsterdam and Philadelphia), 1986, pp 9–51) to have omitted references to the American poet Randall Jarrell's use of the term in a review of Robert Lowell's Lord Weary's Castle of 1946, and to John Berryman's use of it following Jarrell as well as several later uses. (See Fokkema and Bertens, *Approaching Postmodernism*, pp 12 ff.)
72 Koehler's references to the use of the term 'postmodernism' in visual art criticism include that to John Perreault mentioned previously, and to Brian O'Doherty's May–June 1971 edition of *Art in America*, in which he had put the question 'What is Post-modernism?'. Koehler adds, however, that the question was largely rhetorical, as O'Doherty could give 'no satisfactory answer'. (See Koehler, ''Postmodernismus'', p 13.)
73 Bernard Smith provided this information when I asked him in April 1989 about his use of the term 'post-Modernist'. As noted previously, Arnold J Toynbee had used the term 'Post-Modern' in volume V of his *A Study of History* of 1939, p 43, to describe the period following the First World War, while he later wrote it in the form 'post-Modern' in the 1954 volumes of his study to refer to the new 'post-middle class' age following the year 1875. Although written before the publication of these later volumes of Toynbee's study, Smith's 'post-Modernism' also appears to be dealing with a 'post-bourgeois' set of artists, in so far as all of those listed by Smith had some connection with communist or socialist beliefs, while their art was concerned with the depiction of workers and their impoverished conditions, rather than with what was understood to be a middle-class way of life.
74 See, for example, Bernard Smith, *Place, Taste and Tradition* (Oxford), 1979, pp 277.
75 Ibid, p 255.
76 See Toynbee, *A Study of History*, volume V, p 482.
77 Later, in April 1989, after writing an attack on contemporary post-modernism, Smith claimed that he had used the word 'post-Modernism' in 1944/5 because the art to which it was applied appeared to be doing something different from other modernist works. (And see also note 80.)
78 See the previous page on Toynbee for further explanation of this point.
79 While Koehler has also claimed (''Postmodernismus'', p 9) that the use of the prefix 'post' had become more frequent following its use in the term 'post-war' (dated by the *OED* from 1908), one other use of the prefix 'post' in art criticism had been the use of it in the term 'Post-Impressionism' from around the same time.
80 The styles of Counihan, Bergner and O'Conner had, as Smith has noted, combined elements of modernist Expressionism with the subject matter typical of Social Realism. For Smith (conversation of April 1989) their 'post-Modernism had therefore seemed to be doing something different from ''other forms of Modernism'''. By the time of Smith's *Australian Painting* 1733–1970 (Oxford), 1962, (see pp 233–9 of the second edition of 1971) the Social Realism discussed above is, however, being described as something which 'as a creative trend in Australian art barely survived the war' and the postwar years as 'ones which did not favour a realistic approach to art'.
81 Smith could not at first recall having used the term 'post-Modernism' in his 1945 text when asked about it in April 1989, and had by then also used it in a review of Peter Fuller's *Theoria* (in *Australian Society*, March 1989, p 41) to write that 'a central weakness of post-modernism has been to treat tradition as a load of old junk to be dismissed or ruthlessly exploited'.

82 Here it should, however, also be noted that Smith's final target in his 1944/5 work was not simply modernist abstraction but the fascism of the time and its aesthetics. Hence Smith concluded his 1945 book (*Place, Taste and Tradition*, pp 280–1) by quoting from Melvin Rader's attack on fascist aesthetics in his *No Compromise* of 1939: 'It is important to remember that there is a tradition, embodied in the works of men like Ruskin, Morris, Wright, Gropius, and Mumford, which insists upon the democratic functional and collective nature of art.'

PART 2   Literature and Architecture

The Literature of Replenishment

John Barth

In this text, John Barth offers a historical journey through premodernist, modernist and postmodernist literature, citing Italo Calvino and Gabriel García Márquez as exemplary postmodern authors. Barth defines post-modern literature not so much as the extension or complete repudiation of modern literature, but rather as something that is in between the pre-modernist and the modernist, in between realism and irrealism. Within his essay, Barth tries to answer questions such as 'Who are the postmodernists?' and 'What is postmodernism?' always in relation to literature and its related media.

The American novelist and short-story writer John Barth (1930–) is known as one of the foremost practitioners of postmodernism and metafiction. Before retiring in 1995, Barth taught at Penn State University, SUNY Buffalo, Boston University and Johns Hopkins University. Barth started his career with novels such as *The Floating Opera* (1957), *The End of the Road* (1958), *The Sot-Weed Factor* (1960) and *LETTERS* (1980), and has published more than 15 novels, his latest one being *The Development* (2008). *LCS*

The world is not yet in our standard dictionaries and encyclopedias, but since the end of the Second World War, and especially in the United States in the late 1960s and the 1970s, 'postmodernism' has enjoyed a very considerable currency, particularly with regard to our contemporary fiction. There are university courses in the American postmodernist novel; at least one quarterly journal is devoted exclusively to the discussion of postmodernist literature; at the University of Tübingen last June, the annual meeting of the Deutsche Gesellschaft für Amerikastudien took as its theme 'America in the 1970s', with particular emphasis on American postmodernist writing. Three alleged practitioners of that mode – William Gass, John Hawkes and I – were even there as live exhibits. The December annual convention of the Modern Language Association, just held in San Francisco, likewise scheduled a symposium on 'the self in postmodernist fiction', a subtopic that takes the larger topic for granted.

From all this, one might innocently suppose that such a creature as postmodernism, with defined characteristics, is truly at large in our land. So I myself imagined when, in preparation for the Tübingen conference, and in response to being frequently labelled a postmodernist writer, I set about to learn what postmodernism is. I had a sense of *déjà vu*: about my very first published fiction, a 1950 undergraduate effort printed in my university's quarterly magazine, a graduate-student critic wrote, 'Mr Barth alters that modernist dictum, "the plain reader be dammed": he removes the adjective.' Could that, I wondered now, be postmodernism? What I quickly discovered is that while some of the writers tagged as postmodernist, myself included, may happen to take the tag with some seriousness, a principal activity of postmodernist critics (also called 'metacritics' and 'paracritics'), writing in postmodernist journals or speaking at postmodernist symposia, consists in disagreeing about what postmodernism is or ought to be, and thus about who should be admitted to the club – or clubbed into admission, depending on the critic's view of the phenomenon and of particular writers.

Who are the postmodernists? By my count, the American fictionists most commonly included in the canon, besides the three of us at Tübingen, are Donald Barthelme, Robert Coover, Stanley Elkin, Thomas Pynchon and Kurt Vonnegut, Jr. Several of the critics I read widen the net to include Saul Bellow and Norman Mailer, different as those two writers would appear to be. Others look beyond the United States to Samuel Beckett, Jorge Luis Borges and the late Vladimir Nabokov as engendering spirits of the 'movement'; others yet insist upon including the late Raymond Queneau, the French 'new novelists' Michael Butor, Alain Robbe-Grillet and Claude Mauriac, the even newer French writers of the *Tel Quel* group, the Englishman John Fowles and the expatriate Argentine Julio Cortázar. Some assert that such film makers as Michelangelo Antonioni, Federico Fellini, Jean-Luc Godard and Alain Resnais are postmodernists. I myself will not join any literary club that doesn't include the expatriate Colombian Gabriel García Márquez and the semi-expatriate Italian Italo Calvino, of both of whom more presently. Anticipations of the 'postmodernist literary aesthetic' have duly been traced through the great modernists of the first half of the 20th century – TS Eliot, William Faulkner, André Gide, James Joyce, Franz Kafka, Thomas Mann, Robert Musil, Ezra Pound, Marcel Proust, Gertrude Stein, Miguel Unamuno, Virginia Woolf – through *their* 19th-century predecessors – Alfred Jarry, Gustave Flaubert, Charles Baudelaire, Stéphane Mallarmé and ETA Hoffmann – back to Laurence Sterne's *Tristram Shandy* (1767) and Miguel Cervantes's *Don Quixote* (1615).

On the other hand, among certain commentators the sifting gets exceedingly fine. Professor Jerome Klinkowitz of Northern Iowa, for example, hails Barthelme and Vonnegut as the exemplary 'postcontemporaries' of the American 1970s and consigns Mr Pynchon and me to some 1960-ish outer darkness. I regard the novels of John Hawkes as examples of fine late modernism rather than of postmodernism (and I admire them no less for that). Others might regard most of Bellow, and the Mailer of *The Naked and the Dead*, as comparatively *pre*modernist, along with the works of such more consistently traditionalist American writers as John Cheever, Wallace Stegner, William Styron and John Updike, for example, or those of most of the leading British writers of this century (as contrasted with the Irish), or those of most of our contemporary American women writers of fiction, whose main literary concern, for better or worse, remains the eloquent issuance of what Richard Locke has called 'secular news reports'.

Even among the productions of a given writer, distinctions can be and often are invoked. Joyce Carol Oates writes all over the aesthetical map. John Gardner's first two published novels I would call distinctly modernist works; his short stories dabble in postmodernism; his polemical nonfiction is aggressively reactionary. Italo

Calvino, on the other hand, began as an Italian neo-Realist (in *The Path to the Nest of Spiders*, 1947) and matured into an exemplary postmodernist (with *Cosmicomics*, 1965 and *The Castle of Crossed Destinies*, 1974) who on occasion rises, sinks or merely shifts to modernism (*Invisible Cities*, 1972). My own novels seem to me to have both modernist and postmodernist attributes; my short story series, *Lost in the Funhouse*, strikes me as mainly late-modernist, though some critics have praised or damned it as conspicuously postmodernist. My most recent novel *LETTERS*, is postmodernist by my own definition, not, however, without traces or taints of the modernist mode, even of the premodernist mode.

One certainly does have a sense of having been through this before. Indeed some of us who have been publishing fiction since the 1950s have the interesting experience of being praised or damned in that decade as existentialists and in the early 1960s as black humorists. Had our professional careers antedated the Second World War, we would no doubt have been praised or damned as modernists, in the distinguished company listed above. Now we are praised or damned as postmodernists.

Well, but what *is* postmodernism? When one leaves off the recitation of proper names, and makes due allowance for the differences among any given author's works, do the writers most often called postmodernist share any aesthetic principles or practices as significant as the differences between them? The term itself, like 'postimpressionism', is awkward and faintly epigonic, suggestive less of a vigorous or even interesting new direction in the old art of storytelling than of something anticlimactic, feebly following a very hard act to follow. One is reminded of the early James Joyce's fascination with the word *gnomon* in its negative geometrical sense: the figure that remains when a parallelogram has been removed from a similar but larger parallelogram with which it shares a common corner.

My Johns Hopkins colleague Professor Hugh Kenner, though he does not use the term postmodernist, clearly feels that way in his study of American modernist writers (*A Homemade World*, 1975): after a chapter on William Faulkner entitled 'The Last Novelist', he dismisses Nabokov, Pynchon and Barth with a sort of sigh. The later John Gardner goes even further in his tract *On Moral Fiction* (1978), an exercise in literary kneecapping that lumps modernists and postmodernists together without distinction and consigns us all to hell with the indiscriminate fervour characteristic of late converts to the right. Irving Howe (*The Decline of the New*, 1969) and George P Elliott (*Conversion: Literature and the Modernist Deviation*, 1971) would applaud – Professor Howe perhaps less enthusiastically than Professor Elliott. Professor Gerald Graff of Northernwestern University, writing in *Tri-Quarterly* in 1975, takes a position somewhat similar to Kenner's, as the title of two of his admirable essays make clear: 'The Myth of the Postmodernist Breakthrough' (*Tri-Quarterly* 26) and 'Babbitt at the Abyss' (*Tri-Quarterly* 33). Professor Robert Alter of Berkeley, in the same magazine, subtitles *his* essay on postmodernist fiction 'Reflections on the Aftermath of Modernism'. Both critics proceed to a qualified sympathy for what they take to be the postmodernist programme (as does Professor Ihab Hassan of the University of Wisconsin-Milwaukee in his 1971 study *The Dismemberment* of Orpheus: Toward a Postmodern Literature*), and both rightly proceed from the premise that the programme is in some respects an extension of the programme of modernism, in other respects a reaction against it. The term *postmodernism* clearly suggests both; any discussion of it must therefore either presume that modernism in its turn, at this hour of the world, needs no definition (surely everybody knows what modernism is!) or else must attempt after all to define or redefine that predominant aesthetic of Western literature (and music, painting, sculpture, architecture and the rest) in the first half of this century.

Professor Alter takes the former course: his aforementioned essay opens with the words 'Over the past two decades, as the high tide of modernism ebbed and its masters died off …' and proceeds without further definition to the author's reflections upon the ensuing low tide. Professor Graff, on the other hand, borrowing from Professor Howe, makes a useful quick review of conventions of literary modernism before discussing the mode of fiction which, in his words, 'departs not only from realistic conventions but from modernist ones as well'.

It is good that he does, for it is not only *post*modernism that lacks definition in our standard reference books. My *Oxford English Dictionary* attests *Modernism* to 1737 (Jonathan Swift, in a letter to Alexander Pope) and *Modernist* to 1588, but neither term in the sense we mean. My *American Heritage Dictionary* (1973) gives as its fourth and last definition of lower-case *modernism* 'the theory and practice of modern art', a definition which does not take us very far into our American heritage. My *Columbia Encyclopedia* (1975) discusses modernism only in the theological sense – the reinterpretation of Christian doctrine in the light of modern psychological and scientific discoveries – and follows this with an exemplary entry on *el modernismo*, a 19th-century Spanish literary movement which influenced the 'Generation of 98' and inspired the *ultraísmo* of which Jorge Luis Borges was a youthful exponent. Neither my Reader's *Encyclopedia* (1948) nor my Reader's *Guide to Literary Terms* (1960) enters *modernism* by any definition whatever, much less *postmodernism*.

Now, as a working writer who cut his literary teeth on Eliot, Joyce, Kafka and the other great modernists, and who is currently branded as a postmodernist, and who in fact has certain notions, no doubt naive, about what the term might conceivably mean if it is to describe anything very good very well, I am grateful to the likes of Professor Graff for not regarding his categories as self-defining. It is quite one thing to compare a line of Verdi or Tennyson or Tolstoy with a line of Stravinsky or Eliot or Joyce and to recognise that you have put the 19th century behind you:

Happy families are all alike; every unhappy family is unhappy in its own way.
(Leo Tolstoy, *Anna Karenina*, trans Constance Garnett)

riverrun, past Eve's and Adam's, from swerve of shore to bend of bay, brings us by a commodius vicus of recirculation back to Howth Castle and Environs.
(James Joyce, *Finnegans Wake*).

It is quite another thing to characterise the differences between those two famous opening sentences, to itemise the aesthetic principles – premodernist and modernist – from which each issues, and then to a great *post*modernist opening sentence [*sic*] and show where its aesthetics resemble and differ from those of its parents, so to speak, and those of its grandparents, respectively:

> Many years later, as he faced the firing squad, Colonel Aureliano Buendía was to remember that distant afternoon when his father took him to discover ice. (Gabriel García Márquez, *One Hundred Years of Solitude*, trans Gregory Rabassa).

Professor Graff does not do this, exactly, though no doubt he could if pressed. But I shall borrow his useful checklist of the characteristics of modernist fiction, add a few items to it, summarise as typical his and Professor Alter's differing characterisations of *post*modernist fictions, disagree with them respectfully in some particulars, and then fall silent, except as a storyteller.

The ground motive of modernism, Graff asserts, was criticism of the 19th-century bourgeois social order and its worldview. Its artistic strategy was the self-conscious overturning of the conventions of bourgeois realism by such tactics and devices as the substitution of a 'mythical' for a 'realistic' method and the 'manipulation of conscious parallels between contemporaneity and antiquity' (Graff is here quoting TS Eliot on James Joyce's *Ulysses*); also the radical disruption of the linear flow of narrative; the frustration of conventional expectations concerning unity and coherence of plot and character and the cause-and-effect 'development' thereof; the deployment of ironic and ambiguous juxtapositions to call into question the moral and philosophical 'meaning' of literary action; the adoption of a tone of epistemological self-mockery aimed at the naive pretensions of bourgeois rationality; the opposition of inward consciousness to rational, public, objective discourse; and an inclination to subjective distortion to point up the evanescence of the objective social world of the 19th-century bourgeoisie.

This checklist strikes me as reasonable, if somewhat depressing from our historical perspective. I would add to it the modernists' insistence, borrowed from their romantic forebears, on the special, usually alienated role of the artist in his society, or outside it: James Joyce's priestly, self-exiled artist-hero; Thomas Mann's artist as charlatan, or mountebank; Franz Kafka's artist as anorexic, or bug. I would add, too, what is no doubt implicit in Graff's catalogue, the modernists' foregrounding of language and technique as opposed to straightforward traditional 'content': we remember Thomas Mann's remark (in *Tonio Kröger*, 1903), '… what an artist talks *about* is never the main point;' a remark which echoes Gustave Flaubert's to Louise Colet in 1852 – '… what I could like to do, is write a book about nothing …' – and which anticipates Alain Robbe-Grillet's *obiter dictum* of 1957: '… the genuine writer has nothing to say … He has only a way of speaking.' Roland Barthes sums up this 'fall from innocence' and ordinary content on the part of modernist literature in *Writing Degree Zero* (1953):

... the whole of literature, from Flaubert to the present day, became the problematics of language.

This is French hyperbole: it is enough to say that one cardinal preoccupation of the modernists was the problematics, not simply of language, but of the medium of literature.

Now, for Professor Alter, Professor Hassan and others, *post*modernist fiction merely emphasises the 'performing' self-consciousness and self-reflexiveness of modernism, in a spirit of cultural subversiveness and anarchy. With varying results, they maintain, postmodernist writers write a fiction that is more and more about itself and its processes, less and less about objective reality and life in the world. For Gerald Graff, too, postmodern fiction simply carries to its logical and questionable extremes the anti-rationalist, anti-realist, anti-bourgeois programme of modernism, but with neither a solid adversary (the bourgeois having now everywhere coopted the trappings of modernism and turned its defiant principles into mass-media kitsch) nor solid moorings in the quotidien realism it defines itself against. From this serious charge Graff exempts certain postmodernist satire, in particular the fiction of Donald Barthelme, Saul Bellow and Stanley Elkin, as managing to be vitalised by the same kitschy society that is its target.

I must say that all this sounds persuasive to me – until I examine more closely what I'm so inclined to nod my head yes to. It goes without saying that critical categories are as more or less fishy as they are less or more useful. I happen to believe that just as an excellent teacher is likely to teach well no matter what pedagogical theory he suffers from, so a gifted writer is likely to rise above what he takes to be his aesthetic principles, not to mention what *others* take to be his aesthetic principles. Indeed, I believe that a truly splendid specimen in whatever aesthetic mode will pull critical ideology along behind it, like an ocean liner trailing seagulls. Actual artists, actual texts, are seldom more than more or less modernist, postmodernist, formalist, symbolist, realist, surrealist, politically committed, aesthetically 'pure', 'experimental', regionalist, internationalist, what have you. The particular work ought always to take primacy over contexts and categories. On the other hand, art lives in human time and history, and general changes in its modes and materials and concerns, even when not obviously related to changes in technology, are doubtless as significant as changes in a culture's general attitudes, which its arts may both inspire and reflect. Some are more or less trendy and superficial, some may be indicative of more or less deep malaises, some are perhaps healthy correctives of or reactions against such malaises. In any case, we can't readily discuss what artists aspire to do and what they end up doing except in terms of aesthetic categories, and so should look further at this approximately shared impulse called postmodernism.

In my view, if it has no other and larger possibilities than those noted by, for example, Professors Alter, Graff and Hassan, then postmodernist writing is indeed a kind of pallid, last-ditch decadence, of no more than minor symptomatic interest. There is no want of actual texts illustrative of this view of the 'postmodernist breakthrough'; but that is only to remind us that what Paul Valéry remarked of an earlier generation applies to ours as well:

'Many ape the postures of modernity, without understanding their necessity.' The proper programme for postmodernism is neither a mere extension of the modernist programme as described above, nor a mere intensification of certain aspects of modernism, nor on the contrary a wholesale subversion or repudiation of either modernism or what I'm calling premodernism – 'traditional' bourgeois realism.

To go back a moment to our catalogue of the field-identification marks of modernist writing: two other conspicuous ones are not yet there acknowledged, except by implication. On the one hand, James Joyce & Co set very high standards of artistry, no doubt implicit in their preoccupation with the special remove of the artist from his or her society. On the other hand, we have their famous relative difficulty of access, inherent in their anti-linearity, their aversion to conventional characterisation and cause-and-effect dramaturgy, their celebration of private, subjective experience over public experience, their general inclination to 'metaphoric' as against 'metonymic' means. (But this difficulty is *not* inherent, it is important to note, in their high standards of craftsmanship.)

And from this relative difficulty of access, what Hassan calls their aristocratic cultural spirit, comes of course the relative unpopularity of modernist fiction, outside of intellectual circles and university curricula, by contrast with the fiction of, say, Dickens, Twain, Hugo, Dostoevsky, Tolstoy. From it comes also and notoriously the engenderment of a necessary priestly industry of explicators, annotators, allusion-chasers, to mediate between the text and the reader. If we need a guide, or a guidebook, to steer us through Homer or Aeschylus, it is because the world of the text is so distant from our own, as it presumably was not from Aeschylus's and Homer's original audiences. But with *Finnegans Wake* or Ezra Pound's *Cantos*, we need a guide because of the inherent and immediate difficulty of the text. We are told that Bertold Brecht, out of socialist conviction, kept on his writing desk a toy donkey bearing the sign *Even I must understand it*; the high modernists might aptly have put on their desks a professor of literature doll bearing, unless its speciality happened to be the literature of high modernism, the sign *Not even I can understand it.*

I do not say this in deprecation of these great writers and their sometimes brilliant explicators. If modernist works are often forbidding and require a fair amount of help and training to appreciate, it does not follow that they are not superbly rewarding, as climbing Mount Matterhorn must be, or sailing a small boat around the world. To return to our subject: let us agree with the commonplace that the rigidities and other limitations of 19th-century bourgeois realism, in the light of turn-of-the-century theories and discoveries in physics, psychology, anthropology and technology, prompted or fuelled the great adversary reaction called modernist art – which came to terms with our new ways of thinking about the world at the frequent expense of democratic access, of immediate or at least ready delight, and often of political responsibility (the politics of Eliot, Joyce, Pound, Nabokov and Borges, for example, are notoriously inclined either to nonexistence or to the far right). But in North America, in western and northern Europe, in the United Kingdom, and in some of Central and South America, at least, these 19th-century rigidities are virtually no more. The modernist aesthetic is in my opinion unquestionably the characteristic aesthetic of the first half of our century – and in my opinion it *belongs* to the first half of our century. The present reaction against it is perfectly understandable and to be sympathised with, both because the modernist coinages are by now more or less debased common currency and because we really don't *need* more *Finnegans Wakes* or *Pisan Cantos*, each with its staff of tenured professors to explain it to us.

But I deplore the artistic and critical cast of mind that repudiates the whole modernist enterprise as an aberration and sets to work as if it hadn't happened; that rushes back into the arms of 19th-century middle-class realism as if the first half of the 20th century hadn't happened. It *did* happen: Freud and Einstein and two world wars and the Russian and sexual revolutions and automobiles and aeroplanes and telephones and radios and movies and urbanisation, and now nuclear weaponry and television and microchip technology and the new feminism and the rest, and there's no going back to Tolstoy and Dickens & Co except on nostalgia trips. As the Russian writer Yevgeny Zamyatin was already saying in the 1920s (in his essay 'On Literature, Revolution, and Entropy'): 'Euclid's world is very simple, and Einstein's world is very difficult; nevertheless, it is now impossible to return to Euclid's.'

On the other hand, it is no longer necessary, if it ever was, to repudiate *them*, either: the great premodernists. If the modernists, carrying the torch of Romanticism, taught us that linearity, rationality, consciousness, cause and effect, naive illusionism, transparent language, innocent anecdote and middle-class moral conventions are not the whole story, then from the perspective of these closing decades of our century we may appreciate that the contraries of these things are not the whole story either. Disjunction, simultaneity, irrationalism, anti-illusionism, self-reflexiveness, medium-as-message, political olympianism and a moral pluralism approaching moral entropy – these are not the whole story either.

A worthy programme for postmodernist fiction, I believe, is the synthesis or transcension of these antitheses, which may be summed up as premodernist and modernist modes of writing. My ideal postmodernist author neither merely repudiates nor merely imitates either his 20th-century modernist parents or his 19th-century premodernist grandparents. He has the first half of our century under his belt, but not on his back. Without lapsing into moral or artistic simplism, shoddy craftsmanship, Madison Avenue venality, or either false or real naivety, he nevertheless aspires to a fiction more democratic in its appeal than such late-modernist marvels (by my definition and in my judgement) as Beckett's *Stories and Texts for Nothing* or Nabokov's *Pale Fire*. He may not hope to reach and move the devotees of James Michener and Irving Wallace – not to mention the lobotomised mass-media illiterates. But he *should* hope to reach and delight, at least part of the time, beyond the circle of what Mann used to call the Early Christians: professional devotees of high art.

I feel this in particular for practitioners of the novel, a genre whose historical roots are famously and honourably in middle-class popular culture. The ideal postmodernist novel will somehow rise above the quarrel between Realism and Irrealism, Formalism and 'Contentism', pure and committed literature, coterie fiction and junk fiction. Alas for professors of literature, it may not need as much *teaching* as Joyce's or Nabokov's or Pynchon's books, or some of my own. On the other hand, it will not wear its heart on its sleeve either; at least not its whole heart. (In a recent published exchange between William Gass and John Gardner, Gardner declares that he wants everybody to love his books; Gass replies that he would no more want his books to be loved by everybody than he'd want his daughter to be loved by everybody, and suggests that Gardner is confusing love with promiscuity.) My own analogy would be with good jazz or classical music: one finds much on successive listenings or close examination of the score that one didn't catch the first time through; but the first time through should be so ravishing – and not just to specialists – that one delights in the replay.

Lest this postmodern synthesis sound both sentimental and impossible of attainment, I offer two quite different examples of works that I believe approach it, as perhaps such giants as Dickens and Cervantes may be said to anticipate it. The first and more tentative example (it is not meant to be a blockbuster) is Italo Calvino's *Cosmicomics* (1965): beautifully written, enormously appealing space-age fables – 'perfect dreams', John Updike has called them – whose materials are as modern as the new cosmology and as ancient as folk tales, but whose themes are love and loss, change and permanence, illusion and reality, including a good deal of specifically Italian reality. Like all fine fantasists, Calvino grounds his flights in local, palpable detail: along with the nebulae and the black holes and the lyricism, there is a nourishing supply of pasta, bambini and good-looking women sharply glimpsed and gone for ever. A true postmodernist, Calvino keeps one foot always in the narrative past – characteristically the Italian narrative past of Boccaccio, Marco Polo or Italian fairy tales – and one foot in, one might say, the Parisian Structuralist present; one foot in fantasy, one in objective reality. It is appropriate that he has, I understand, been chastised on the left by the Italian Communist critics and on the right by the Italian Catholic critics; it is symptomatic that he has been praised by fellow authors as divergent as John Updike, Gore Vidal and myself. I urge everyone to read Calvino at once, beginning with *Cosmicomics* and going right on, not only because he exemplifies my postmodernist programme, but because his fiction is both delicious and high in protein.

An even better example is Gabriel García Márquez's *One Hundred Years of Solitude* (1967), as impressive a novel as has been written so far in the second half of our century and one of the splendid specimens of that splendid genre from any century. Here the synthesis of straightforwardness and artifice, realism and magic and myth, political passion and nonpolitical artistry, characterisation and caricature, humour and terror, are so remarkably sustained that one recognises with exhilaration very early on, as with *Don Quixote* and *Great Expectations* and *Huckleberry Finn*, that one is in the presence of a masterpiece not only artistically admirable but humanly wise, loveable, literally marvellous. One had almost forgotten that new fiction could be so *wonderful* as well as so merely important. And the question whether my programme for postmodernism is achievable goes happily out the window, like one of García Márquez's characters on flying carpets. Praise be to the Spanish language and imagination! As Cervantes stands as an exemplar of premodernism and a great precursor of much to come, and Jorge Luis Borges as an exemplar of *dernier cri* modernism and at the same time as a bridge between the end of the 19th century and the end of the 20th, so Gabriel García Márquez is in that enviable succession: an exemplary postmodernist and a master of the storyteller's art.

A dozen years ago, I published in *The Atlantic* a much-misread essay called 'The Literature of Exhaustion', occasioned by my admiration for the stories of Señor Borges and by my concern, in that somewhat apocalyptic place and time, for the ongoing health of narrative fiction. (The time was the latter 1960s; the place Buffalo, New York, on a university campus embattled by tear-gassing riot police and tear-gassed Vietnam War protesters, while from across the Peace Bridge in Canada came Marshall McLuhan's siren song that we 'print-oriented bastards' were obsolete.) The simple burden of my essay was that the forms and modes of art live in human history and are therefore subject to used-upness, at least in the minds of significant numbers of artists in particular times and places; in other words, that artistic conventions are liable to be retired, subverted, transcended, transformed, or even deployed against themselves to generate new and lively work. I would have thought that point unexceptionable. But a great many people – among them, I fear, Señor Borges himself –mistook me to mean that literature, at least fiction, is *kaput*; that has all been done already; that there is nothing left for contemporary writers but to parody and travesty our great predecessors in our exhausted medium – exactly what some critics deplore as postmodernism.

Leaving aside the celebrated fact that, with *Don Quixote*, the novel may be said to *begin* in self-transcendent parody and has often returned to that mode for its refreshment, let me say at once and plainly that I agree with Borges that literature can never be exhausted, if only because no single literary text can ever be exhausted – its 'meaning' residing as it does in its transactions with individual readers over time, space and language. I like to remind misreaders of my earlier essay that written literature is in fact about 4,500 years old (give or take a few centuries depending on one's definition of literature), but that we have no way of knowing whether 4,500 years constitutes senility, maturity, youth or mere infancy. The number of splendid sayable things – metaphors for the dawn or the sea, for example – is doubtless finite; it is also doubtless very large, perhaps virtually infinite. In some moods we writers may feel that Homer had it easier than we, getting there early with his rosy-fingered dawn and his wine-dark sea. We should console ourselves that one of the earliest extant literary texts (an Egyptian papyrus of *c* 2000 BC, cited by Walter Jackson Bate in his 1970 study *The Burden of the Past and the English Poet*) is a complaint by the scribe Khakheperresenb that he has arrived on the scene too late:

> Would I had phrases that are not known, utterances that are strange, in new language that has not been used, free from repetition, not an utterance that has gown stale, which men of old have spoken.

What my essay 'The Literature of Exhaustion' was really about, so it seems to me now, was the effective 'exhaustion' not of language or of literature but of the aesthetic of high modernism: that admirable, not-to-be-repudiated, but essentially completed 'programme' of what Hugh Kenner has dubbed 'the Pound era'. In 1966/67 we scarcely had the term *postmodernism* in its current literary-critical usage – at least I hadn't heard it yet – but a number of us, in quite different ways and with varying combinations of intuitive response and conscious deliberation, were already well into the working out, not of the next-best thing after modernism, but of the *best next* thing: what is gropingly now called postmodernist fiction; what I hope might also be thought of one day as a literature of replenishment.

John Barth, 'The Literature of Replenishment: Postmodernist Fiction', first published in *The Atlantic Monthly* 254, 1 January 1980. Copyright 1980 The Atlantic Media Co, as first published in *The Atlantic Monthly.*

The Postscript to *The Name of the Rose*
Postmodernism, Irony, the Enjoyable

Umberto Eco

In 1980, the novel *Il Nome della Rosa* was published in Italian and was translated into English three years later. It quickly became a bestseller and was closely identified with the growing tradition of postmodern literature. The essay from which the excerpt published here is taken followed the novel in 1984 and also became a classic definition of postmodern attitudes, particularly that of irony. Initially conceived as a lengthy article on the role of the reader, it gave some amusing and informative examples of the writing process behind Eco's novel, shedding much light on how he worked. Here Eco explains that postmodernism should not be defined chronologically, but rather should be seen as a metahistorical category recurring in many periods. He prescribes a mode of operation based on the idea that if the past cannot be either reborn or denied, then it must be revisited with irony. For Eco, postmodern work accepts the 'already said', but does so with knowing humour and the acknowledgement of quotation marks.

Umberto Eco (1932–) is internationally known as a significant writer and theorist. A polymath, he is also a medievalist, semiotician, aesthetician, philosopher, literary critic and novelist. After the success of *The Name of the Rose* (1983), Eco published *Foucault's Pendulum* (1989), *The Island of the Day Before* (1995), *Baudolino* (2001) and *The Mysterious Flame of Queen Loana* (2005). Today, Umberto Eco is President of the Scuola Superiore di Studi Umanistici, University of Bologna. *LCS*

Between 1965 and today, two ideas have been definitively clarified: that plot could be found also in the form of quotation of other plots, and that the quotation could be less escapist than the plot quoted. In 1972 I edited the *Almanacco Bompiani*, celebrating 'The Return to the plot', though this return was via an ironic re-examination (not without admiration) of Ponson du Terrail and Eugène Sue, and admiration (with very little irony) of some of the great pages of Dumas. The real problem at stake then was, could there be a novel that was not escapist and, nevertheless, still enjoyable?

This link, and the rediscovery not only of plot but also of enjoyability, was to be realised by the American theorists of postmodernism.

Unfortunately, 'postmodern' is a term *bon à tout faire*. I have the impression that it is applied today to anything the user of the term happens to like. Further, there seems to be an attempt to make it increasingly retroactive: first it was apparently applied to certain writers or artists active in the last 20 years, then gradually it reached the beginning of the century, then still further back. And this reverse procedure continues; soon the postmodern category will include Homer.

Actually, I believe that postmodernism is not a trend to be chronologically defined but, rather, an idea category – or, better still, a *Kunstwollen*, a way of operating. We could say that every period has its own postmodernism, just as every period would have its own Mannerism (and, in fact, I wonder if postmodernism is not the modern name for Mannerism as metahistorical category). I believe that in every period there are moments of crisis like those described by Nietzsche in his *Thoughts Out of Season*, in which he wrote about the harm done by historical studies. The past conditions us, harries us, blackmails us. The historic avant-garde (but here I would also consider avant-garde a metahistorical category) tries to settle scores with the past. 'Down with moonlight' – a Futurist slogan – is a platform typical of every avant-garde; you have only to replace 'moonlight' with whatever noun is suitable. The avant-garde destroys, defaces the past: *Les Demoiselles d'Avignon* is a typical avant-garde act. Then the avant-garde goes further, destroys the figure, cancels it, arrives at the abstract, the informal, the white canvas, the slashed canvas, the charred canvas. In architecture and the visual arts, it will be the curtain wall, the building as stele, pure parallelepiped, minimal art; in literature, the destruction of the flow of discourse, the Burroughs-like collage, silence, the white page; in music, the passage from atonality to noise to absolute silence (in this sense, the early Cage is modern).

But the moment comes when the avant-garde (the modern) can go no further, because it has produced a metalanguage that speaks of its impossible texts (conceptual art). The postmodern reply to the modern consists of recognising that the past, since it cannot really be destroyed, because its destruction leads to silence, must be revisited; but with irony, not innocently. I think of the postmodern attitude as that of a man who loves a very cultivated woman and knows he cannot say to her, 'I love you madly', because he knows that she knows (and that she knows that he knows) that these words have already been written by Barbara Cartland. Still, there is a solution. He can say, 'As Barbara Cartland would put it, I love you madly.' At this point, having avoided false innocence, having said clearly that it is no longer possible to speak innocently, he will nevertheless have said what he wanted to say to the woman: that he loves her, but he loves her in an age of lost innocence. If the woman goes along with this, she will have received a declaration of love all the same. Neither of the two speakers will feel innocent, both will have accepted the challenge of the past, of the already said, which cannot be eliminated; both will consciously and with pleasure play the game of irony ... But both will have succeeded, once again, in speaking of love.

Irony, metalinguistic play, enunciation squared. Thus, with the modern, anyone who does not understand the game can only reject it, but with the postmodern, it is possible not to understand the game and yet to take it seriously. Which is, after all, the quality (the risk) of irony. There is always someone who takes ironic discourse seriously. I think that the collages of Picasso, Juan Gris and Braque were modern: this is why normal people would not accept them. On the other hand, the collages of Max Ernst, who pasted together bits of 19th-century engravings, were postmodern: they can be read as fantastic stories, as the telling of dreams, without any awareness that they amount to a discussion of the nature of engraving, and perhaps even of collage. If 'postmodern' means this, it is clear why Sterne and Rabelais were postmodern, why Borges surely is, and why in the same artist the modern moment and the postmodern moment can coexist, or alternate, or follow each other closely. Look at Joyce. *The Portrait* is the story of an attempt at the modern. *Dubliners*, even if it comes before, is more modern than *Portrait*. *Ulysses* is on the borderline. *Finnegans Wake* is already postmodern, or at least it initiates the postmodern discourse: it demands, in order to be understood, not the negation of the already said, but its ironic rethinking.

On the subject of the postmodern nearly everything has been said, from the very beginning (namely, in essays like 'The Literature of Exhaustion' by John Barth, which dates from 1967). Not that I am entirely in agreement with the grades that the theoreticians of postmodernism (Barth included) give to writers and artists, establishing who is postmodern and who has not yet made it. But I am interested in the theorem that the trend's theoreticians derive from their premises:

> My ideal postmodernist author neither merely repudiates nor merely imitates either his twentieth-century modernist parents or his nineteenth-century premodernist grandparents. He has the first half of our century under his belt, but not on his back … He may not hope to reach and move the devotees of James Michener and Irving Wallace – not to mention the lobotomized mass-media illiterates. But he *should* hope to reach and delight, at least part of the time, beyond the circle of what Mann used to call the Early Christians: professional devotees of high art. …The ideal postmodernist novel will somehow rise above the quarrel between realism and irrealism, formalism and 'contentism', pure and committed literature, coterie fiction and junk fiction. … My own analogy would be with good jazz or classical music: one finds much on successive listenings or close examination of the score that one didn't catch the first time through; but the first time through should be so ravishing – and not just to specialists – that one delights in the replay.

This is what Barth wrote in 1980, resuming the discussion, but this time under the title 'The Literature of Replenishment: Postmodernist Fiction'. Naturally, the subject can be discussed further, with a greater taste for paradox; and this is what Leslie Fiedler does. In 1980 *Salmagundi* (number 50–1) published a debate between Fiedler and other American authors. Fiedler, obviously, is out to provoke. He praises *The Last of the Mohicans*, adventure stories, Gothic novels, junk scorned by critics that was nevertheless able to create myths and capture the imagination of more than one generation. He wonders if something like *Uncle Tom's Cabin* will ever appear again, a book that can be read with equal passion in the kitchen, the living room and the nursery. He includes Shakespeare among those who knew how to amuse, along with *Gone with the Wind*. We all know he is too keen a critic to believe these things. He simply wants to break down the barrier that has been erected between art and enjoyability. He feels that today reaching a vast public and capturing its dreams perhaps means acting as the avant-garde, and he still leaves us free to say that capturing readers' dreams does not necessarily mean encouraging escape: it can also mean haunting them.

From Umberto Eco, Postcript to *The Name of the Rose*, Harcourt Brace Jovanovich (New York), 1984. © 1983 by Umberto Eco, English translation copyright © 1984 by Harcourt Brace Jovanovich, Inc, reprinted by permission of the publisher.

Theorising the Postmodern
Towards a Poetics

Linda Hutcheon

Linda Hutcheon aims at defining postmodernism, a challenging concept that, far from being merely a synonym for contemporary, is primarily European and American. To do so, she starts by saying that postmodernism is a cultural activity that is fundamentally contradictory, resolutely historical and inescapably political. She argues that postmodernism aims at challenging – but not denying – the uniformisation of mass culture. For Hutcheon, the 1960s witnessed ideological formations that made postmodernism possible and it is in architecture that we can find the best model for a poetics of postmodernism. Here she quotes architects and critics such as Paolo Portoghesi and Charles Jencks, and refers to architectural projects such as Charles Moore's famous Piazza d'Italia, to show how the return to history through ironic parody – the privileged mode of postmodern formal self-reflexivity – does not completely negate modernism.

Linda Hutcheon (1947–) is a Canadian academic working in the fields of literary theory and criticism, opera and Canadian Studies. She is presently professor of English literature and a member of the Centre for Comparative Literature at the University of Toronto. Hutcheon is particularly known for her influential theories of postmodernism. After *A Poetics of Postmodernism: History, Theory, Fiction* (1988) she published *The Politics of Postmodernism* (1989), *The Canadian Postmodern: A Study of Contemporary English–Canadian Fiction* (1992), *Irony's Edge: The Theory and Politics of Irony* (1995) and *A Theory of Adaptation* (2006) as well as many articles on postmodernism. *LCS*

Clearly, then, the time has come to theorise the term [postmodernism], if not to define it, before it fades from awkward neologism to derelict cliché without ever attaining to the dignity of a cultural concept. (Ihab Hassan)

Of all the terms bandied about in both current cultural theory and contemporary writing on the arts, postmodernism must be the most over- and underdefined. It is usually accompanied by a grand flourish of negativised rhetoric: we hear of discontinuity, disruption, dislocation, decentring, indeterminacy and anti-totalisation. What all of these words literally do (precisely by their disavowing prefixes – *dis, de, in, anti*) is incorporate that which they aim to contest – as does, I suppose, the term postmodernism itself. I point to this simple verbal fact in order to begin 'theorising' the cultural enterprise to which we seem to have given such a provocative label. Given all the confusion and vagueness associated with the term itself,[1] I would like to begin by arguing that, for me, postmodernism is a contradictory phenomenon, one that uses and abuses, installs and then subverts, the very concepts it challenges – be it in architecture, literature, painting, sculpture, film, video, dance, TV, music, philosophy, aesthetic theory, psychoanalysis, linguistics or historiography. These are some of the realms from which my 'theorising' will proceed, and my examples will always be specific, because what I want to avoid are those polemical generalisations – often by those inimical to postmodernism[2] – that leave us guessing about just what it is that is being called postmodernist, though never in doubt as to its undesirability. Some assume a generally accepted 'tacit definition',[3] others locate the beast by temporal (after 1945? 1968? 1970? 1980?) or economic signposting (late capitalism). But in as pluralist and fragmented a culture as that of the Western world today, such designations are not terribly useful if they intend to generalise about all the vagaries of our culture. After all, what does television's *Dallas* have in common with the architecture of Ricardo Bofill? What does John Cage's music share with a play (or film) like *Amadeus*?

In other words, postmodernism cannot simply be used as a synonym for the contemporary.[4] And it does not really describe an international cultural phenomenon, for it is primarily European and American (North and South). Although the concept of *modernism* is largely an Anglo-American one,[5] this should not limit the poetics of postmodernism to that culture, especially since those who would argue that very stand are usually the ones to find room to sneak in the French *nouveau roman*.[6] And almost everyone[7] wants to be sure to include what Severo Sarduy[8] has labelled – not postmodern – but 'neo-baroque' in a Spanish culture where 'modernism' has a rather different meaning.

I offer instead, then, a specific, if polemical, start from which to operate: as cultural activity that can be discerned in most art forms and many currents of thought today what I want to call postmodernism is fundamentally contradictory, resolutely historical and inescapably political. Its contradictions may well be those of late capitalist society, but whatever the cause, these contradictions are certainly manifest in the important postmodern concept of 'the presence of the past'. This was the title given to the 1980 Venice Biennale which marked the institutional recognition of postmodernism in architecture. Italian architect Paolo Portoghesi's[9] analysis of the 20 facades of the 'Strada Novissima' – whose very newness lay paradoxically in its historical parody – shows how architecture has been rethinking modernism's purist break with history. This is not a nostalgic return; it is a critical revisiting, an ironic dialogue with the past of both art and society, a recalling of a critically shared vocabulary of architectural forms. 'The past whose presence we claim is not a golden age to be recuperated' argues Portoghesi.[10] Its aesthetic forms and its social formations are problematised by critical reflection. The same is true of the postmodernist rethinking of figurative painting in art and historical narrative in fiction and poetry: it is always a critical reworking, never a nostalgic 'return'.[11] Herein lies the governing role of irony in postmodernism. Stanley Tigerman's dialogue with history in his projects for family houses modelled on Raphael's palatial Villa Madama is an ironic one: his miniaturization of the monumental forces a rethinking of the social function of architecture – both then and now. [...]

[...] Most theorists of postmodernism who see it as a 'cultural dominant'[12] agree that it is characterised by the results of late-capitalist dissolution of bourgeois hegemony and the development of mass culture.[13] I would agree and, in fact, argue that the increasing uniformisation of mass culture is one of totalising forces that postmodernism exists to challenge. Challenge, but not deny. But it does seek to assert difference, not homogeneous identity. Of course, the very concept of difference could be said to entail a typically postmodern contradiction: 'difference', unlike 'otherness', has no exact opposite against which to define itself. Thomas Pynchon allegorises otherness in *Gravity's Rainbow* through the single, if anarchic, 'we-system' that exists as the counterforce of the totalising 'They-system' (though also implicated in it). Postmodern difference, or rather differences in the plural, are always multiple and provisional.

Postmodern culture, then, has a contradictory relationship to what we usually label our dominant, liberal humanist culture. It does not deny it, as some have asserted.[14] Instead it contests it from within its own assumptions. Modernists like Eliot and Joyce have usually been seen as profoundly humanistic[15] in their paradoxical desire for stable aesthetic and moral values, even in the face of their realisation of the inevitable absence of such universals. Postmodernism differs from this, not in its humanistic contradictions, but in the provisionality of its response to them; it refuses to posit any structure or, what Lyotard calls, master narrative[16] – such as art or myth – which, for such modernists, would have been consolatory. It argues that such systems are indeed attractive, perhaps even necessary; but this does not make them any less illusory. For Lyotard, postmodernism is characterised by exactly this kind of incredulity towards master or metanarratives: those who lament the 'loss of meaning' in the world or in art are really mourning the fact that knowledge is no longer primarily narrative knowledge of this kind.[17] This does not mean that knowledge somehow disappears. There is no radically new paradigm here, even if there is change.

It is no longer big news that the master narratives of bourgeois liberalism are under attack. There is a long history of many such sceptical sieges to positivism and humanism, and today's foot soldiers of theory – Foucault, Derrida, Habermas, Vattimo, Baudrillard – follow in the footsteps of Nietzsche, Heidegger, Marx and Freud, to name but a few, in their attempts to challenge the empiricist, rationalist, humanist assumptions of our cultural systems, including those of science.[18] [...]

[...] Perhaps it is another inheritance from the 1960s to believe that challenging and questioning are positive values (even if solutions to problems are not offered), for the knowledge derived from such inquiry may be the only possible condition of change. In the late 1950s in *Mythologies*,[19] Roland Barthes had prefigured this kind of thinking in his Brechtian challenges to all that is 'natural' or 'goes without saying' in our culture – that is, all that is considered universal and eternal, and therefore unchangeable. He suggested the need to question and demystify first, and then work for change. The 1960s were the time of ideological formation for many of the postmodernist thinkers and artists of the 1980s and it is now that we can see the results of that formation.

Perhaps, as some have argued, the 1960s themselves (that is, at the time) produced no enduring innovation in aesthetics, but I would argue that they did provide the background, though not the definition, of the postmodern,[20] for they were crucial in developing a different concept of the possible function of art, one that would contest the 'Arnoldian' or humanist moral view with its potentially elitist class bias.[21] One of the functions of art in mass culture, argued Susan Sontag, would be to 'modify consciousness'.[22] And many cultural commentators since have argued that the energies of the 1960s have changed the framework and structure of how we consider art.[23] The conservatism of the late 1970s and 1980s may have their impact when the thinkers and artists being formed now begin to produce their work,[24] but to call Foucault or Lyotard a neo-conservative – as did Habermas[25] – is historically and ideologically inaccurate.[26]

The political, social, and intellectual experience of the 1960s helped make it possible for postmodernism to be seen as what Kristeva calls 'writing-as-experience-of-limits':[27] limits of language, of subjectivity, of sexual identity, and we might also add: of systematisation and uniformisation. This interrogating (and even pushing) of limits has contributed to the 'crisis in legitimation' that Lyotard and Habermas see (differently) as part of the postmodern condition. It has certainly meant a rethinking and putting into question of the bases of our Western modes of thinking that we usually label, perhaps rather too generally, as liberal humanism.

Modelling the Postmodern: Parody and Politics

> That postmodern theses have deep roots in the present human condition is confirmed today in the document on architecture issued by the Polish union Solidarity. This text accuses the modern city of being the product of an alliance between bureaucracy and totalitarianism, and singles out the great error of modern architecture in the break of historical continuity. Solidarity's words should be meditated upon, especially by those who have confused a great movement of collective consciousness [postmodernism] with a passing fashion.
> (Paolo Portoghesi)

We have seen that what both its supporters and its detractors seem to want to call 'postmodernism' in art today – be it in video, dance, literature, painting, music, architecture or any other form – seems to be art marked paradoxically by both history and internalised, self-reflexive investigation of the nature, the limits and the possibilities of the discourse of art. On the surface, postmodernism's main interest might seem to be in the processes of its own production and reception, as well as in its own parodic relation to the past. But I want to argue that it is precisely parody – that seemingly introverted Formalism – that paradoxically brings about a direct confrontation with the problem of the relation of the aesthetic to a world of significance external to itself, to a discursive world of socially defined meaning systems (past and present) – in other words, to the political and the historical.

My focus in this chapter will be on what I think offers the best model for a poetics of postmodernism: postmodern architecture, the one art form in which the label seems to refer, uncontested, to a generally agreed upon corpus of works, Throughout, my (nonspecialist) discussion will be clearly indebted to the work of architect/theorists like Charles Jencks and Paolo Portoghesi, the major voices in the postmodern debates. This will be my model, because the characteristics of this architecture are also those of postmodernism at large – from historiographic metafictions like Christa Wolf's *Cassandra* or EL Doctorow's *The Book of Daniel* to metafilmic historical movies like Peter Greenway's *The Draughtsman's Contract*, from the video art of Douglas Davis to the photography of Vincent Leo. And all of these artworks share one major contradictory characteristic: they are all overtly historical and unavoidably political, precisely because they are formally parodic. I will argue throughout this study that postmodernism is a fundamentally contradictory enterprise: its art forms (and its theory) at once use and abuse, install and then destabilise convention in parodic ways, self-consciously pointing both to their own inherent paradoxes and provisionality and, of course, to their critical or ironic rereading of the art of the past. In implicitly contesting in this way such concepts as aesthetic originality and textual closure, postmodernist art offers a new model for mapping the borderland between art and the world, a model that works from a position within both and yet not totally within either, a model that is profoundly implicated in, yet still capable of criticising, that which it seeks to describe.

As we have seen, such a paradoxical model of *post*modernism is consistent with the very name of the label for postmodernism signals its contradictory dependence upon and independence from the modernism that both historically preceded it and literally made it possible. Philip Johnson probably could not have built the postmodern Transco Tower in Houston if he had not first designed the modernist Purist form of Pennzoil Place – and if he had not begun his career as an architectural historian. All architects know that, by their art's very nature as the shaper of public space, the act of designing a building is an unavoidably social act. Parodic references to the history of architecture textually reinstate a dialogue with the past and – perhaps inescapably – with the social and ideological context in which architecture is (and has been) both produced and lived. In using parody in this way, postmodernist forms want to work towards a public discourse that would overtly eschew modernist aestheticism and hermeticism and its attendant political self-marginalisation.

[…] Postmodernist art is precisely that which casts 'the contradictions of modernism in an explicitly political light'. In fact, as architect Paolo Portoghesi reminds us, it has risen from the very conjunction of modernist and avant-garde politics and forms.[28] But it also suggests that we must be critically conscious of the myths of both the modernists and the late-Romantic avant-garde. The 'elitism' of Dada and of Eliot's verse is exactly what postmodernism paradoxically seeks to exploit and to undercut. But the theorist/practitioners of postmodernism in all the arts – from Umberto Eco to Karlheinz Stockhausen – are emphatic in their commitment to the formation (or recollection) of a more generally shared collective aesthetic code. They insist: 'It is not just the cry of rage of a minority of intellectuals who want to teach others how to live, and who celebrate their own solitude and separateness.'[29]

* * *

Whatever modernism's historical and social ideals at its inception, by the end of the Second World War its innovatory promises had become symbols and causes – of alienation and dehumanisation. Modernism in architecture had begun as a 'heroic attempt after the Great War and the Russian Revolution to rebuild a war-ravaged Europe in the image of the new, and to make building a vital part of the envisioned renewal of society'.[30] In reaction against what modernist ahistoricism then led to, however, postmodern parodic revisitations of the history of architecture interrogate the modernist totalising ideal of progress through rationality and Purist form.[31]

As a way of textually incorporating the history of art, parody is the formal analogue to the dialogue of the past and present that silently but unavoidably goes on at a social level in architecture, because the relation of form to function, shape to use of space, is not a new problem for architects. It is in this way that parodic postmodern buildings can be said to parallel, in their form and their explicitly social contextualizing, contemporary challenges on the level of theory. Any study of the actual aesthetic practice of postmodernism quickly makes clear its role in the crises of *theoretical* legitimation that have come to our attention in the now infamous Lyotard-Habermas-Rorty debate.[32] Perhaps it is at this level that the ideological status of postmodernist art should be argued out, instead of at that of an understandable, if knee-jerk, reaction against its implication in the mass culture of late capitalism.

To rage, as so many do, following Adorno, against mass culture as only a negative force may be, as one architect/critic has remarked, 'simply continuing to use an aristocratic viewpoint and not knowing how to grasp the liberating result and the egalitarian charge of this [postmodernist] profanation of the myth' of elitist Romantic/modernist originality and unique genius.[33] In fact the architecture of the 1970s from the start signalled a conscious move away from the modern movement of the International Style as much for overtly ideological as for aesthetic reasons. The social failure of the great modernist housing projects and the inevitable economic association of 'heroic' modernism with large corporations combined to create a demand for new architectural forms that would reflect a changed and changing social awareness. These new forms were not, by any means, monolithic. They did, however, mark a shared return to such rejected forms as the vernacular (that is, to local needs and local architectural traditions), to decoration and a certain individualism in design, and most importantly, to the past, to history. Modernism's great Purist monuments to the corporate elite and to the cultural seats of power (museums, theatres) gave way, for example, to the Centre Pompidou's (at least stated) desire to make culture part of the business of everyday living.

What soon became labelled as postmodernism challenged the survival of modernism by contesting its claims to universality: its transhistorical assertions of value were no longer seen as based – as claimed – on reason or logic, but rather on a solid alliance with power, with what Portoghesi calls its 'identification with the productive logic of the industrial system'.[34] In addition, any feeling of 'inevitability'[35] of form was shown to be historically and culturally determined. The 'inevitable' was not eternal, but learned. Peter Eisenman's houses deliberately undercut our 'natural' reactions to space in order to reveal to us that these reactions are, in fact, cultural. And, just as modernism (oedipally) had to reject historicism and to pretend to a parthenogenetic birth fit for the new machine age, so postmodernism, in reaction, returned to history, to what I have been calling 'parody', to give architecture back its traditional social and historical dimension, though with a new twist this time.

What I mean by 'parody' here – as elsewhere in this study – is *not* the ridiculing imitation of the standard theories and definitions that are rooted in 18th-century theories of wit. The collective weight of parodic practice suggests a redefinition of parody as repetition with critical distance that allows ironic signalling of difference at the very heart of similarity. In historiographic metafiction, in film, in painting, in music and in architecture, this parody paradoxically enacts both change and cultural continuity: the Greek prefix *para* can mean both 'counter' or 'against' and 'near' or 'beside'. Jameson argues that in postmodernism 'parody finds itself without a vocation',[36] replaced by pastiche, which he (bound by a definition of parody as ridiculing imitation) sees as neutral or blank parody. But the looking to both the aesthetic and historical past in postmodernist architecture is anything but what Jameson describes as pastiche, that is 'the random cannibalisation of all the styles of the past, the play of random stylistic allusion'. There is absolutely nothing random or 'without principle' in the parodic recall and re-examination of the past by architects like Charles Moore or Ricardo Bofill. To include irony and play is never necessarily to exclude seriousness and purpose in postmodernist art. To misunderstand this is to misunderstand the nature of much contemporary aesthetic production – even if it does make for neater theorising.

> O Beautiful, for spacious skies, for amber waves of grain, has there ever been another place on earth where so many people of wealth and power have paid for and put up with so much architecture they detested as within thy blessed borders today? (Tom Wolfe)

In order to understand why ironic parody should, seemingly paradoxically, become such an important form of postmodernist architecture's desire to reinstate a 'worldly' connection for its discourse, we should remind ourselves of what the tyranny of 'heroic' or high modernism has meant in the 20th century. There have been two kinds of reactions to this modernist hegemony: those from architects themselves and those from the public at large. Perhaps the most eloquent and polemical of the recent public responses has been that of Tom Wolfe in his *From Bauhaus to Our House*, which opens with the wonderfully parodic American lament quoted above. Wolfe's is a negative aesthetic response to what he amusingly calls 'the whiteness & lightness & leanness & cleanness & bareness & sparseness of it all'.[37] But it is also an ideological rejection of what can only be called the modernist architects' 'policing' of the impulses of both the clients and the tenants of their buildings. This is the tyranny of the European theorists working in their 'compounds' (be they the Bauhaus or, later, the American universities). This is a tyranny – both moral and aesthetic – over American clients. In Wolfe's terms: 'No alterations, special orders, or loud talk from the client permitted. We know best. We have exclusive possession of the true vision of the future of architecture.'[38] The clients – even if they did foot the bill – were still considered the 'bourgeois' to be despised and, if possible, confounded by the architectural clerisy's elitist esoteric theories. [...]

[...] What we should not forget is that the act of designing and building is always a gesture in a social context,[39] and this is one of the ways in which formal parody meets social history. Architecture has both an aesthetic (form) and social (use) dimension. The odd combination of the empirical and the rational in modernist theory was meant to suggest a scientific determinism that was to combat the cumulative power and weight of all that had been inherited from the past. Faith in the rational, scientific mastery of reality implicitly – then explicitly – denied the inherited, evolved cultural continuity of history. It is perhaps a loss of faith in these modernist values that has led to postmodernist architecture today. The practitioners of this new mode form an eclectic grouping, sharing only a sense of the past (though not a 'random' one) and a desire to return to the idea of architecture as both communication and community (despite the fact that both of these concepts, from a postmodern perspective, now have a distinctly problematic and decentralised ring to them). The two major theoretical spokesmen of this mixed group have been Paolo Portoghesi and Charles Jencks – both practising architects.

As early as 1974, in *Le inibizioni dell'architettura moderna*, Portoghesi argued for the return of architecture to its roots in practical needs and in the (now problematised) aesthetic and social sense of continuity and community. Memory is central to this linking of the *past* with the *lived*. As an architect working in Rome, Portoghesi cannot avoid direct confrontation with the layers of history in his city and with the example of the Baroque architects before him. History is not, however, a repository of models: he is not interested in copying or in straight revivalism. Like all the *postmodernists* (and this is the reason for the label) he knows he cannot totally reject modernism, especially its material and technological advances, but he wants to integrate with these positive aspects of the immediate past the equally positive aspects of the more remote and repressed history of forms. All must be used; all must also be put into question, as architecture 'writes' history through its modern recontextualising of the forms of the past. Surely this is exactly what Jameson and Eagleton are calling for,[40] but failing to see in postmodernist architecture, where the collective architectural language of postmodernism is put into ironic contact with 'the entire historical series of its past experiences' in order to create an art that is 'paradoxical and ambiguous but vital'.[41] (Portoghesi refuses to limit this historical borrowing to post-industrial periods and has been accused of being reactionary for it.[42])

[...] The implication of this kind of relationship to the historical forms of the past is perhaps best expressed by architect Aldo van Eyck:

Man after all, has been accommodating himself physically in this world for thousands of years. His natural genius has neither increased nor decreased during that time. It is obvious that the full scope of this enormous environmental experience cannot be contained in the present unless we telescope the past, ie the entire human effort, into it. This is not historical indulgence in a limited sense, not a question of travelling back, but merely of being aware of what 'exists' in the present – what has travelled into it.[43]

The naivety of modernism's ideologically and aesthetically motivated rejection of the past (in the name of the future) is not countered here by an equally naive antiquarianism, as Jameson and Eagleton assert. On the contrary, what does start to look naive … is this reductive notion that any recall of the past must, by definition, be sentimental nostalgia.

By its doubly parodic, double-coding (that is, as parodic of both modernism and something else), postmodernist architecture also allows for that which was rejected as uncontrollable and deceitful by both modernism's *Gesamtkünstler* and its 'life-conditioner': that is, ambiguity and irony. Architects see themselves as no longer above or outside the experience of the users of their buildings; they are now in it, subject to its echoing history and its multivalent meanings – both the results of the 'recycling and creative transformation of any number of prototypes which [have] survived in the western world for centuries'.[44] In Portoghesi's words: 'It is the loss of memory, not the cult of memory, that will make us prisoners of the past'.[45] To disregard the collective memory of architecture is to risk making the mistakes of modernism and its ideology of the myth of social reform through purity of structure. Jane Jacobs has clearly documented the failure of this myth in her *Death and Life of Great American Cities*[46] and even the opponents of postmodernism agree on the social and aesthetic effects of modernism on major urban centres.

Yet postmodernism does not entirely negate modernism. It cannot. What it does do is interpret it freely; it 'critically reviews it for its glories and its errors'.[47] Thus modernism's dogmatic reductionism, its inability to deal with ambiguity and irony, and its denial of validity of the past were all issues that were seriously examined and found wanting. Postmodernism attempts to be historically aware, hybrid and inclusive. Seemingly inexhaustible historical and social curiosity and a provisional and paradoxical stance (somewhat ironic, yet involved) replaced the prophetic, prescriptive posture of the great masters of modernism. An example of this new collaborative position would be Robert Pirzio Biroli's rebuilding of the town hall in Venzone, Italy, following a recent earthquake. An elegant rereading of the local structural models (mostly Palladian) of the Veneto region is here filtered through both the modernist technology best suited to a structure built in a seismic area and the particular needs of a modern administrative centre. Even more significantly, perhaps, this building was designed with the help of a cooperative formed by the inhabitants of the destroyed village – who also literally worked at the rebuilding themselves. Here memory played a central role: both the material and cultural memory of the users of the site and the collective architectural memory of the place (and architect).

This is not to deny that there is also kitsch, kitsch that is being labelled as postmodernism: the tacking of classical arches onto the front of modernist skyscrapers, for instance. This trendy attempt to capitalise on the popularity of postmodern historicism is not the same as postmodernism itself, but is a sign of its (perhaps inevitable) commodification. Just as modernist techniques and forms became debased by dilution and commercialisation, so the same has happened to the postmodern. This does not, however, undermine the positive potential value of postmodernist architecture as a whole and its salutary and necessary critique of some of the 'unexamined cant' of modernism.[48] A young Toronto architect, Bruce Kuwabara, recently pointed to the importance of the postmodern breaking up of modernist dogma and its reconsideration of the urban heritage of the city.[49] Another architect, Eberhardt Zeidler, has compared this postmodern shattering of the doxa to that of Mannerism's challenge to the classical order of architecture.[50] Neither is in itself radically new, but both open things up to the possibility of the new.

There are always two ways of reading the contradictions of postmodernism, though. What Tom Wolfe sees as postmodernism's failure to break completely with modernism is interpreted by Portoghesi as a necessary and often even affectionate 'dialogue with a father'.[51] What Wolfe sees as Robert Venturi's empty ironic references, Portoghesi sees as a way of involving the decoding observer in the process of meaning-generating through ambiguity and multivalence.[52] It is also a way to mark an ideological stance: the Venturis, in their work on Las Vegas, for instance, can be seen – as Jencks notes – to:

> express, in a gentle way, a mixed appreciation for the American Way of Life. Grudging respect, not total acceptance. They don't share all the values of a consumer society, but they want to speak to this society, even if partially in dissent.[53]

What to Wolfe is just camp historical reference in the work of Charles Moore is seen by Portoghesi as revealing the nearly limitless possibilities for recycling historic forms.[54] Moore's famous Piazza d'Italia in New Orleans is perhaps the best example of what novelist John Fowles once called both a homage and a kind of ironic thumbed nose to the past.[55] With none of modernism's iconoclasm, this parodic project shows both its critical awareness and its love of history by giving new meaning to old forms, though often not without irony. We are clearly dealing here with classical forms and ornamentation, but with a new and different twist: there is no handcrafted decoration at all (this is not a celebration of Romantic individuality or even Gothic craftsmanship). The ornamentation is here, but it is of a new kind, one that partakes, in fact, of the machine-tooled impersonality and standardisation of modernism.

Because this is a public area for the Italian community of the city, Moore encodes signs of local Italian ethnic identity – from Latin inscriptions to a parody of the Trevi fountain. That particular corner of Rome is a complex mix of theatrical stage, palace, sculpture and nature (rocks and water). In Moore's parodic rendition, the same elements are retained, but are now executed in new media. Sometimes even structures are refashioned and 're-functioned': a Tuscan column becomes a fountain, with water running down it. Despite the use of modernist materials like neon, concrete and stainless steel, there is still a challenge to modernism. This appears not just in the eclectic (but never random) classical echoing, but also in the use of colour and ornament in general. The same challenge is also to be seen in the deliberate contextualising of the piazza into the local architecture. From a nearby skyscraper, Moore took the black and white colouring of concentric rings, themselves reminiscent of the Place des Victoires in Paris. But what he did with these rings is new: the bull's-eye form draws the eye towards the centre, leading us to expect symmetry. But this symmetry is denied by the incompletion of the circles. As in much postmodernist art, the eye is invited to complete the form for itself; such counter-expectation urges us to be active, not passive, viewers.

In another implicitly anti-modernist gesture, Moore takes the actual social use of the square into account. The shape that interrupts the concentric circles is a familiar boot-shaped map of Italy, with Sicily at the point of the bull's eye. Such a focus is apt because most of the Italians in New Orleans are, in fact, Sicilian. On that spot there is a podium for speeches on St Joseph's day. Piazza d'Italia is meant as a return to the idea of architecture as intimately related to the *res publica*, and the awareness of this social and political function is reflected in its echoing of classical forms – that is, an echoing of a familiar and accessible public idiom. In an implied attack on the earnest seriousness of high modernism, such relevance and function here go together with irony: the boot shape is constructed as a new Trevi fountain, a cascade of broken forms in which (when it works properly) water flows from the highest point (the Alps) to the lowest, along the Po, Arno and Tiber rivers. This celebration of ethnic public identity is brought about by a formal reworking of the structures and functions of both classical and modernist architecture. The dialogue of past and present, of old and new, is what gives formal expression to a belief in change within continuity. The obscurity and hermeticism of modernism are abandoned for a direct engagement of the viewer in the processes of signification through recontextualised social and historical references.

> Those who fear a wave of permissiveness would do well to remember that the ironic use of quotation and the archaeological artifact as an *objet trouvé* are discoveries of the figurative avant-garde of the twenties that have landed on the island of architecture sixty years late. (Paolo Portoghesi)

The other major theorist of postmodernism has been Charles Jencks, upon whose descriptions of Moore's work I have just been drawing. Influenced by modern semiotics, Jencks sees architecture as conveying meaning through language and convention. It is in this context that he situates the parodic recall of the past, the context of the need to look to history to enlarge the available vocabulary of forms. His description of Robert Stern's design for the Chicago Tribune Tower is typical in revealing his interest in the language and rhetoric of architecture:

The skycolumn, one of the oldest metaphors for the tall building, is used very effectively here to accentuate the vertical dimension and emphasise the top. Unlike the [Adolf] Loos [1922] entry, from which Stern's tower derives, it ends with a flourish ... Unlike the Michelangelo pilasters [from the Palazzo Farnese in Rome], to which it also relates, it sets horizontal and vertical faces into extreme opposition by changing the colour and texture ... the building seems to ripple and then burst upwards towards its 'shower' of grey, gold, white and red – its entablature and advertisement. Since the building is to be made from coloured glass, one would experience an odd oxymoronic contradiction – 'glass/masonry' – that, in a way, is as odd as the basic conceit: the skycolumn which supports the sky.[56]

The pun on newspaper columns is deliberate; the black and white of the building are meant to suggest print lines and, of course, the *Chicago Tribune* is red/read all over. The same punning occurs in Thomas Vreeland's World Savings and Loan Association Building in California. The formal echoing of the black and white marble stripes of the campanile of the cathedral in Sienna gives an ironic religious edge to the bank building's large and simple sign: 'World Savings.'

That such a complex combination of verbal and architectural languages also has direct social implications goes without saying to Jencks. Even without the verbal connection, the ideological dimension is clear. For instance, in his discussion of late-modern architecture (which Jameson confuses with postmodernism[57]), Jencks points out how the 'Slick-Tech' forms of 'Corporate Efficiency' imply effortless mechanical control of the users of the buildings.[58] But this industrial aesthetic of utility, exchange and efficiency has been challenged by a postmodernist return to the historical and semantic awareness of architecture's relationship to the *res publica*, for example, with its very different associations of communal power, political process and social vision.[59] In other words, the self-reflexive parodic introversion suggested by a turning to the aesthetic past is itself what makes possible an ideological and social intervention. Philip Johnson returned the city street to its users in the plaza of his AT&T Building in New York precisely through his parodic historical recalling of the loggia as shared public spare.

There are obviously borderline cases, however, where the contradictions of the postmodern use and abuse of conventions may, in fact, be rather problematic. Jencks has trouble dealing with Michael Graves's Fargo/Moorhead Cultural Bridge with its admitted echoes of Ledoux, Castle Howard, Serliana, [Gordon] Wilson's architecture at Kew, Asplund, Borromini and others. He adds other parodic reworkings which Graves does not mention, but which he himself notices: of modernist concrete construction, of Mannerist broken pediments and of Cubist colours. Jencks acknowledges that the meaning of these historical references would likely be lost on the average citizen of the American Midwest. He seems to want to call this esoteric, private game-playing, but then stops and claims, after all, that 'there is a general penumbra of historical meaning which would, I believe, be perceived'.[60] Like all parody, postmodernist architecture can certainly be elitist, if the codes necessary for its comprehension are not shared by both encoder and decoder. But the frequent use of a very common and easily recognised idiom – often that of classical architecture – works to combat such exclusiveness.

In 'postmodern Classicism', to use Jencks's phrase, such explicit clues as columns and arches should be obvious enough to counteract any tendency to privacy of meaning. Like the 'misprision' of Harold Bloom's poets,[61] burdened by the 'anxiety of influence', postmodern classicists 'try hard to misread their classicism in a way which is still functional, appropriate and understandable'.[62] It is this concern for 'being understood' that replaces the modernist concern for purism of form. The search is now for a public discourse that will articulate the present in terms of the 'presentness' of the past and of the social placement of art in cultural discourse – then and now. Parody of the classical tradition offers a set of references that not only remain meaningful to the public but also continue to be compositionally useful to architects. [...]

[...] Parody has perhaps come to be a privileged mode of postmodern formal self-reflexivity because its paradoxical incorporation of the past into its very structures often points to these ideological contexts somewhat more obviously, more didactically, than other forms. Parody seems to offer a perspective on the present and the past which allows an artist to speak *to* a discourse from *within* it, but without being totally recuperated by it. Parody appears to have become, for this reason, the mode of what I have called the 'ex-centric', of those who are marginalised by a dominant ideology. This is clearly true of contemporary architects trying to combat the hegemony of modernism in our century. But parody has also been a favourite postmodern literary form of writers in places like Ireland and Canada, working as they do from both inside and outside a culturally different and dominant context. And parody has certainly become a most popular and effective strategy of the other ex-centrics – of black, ethnic, gay and feminist artists – trying to come to terms with and to respond, critically and creatively, to the still predominantly white, heterosexual, male culture in which they find themselves. For both artists and their audiences, parody sets up a dialogical relation between identification and distance. Like Brecht's *Verfremdungseffekt*, parody works to distance and, at the same time, to involve both artist and audience in a participatory hermeneutic activity. *Pace* Eagleton and Jameson, only on a very abstract level of theoretical analysis – one which ignores actual works of art – can it be dismissed as a trivial and depthless mode.

David Caute has argued that if art wants to make us question the 'world', it must question and expose itself first, and it must do so in the name of public action.[63] Like it or not, contemporary architecture cannot evade its representative social function. As Jencks explains: 'Not only does it express the values (and land values) of a society, but also its ideologies, hopes, fears, religion, social structure, and metaphysics.'[64] Because architecture both is and represents this state of affairs, it may be the most overt and easily studied example of postmodernist discourse, a discourse which may, in Charles Russell's words, perhaps at first appear to be merely the next logical step in accepted art history, but which subsequently must be seen as revealing the fatal limitations of current patterns of seeing or reading, and as having, in fact, effected a fundamental transformation of the practices of art.[65]

Postmodern architecture seems to me to be paradigmatic of our seeming urgent need, in both artistic theory and practice, to investigate the relation of ideology and power to all of our present discursive structures, and it is for this reason that I will be using it as my model throughout this study.

Notes

1   See Janet Paterson, 'Le Roman "Postmoderne": mise au point et perspectives', *Canadian Review of Comparative Literature* 13, 2, pp 238–55.

2   Fredric Jameson, 'Postmodernism, Or The Cultural Logic of Late Capitalism', *New Left Review* 146, 1984, pp 53–92; Terry Eagleton, 'Capitalism, Modernism: and Postmodernism', *New Left Review* 152, 1985, pp 60–73; Charles Newman, *The Post-Modern Aura: The Act of Fiction in an Age of Inflation*, Northwestern University Press (Evanston, IL), 1985.

3   Charles Caramello, *Silverless Mirrors: Book, Self and Postmodern American Fiction*, University Presses of Florida (Tallahassee), 1983.

4   Cf Arthur Kroker and David Cooke, *The Postmodern Scene: Excremental Culture and Hyper-Aesthetics*, New World Perspectives (Montreal), 1986.

5   Susan Rubin Suleiman, 'Naming a Difference: Reflections on "Modernism versus Postmodernism" in Literature', *Approaching Postmodernism*, eds Dowe Fokkema and Hans Bertens, John Benjamins, (Amsterdam and Philadelphia), 1986, pp 255–70.

6   Alan Wilde, *Horizons of Assent: Modernism, Postmodernism, and the Ironic Imagination*, Johns Hopkins University Press (Baltimore), 1981; Christine Brooke-Rose, *A Rhetoric of the Unreal: Studies in Narrative and Structure, Especially of the Fantastic*, Cambridge University Press (Cambridge and New York), 1981; David Lodge, *The Modes of Modern Writing: Metaphor, Metonymy, and the Typology of Modern Literature*, Edward Arnold (London), 1977.

7   Eg John Barth, 'The Literature of Replenishment: Postmodernist Fiction', *The Atlantic* 145, 1, pp 65–71 (reproduced in this volume).

8   Severo Sarduy, 'El barroco y el neobarroco', *América Latina en su Literatura*, ed César Fernández Moreno, second edition, Siglo XXI (Buenos Aires), 1974, pp 167–84.

9   Paolo Portoghesi, *Postmodern: The Architecture of the Postindustrial Society*, Rizzoli (New York), 1983.

10 Ibid, p 26.

11 See Marjorie Perloff, *The Dance of the Intellect: Studies in the Poetry of the Pound Tradition*, Cambridge University Press (Cambridge), 1985.

12 Fredric Jameson, 'Postmodernism, Or The Cultural Logic of Late Capitalism', p 56.

13 Ibid, via Henri Lefebvre, *La Vie quotidienne dans le monde moderne*, Gallimard (Paris), 1968; Charles Russell, 'The Context of the Concept', *Romanticism, Modernism, Postmodernism*, ed Harry R Garvin, Bucknell University Press (Lewisburg), 1980, pp 181–93; Donald D Egbert, *Social Radicalism and the Arts*, Knopf (New York), 1970; Matei Calinescu, *Faces of Modernity*, Indiana University Press (Bloomington), 1977.

14 Newman, *The Post-Modern Aura*, p 42; Richard E Palmer, 'Postmodernity and Hermeneutics', *Boundary* 2 5, 2, 1977 pp 636–93.

15 Eg Daniel Stern, 'The Mysterious New Novel', *Liberations: New Essays on the Humanities in Revolution*, ed Ihab Hassan, Wesleyan University Press (Middletown), 1971, p 26.

16 Jean-François Lyotard, *The Postmodern Condition: A Report on Knowledge*, trans Geoff Bennington and Brian Massumi, University of Minnesota Press (Minneapolis), 1984.

17 Ibid, p 26.

18 Joseph F Graham, 'Critical Persuasion; In Response to Stanley Fish', *The Question of Textuality: Strategies of Reading in Contemporary American Criticism*, eds William V Spanos, Paul A Bové and Daniel O'Hara, Indiana University Press (Bloomington), 1982, p 148; Stephen Toulmin, *Human Understanding*, Princeton University Press (Princeton), 1972.

19 Roland Barthes, *Mythologies*, trans Annette Lavers, Granada (London), 1973.

20 Cf Hans Bertens, 'The Postmodern Weltanschauung and its Relation with Modernism: An Introductory Survey', *Approaching Postmodernism*, p 17.

21   See Raymond Williams, *Culture and Society 1780–1950*, Doubleday (Garden City, NY), 1960, p xiii.

22   Susan Sontag, *Against Interpretation and Other Essays*, Dell (New York), 1967, p 304.

23   Richard Wasson, 'From Priest to Prometheus; Culture and Criticism in the Post-Modernist Period', *Journal of Modern Literature* 3, 5, pp 1,188–202.

24   Cf McCaffery, *Metafictional Muse*.

25   Jurgen Habermas, 'Modernity – An Incomplete Project', *The Anti-Aesthetic: Essays on Postmodern Culture*, ed Hal Foster, Bay Press (Port Townsend), 1983, pp 3–15.

26   See also Matei Calinescu. 'Postmodernism and Some Paradoxes of Periodization', *Approaching Postmodernism*, eds Fokkema and Bertens, p 246; Anthony Giddens, 'Modernism and Post-Modernism', *New German Critique* 22, pp 15–18.

27   Julia Kristeva, 'Postmodernism?' *Romanticism, Modernism, Postmodernism*, ed Harry R Garvin, Bucknell University Press (Lewisburg), Associated University Press (London), 1980, p 137.

28   Paolo Portoghesi, *Postmodern: The Architecture of the Postindustrial Society*, p 35.

29   Ibid, p 81.

30   Andreas Huyssen, *After the Great Divide: Modernism, Mass Culture, Postmodernism*, Indiana University Press (Bloomington), 1986, p 186.

31   Jean-François Lyotard, *Le Postmoderne expliqué aux enfants: Correspondance 1982–1985*, Galilée (Paris), 1986, p 120.

32   See Jean-François Lyotard, *Postmodern Condition*; Habermas, 'Modernity – An Incomplete Project'; Richard Rorty, 'Habermas, Lyotard et la postmodernité', *Critique* 442, 1984, pp 181–97.

33   Paolo Portoghesi, *Postmodern: The Architecture of the Postindustrial Society*, p 28.

34   Paolo Portoghesi, *After Modern Architecture*, trans Meg Shore, Rizzoli (New York), 1982, p 3.

35   William Hubbard, *Complicity and Conviction: Steps Toward an Architecture of Convention*, MIT Press (Cambridge, MA, and London), 1980.

36   Fredric Jameson, 'Postmodernism, Or The Cultural Logic of Late Capitalism', p 65.

37   Tom Wolfe, *From Bauhaus to Our House*, Farrar, Strauss & Giroux (New York), 1981, p 4.

38   Ibid, p 17.

39   Baird, '"La Dimension Amoureuse" in Architecture', p 81.

40   Fredric Jameson, 'Postmodernism, Or The Cultural Logic of Late Capitalism', p 85; Terry Eagleton, 'Capitalism, Modernism: and Postmodernism', p 73.

41   Paolo Portoghesi, *Postmodern: The Architecture of the Postindustrial Society*, pp 10–11.

42   Frampton, 'Towards a Critical Regionalism', p 20.

43   Aldo van Eyck, 'The Interior of Time', *Meaning in Architecture*, eds Jencks and Baird, p 171.

44   Paolo Portoghesi, *After Modern Architecture*, p 5.

45   Ibid, p 111.

46   Jane Jacobs, *The Death and Life of Great American Cities*, Vintage (New York), 1961.

47   Paolo Portoghesi, *After Modern Architecture*, p 28.

48   William Hubbard, *Complicity and Conviction*, p 8.

49   Bruce Kuwabara, 'A Problem for Post-Modern Architecture: Which Heritage to Preserve?', panel at University College Symposium on 'Our Postmodern Heritage', Toronto, 1987.

50   Eberhardt Zeidler, 'Post-Modernism: From the Past into the Future' panel at University College Symposium on 'Our Postmodern Heritage', Toronto, 1987.

51   Tom Wolfe. *Bauhaus to Our House*, pp 127–9; Paolo Portoghesi, *After Modern Architecture*, p 80.

52   Ibid, p 86.

53   Charles Jencks, T*he Language of Postmodern Architecture*, Academy (London), 1977, p 70.

54   Paolo Portoghesi, *After Modern Architecture*, p 77.

55   John Fowles, *Tbe Ebony Tower*, Little, Brown (Boston, MA, and Toronto), 1974.

56   Charles Jencks, *Post-Modern Classicism: The New Synthesis*, Academy (London), 1980, p 35.

57   Fredric Jameson, 'Postmodernism, Or The Cultural Logic of Late Capitalism', pp 80–3.

58   Charles Jencks, *Architecture Today*, Abrams (New York), 1982, p 50.

59   Ibid, p 92.

60   Charles Jencks, *Late-Modem Architecture and Other Essays*, Academy (London), 1980.

61   Harold Bloom, *The Anxiety of Influence*, Oxford University Press (New York), 1973.

62   Charles Jencks, *Post-Modern Classicism*, p 12.

63   David Caute, *The Illusion*, Harper and Row (New York), 1972.

64   Charles Jencks, *Architecture Today*, p 178; see also Fredric Jameson, 'Postmodernism, Or The Cultural Logic of Late Capitalism', p 56.

65   Charles Russell, 'The Context of the Concept', *Romanticism, Modernism, Postmodernism*, ed Harry R Garvin, Bucknell University Press (Lewisburg), p 182.

From Postmodernism to Postmodernity
The Local/Global Context

Ihab Hassan

The debate about postmodernism continues in this essay by Ihab Hassan. Here Hassan looks back at 30 years of writing on the subject, and summarises his most recent views on the controversy. He continues his quest to define the elusive concept and periodisation, in terms of listing the attributes and values of what he considers postmodernism. Among these are deconstruction, High Tech and the compositions of the exemplary musician John Cage, characteristics and characters Jencks has seen as being more in the Late-Modern camp. Still, both sides of this argument acknowledge there is overlap in their views as well as clear distinctions between them, and that it is also true that pluralism remains common to virtually all definitions. Here Hassan is contributing to the debate by highlighting the connections of postmodernism with postmodernity, and more importantly how they differ from each other. Like Jencks he points out that many people confuse the two: the cultural movement and the social and economic condition.

Ihab Hassan was born in Egypt in 1925. Originally educated as an engineer he emigrated to the United States in 1946 where he studied literature and had gained a PhD in English by 1953. He taught at the University of Wisconsin in Milwaukee for 29 years and received many international honours. He has written extensively on postmodernism and was one of the first to start writing positively on the subject within a literary context in his essay 'Postmodernism' (1971). *EB*

What Was Postmodernism?

What was postmodernism, and what is it still? I believe it is a revenant, the return of the irrepressible; every time we are rid of it, its ghost rises back. And like a ghost, it eludes definition. Certainly, I know less about postmodernism today than I did 30 years ago, when I began to write about it. This may be because postmodernism has changed, I have changed, the world has changed.

But this is only to confirm Nietzsche's insight, that if an idea has a history, it is already an interpretation, subject to future revision. What escapes interpretation and reinterpretation is a Platonic Idea or an abstract analytical concept, like a circle or a triangle. Romanticism, modernism, postmodernism, however, like humanism or realism, will shift and slide continually with time, particularly in an age of ideological conflict and media hype.

All this has not prevented postmodernism from haunting the discourse of architecture, the arts, the humanities, the social and sometimes even the physical sciences; haunting not only academic but also public speech in business, politics, the media and entertainment industries; haunting the language of private lifestyles like postmodern cuisine – just add a dash of raspberry vinegar. Yet no consensus obtains on what postmodernism really means.

The term, let alone the concept, may thus belong to what philosophers call an essentially contested category. That is, in plainer language, if you put in a room the main discussants of the concept – say Leslie Fiedler, Charles Jencks, Jean-François Lyotard, Bernard Smith, Rosalind Krauss, Fredric Jameson, Marjorie Perloff, Linda Hutcheon and, just to add to the confusion, myself – locked the room and threw away the key, no consensus would emerge between the discussants after a week, but a thin trickle of blood might appear beneath the sill.

Let us not despair: though we may be unable to define or exorcise the ghost of postmodernism, we can approach it, surprising it from various angles, perhaps teasing it into a partial light. In the process, we may discover a family of words congenial to postmodernism. Here are some current uses of the term:

1   Frank Gehry's Guggenheim Museum in Bilbao (Spain), Ashton Raggatt McDougall's Storey Hall in Melbourne (Australia) and Arata Isozaki's Tsukuba Center (Japan) are considered examples of postmodern architecture: they depart from the pure angular geometries of the Bauhaus, the minimal steel and glass boxes of Mies van der Rohe, mixing aesthetic and historical elements, flirting with fragments, fantasy and even kitsch.

2   In a recent encyclical, titled *Fides et Ratio*, Pope John Paul II actually used the word postmodernism to condemn extreme relativism in values and beliefs, acute irony and scepticism toward reason, and the denial of any possibility of truth, human or divine.

3   In cultural studies, a highly politicised field, the term postmodernism is often used in opposition to postcolonialism, the former deemed historically feckless, being unpolitical, or worse, not politically correct.

4   In Pop culture, postmodernism – or Po-Mo as Yuppies call it insouciantly – refers to a wide range of phenomena, from Andy Warhol to Madonna, from the colossal plaster Mona Lisa I saw advertising a *pachinko* parlor in Tokyo to the giant, cardboard figure of Michelangelo's David – pink dayglo glasses, canary shorts, a camera slung across bare, brawny shoulders – advertising KonTiki Travels in New Zealand.

What do all these have in common? Well, fragments, hybridity, relativism, play, parody, pastiche, an ironic, anti-ideological stance, an ethos bordering on kitsch and camp. So, we have begun to build a family of words applying to postmodernism; we have begun to create a context, if not a definition, for it. More impatient or ambitious readers can consult Hans Bertens's *The Idea of the Postmodern*, the best and fairest introduction I know to the topic.

But now I must make my second move or feint to approach postmodernism from a different perspective.

Postmodernism/Postmodernity

I do so by making a distinction I did not sufficiently stress in my earlier work: between postmodernism and postmodernity. This is the distinction that constitutes the main thrust of this statement, and to which I will later return.

For the moment, let me simply say that I mean postmodernism to refer to the cultural sphere, especially literature, philosophy and the various arts, including architecture, while postmodernity refers to the geopolitical scheme, less order than disorder, which has emerged in the last decades. The latter, sometimes called postcolonialism, features globalisation *and* localisation, conjoined in erratic, often lethal, ways.

This distinction is not the defunct Marxist difference between superstructure and base, since the new economic, political, religious and technological forces of the world hardly conform to Marxist 'laws'. Nor does postmodernity equal postcolonialism, though the latter, with its concern for colonial legacies, may be part of the former.

Think of postmodernity as a world process, by no means identical everywhere yet global nonetheless. Or think of it as a vast umbrella under which stand various phenomena: postmodernism in the arts, poststructuralism in philosophy, feminism in social discourse, postcolonial and cultural studies in academe, but also multinational capitalism, cybertechnologies, international terrorism, assorted separatist, ethnic, nationalist and religious movements – all standing under, but not causally subsumed by, postmodernity.

From what I have said, we can infer two points: first, that postmodernism (the cultural phenomenon) applies to affluent, High Tech, consumer, media-driven societies; and second, that postmodernity (the inclusive geopolitical process) refers to an interactive, planetary phenomenon wherein tribalism and imperialism, myth and technology, margins and centres – these terms are not parallel – play out their conflictual energies, often on the Internet.

I have said that I did not stress enough the distinction between postmodernism and postmodernity in my earlier work. But in fairness to the subject – and perhaps to myself – I should note that an internal distinction I made *within postmodernism itself* points to a crucial characteristic of postmodernity in its planetary context.

In an essay titled 'Culture, Indeterminacy, and Immanence: Margins of the (Postmodern) Age' (1977), I coined the term 'indetermanence' – that is, indeterminacy combined with immanence – to describe two disparate tendencies within postmodernism: that of cultural indeterminacy, on the one hand, and that of technological immanence, on the other. These tendencies are contrastive rather than dialectical: they ensue in no Hegelian or Marxist synthesis. (I can think of no one less postmodern than either.)

By indeterminacy, or better still, indeterminacies, I mean a combination of trends that include openness, fragmentation, ambiguity, discontinuity, decentrement, heterodoxy, pluralism, deformation, all conducive to indeterminacy or under-determination. The latter concept alone, deformation, subsumes a dozen current terms like deconstruction, decreation, disintegration, displacement, difference, discontinuity, disjunction, disappearance, de-definition, demystification, detotalisation, delegitimation, decolonisation. Through all these concepts moves a vast will to undoing, affecting the body politic, the body cognitive, the erotic body, the individual psyche, the entire realm of discourse in the West. In literature alone, our ideas of author, audience, reading, writing, book, genre, critical theory, and of literature itself, have all suddenly become questionable – *questionable but far from invalid, reconstituting themselves in various ways.*

These uncertainties or indeterminacies, however, are also dispersed or disseminated by the fluent imperium of technology. Thus I call the second major tendency of postmodernism *immanences*, a term that I employ without religious echo to designate the capacity of mind to generalise itself in symbols, intervene more and more into nature, act through its own abstractions, and project human consciousness to the edges of the cosmos. This mental tendency may be further described by words like diffusion, dissemination, projection, interplay, communication, which all derive from the emergence of human beings as language animals, *homo pictor* or *homo significans*, creatures constituting themselves, and also their universe, by symbols of their own making. Call it gnostic textualism, if you must. Meanwhile, the public world dissolves as fact and fiction blend, history becomes a media happening, science takes its own models as the only accessible reality, cybernetics confronts us with the enigma of artificial intelligence (Deep Blue contra Kasparov), and technologies project our perceptions to the edge of matter, within the atom or at the rim of the expanding universe.

No doubt, these tendencies, I repeat, may seem less prevalent in some countries than others like America or Australia, Germany or Japan, where the term postmodernism has become familiar both in and outside the university. But the fact in most developed societies remains: as a cultural phenomenon, postmodernism evinces the double tendency I have dubbed 'indetermanence' – its forms cognate to labyrinths, networks, the rhizomes of Deleuze and Guattari.

The earth, however, is larger and more significant than Planet Hollywood, Deutsche Bank or Mitsubishi. Hence the relevance of postmodernity. For the indetermanences of cultural postmodernism seem to have mutated into the local-global conflicts of postmodernity, including the genocides of Bosnia, Kosovo, Ulster, Rwanda, Chechnya, Kurdistan, Sudan, Sri Lanka, Tibet. ... At the same time, cultural postmodernism itself has metastasised into sterile, campy, kitschy, jokey, dead-end games or sheer media stunts.

Here, then, are some new terms to add to our family of words about postmodernism: indeterminacy, immanence, textualism, networks, High Tech, consumer, media-driven societies, and all the subvocabularies they imply. Have we nudged the ghost of postmodernism toward the light?

Perhaps we need to nudge it further by raising a different question: isn't the statement of this essay, so far, a mark of historical introspection? Doesn't it suggest that the postmodern mind inclines to self-apprehension, self-reflection, as if intent on writing the equivocal autobiography of an age?

The Equivocal Autobiography of an Age

In 1784, Immanuel Kant published an essay called *Was Ist Aufklärung?* ('What is Enlightenment?'). Some thinkers, especially Michel Foucault, have taken this essay to be the first time a philosopher asks self-reflexively: who are we, historically speaking, and what is the meaning of our contemporaneity? Certainly, many of us wonder nowadays: *Was ist Postmodernismus?* But as Foucault fails to note – he fails in other respects too – we ask the question without Kant's confidence in the possibilities of knowledge, his historical self-assurance.

Children of an equivocal Chronos, versed in aporia, suspicion, incredulity, votaries of decenterment and apostles of multiplicity, pluralist, parodic, pragmatic and polychronic, we could hardly privilege postmodernism as Kant privileged the Enlightenment. Instead, we betray an abandon of belatedness, a seemingly limitless anxiety of self-nomination. Hence the weird terms and nomenclatures surrounding postmodernism, terms like classical postmodernism, high, pop, Po-Mo, revisionary, deconstructive, reconstructive, insurrectional, pre- and post-postmodernism – neologisms suggesting an explosion in a word factory.

In any case, we can hardly imagine any other epoch agonising so much about itself, only to devise so clunky a moniker, so awkward a name as postmodernism. (In this, I share the blame.) Perhaps, after all, postmodernism can be 'defined' as a continuous inquiry into self-definition. This impulse is by no means restricted to the so-called West. The more interactive the globe, the more populations move, jostle and grapple – this is the age of diasporas – the more questions of cultural, religious and personal identity become acute – and sometimes specious. In still another transposition of postmodernism into postmodernity, you can hear the cry around the world: 'Who are we? Who am I?'

So, once again, here are some more words accruing to our family of words about postmodernism: historical and epistemic self-reflexivity, anxiety of self-nomination, a polychronic sense of time (linear, cyclical, sidereal, cybernetic, nostalgic, eschatological, visionary times are all in there), massive migrations, forced or free, a crisis of cultural and personal identities.

Brief History of the Term

This attempt at self-apprehension – what I called the equivocal autobiography of an age – appears reflected in the erratic history of the word postmodernism itself, a history, nonetheless, that helps to clarify the concept currently in use. I must be ruthlessly selective here, particularly since Charles Jencks and Margaret Rose have given detailed accounts of that history elsewhere.

It seems that an English salon painter, John Watkins Chapman, used the term, back in the 1870s, in the sense that we now speak of Post-Impressionism. Jump to 1934, when Federico de Onís uses the word *postmodernismo* to suggest a reaction against the difficulty and experimentalism of modernist poetry. In 1939, Arnold Toynbee takes up the term in a very different sense, proclaiming the end of the 'modern', Western bourgeois order dating back to the 17th century. Then, in 1945, Bernard Smith employs the word to suggest a movement in painting, beyond abstraction, which we call Socialist Realism. In the 1950s in America, Charles Olson, in conjunction with poets and artists at Black Mountain College, speaks of a postmodernism that reverts more to Ezra Pound and

William Carlos Williams than to Formalist poets like TS Eliot. By the end of that decade, in 1959 and 1960, Irving Howe and Harry Levin respectively argue that postmodernism intimates a decline in high modernist culture.

Only in the late 1960s and early 1970s, in various essays by Leslie Fiedler and myself, among others, does postmodernism begin to signify a distinct, sometimes positive, development in American culture, a critical modification, if not actual end, of modernism. It is in this latter sense, I believe, changing masks and changing faces, that postmodern theory persists today.

Why do I make such a seemingly self-serving claim? Consider the 1960s for a moment, all the openings and breaks that occurred in developed, consumer societies (we are speaking of postmodernism). Andreas Huyssen called that decade, straddling the 1960s and 1970s really, the 'great divide'. Within 10 or 15 years, the United States experienced an astonishing succession of liberation and countercultural movements: the Berkeley Free Speech, Vietnam Anti-War, Black Power, Chicano Power, Women's Lib, Gay Pride, Gray Panther, Psychedelic and Ecological Movements, to mention but a few. Street theatre, happenings, rock music, aleatory composition, concrete poetry, the L=A=N=G=U=A=G=E group, Pop art and multimedia events spread, blurring the borders of high and popular culture, art and theory, text and metatext and paratext (my Paracriticism, for instance). Hippies and Yippies, Flower Children and Minute Men, Encounter Groups and Zen Monks crowded the landscape. Elitism and hierarchy were out, participation and anarchy, or at least pseudo-anarchy, were in. The forms of thought and art shifted from static to performative, from the hypotactical to paratactical – or so it seemed. Not Heidegger but Derrida; not Matisse but Duchamp; not Schönberg but Cage; not Hemingway but Barthelme – and again, most visibly, not Gropius, Mies or Le Corbusier, but Gehry, Renzo Piano and Isozaki in architecture, among countless others. (Note, however, that postmodernism in the various arts is not necessarily homologous, as I will later discuss.)

In this climate of cultural 'indetermanence' and social 'delegitimation' (this latter, Lyotard's term), postmodernism grew, assuming its latest guise. Grew and I think died, though its spectre still haunts Europe, America, Australia, Japan. … But that spectre may now find a new life and a new name. Clicking 'postmodernism' in a search engine, my cybermaven colleague Cam Tatham assures me, yields 92,000 links in .06 seconds.

Conceptual Difficulties

The spectre still haunts, but it does so ineffectually; for it is conceptually flawed, and time's wingless chariot awaits no one. Since the theoretical difficulties of postmodernism are themselves revealing, I will mention at least five:

1   The term postmodernism is not only awkward; it is also Oedipal, and like a rebellious but impotent adolescent, it cannot separate itself completely from its parent. It cannot invent for itself a new name like Baroque, Rococo, Romantic, Symbolist, Futurist, Cubist, Dadaist, Surrealist, Constructivist, Vorticist and so

on. In short, the relation of postmodernism to modernism remains ambiguous, Oedipal or parasitical if you wish; or as Bernard Smith remarks in *Modernism's History*, it remains a conflictual dialogue with the older movement, which he would rather call 'Formalesque' – a term with problems of its own.

2   Postmodernism, misnamed, Smith would insist, relates itself to a modernism no longer modern; for the latter can no longer describe the high cultural achievement of the years, say, between 1890 and 1940. That is because the term modern, in its typological sense, keeps moving forward at the cutting edge of history, and has done so from Abbot Suger and Shakespeare, who both used the word, to our time.

3   The term postmodernism, triply inadequate, seems very un-postmodern because postmodern, specifically poststructuralist, thought rejects linear time, from past to present to future as the prefixes pre- and post- imply. Postmodern time, I have said, is polychronic. As such, it avoids categorical and linear periodisation: for instance, in English literary history, that useful and familiar sequence of Elizabethan, Jacobean, Neoclassical, Romantic, Victorian, Edwardian, Modern, Postmodern.

4   More importantly, postmodernism cannot serve simply as a period, as a temporal, chronological or diachronic construct; it must also function as a theoretical, phenomenological or synchronic category. Older or dead writers, like Samuel Beckett or Jorge Luis Borges or Raymond Roussel or Vladimir Nabokov, can be postmodern, while younger ones, still alive like John Updike or Toni Morrison or VS Naipaul, may not be postmodern (the distinction carries no literary value judgments). And so, we cannot claim that everything before 1960 is modern, everything after, postmodern. Beckett's *Murphy* appeared in 1938, Joyce's *Finnegans Wake* in 1939, both, in my view, pre-eminently postmodern. Nor can we simply say that Joyce is modern or postmodern. Which Joyce? That of *Dubliners* (pre-modern), *Portrait of the Artist as a Young Man* (modern), *Ulysses* (modern shading into postmodern), *Finnegans Wake* (postmodern)?

5   All this is to say that a persuasive model of postmodernism requires a constellation of particular styles, features, attitudes, *placed in a particular historical context*. Any one of these features alone – say parody, self-reflection or black humor – may find antecedents a hundred or a thousand years ago, in Euripides or Sterne. But together, in their present historical context, these features may cohere into a working model of the phenomenon called postmodernism.

6   Having constructed such a model, does postmodernism develop along the same lines in every artistic or cultural field? Does it manifest itself identically in architecture, painting, music, dance, literature – and in the latter alone, in poetry, fiction, drama, the essay? What are the correspondences and symmetries, but

also disjunctions and asymmetries, in various artistic genres, indeed in distinct fields like science, philosophy, politics, popular entertainment? Obviously, the challenges to a comprehensive model of postmodernism are daunting. Do we need such a model? Do we still need the word?

Postmodernism as Interpretive Category

At this point, we might as well ask – whether in Cairo, Sydney, Milwaukee or Kuala Lumpur – why bother with postmodernism at all?

One answer, I have suggested, is that postmodernism mutates into postmodernity, which is our global/local condition. I will shortly return, and indeed conclude, with this theme. But there is another, more immediate answer: postmodernism has become, consciously or unconsciously, for better or for worse, an interpretive category, a hermeneutic tool. As such, it impinges on our business as students of culture, literature, the arts.

Why is that? More than a period, more even than a constellation of artistic trends and styles, postmodernism has become, even after its partial demise, a way we view the world. Bernard Smith may be right in saying that postmodernism amounts to little more than a struggle with the modernist 'Formalesque'. But this dialogue or struggle also becomes a filter through which we view history, interpret reality, see ourselves; postmodernism is now our shadow.

Every generation, of course, reinvents, reinvests, its ancestors – this, too, is hermeneutics. And so we look back on Lawrence Sterne's *Tristram Shandy* (1759–67) and say, here is an instance, or an antecedent, of postmodernism. We can say the same of Franz Kafka's *The Castle* (1926) or Jean-Paul Sartre's *Nausea* (1938) or James Joyce's *Finnegans Wake* (1939). But all this simply means that we have internalised some of the assumptions and values of postmodernism and that we now reread the past – indeed, re-appropriate it – in their terms.

This tendency, inevitable perhaps and sometimes enabling, can become offensive when postmodern ideologies cannibalise the past, incorporating it wholly into their flesh. Put more equably, we need to respect the otherness of the past, though we may be condemned to revise it even as we repeat it. In this, as in literary studies generally, postmodern theory, at its best, can prove beneficial: it can become a heightened mode of self-awareness, self-critical of its own assumptions, its own bleached myths and invisible theologies, and tolerant of what is not itself. But this calls for pragmatism, to avoid the extremes of dogma and scepticism. For the latter, as TS Eliot said in his *Notes Toward a Definition of Culture*, can be a highly civilised trait, though when it declines into pyrrhonism, it becomes a trait from which civilisations can die.

Postmodernism and Pragmatism

Here I must make an excursus on philosophical pragmatism, one more crucial word to add to our growing verbal family. By 1987, when I published *The Postmodern Turn*, I had begun to wonder, like others, how to recover the creative impulse of postmodernism without atavism or reversion, without relapse into enervated forms or truculent dogmas, without cynicism or fanaticism. Facile scepticism lacked conviction; ideological politics was full of passionate mendacity. I turned then to the philosophical pragmatism of William James and returned to the artistic pragmatism of John Cage. Both allowed a place for belief, indeed for unabashed spirituality, in works like *The Will to Believe* and *A Year from Monday*.

Philosophical pragmatism, of course, offers no panacea. But its intellectual generosity; its epistemic or noetic pluralism; its avoidance of stale debates (about mind and matter, for instance, freedom and necessity, nurture and nature); and its affinities with open, liberal, multicultural societies, where issues must be resolved by mediation and compromise rather than dictatorial power or divine decree – all these make it congenial to postmodernism without acceding to the latter's potential for nihilism, its spirit of feckless and joyless 'play'.

But the virtues of Emersonian and Jamesian – far more than Rortian – pragmatism affect literary studies generally, not only postmodern theory. (The topic warrants a monograph in itself.) Perhaps, in anticipation of my conclusion, I can say simply this: such virtues are inward with reality. They resist the hubris of theory, the impatience of ideology, the rage of our desires and needs – in short, they nurture that 'negative capability' Keats considered essential to great literature.

As for Cage, that genius of postmodern avant-gardes in music, dance, the visual arts, literature, he carried negative capability to the thresholds of nondiscrimination. A pragmatist, a descendant of American Transcendentalism withal, a disciple of Zen, Cage's sacramental vision of dispossession, of egolessness, perfuses his work from first to last. Who has not heard rise from his aleatory pages – often composed by chance operations applied to the *I Ching* – Cage's happy, open-mouthed laugh, echoing the practical hilarity of holy fools in times past as well as the robust, expansive amiability of William James?

That is the sound of pragmatism, I submit, whose cadences may calm and inspire us all, especially in cultural and postcolonial studies.

Beyond Postmodernism: An Inconclusion

Throughout this paper, the latent question has been: what lies beyond postmodernism? Of course, no one really knows. But my tacit answer has been: postmodernity, pulsing on the Internet. This is no cause to cheer.

Realism teaches us that historical crises do not always come to happy resolution; we need to learn what history can and cannot teach. Still, though inequities and iniquities of existence may be indurate, they are not all irremediable *in the particular forms they take*.

Two factors aggravate the ordeals of postmodernity in our time: the glaring disparities of wealth among and *within* nations, and the furies of nationalism, collective identity, mass feelings. About the first subject, crucial as it may be, I will say little: it engages the dismal sciences of economics and geopolitics, beyond my reach. About the second, I will hazard a few remarks.

Much is said about difference, about otherness, and much of that is in the hortatory mode. But those who demand respect for their kind do not always accord it to other kinds. The fact is that the human brain exploded mysteriously into evolution a million or so years ago, devising hasty strategies for survival, which include the distinction between Self and Other, We and Them.

The division is manifest in the biological world, not only interspecies (between different species), but also intraspecies (between individuals of the same species). That is the miracle of our immune systems which distinguish immediately, electrochemically, between home bodies and 'invaders'. Such systems, though, can be fooled sometimes into attacking friends and ignoring foes – but that is another story. The division between Self and Other is also manifest in nearly all our languages, in the deep structures of grammar and in the vocabularies of the different pronouns. Hence the distinctions we make between I and You, Us and Them, We and They, and so forth. Furthermore, the division is active in the layers of the psyche, as Freudians and Lacanians know, in the distinction between Ego Instincts (self-centered) and Object or Erotic Instincts (centered on others), as well as in Lacan's Mirror Stage and Symbolic Order. Most pertinent to our topic, however, the division is clear in the evolutionary and historical development of the family, the group, the tribe. Human beings would have perished long ago in the struggle for evolution – to faster, stronger, fiercer animals like the sabre-toothed tiger – were it not for the human brain, human languages and human social organisations. Hence the profound instinct of tribalism, which develops into nationalisms of different kinds, including ethnic, religious, cultural and political nationalism.

This instinct is primal – but also primitive. The Bulgarian Nobelist Elias Canetti wrote, in *Auto-da-Fé*, about the 'mass-soul in ourselves', which foams like a huge, wild, full-blooded animal. More soberly, the great biologist EO Wilson describes, in *Consilience*, the 'epigenitic rules' governing the practices of kinship, cooperation and reciprocal altruism in human societies.

Now, the mass-soul, the herd or tribal instinct, may be primal. But so is imagination, so is love, so is the power of sympathy – in short, the power to vault over distinctions and identify with others. Moreover, though the division between Self and Other may have been once essential to survival, it may be less so now, may need to assume different shapes, in our interactive, interdependent, cybernetic and 'glocal' age – this hideous neologism can be used only once – the age of postmodernity.

Still, I do not think that divisions between Self and Other, Us and Them, will soon vanish, especially if the discrepancies of wealth and power persist in their flagrant forms. But I do think that, instead of wishing or talking the distinction away, *we can make it more conscious of itself in our lives*. This requires absolute candor, the courage to speak the truth to ourselves and not only to others. Beyond that, we need to cultivate a keener, livelier, more dialogical sense of ourselves in relation to diverse cultures, diverse natures, the whole universe itself. And we need to discover modes of self-transcendence, especially for the 'wretched of the earth', that avoid blind identification with collectives premised on exclusion of other groups. This, I realise, is far easier said than done, especially for the mass-minded in every clime. Still, I would maintain, *that is the spiritual project of postmodernity*, a project to which literature and all the arts remain vital.

Of course, we can define the project of postmodernity simply in political terms as an open dialogue between local and global, margin and centre, minority and majority, concrete and universal – and not only between those but also between local and local, margin and margin, minority and minority, and further still, between universals of different kinds. But there is never surety that a political dialogue, even the most open, will not erupt into violence.

To this ancient stain of human violence, I have no remedy. But I wonder: can postmodern pragmatism serve us in a small way? Can the imagination serve us in larger ways? Will spirit become the ground from which new ecological and planetary values spring? Can the Internet – more conjunctive than disjunctive despite current parodies of Teilhard.com – abet a noetic, holistic apprehension of reality, which I called in *Paracriticisms* 'the new gnosticism'? This I know: without spirit, the sense of cosmic wonder, of being and mortality at the widest edge, which we all share, existence quickly reduces to mere survival. Something we need to release us from the prison-house of tribal identity, and from the terrible grip of self-concern. That is spirit.

In this universe, not all the music is of our own making.

References

Bertens, Hans, *The Idea of the Postmodern: A History*, Routledge (London and New York), 1995.
Cage, John, *A Year From Monday*, Wesleyan University Press (Middletown, CT), 1967.
Canetti, Elias, *Auto-da-Fé*, trans CV Wedgwood, Seabury Press (New York), 1979.
Deleuze, Gilles, and Guattari, Félix, *Rhizome*, Les Éditions de Minuit (Paris), 1976.
Eliot, TS, *Notes Toward the Definition of Culture*, Faber and Faber (London), 1948.
Foucault, Michel, *Michel Foucault: Beyond Structuralism and Hermeneutics*, eds Hubert L Dreyfus and Paul Rabinow, University of Chicago Press (Chicago), 1982.
Hassan, Ihab, *Paracriticisms: Seven Speculations of the Times*, University of Illinois Press (Urbana), 1975.
Hassan, Ihab, *The Postmodern Turn: Essays in Postmodern Theory and Culture*, Ohio State University Press (Columbus), 1987.
Huyssen, Andreas, *After the Great Divide: Modernism, Mass Culture, Postmodernism*, Indiana University Press (Bloomington), 1986.
James, William, *Pragmatism*, Meridian Books (New York), 1955.
James, William, *The Will to Believe and Other Essays*, Dover (New York), 1956.
Jencks, Charles, *What Is Postmodernism?* fourth edition, Academy Editions (London), 1996.
Kant, Immanuel, "Was Ist Aufklärung?" *Berlinische Monatschrift*, November 1784.
Keats, John, *The Selected Letters of John Keats*, ed Lionel Trilling, Farrar, Straus, & Young (New York), 1951.
Lyotard, Jean-François, *La Condition postmoderne*, Les Editions de Minuit (Paris), 1979.
Nietzsche, Friedrich, *The Will to Power*, ed Walter Kaufmann, trans Walter Kaufmann and RJ Hollingdale, Random House (New York), 1967.
Rose, Margaret, *The Post-Modern and the Post-Industrial*, Cambridge University Press (Cambridge), 1991.
Smith, Bernard, *Modernism's History*, Yale University Press (New Haven), 1998.
Wilson, EO, *Consilience: the Unity of Knowledge*, Random House (New York), 1998.

Ihab Hassan, 'From Postmodernism to Postmodernity, earlier versions of this essay have been published in *Artspace*, Critical Issues Series No 3, 2000, and *Philosophy and Literature* 25, 1 (Spring 2001). The current text has previously been published on the author's website: http://www.ihabhassan.com/postmodernism_to_postmodernity.htm. © Ihab Hassan.

Pillars and Posts
Foundations and Future of Post-Modernism

Felipe Fernández-Armesto

Here Fernández-Armesto traces the pivotal historical events around the emergence of Post-Modernism by investigating at which point the various disciplines start to question their accepted ideas of reality. He argues that Post-Modernism had been developing as a phenomenon much earlier than it was identified by name and agrees with Jencks that Post-Modernism is not a reactionary movement away from Modernism, but a development that is intimately linked to it, growing out of it. In this overview, Fernández-Armesto shows that Modernists had already questioned the foundations of ultimate truth in the early decades of the 20th century and continued to do so into the 1960s, claiming that these were speculations more than stable concepts. The line of inquiry moves from Albert Einstein to Henri Poincaré in science, Franz Boas in anthropology, Ferdinand de Saussure in linguistics, William James in philosophy and Kurt Gödel in mathematics. Then, returning to philosophy and linguistics with Ludwig Wittgenstein, it recommences with Jane Jacobs in architecture and urban planning, and finally finishes with the opening up of the Catholic Church to a liturgical pluralism with the Second Vatican Council.

Felipe Fernández-Armesto was born in London in 1950 and received a DPhil in History from Oxford University. He holds teaching positions at Notre Dame, Tufts, the Universidad Complutense de Madrid and Queen Mary, University of London and has numerous academic distinctions. His research has been published in 25 languages and he contributes not only to the world of academia, but also to popular culture as a food writer, a presenter on Radio 4 and as a screen writer for BBC2, Channel 4 and CNN; he has been called a Renaissance Man of history writing. *EB*

If this were a post-modern paper on Post-Modernism, I should not speak of 'origins' but of 'genealogy' or 'archaeology': the blood-lines that lead to the relevant texts, or the stratigraphy that underlies them. I have no hope of reaching the *Ursprung* or the bedrock. Instead, I shall describe a tradition, not only in the arts but in the glutinous intellectual and cultural contexts in which the arts are always embedded, linking Post-Modernism to movements which preceded it, and speculating briefly about where the tradition might lead in future.

In trying to trace what Charles Jencks describes in the introduction to this anthology as a 'golden thread of continuity' that joins Post-Modernism to its Modernist origins, I feel less like Ariadne in the labyrinth than Piglet hunting the heffalump: tracking an indescribable

Subodh Gupta, *Line of Control*, 2008. A mushroom cloud of pots, pens and kitchen equipment. Although such work was shown under the title of *Altermodernism*, the metaphor critical of the atomic bomb (of Modernism) and the use of ready-made material not to mention the high-low imagery were all essential to the Post-Modern canon. © Charles Jencks.

beast through undecipherable prints. In rival characterisations, the postmodern seems full of ill-assorted particularities, from 'punk rock to the death of metanarrative, fanzines to Foucault',[1] yet no easy generalisations describe it. 'Postmodernism', streamlined, is used as a name for the feeling that a historical period, which, rather uninventively, we have called 'modern', has recently ended, or is coming to an end. It is also used for a sensibility drawn towards the mysteries of nonbeing and 'becoming', rather as Romanticism was attracted to the delicious frustrations of experience unfulfilled. A postmodern sensibility responds to the elusive, the uncertain, the absent, the undefined, the fugitive, the silent, the inexpressible, the meaningless, the unclassifiable, the unquantifiable, the intuitive, the ironic, the inexplicit, the random, the transmutative or transgressive, the incoherent, the ambiguous, the chaotic, the plural, the prismatic: whatever hard-edged modern sensibilities cannot enclose.

Post-Modernism – hyphenated and capitalised, the proper subject of the present anthology – is a movement or group of movements that embodies those sensibilities and proposes creative values that reflect them in ways variable from discipline to discipline and art to art. In architecture, Post-Modernism, thanks to Charles Jencks, has become identified with 'double-coding'. In other visual arts, it is associated with the abjuration of such hallowed values as creativity, originality, uniqueness, meaning and form.[2] In ethics it has come to mean, or at least to include, moral relativism; in epistemology, it suggests scepticism about the validity of the concepts of reality and truth. In the humanities generally it refers to methodologies affected by the 'linguistic turn'. And what is said to be Post-Modern science is 're-enchanted' or 'organicist' or deflected by the 'oriental turn', which represents an attempt to incorporate the insights – holistic and mystical – of supposedly Eastern wisdom into Western thought.[3] One thing all manifestations of Post-Modernism are widely supposed to have in common is political radicalism. It is therefore tempting to understand it in a political context and trace its origins via the history of leftist schisms and heresies. A lot of Post-Modernist work, however, especially in the visual arts, seems aggressively nonpolitical or anti-political; and while this may be the outcome of another radical tradition – anarchism – it does not seem fair to assume so in advance.

I propose to treat Post-Modernism by analogy with other commonly identified movements in Western art and thought. Such movements have sometimes been revolutionary in their effects but are always traditional in their origins: they grow out of what precedes them. The Renaissance, the Reformation, the Scientific Revolution, the Enlightenment, Romanticism and what – to avoid 'Modernism' and 'modernity' – I prefer to call 'the modern movements' all grew, one out of the other. The Reformation was an outgrowth of Renaissance humanism and medieval piety; the Scientific Revolution owed a great deal to the Renaissance 'Hermetic tradition'. The Enlightenment got the cult of reason from the Renaissance and faith in empiricism from the Scientific Revolution. The late Enlightenment and early Romanticism, late Romanticism and the early modern movements, all overlapped and blended into one another. We should therefore expect to find Post-Modernism, prefigured and emergent, before it acquired a name.

Nor should we allow that name to mislead us. *Soi-disant* Post-Modernists frequently express what makes them postmodern in terms of sequences of dilemmatically paired or contrasting terms or sharp distinctions from supposedly modern values. The most representative contrasts are: modern is urbanist, postmodern ecological; modern is authorial, postmodern is self-reflexive; modern is meaningful, postmodern is absurd; modern is transcendent, postmodern is immanent; modern is identity, postmodern is difference; modern is elitism, postmodern is vernacular.[4] In the past, this habit of pairing apparent contrasts encouraged the assumption that Post-Modernism and the modern are mutually exclusive, whereas they are better understood symbiotically, as Charles Jencks's tabulated pairings tend to show in the introduction to this volume. In famous lines, Baudelaire defined the modern as 'the ephemeral, the fugitive, the contingent, the half of art whose other half is the eternal and the immutable'.[5] It is tempting to adapt this phrase and say that the postmodern is the ephemeral, fugitive and contingent half of the modern, whose other half is the eternal and the immutable.

I therefore see the early years of the 20th century – the time of the modern movements' most intense and creative dynamism – as the founding moment of the tradition to which Post-Modernism belongs. In historians' work, the years preceding the First World War often appear as a period of inertia when nothing much happened – a golden afterglow of the Romantic age, which would be turned blood-red by the real agent of change: the war itself. As soon as one looks beyond political history to culture one realises how inadequate an account that is. The period between 1900 and the outbreak of the war was explosively innovative – in part, perhaps, because the new century dissipated *fin-de-siècle* inhibitions.

During that decade or so, three contexts in particular influenced potentially Post-Modernist trends in art and thought: first, what I call the scientific counter revolution, which exploded certainties inherited from 17th- and 18th-century science; second, a revolution in social anthropology, which made cultural relativism the only credible basis on which a serious study of human societies could be pursued; finally, a philosophical climate which eroded confidence in traditional notions about language, reality and the links between them. Each of these contexts can be evoked through the figure of an individual contributor to the novelties of the decade.

The scientific counter revolution is associated, in most people's minds, with Einstein. In 1905, he emerged from obscurity, like a burrower from a mine, to detonate a terrible charge: but the impact of the explosion was registered only very gradually, as the theory of relativity was elaborated, and knowledge of it spread. 'The spirit of unrest', – it could be said by 1919 – had 'invaded science'.[6] But it was a case of delayed shock and it belonged in the context of other rumblings: relativity, as Einstein said, was 'waiting to be discovered'. The scientific thinker who really changed the world in the first decade of the 20th century is little remarked today but, at the time, was unrivalled for fame and popular eminence: Henri Poincaré.

In 1902 he published *La Science et l'hypothèse*, in which he questioned what had previously been the defining assumption of scientific method: the link between hypothesis and evidence. Any number of hypotheses, he said, could fit the results of experiments.

Scientists chose between them by convention – or even, in a formulation Poincaré used in 1901, according to 'the idiosyncracies of the individual'.[7] Among examples he examined were Newton's laws and the traditional concepts of space and time: the very heritage Einstein's theory questioned. His work is a window on a scientific world puzzled by rogue results, confused by self-questioning – a laboratory transformable by the magic of a sorcerer's apprentice. It helps to explain why a *méchant* like Einstein could be accepted. Poincaré provided reasons for doubting everything formerly regarded as demonstrable. He likened a physicist to 'an embarrassed theologian, ... chained' to contradictory propositions.[8] His scepticism was both representative and formative of his age. His books sold in scores of thousands.[9] He was 'an international celebrity at the age of 35'.[10] He made frequent appearances on popular platforms and in the press.

For a sense of the impact of Poincaré it is sufficient to quote some of the popular misreadings he felt compelled to abjure. He had to dissent from the view that 'scientific fact was created by the scientist'[11] and deny that 'Science consists only of conventions, and ... the facts of science and a fortiori its laws are the artificial work of the scientist'.[12] When he injudiciously remarked that '"the earth turns round" and "it is more convenient to suppose that the earth turns round" have one and the same meaning', he complained that his public saw in these words 'the rehabilitation of Ptolemy's system, and perhaps the justification of Galileo's condemnation'.[13] Poincaré, like Einstein, was an upholder of traditional scientific values and a resolute believer in the reality of its objects of study. But unlike Einstein, he nourished popular scepticism about meanings and facts.

Among the most powerful of the supposedly scientific certainties treasured in the late 19th-century West was that of the superior evolutionary status of some peoples and some societies: an image of the world sliced and stacked in order of race. It was upset largely thanks to the anthropology of Franz Boas, who not only dethroned the fallacies of racist craniology but also outlawed the notion that societies could be ranked in terms of a developmental model of thought. People, he concluded, think differently in different cultures not because some have superior mental equipment but because all thought reflects the traditions to which it is heir, the society by which it is surrounded and the environment to which it is exposed. At the end of the first decade of the 20th century, he summarised the findings or principles of the work in progress under his guidance: 'The mental attitude of individuals who ... develop the beliefs of a tribe is exactly that of the civilized philosopher'.[14] And 'the general theory of valuation of human activities, as developed by anthropological research, teaches us a higher tolerance than the one we now profess'.[15] Boas was a fieldworker in his youth and a museum keeper in maturity – always in touch with the people and artefacts he sought to understand. His pupils had native American peoples to study within little more than a railway's reach. The habit of fieldwork clinched the conclusion that cultural relativism was inescapable. It reinforced the relativistic tendency by piling up enormous quantities of diverse data intractable to the crudely hierarchical schemes of the 19th century.

To disquiet about previously supposed scientific and anthropological certainties, Ferdinand de Saussure, meanwhile, added potentially devastating philosophical malaise:

doubt about the accessibility of truth to language. He began his lectures in Geneva in 1907,[16] following the first version of Einstein's theory by a couple of years; but it is hard to tell how, at first hearing, they fitted into the epistemological revolution of the early 20th century. They were much modified in later courses and were not published until after his death, in a form perfected or distorted by his pupils. To judge from notes taken at the time, the first course was largely concerned with the traditional problems of the morphology of sounds, which separates written from spoken language. Though Saussure also emphasised an intriguing novelty – the distinction between social speech and subjective language – there seems to have been little in his work, at this stage, which made him later acclaimed as a founding father of Post-Modernism.[17]

The figure of the time who really does deserve emphasis is, at first sight, a much less likely candidate. William James wanted a distinctively American philosophy, reflecting the values of business and hustle. It is hard to think of a more representatively 'modern' thinker. But contradictions rippled his life. He struggled against insanity and abandoned successive vocations. He preferred sentiment to reason. He dabbled in Christian Science and psychical research. He had flashes of mysticism, even while cultivating a 'tough-minded' approach to philosophy. On the recoil from the sublime and ineffable, he tried to make a home for himself in the grimy world of Mr Gagrind. 'Go back into reason,' he advised, 'and you come at last to fact, nothing more.'[18] This was where he found pragmatism. The work in which he popularised it in 1907 was hailed as 'the philosophy of the future'.[19] James's claim that truth is a matter not of the reality of what is claimed, but its conformity to a particular purpose was one of the most subversive claims ever made by a philosopher. He had set out as an apologist for Christianity: he ended by undermining it by relativising truth.[20]

So the first decade of the 20th century was a graveyard and a cradle: a graveyard of certainties, the cradle of a civilisation of crumbling confidence, in which it would be hard to be sure of anything. The effect of this unsettling decade can be seen – literally, seen – in the work of artists. Never more than in the 20th century, painters tend to paint not the world as they see it directly, but as science and philosophy display it for their inspection. The revolutions of 20th-century art, the chronologies of changing perceptions in painting, exactly match the jolts and shocks administered by science and philosophy. In 1907 Cubism began to hold up to the world images of itself reflected as if in a distorting mirror, shivered into fragments. Picasso and Braque denied they had ever heard of Einstein – but their work breathed the same Zeitgeist as his, and scientific vulgarisations, especially of course of the work of Poincaré, reached them through the press. As painters of an elusive reality from a multiplicity of perspectives they were reflecting the science and philosophy of their decade.

Marcel Duchamp, whom Post-Modernists are usually happy to acknowledge as a predecessor or even a progenitor, called his *Nude Descending a Staircase* of 1912 an expression of 'time and space through the abstract presentation of motion'.[21] The depth of his study of relativity would be fully revealed in the next decade in his notes on the *Large Glass*. Even Mondrian – the artist whom we think of as unqualifiably representative of Modernism, whose work so perfectly captured the angularities of modern taste that he represented the syncopations of boogie-woogie as a rectilinear grid and Broadway as a straight line – had a shivered-mirror phase in the very early years of the second decade of the century, when the trees along the river Geyn, which he had loved to paint with Romantic fidelity, were splayed and atomised in new versions. Meanwhile, in 1911, Kandinsky read Rutherford's description of the atom, 'The discovery hit me with frightful force, as if the end of the world had come. All things become transparent, without strength or certainty.'[22] The effects fed into the new style he was creating, in which he attempted to suppress every reference to or reminiscence of real objects in his work. The effects of anthropology on the art of the time are even more explicit than those of physics: in admiring and copying the arts of 'primitive' cultures, Brücke, Picasso, Braque, Brancusi and the Blue Rider school were effectively championing cultural relativism, demonstrating the validity of alien aesthetics, drawing the lessons to be learned from the formerly despised. Charles Jencks's introduction to this volume 'What Then Is Post-Modernism?', adds examples of artists and writers whom we think of as exemplars of the modern but who could almost equally well pass for Post-Modernists *avant la lettre*.

If the picture I have drawn so far is accurate, why did Post-Modernism take so long after its founding period to speak its name and become self-aware? Usually, the crystallisation of the movement in the 1960s and 1970s is explained in one of three ways. First comes the Marxist explanation: worth hearing with respect, since Marxists need to explain the forms of radicalism with which they are out of sympathy. For them, 'late capitalist' shift in the means of production was decisive: from industrial to post-industrial economies, from the energy age to the information age.[23] Rather than simply identifying Post-Modernisms as the ideology of a new 'knowledge class',[24] which replaced industrial bosses, Fredric Jameson argued that the demise of the industrial economy changed society by way of its effects on collective psychology:

> As a service economy, we are … so far removed from the realities of production and work that we inhabit a dream world of artificial stimuli and televised experience: never in any previous civilization have the great metaphysical preoccupations, the fundamental questions of being and of the meaning of life, seemed so utterly pointless.[25]

The artist Ilya Kabakov – not a doctrinaire or consistent Post-Modernist, since his installations are storytelling devices which break the Post-Modernist taboo on narrative – explained, 'The postmodern consciousness arises in a society that doesn't need new discoveries, a society that exchanges information …'[26]

Second, there is the explanation associated with Terry Eagleton, who is also a heretical Marxist or ex-Marxist or a Marxist who, in postmodern fashion, has 'become' something else:

> Wherever else postmodernism may spring from – 'post-industrial' society, the final discrediting of modernity, the recrudescence of the avant-garde, the

commodification of culture, the emergence of vital new political forces, the collapse of certain classical ideologies of society and the subject – it is also, and centrally, the upshot of a political failure.[27]

Post-Modernism, in some versions of this line of thought, was the invention of failed revolutionaries of 1968 in self-consolation, or in retreat from the streets into theory – 'from political activism into academic discourse'.[28] But the chronology of events does not fit the theory. Texts of the late 1950s and early 1960s record a crystallising sense that a postmodern age had begun.[29] The texts which galvanised the movement – the early contributions of Ihab Hassan, Robert Venturi – dated from before 1968, in a period when the revolutionary optimism of the left was cresting.[30]

Third, Post-Modernism is represented as revulsion from Modernism under the impact of distressing events and new opportunities: the war, genocide, Stalinism, Hiroshima, the tawdry utopias created by the architectural modern movements, the dreariness of the overplanned societies Europeans inhabited in the postwar years. The alienated had to reclaim culture: the breakneck technology of electronically generated entertainment helped them do it. In part, against this background, Post-Modernism was a generational effect. The baby boomers could repudiate a failed generation and embrace sensibilities suited to a postcolonial, multicultural, pluralistic era. The contiguities and fragility of life in a crowded world and a global village encouraged or demanded multiple perspectives, as neighbours adopted or sampled each others' points of views. Hierarchies of value had to be avoided, not because they are false but because they are conflictive. Post-Modernism, according to this approach, arose in accordance with its own predictions about other 'hegemonic' ways of thought: it was the socially constructed, culturally engineered formula imposed by our own historical context.

In the attempt to understand the rise of Post-Modernism, insights from all these approaches are useful; but they are incomplete unless Post-Modernism is seen for what it is: an intellectual and artistic movement, which resembles others in the way they unfold. Movements of this kind usually take a long time to mature into self-consciousness. For Post-Modernism to develop out of its early 20th-century cocoons, the ideas of the scientific, anthropological and philosophical revolutions of the first decade had to be transmitted and extended.

Between the wars, the key events in the extension of the tradition were the formulations of the Uncertainty Principle and of Gödel's theorem. The Uncertainty Principle was a response to one of the paradoxes of quantum mechanics: when the motion of subatomic particles is plotted, their positions tend to seem irreconcilable with their momentum. Interpreters, however, made a reasonable inference: the world of big objects is continuous with the subatomic world and both are part of the same nature. Experiments in both spheres are vitiated by similar limitations. The observer is part of every observation, and there is no level of inspection at which his findings are objective. As popularly understood, the Uncertainty Principle threatened to put scientists back on par with their predecessors, the alchemists, who, because they worked with impractically complex distillations under the influence of the stars, could never repeat the conditions of an experiment and therefore never predict its results.[31]

Even after the formulation of the Uncertainty Principle, it was still possible to pick a way among the pits dug in the graveyard of certainty. Mathematics and logic, at least, seemed uncorrupted by the sublunar, subatomic world of quantum contradictions. Kurt Gödel believed in mathematics, but the effect of his work was to undermine the faith of others. He accepted Kant's view that numbers were known by apprehension, but he helped inspire others to doubt it. He felt certain – as certain as Plato or Pythagoras – that numbers really exist as objective entities, independent of thought, but he gave succour to those who dismissed them as merely conventional. He excited doubts as to whether they were known at all, rather than just assumed. He undermined a traditional way of understanding arithmetic as a formal system of reasoning similar to or identical with logic, and he inspired an unintended effect, encouraging philosophers of mathematics to devise new arithmetics in defiance of logic – rather as non-Euclidean geometries had been devised in defiance of traditional physics. He thought the truths of mathematics were non-negotiable, but by severing them from logic he encouraged a trend towards 'intuitionist' mathematics, which he abhorred. Intuitionist mathematics comes close, at the extremes, to saying that every man has his own mathematics and that a theorem proved is proved to the satisfaction of the prover. 'That which puts its trust in measurement and reckoning,' said Plato, 'must be the best part of the soul', and the study of numbers 'obviously compels the mind to use pure thought in order to get at the truth'.[32] To lose that trust and forego that compulsion, was a terrible forfeiture. The effect of Gödel's demonstrations on the way the world thinks was comparable to that of termites in a vessel formerly treated as watertight by those aboard it: the shock of the obvious. If maths and logic were leaky, the world was a ship of fools.[33]

After the war, the most significant boost to the tradition came with the publication of Wittgenstein's *Philosophical Investigations* in 1953. The printed pages still have the flavour of lecture notes, full of unresolved prompts and queries to himself and anticipated questions or dialogue from the audience. In them roams a potentially annihilating virus. For those of us who want to tell the truth, language is an attempt to refer to things. After reading Wittgenstein's last work, one finds it hard to go on believing that this is possible. His argument that we understand language not because it corresponds to reality but because it obeys rules of usage seems unanswerable. Therefore, when we understand language, we do not necessarily know what it refers to, except its own terms. Wittgenstein imagined a student asking, 'So you are saying that human agreement decides what is true and what is false?', and again, 'Aren't you at bottom really saying that everything except human behaviour is a fiction?' These were forms of scepticism anticipated by pragmatists and existentialists respectively. Wittgenstein tried to distance himself from them: 'if I do speak of a fiction, it is of a grammatical fiction.' The impact of a writer's work, however, often exceeds his intention. When he drove a wedge into what he called 'the model of object and name', he parted language from meaning. He even anticipated the absurdity in which postmodern pedagogy revels: 'My aim', he told his students, 'is to teach you to pass from a piece of disguised nonsense to something that is patent nonsense.'[34]

Specific events of the 1960s helped Post-Modernism crystallise. Students became aware that the currently prevailing scientific picture of the cosmos was riven by contradictions and that, for example, relativity theory and quantum theory – the most-prized intellectual achievements of our century – could not both be correct. The work of Jane Jacobs voiced disillusionment with the modern vision of utopia, embodied in architecture and urban planning.[35] Thomas Kuhn and chaos theory completed the scientific counter revolution of our century. The ordered image of the universe inherited from the past was replaced by the image we live with today: chaotic, contradictory, full of unobservable events, untrackable particles, untraceable causes and unpredictable effects. The contribution of the Catholic Church – the world's biggest and most influential communion – is not often acknowledged. But in the Second Vatican Council, the formerly most confident human repository of confidence dropped its guard: the church licensed liturgical pluralism, showed unprecedented deference to multiplicity of belief, and compromised its structures of authority by elevating bishops closer to the pope and the laity closer to the priesthood.

The result of this combination of traditions and circumstances was a brief postmodern age, which convulsed and coloured the worlds of academia and the arts and – in as far as civilisation belongs to intellectuals and artists – deserved to be inserted into the roll call of periods into which we divide our history. And yet, if there has been a post-modern age, it seems to have been suitably evanescent. We have passed rapidly in the last 20 years or so, from Post-Modernism to post-mortemism. Ihab Hassan recoiled in *ennui* and denounced fellow Post-Modernists for taking 'the wrong turn'.[36] Lyotard turned with a shrug or a *moue*, telling us – ironically, no doubt – that it was all a joke. Derrida rediscovered the virtues of Marxism and embraced its 'spectres'. Charles Jencks's redefinitions of Post-Modernism gutted some supposedly defining features: he has proposed reconstruction to replace deconstruction, excoriated pastiche, and rehabilitated canonical Modernists in art, architecture and literature. Many Post-Modernists seem to have yielded something to 'the return of the real'.[37]

Yet just as Modernism survived in the postmodern era, so does Post-Modernism survive the end of its brief supremacy. Charles Jencks, in 'What Then Is Post-Modernism?', describes the result as a hybrid world. That is as it should be. Modernism and Post-Modernism have a symbiotic relationship, evoked for Jencks by the coexistence of fractals and Fordism, or the image of Madonna, materialistically modern and pluralistically Po-Mo all at once. Even so, a hundred years after the first generation of 20th-century iconoclasts began to dismantle Modernist assumptions about reality, it is proper to ask whether the foundations of any equally subversive movement are discernible today. Could a new movement replace Post-Modernism or have the same breadth of influence or depth of impact?

Two possibilities are worth considering: something different from both could emerge, in theory, from the miscegenation of Modernism and Post-Modernism, as their progeny or synthesis. Or a reaction against the hybrid world we inhabit could inspire a revanchiste Modernism, rigid and dogmatic, rather as Futurism, with its trenchancy and stridency, emerged in the very decade I have claimed as Post-Modernism's founding era. So far, the only movement in the arts whose followers have enough chutzpah to claim to replace Post-Modernism is Altermodernism. Announcing 'the end of postmodernism', Nicolas Bourriaud proposed the term in 2005, calling for an 'alternative Modernism' that would reflect the new or newly impactful features of the new century – cosmopolitanism, the permeability of boundaries, the interpenetration of global cultures, and the open-mindedness and open-endedness of the Internet. Three years later, artists who responded to his call contributed to a huge and spectacular exhibition at Tate Britain. But the location of some very old work by Gustav Metzger at the centre of the exhibition – later justified by Bourriaud on the grounds that Metzger was 'the father figure' of Altermodernism[38] – suggested that the new movement was not so much an abjuration of Modernisim and Post-Modernism as a further manifestation of their durability. The signature piece of the show, which greeted exhibition goers and set the tone for the whole experience, was Subodh Gupta's stunning stunted mushroom-cloud made of stainless-steel pots and pans – a work that any self-respecting Post-Modernist would have been equally proud to include. The exhibition was full of the themes Bourriaud had emphasised – themes transgressive of boundaries of space and time – but looks, styles, feels, textures and techniques all evoked continuity with Modernist and Post-Modernist work.[39]

If anything threatens the continuities that characterise our hybrid world, it is more likely to come from outside the arts than from within them: artists are too steeped in the work of their predecessors to effect a real rupture. Even when they react, they always refer. In a sense, there has not really been a post-modern age at all, except among intellectuals, academics and artists. While we have been worrying about the corrosive effects of sceptics, who deny everything, the world beyond the arts and academe has been the prey of fanatics who think they know it all. While we have been exchanging subtle persuasion with relativists, for whom truth can never be known, dogmatists, who are convinced they have found it, have been gathering strength and spreading falsehood.

Dogmatism is incompatible with Post-Modernism, and represents a reversion to an early phase of modernity, before the subversion of certainty. In its currently powerful forms it has two curiously complementary aspects. Scientistic reductionism, though annoying to people who value metaphysics, transcendence and spirituality, is a largely academic vice that can be comfortably accommodated in a plural world without threatening to swamp or eliminate rival worldviews. A more corrosive form of certainty is religious fundamentalism, which is more powerful than scientistic dogma because it is more popular. Often misunderstood as a kind of pre-modern superstition, it is quintessentially modern, because it apes science in its search for verifiable certainty.[40] Post-modernism, considered from one perspective, is uncertainty about what is true. Fundamentalism is certainty on behalf of what is false – which is and will continue to be far harder to fit into a plural and unruptured world.

Notes

1 T Eagleton, *The Illusions of Postmodernism* (Oxford) 1996, p 21.
2 Brilliantly summarised in I Sandler, *Art of the Postmodern Era: from the late 1960s to the early 1990s* (New York), 1996, pp 332–74.
3 DR Griffin, *The Reenchantment of Science* (Albany), 1988; D Hall, 'Modern China and the Postmodern West', in *Culture and Modernity: east-west philosophic perspectives,* ed E Deutsch, (Honolulu), 1991, pp 57–62. Influential examples of attempts to use oriental models in explaining problems in physics include F Capra, *The Tao of Physics* (London), 1975, and G Zukav, *The Dancing Wu Li Masters: an overview of the new physics* (London), 1979. There is some support, too, for the term 'ironic science', owed – or, at least, its popularity is owed – to J Horgan, *The End of Science: facing the limits of knowledge in the twilight of the scientific age* (London), 1998, which substitutes speculation for science, just as postmodern literary and artistic criticism is often said to substitute theory for content.
4 Ihab Hassan, 'POSTmodernISM: a Paracritical Bibliography', *Paracriticisms: seven speculations of the times* (Urbana), 1975, pp 39–59; C Jencks, *The Language of Post-Modern Architecture* (New York), 1978, pp 6–8.
5 C Baudelaire, 'The Painter of Modern Life', trans J Mayne, *The Painter of Modern Life and Other Essays* (London), 1964, p 8.
6 *The New York Times*, quoted G Holton, *Einstein and the Cultural Roots of Modern Science* (Cambridge, MA), 1997, p 8.
7 Quoted T Dantzig, *Henri Poincaré, critic of crisis* (New York and London), 1954, p 11.
8 H Poincaré, *The Foundations of Science* (Lancaster, PA), 1946, p 142.
9 *Science and Hypothesis* sold over 20,000 copies. GB Halsted in ibid, p x.
10 T Dantzig, *Henri Poincaré*, p 1.
11 H Poincaré, *The Foundations of Science*, p 208.
12 Ibid, p 321.
13 Ibid, p 353.
14 F Boas, *The Mind of Primitive Man* (New York), 1913, p 113.
15 Ibid, pp 208–9.
16 Not 1906, as commonly asserted. F de Saussure, *Premier cours de linguistique générale (1907), d'après les cahiers d'Albert Riedlinger*, ed and trans E Komatsu and G Wolf (Oxford), 1996.
17 F Fernández-Armesto, *Truth* (London), 1997, pp 195–7.
18 Ibid, p 415.
19 RB Perry, *The Thought and Character of William James*, ii (London, nd), p 621.
20 F Fernández-Armesto, *Truth*, pp 179–81.
21 P Conrad, *Modern Times, Modern Places* (London), 1998, p 82.
22 Ibid, p 83.
23 F Jameson, *Postmodernism or the Cultural Logic of Late Capitalism* (Durham, NC), 1991, p 5.
24 D Bell, *The Coming of Post-Industrial Society* (New York), 1976, p xiv.
25 F Jameson, *Marxism and Form* (Princeton), 1971, p xviii.
26 I Sandler, *Art of the Postmodern Era*, p 357.
27 T Eagleton, *The Illusions of Postmodernism*, p 21.
28 I Sandler, *Art of the Postmodern Era*, p 333.
29 C Wright Mills, *The Sociological Imagination* (New York), 1959, pp 165–7; I Howe, 'Mass Society and Post-modern Fiction' [1959], *The Decline of the New* (New York), 1970, pp 190–207. For these and other references to work of the same period see P Anderson, *The Origins of Postmodernity* (London and New York), 1998, p 13.
30 R Venturi, *Complexity and Contradiction in Architecture* (New York), 1966; I Hassan's 'The Dismemberment of Orpheus' first appeared in *American Scholar*, xxxiii in 1963.
31 F Fernández-Armesto, *Truth*, p 186.
32 *Republic*, ed D Lee (Harmondsworth), 1974, p 333.
33 F Fernández-Armesto, *Truth*, pp 188–90.
34 Ibid, p 200; L Wittgenstein, *Philosophical Investigations* (Oxford), 1953, pp 88, 100, 102–3, 133, 241, 293, 307, 464.
35 Jane Jacobs, *The Death and Life of Great American Cities* (New York), 1961.
36 I Hassan, *The Postmodern Turn* (Ithaca), 1987, p 211.

37   H Foster, *The Return of the Real: the avant-garde at the end of the century* (Cambridge, MA, and London), 1996, pp 205–6.

38   http://www.artinamericamagazine.com/news-opinion/conversations/2009-03-17/altermodern-a-conversation-with-nicolas-bourriaud, as on 11 September 2009.

39   See N Bourrillaud, ed, *Altermodern: Tate Triennial, 2009* (London), 2009.

40   K Armstrong, *The Battle for God: Fundamentalism in Christianity, Judaism, and Islam* (New York), 2000; C Taylor, *A Secular Age* (Cambridge, MA), 2009.

The Kind of Problem a City Is

Jane Jacobs

> Because of her seminal book, *The Death and Life of Great American Cities,* Jane Jacobs is the most influential contributor to the rethinking of American city planning in the second part of the 20th century. The book is a substantial critique of Modern ideas of slum clearance and large-scale redevelopment as advocated by Le Corbusier et al. This call to arms changed architectural and planning theory and ushered in Post-Modern urbanism. In this, the last chapter, Jacobs adopts the idea of 'organized complexity', as described by Warren Weaver, for her analysis of city planning. Following leads from the natural sciences, she posits the city as a growing organism that cannot be reduced to a combination of separate functions considered statistically, nor segregated into sterile townscapes and suburbs.
>
> Jane Jacobs was born in 1916 in Pennsylvania and died in 2006 in Toronto, Canada. She worked as a journalist and was the editor of *Architectural Forum* where, eventually, she became disillusioned with the new urban developments she was writing about. *EB*

Thinking has its strategies and tactics too, much as other forms of action have. Merely to think about cities and get somewhere, one of the main things to know is what *kind* of problem cities pose, for all problems cannot be thought about in the same way. Which avenues of thinking are apt to be useful and help to yield the truth depends not on how we might prefer to think about a subject, but rather on the inherent nature of the subject itself.

Among the many revolutionary changes of this century, perhaps those that go deepest are the changes in the mental methods we can use for probing the world. I do not mean new mechanical brains, but methods of analysis and discovery that have got into human brains: new strategies for thinking. These have developed mainly as methods of science. But the mental awakenings and intellectual daring they represent are gradually beginning to affect other kinds of inquiry too. Puzzles that once appeared unanalysable become more susceptible to attack. What is more, the very nature of some puzzles are no longer what they once seemed.

To understand what these changes in strategies of thought have to do with cities, it is necessary to understand a little about the history of scientific thought. A splendid summary and interpretation of this history is included in an essay on science and complexity in the 1958 *Annual Report of the Rockefeller Foundation*, written by Dr Warren Weaver upon his retirement as the foundation's Vice-President for the Natural and Medical Sciences. I shall quote from this essay at some length, because what Dr Weaver says has direct pertinence to thought about cities. His remarks sum up, in an oblique way, virtually the intellectual history of city planning.

Dr Weaver lists three stages of development in the history of scientific thought: (1) ability to deal with problems of simplicity; (2) ability to deal with problems of disorganized complexity; and (3) ability to deal with problems of organized complexity.

Problems of simplicity are problems that contain two factors which are directly related to each other in their behaviour – two variables – and these problems of simplicity, Dr Weaver points out, were the first *kinds* of problems that science learned to attack:

> Speaking roughly, one may say that the seventeenth, eighteenth, and nineteenth centuries formed the period in which physical science learned how to analyse two-variable problems. During that three hundred years, science developed the experimental and analytical techniques for handling problems in which one quantity – say a gas pressure – depends primarily upon a second quantity – say, the volume of the gas. The essential character of these problems rests in the fact that … the behaviour of the first quantity can described with a useful degree of accuracy by taking into account only its dependence upon the second quantity and by neglecting the minor influence of other factors.
>
> These two-variable problems are essentially simple in structure … and simplicity was a necessary condition for progress at that stage of [the] development of science.
>
> It turned out, moreover, that vast progress could be made in the physical sciences by theories and experiments of this essentially simple character … It was this kind of two-variable science which laid, over the period up to 1900, the foundations for our theories of light, of sound, of heat, and of electricity … which brought us the telephone and the radio, the automobile and the airplane, the phonograph and the moving pictures, the turbine and the Diesel engine and the modern hydro-electric power plant …

It was not until after 1900 that a second method of analysing problems was developed by the physical sciences:

> Some imaginative minds [Dr Weaver continues] rather than studying problems which involved two variables or at most three or four, went to the other extreme, and said, 'Let us develop analytical methods which can deal with two billion variables.' That is to say, the physical scientists (with the mathematicians often in the vanguard) developed powerful techniques of probability theory and of statistical mechanics which can deal with what we may call problems of *disorganized complexity* …
>
> Consider first a simple illustration in order to get the flavour of the idea. The classical dynamics of the nineteenth century was well suited for analysing and predicting the motion of a single ivory ball as it moves about on a billiard table … One can, but with a surprising increase in difficulty, analyse the motion of two or even three balls on a billiard table … But as soon as one tries to analyse

the motion of ten or fifteen balls on the table at once, as in pool, the problem becomes unmanageable, not because there is any theoretical difficulty, but just because the actual labour of dealing in specific detail with so many variables turns out to be impractical.

Imagine, however, a large billiard table with millions of balls flying about on its surface … The great surprise is that the problem now becomes easier: the methods of statistical mechanics are now applicable. One cannot trace the detailed history of one special ball, to be sure; but there can be answered with useful precision such important questions as: On the average how many balls per second hit a given stretch of rail? On the average how far does a ball move before it is hit by some other ball? …

… The word 'disorganized' [applies] to the large billiard table with the many balls … because the balls are distributed, in their positions and motions, in a helter-skelter way … But in spite of this helter-skelter or unknown behaviour of all the individual variables, the system as a whole possesses certain orderly and analysable average properties …

A wide range of experience comes under this label of disorganized complexity … It applies with entirely useful precision to the experience of a large telephone exchange, predicting the average frequency of calls, the probability of overlapping calls of the same number, etc. It makes possible the financial stability of a life insurance company … The motions of the atoms which form all matter, as well as the motions of the stars which form the universe, all come under the range of these new techniques. The fundamental laws of heredity are analysed by them. The laws of thermodynamics, which describe basic and inevitable tendencies of all physical systems, are derived from statistical considerations. The whole structure of modern physics … rests on these statistical concepts. Indeed, the whole question of evidence, and the way in which knowledge can be inferred from evidence, is now recognized to depend on these same ideas … We have also come to realize that communication theory and information theory are similarly based upon statistical ideas. One is thus bound to say that probability notions are essential to any theory of knowledge itself.

However, by no means all problems could be probed by this method of analysis. The life sciences, such as biology and medicine, could not be, as Dr Weaver points out. These sciences, too, had been making advances, but on the whole they were still concerned with what Dr Weaver calls preliminary stages for application of analysis; they were concerned with collection, description, classification and observation of apparently correlated effects. During this preparatory stage, among the many useful things that were learned was that the life sciences were neither problems of simplicity nor problems of disorganized complexity; they inherently posed still a different kind of problem, a kind of problem for which, says Dr Weaver, methods of attack were still very backward as recently as 1932.

Describing this gap, he writes:

One is tempted to oversimplify and say that scientific methodology went from one extreme to the other ... and left untouched a great middle region. The importance of this middle region, moreover, does not depend primarily on the fact that the number of variables involved is moderate – large compared to two, but small compared to the number of atoms in a pinch of salt ... Much more important than the mere numbers or variables is the fact that these variables are all interrelated ... These problems, as contrasted with the disorganized situations with which statistics can cope, *show the essential feature of organization*. We will therefore refer to this group of problems as those of *organized complexity*.

What makes an evening primrose open when it does? Why does salt water fail to satisfy thirst? ... What is the description of ageing in biochemical terms? ... What is a gene, and how does the original genetic constitution of a living organism express itself in the developed characteristics of the adult? ...

All these are certainly complex problems. But they are not problems of disorganized complexity, to which statistical methods hold the key. They are all problems which involve dealing simultaneously with a *sizeable number of factors which are interrelated into an organic whole*.

In 1932, when the life sciences were just at the threshold of developing effective analytical methods for handling organized complexity, it was speculated, Dr Weaver tells us, that if the life sciences could make significant progress in such problems, 'then there might be opportunities to extend these new techniques, if only by helpful analogy, into vast areas of the behavioural and social sciences'.

In the quarter-century since that time, the life sciences have indeed made immense and brilliant progress. They have accumulated, with extraordinary swiftness, an extraordinary quantity of hitherto hidden knowledge. They also acquired vastly improved bodies of theory and procedure – enough to open up great new questions, and to show that only a start has been made on what there is to know.

But this progress has been possible only because the life sciences were recognized to be problems in organized complexity, and were thought of and attacked in ways suitable to understanding that *kind* of problem.

The recent progress of the life sciences tells us something tremendously important about other problems of organized complexity. It tells us that problems of this kind can be analysed – that it is only sensible to regard them as capable of being understood, instead of considering them, as Dr Weaver puts it, to be 'in some dark and foreboding way, irrational'.

Now let us see what this has to do with cities.

Cities happen to be problems in organized complexity, like the life sciences. They present 'situations in which a half-dozen or even several dozen quantities are all varying simultaneously and in *subtly interconnected ways*'. Cities, again like the life sciences, do not exhibit *one* problem in organized complexity, which if understood explains all. They can be analysed into many such problems or segments which, as in the case of the life sciences, are also related with one another. The variables are many, but they are not helter-skelter; they are 'interrelated into an organic whole'.

Consider again, as an illustration, the problem of a city neighbourhood park. Any single factor about the park is slippery as an eel; it can potentially mean any number of things, depending on how it is acted upon by other factors and how it reacts to them. How much the park is used depends, in part, upon the park's own design. But even this partial influence of the park's design upon the park's use depends, in turn, on who is around to use the park, and when, and this in turn depends on uses of the city outside the park itself. Furthermore, the influence of these uses on the park is only partly a matter of how each affects the park independently of the other; it is also partly a matter of how they affect the park in combination with one another, for certain combinations stimulate the degree of influence from one another among their components. In turn, these city uses near the park and their combinations depend on still other factors, such as the mixture of age in buildings, the size of blocks in the vicinity, and so on, including the presence of the park itself as a common and unifying use in its context. Increase the park's size considerably, or else change its design in such a way that it severs and disperses users from the streets about it, instead of uniting and mixing them, and all bets are off. New sets of influences come into play, both in the park and in its surroundings. This is a far cry from the simple problem of ratios of open space to ratios of population; but there is no use wishing it were a simpler problem or trying to make it a simpler problem, because in real life it is not a simpler problem. No matter what you try to do to it, a city park *behaves* like a problem in organized complexity, and that is what it is. The same is true of all other parts or features of cities. Although the interrelations of their many factors are complex, there is nothing accidental or irrational about the ways in which these factors affect each other.

Moreover, in parts of cities which are working well in some respects and badly in others (as is often the case), we cannot even analyse the virtues and the faults, diagnose the trouble or consider helpful changes, without going at them as problems of organized complexity. To take a few simplified illustrations, a street may be functioning excellently at the supervision of children and at producing a casual and trustful public life, but be doing miserably at solving all other problems because it has failed at knitting itself with an effective larger community, which in turn may or may not exist because of still other sets of factors. Or a street may have, in itself, excellent physical material for generating diversity and an admirable physical design for casual surveillance of public spaces, and yet because of its proximity to a dead border, it may be so empty of life as to be shunned and feared even by its own residents. Or a street may have little foundation for workability on its own merits, yet geographically tie in so admirably with a district that is workable and vital that this circumstance is enough to sustain its attraction and give it use and sufficient workability. We may wish for easier, all-purpose analyses, and for simpler magical, all-purpose cures, but wishing cannot change these problems into simpler matters than organized complexity, no matter how much we try to evade the realities and to handle them as something different.

Why have cities not, long since, been identified, understood and treated as problems of organized complexity? If the people concerned with the life sciences were able to identify their difficult problems as problems of organized complexity, why have people professionally concerned with cities not identified the *kind* of problem they had?

The history of modern thought about cities is unfortunately very different from the history of modern thought about the life sciences. The theorists of conventional modern city planning have consistently mistaken cities as problems of simplicity and of disorganized complexity, and have tried to analyse and treat them thus. No doubt this imitation of the physical sciences was hardly conscious. It was probably derived, as the assumptions behind most thinking are, from the general floating fund of intellectual spores around at the time. However, I think these misapplications could hardly have occurred, and certainly would not have been perpetuated as they have been, without great disrespect for the subject matter itself – cities. These misapplications stand in our way; they have to be hauled out in the light, recognized as inapplicable strategies of thought, and discarded.

Garden City planning theory had its beginnings in the late 19th century, and Ebenezer Howard attacked the problem of town planning much as if he were a 19th-century physical scientist analysing a two-variable problem of simplicity. The two major variables in the Garden City concept of planning were the quantity of housing (or population) and the number of jobs. These two were conceived of as simply and directly related to each other, in the form of relatively closed systems. In turn the housing had its subsidiary variables, related to it in equally direct, simple, mutually independent form: playgrounds, open space, schools, community centre, standardized supplies and services. The town as a whole was conceived of, again, as one of the two variables in a direct, simple, town–green-belt relationship. As a system of order, that is about all there was to it. And on this simple base of two-variable relationships was created an entire theory of self-contained towns as a means of redistributing the population of cities and (hopefully) achieving regional planning.

Whatever may be said of this scheme for isolated towns, any such simple systems of two-variable relationships cannot possibly be discerned in great cities – and never could be. Such systems cannot be discerned in a town either, the day after the town becomes encompassed in a metropolitan orbit with its multiplicity of choices and complexities of cross-use. But in spite of this fact, planning theory has persistently applied this two-variable *system of thinking and analysing* to big cities; and to this day city planners and housers believe they hold a precious nugget of truth about the *kind* of problem to be dealt with when they attempt to shape or reshape big-city neighbourhoods into versions of two-variable systems, with ratios of one thing (open space) depending directly and simply upon an immediate ratio of something else (population).

To be sure, while planners were assuming that cities were properly problems of simplicity, planning theorists and planners could not avoid seeing that real cities were not so in fact. But they took care of this in the traditional way that the incurious (or the disrespectful) have always regarded problems of organized complexity: as if these puzzles were, in Dr Weaver's words, 'in some dark and foreboding way, irrational'.[i]

Beginning in the late 1920s in Europe, and in the 1930s here, city planning theory began to assimilate the newer ideas on probability theory developed by physical science. Planners began to imitate and apply these analyses precisely as if cities were problems in disorganized complexity, understandable purely by statistical analysis, predictable by the application of probability mathematics, manageable by conversion into groups of averages.

This conception of the city as a collection of separate file drawers, in effect, was suited very well by the Radiant City vision of Le Corbusier, that vertical and more centralized version of the two-variable Garden City. Although Le Corbusier himself made no more than a gesture towards statistical analysis, his scheme assumed the statistical recording of a system of disorganized complexity solvable mathematically; his towers in the park were a celebration, in art, of the potency of statistics and the triumph of the mathematical average.

The new probability techniques, and the assumptions about the kind of problem that underlie the way they have been used in city planning, did not supplant the base idea of the two-variable reformed city. Rather these new ideas were added. Simple, two-variable systems of order were still the aim. But these could be organized even more 'rationally' now, from out of a supposed existing system of disorganized complexity. In short, the new probability and statistical methods gave more 'accuracy', more scope, made possible a more Olympian view and treatment of the supposed problem of the city.

With the probability techniques, an old aim – stores 'properly' related to immediate housing or to a preordained population – became seemingly feasible; there arose techniques for planning standardized shopping 'scientifically'; although it was early realized by such planning theorists as [Clarence] Stein and [Catherine] Bauer that preplanned shopping centres within cities must also be monopolistic or semimonopolistic, or else the statistics would not predict, and the city would go on behaving with dark and foreboding irrationality.

With these techniques, it also became feasible to analyse statistically, by income groups and family sizes, a given quantity of people uprooted by acts of planning, to combine these with probability statistics on normal housing turnover, and to estimate accurately the gap. Thus arose the supposed feasibility of large-scale relocation of citizens. In the form of statistics, these citizens were no longer components of any unit except the family, and could be dealt with intellectually like grains of sand, or electrons, or billiard balls. The larger the number of uprooted, the more easily they could be planned for on the basis of mathematical averages. On this basis it was actually intellectually easy and sane to contemplate clearance of all slums and re-sorting of people in 10 years and not much harder to contemplate it as a 20-year-job.

By carrying to logical conclusions the thesis that the city, as it exists, is a problem in disorganized complexity, housers and planners reached – apparently with straight faces – the idea that almost any specific malfunctioning could be corrected by opening and filling a new file drawer. Thus we get such political party policy statements as this:

---

i   Eg 'a chaotic accident', 'solidified chaos', etc.

The Housing Act of 1959 … should be supplemented to include … a programme of housing for moderate-income families whose incomes are too high for admission to public housing, but too low to enable them to obtain decent shelter in the private market.

With statistical and probability techniques, it also became possible to create formidable and impressive planning surveys for cities – surveys that come out with fanfare, are read by practically nobody, and then drop quietly into oblivion, as well they might, being nothing more nor less than routine exercises in statistical mechanics for systems of disorganized complexity. It became possible also to map out master plans for the statistical city, and people take these more seriously, for we are all accustomed to believe that maps and reality are necessarily related, or that if they are not, we can make them so by altering reality.

With these techniques, it was possible not only to conceive of people, their incomes, their spending money and their housing as fundamentally problems in disorganized complexity, susceptible to conversion into problems of simplicity once ranges and averages were worked out, but also to conceive of city traffic, industry, parks and even cultural facilities as components of disorganized complexity, convertible into problems of simplicity.

Furthermore, it was no intellectual disadvantage to contemplate 'coordinated' schemes of city planning embracing ever greater territories. The greater the territory, as well as the larger the population, the more rationally and easily could both be dealt with as problems of disorganized complexity viewed from an Olympian vantage point. The wry remark that 'A Region is an area safely larger than the last one to whose problems we found no solution' is not a wry remark in these terms. It is a simple statement of a basic fact about disorganized complexity; it is much like saying that a large insurance company is better equipped to average out risks than a small insurance company.

However, while city planning has thus mired itself in deep misunderstandings about the very nature of the problem with which it is dealing, the life sciences, unburdened with this mistake, and moving ahead very rapidly, have been providing some of the concepts that city planning needs: along with providing the basic strategy of recognizing problems of organized complexity, they have provided hints about analysing and handling this *kind* of problem. These advances have, of course, filtered from the life sciences into general knowledge; they have become part of the intellectual fund of our times. And so a growing number of people have begun, gradually, to think of cities as problems in organized complexity – organisms that are replete with unexamined, but obviously intricately interconnected, and surely understandable, relationships. This book is one manifestation of that idea.

This is a point of view which has little currency yet among planners themselves, among architectural city designers, or among the businessmen and legislators who learn their planning lessons, naturally, from what is established and long accepted by planning 'experts'. Nor is this a point of view that has much appreciable currency in schools of planning (perhaps there least of all).

City planning, as a field, has stagnated. It bustles but it does not advance. Today's plans show little if any perceptible progress in comparison with plans devised a generation ago. In transport, either regional or local, nothing is offered which was not already offered and popularized in 1938 in the General Motors diorama at the New York World's Fair, and before that by Le Corbusier. In some respects, there is outright retrogression. None of today's pallid imitations of Rockefeller Center is as good as the original, which was built a quarter of a century ago. Even in conventional planning's *own given terms*, today's housing projects are no improvement, and usually a retrogression, in comparison with those of the 1930s.

As long as city planners, and the businessmen, lenders and legislators who have learned from planners, cling to the unexamined assumptions that they are dealing with a problem in the physical sciences, city planning cannot possibly progress. Of course it stagnates. It lacks the first requisite for a body of practical and progressing thought: recognition of the kind of problem at issue. Lacking this, it has found the shortest distance to a dead end.

Because the life sciences and cities happen to pose the same *kinds* of problems does not mean they are the *same* problems. The organizations of living protoplasm and the organizations of living people and enterprises cannot go under the same microscopes.

However, the tactics for understanding both are similar in the sense that both depend on the microscopic or detailed view, so to speak, rather than on the less detailed, naked-eye view suitable for viewing problems of simplicity or the remote telescopic view suitable for viewing problems of disorganized complexity.

In the life sciences, organized complexity is handled by identifying a specific factor or quantity – say an enzyme – and then painstakingly learning its intricate relationships and interconnexions with other factors or quantities. All this is observed in terms of the behaviour (not mere presence) of other specific (not generalized) factors or quantities. To be sure, the techniques of two-variable and disorganized-complexity analysis are used too, but only as subsidiary tactics.

In principle, these are much the same tactics as those that have to be used to understand and to help cities. In the case of understanding cities, I think the most important habits of thought are these: (1) to think about processes; (2) to work inductively, reasoning from particulars to the general, rather than the reverse; and (3) to seek for 'unaverage' clues involving very small quantities, which reveal the way larger and more 'average' quantities are operating.

If you have got as far as this in this book, you do not need much explanation of these tactics. However, I shall sum them up, to bring out points otherwise left only as implications.

Why think about processes? Objects in cities – whether they are buildings, streets, parks, districts, landmarks or anything else – can have radically differing effects, depending

---

ii Because this is so, 'housers', narrowly specializing in 'housing' expertise, are a vocational absurdity. Such a profession makes sense only if it is assumed that 'housing' per se has important generalized effects and qualities. It does not.

upon the circumstances and contexts in which they exist. Thus, for instance, almost nothing useful can be understood or can be done about improving city dwellings if these are considered in the abstract as 'housing'. City dwellings – either existing or potential – are *specific* and particularized buildings *always involved in differing, specific processes* such as unslumming, slumming, generation of diversity, self-destruction of diversity.[ii]

This book has discussed cities, and their components, almost entirely in the form of processes, because the subject matter dictates this. For cities, processes are of the essence. Furthermore, once one thinks about city processes, it follows that one *must* think of catalysts of these processes, and this too is of the essence.

The processes that occur in cities are not arcane, capable of being understood only by experts. They can be understood by almost anybody. Many ordinary people already understand them; they simply have not given these processes names, or considered that by understanding these ordinary arrangements of cause and effect, we can also direct them if we want to.

Why reason inductively? Because to reason, instead, from generalizations ultimately drives us into absurdities – as in the case of the Boston planner who knew (against all the real-life evidence he had) that the North End had to be a slum because the generalizations that make him an expert say it is.

This is an obvious pitfall because the generalizations on which the planner was depending are themselves so nonsensical. However, inductive reasoning is just as important for identifying, understanding and constructively using the forces and processes that actually are relevant to cities, and therefore are not nonsensical. I have generalized about these forces and processes considerably, but let no one be misled into believing that these generalizations can be used routinely to declare what the particulars, in this or that place, *ought* to mean. City processes in real life are too complex to be routine, too particularized for application as abstractions. They are always made up of interactions among unique combinations of particulars, and there is no substitute for knowing the particulars.

Inductive reasoning of this kind is, again, something that can be engaged in by ordinary, interested citizens, and again they have the advantage over planners. Planners have been trained and disciplined in *deductive* thinking, like the Boston planner who learned his lessons only too well. Possibly because of this bad training, planners frequently seem to be less well equipped intellectually for respecting and understanding particulars than ordinary people, untrained in expertise, who are attached to a neighbourhood, accustomed to using it, and so are not accustomed to thinking of it in a generalized or abstract fashion.

Why seek 'unaverage' clues, involving small quantities? Comprehensive statistical studies, to be sure, can *sometimes* be useful abstracted measurements of the sizes, ranges, averages and medians of this and that. Gathered from time to time, statistics can tell too what has been happening to these figures. However, they tell almost nothing about how the quantities are working in systems of organized complexity.

To learn how things are working, we need pinpoint clues. For instance, all the statistical studies possible about the downtown of Brooklyn, NY, cannot tell us as much about the problem of that downtown and its cause as is told in five short lines of type in a single newspaper advertisement. This advertisement, which is for Marboro, a chain of bookstores, gives the business hours of the chain's five stores. Of the four in Manhattan, three (one near Carnegie Hall, one near the Public Library and not far from Times Square, one in Greenwich Village) stay open until midnight; the fourth, close to Fifth Avenue and Fifty-Ninth Street, stays open until 10 pm. The fifth, in downtown Brooklyn, stays open until 8 pm. Here is a management which keeps its stores open late, if there is business to be had. The advertisement tells us that Brooklyn's downtown is too dead by 8 pm, as indeed it is. No surveys (and certainly no mindless, mechanical predictions projected forward in time from statistical surveys, a boondoggle that today frequently passes for 'planning') can tell us anything so relevant to the composition and to the needs of Brooklyn's downtown as this small, but specific and precisely accurate, clue to the *workings* of that downtown.

It takes large quantities of the 'average' to produce the 'unaverage' in cities. [...]

[...] This awareness of 'unaverage' clues – or awareness of their lack – is, again, something any citizen can practise. City dwellers, indeed, are commonly great informal experts in precisely this subject. Ordinary people in cities have an awareness of 'unaverage' quantities which is quite consonant with the importance of these relatively small quantities. And again, planners are the ones at the disadvantage. They have inevitably come to regard 'unaverage' quantities as relatively inconsequential, because these are *statistically* inconsequential. They have been trained to discount what is most vital.

Now we must dig a little deeper into the bog of intellectual misconceptions about cities in which orthodox reformers and planners have mired themselves (and the rest of us). Underlying the city planners' deep disrespect for their subject matter, underlying the jejune belief in the 'dark and foreboding' irrationality or chaos of cities, lies a long-established misconception about the relationship of cities – and indeed of men – with the rest of nature.

Human beings are, of course, a part of nature, as much so as grizzly bears or bees or whales or sorghum cane. The cities of human beings are as natural, being a product of one form of nature, as are the colonies of prairie dogs or the beds of oysters. The botanist Edgar Anderson has written wittily and sensitively in *Landscape* magazine from time to time about cities as a form of nature. 'Over much of the world,' he comments, 'man has been accepted as a city-loving creature.' Nature watching, he points out, 'is quite as easy in the city as in the country; all one has to do is accept Man as a part of Nature. Remember that as a specimen of *Homo sapiens* you are far and away most likely to find that species an effective guide to deeper understanding of natural history.'

A curious but understandable thing happened in the 18th century. By then, the cities of Europeans had done well enough by them, mediating between them and many harsh aspects of nature, so that something became popularly possible which previously had been a rarity – sentimentalization of nature, or at any rate, sentimentalization of a rustic or a barbarian relationship with nature. Marie Antoinette playing milkmaid was an expression of the sentimentality on one plane. The romantic idea of the 'noble savage' was an even sillier one, on another plane. So, in this country, was Jefferson's intellectual rejection of cities of free artisans and mechanics, and his dream of an ideal republic of self-reliant rural yeomen – a pathetic dream for a good and great man whose land was tilled by slaves.

In real life, barbarians (and peasants) are the least free of men – bound by tradition, ridden by caste, fettered by superstitions, riddled by suspicion and foreboding of whatever is strange. 'City air makes free' was the medieval saying, when city air literally did make free the runaway serf. City air still makes free the runaways from the company towns, from plantations, from factory farms, from subsistence farms, from migrant picker routes, from mining villages, from one-class suburbs.

Owing to the mediation of cities, it became popularly possible to regard 'nature' as benign, ennobling and pure, and by extension to regard 'natural man' (take your pick of how 'natural') as so too. Opposed to all this fictionalized purity, nobility and beneficence, cities, not being fictions, could be considered as seats of malignancy and – obviously – the enemies of nature. And once people begin looking at nature as if it were a nice big St Bernard dog for the children, what could be more natural than the desire to bring this sentimental pet into the city too, so the city might get some nobility, purity and beneficence by association?

There are dangers in sentimentalizing nature. Most sentimental ideas imply, at bottom, a deep if unacknowledged disrespect. It is no accident that we Americans, probably the world's champion sentimentalizers about nature, are at one and the same time probably the world's most voracious and disrespectful destroyers of wild and rural countryside.

It is neither love for nature nor respect for nature that leads to this schizophrenic attitude. Instead, it is a sentimental desire to toy, rather patronizingly, with some insipid, standardized, suburbanized shadow of nature – apparently in sheer disbelief that we and our cities, just by virtue of being, are a legitimate part of nature too, and involved with it in much deeper and more inescapable ways than grass trimming, sunbathing and contemplative uplift. And so, each day, several thousand more acres of our countryside are eaten by the bulldozers, covered by pavement, dotted with suburbanites who have killed the thing they thought they came to find. Our irreplaceable heritage of Grade I agricultural land (a rare treasure of nature on this earth) is sacrificed for highways or supermarket parking lots as ruthlessly and unthinkingly as the trees in the woodlands are uprooted, the streams and rivers polluted and the air itself filled with the gasoline exhausts (products of eons of nature's manufacturing) required in this great national effort to cozy up with a fictionalized nature and flee the 'unnaturalness' of the city.

The semisuburbanized and suburbanized messes we create in this way become despised by their own inhabitants tomorrow. These thin dispersions lack any reasonable degree of innate vitality, staying power or inherent usefulness as settlements. Few of them, and these only the most expensive as a rule, hold their attraction much longer than a generation; then they begin to decay in the pattern of city grey areas. Indeed, an immense amount of today's city grey belts was yesterday's dispersion closer to 'nature'. Of the buildings on the 30,000 acres of already blighted or already fast-blighting residential areas in northern New Jersey, for example, half are less than 40 years old. Thirty years from now, we shall have accumulated new problems of blight and decay over acreages so immense that in comparison the present problems of the great cities' grey belts will look piddling. Nor, however destructive, is this something which happens accidentally or without the use of will. This is exactly what we, as a society, have willed to happen.

Nature, sentimentalized and considered as the antithesis of cities, is apparently assumed to consist of grass, fresh air and little else, and this ludicrous disrespect results in the devastation of nature even formally and publicly preserved in the form of a pet.

* * *

[...] cities, as created or used by city-loving creatures are unrespected by such simple minds because they are not bland shadows of cities suburbanized. Other aspects of nature are equally unrespected because they are not bland shadows of nature suburbanized. Sentimentality about nature denatures everything it touches.

Big cities and countrysides can get along well together. Big cities need real countryside close by. And countryside – from man's point of view – needs big cities, with all their diverse opportunities and productivity, so human beings can be in a position to appreciate the rest of the natural world instead of to curse it.

Being human is itself difficult, and therefore all kinds of settlements (except dream cities) have problems. Big cities have difficulties in abundance, because they have people in abundance. But vital cities are not helpless to combat even the most difficult of problems. They are not passive victims of chains of circumstances, any more than they are the malignant opposite of nature.

Vital cities have marvellous innate abilities for understanding, communicating, contriving and inventing what is required to combat their difficulties. Perhaps the most striking example of this ability is the effect that big cities have had on disease. Cities were once the most helpless and devastated victims of disease, but they became great disease conquerors. All the apparatus of surgery, hygiene, microbiology, chemistry, telecommunications, public health measures, teaching and research hospitals, ambulances and the like, which people not only in cities but also outside them depend upon for the unending war against premature mortality, are fundamentally products of big cities and would be inconceivable without big cities. The surplus wealth, the productivity, the close-grained juxtaposition of talents that permit society to support advances such as these are themselves products of our organization into cities, and especially into big and dense cities.

It may be romantic to search for the salves of society's ills in slow-moving rustic surroundings, or among innocent, unspoiled provincials, if such exist, but it is a waste of time. Does anyone suppose that, in real life, answers to any of the great questions that worry us today are going to come out of homogeneous settlements?

Dull, inert cities, it is true, do contain the seeds of their own destruction and little else. But lively, diverse, intense cities contain the seeds of their own regeneration, with energy enough to carry over for problems and needs outside themselves.

Complexity and Contradiction in Architecture

Robert Venturi

The architectural historian Vincent Scully called *Complexity and Contradiction in Architecture* (Museum of Modern Art, New York, 1966) the most significant book on architecture since *Vers une architecture* by Le Corbusier in 1923. The following excerpts trace Venturi's key ideas on the complexity of architecture inherent in its multiple media and variety of program. He contends that Modern architects oversimplified the problems that their buildings addressed seeking instead a purity of expression and form. They ignore the complexities of everyday life that a successful structure should solve. He argues for an inclusive whole that manages to unify or include many different facets: 'the difficult unity of inclusion.' The thinking, taking seriously the aesthetic of Route 66 and Main Street USA, formed the foundation for many later Post-Modern buildings.

Robert Venturi was born in Philadelphia in 1925 and is married to Denise Scott Brown who is also his partner in thought and building. *EB*

Nonstraightforward Architecture: A Gentle Manifesto

I like complexity and contradiction in architecture. I do not like the incoherence or arbitrariness of incompetent architecture nor the precious intricacies of picturesqueness or Expressionism. Instead, I speak of a complex and contradictory architecture based on the richness and ambiguity of modern experience, including that experience which is inherent in art. Everywhere, except in architecture, complexity and contradiction have been acknowledged, from Gödel's proof of ultimate inconsistency in mathematics to TS Eliot's analysis of 'difficult' poetry and Joseph Albers's definition of the paradoxical quality of painting.[i]

But architecture is necessarily complex and contradictory in its very inclusion of the traditional Vitruvian elements of commodity, firmness and delight. And today the wants of program, structure, mechanical equipment and expression, even in single buildings in simple contexts, are diverse and conflicting in ways previously unimaginable. The increasing dimension and scale of architecture in urban and regional planning add to the difficulties. I welcome the problems and exploit the uncertainties. By embracing contradiction as well as complexity, I aim for vitality as well as validity.

Architects can no longer afford to be intimidated by the puritanically moral language of orthodox Modern architecture. I like elements which are hybrid rather than 'pure',

---

i   Logican Kurt Gödel (1906–78), poet and critic TS Eliot (1888–1965), and painter Joseph Albers (1888–1976).

compromising rather than 'clean', distorted rather than 'straightforward', ambiguous rather than 'articulated', perverse as well as impersonal, boring as well as 'interesting', conventional rather than 'designed', accommodating rather than excluding, redundant rather than simple, vestigial as well as innovating, inconsistent and equivocal rather than direct and clear. I am for messy vitality over obvious unity. I include the non sequitur and proclaim the duality.

I am for richness of meaning rather than clarity of meaning; for the implicit function as well as the explicit function. I prefer 'both-and' to 'either-or', black and white, and sometimes gray, to black or white. A valid architecture evokes many levels of meaning and combinations of focus: its space and its elements become readable and workable in several ways at once.

But an architecture of complexity and contradiction has a special obligation toward the whole: its truth must be in its totality or its implications of totality. It must embody the difficult unity of inclusion rather than the easy unity of exclusion. More is not less.

Complexity and Contradiction vs Simplification or Picturesqueness

Orthodox Modern architects have tended to recognize complexity insufficiently or inconsistently. In their attempt to break with tradition and start all over again, they idealized the primitive and elementary at the expense of the diverse and the sophisticated. As participants in a revolutionary movement, they acclaimed the newness of modern functions, ignoring their complications. In their role as reformers, they puritanically advocated the separation and exclusion of elements, rather than the inclusion of various requirements and their juxtapositions. As a forerunner of the Modern movement, Frank Lloyd Wright,[ii] who grew up with the motto 'Truth against the World', wrote: 'Visions of simplicity so broad and far-reaching would open to me and such building harmonies appear that … would change and deepen the thinking and culture of the modern world. So I believed.'[1] And Le Corbusier, co-founder of Purism, spoke of the 'great primary forms' which, he proclaimed, were 'distinct … and without ambiguity'.[2] Modern architects with few exceptions eschewed ambiguity.

But now our position is different: 'At the same time that the problems increase in quantity, complexity, and difficulty they also change faster than before',[3] and require an attitude more like that described by August Heckscher:

The movement from a view of life as essentially simple and orderly to a view of life as complex and ironic is what every individual passes through in becoming mature. But certain epochs encourage this development; in them the paradoxical or dramatic outlook colors the whole intellectual scene. … Amid simplicity and order rationalism is born, but rationalism proves inadequate in any period of upheaval. Then equilibrium must be created out of opposites. Such inner peace

---

ii   Great American architect (1867–1959).

as men gain must represent a tension among contradictions and uncertainties. …
A feeling for paradox allows seemingly dissimilar things to exist side by side, their
very incongruity suggesting a kind of truth.[4]

Rationalizations for simplification are still current, however, though subtler than the
early arguments. They are expansions of Mies van der Rohe's magnificent paradox, 'less
is more'.[iii] Paul Rudolph has clearly stated the implications of Mies's point of view: 'All
problems can never be solved. … Indeed it is a characteristic of the twentieth century
that architects are highly selective in determining which problems they want to solve.
Mies, for instance, makes wonderful buildings only because he ignores many aspects of a
building. If he solved more problems, his buildings would be far less potent.'[5]

The doctrine 'less is more' bemoans complexity and justifies exclusion for expressive
purposes. It does, indeed, permit the architect to be 'highly selective in determining which
problems [he wants] to solve'. But if the architect must be 'committed to his particular way
of seeing the universe',[6] such a commitment surely means that the architect determines
how problems should be solved, not that he can determine which of the problems he will
solve. He can exclude important considerations only at the risk of separating architecture
from the experience of life and the needs of society. If some problems prove insoluble,
he can express this: in an inclusive rather than an exclusive kind of architecture there is
room for the fragment, for contradiction, for improvisation, and for the tensions these
produce. Mies's exquisite pavilions have had valuable implications for architecture, but
their selectiveness of content and language is their limitation as well as their strength.

I question the relevance of analogies between pavilions and houses, especially
analogies between Japanese pavilions and recent domestic architecture. They ignore
the real complexity and contradiction inherent in the domestic program – the spatial
and technological possibilities as well as the need for variety in visual experience. Forced
simplicity results in oversimplification. In the Wiley House, for instance, in contrast to
his glass house, Philip Johnson attempted to go beyond the simplicities of the elegant
pavilion.[iv] He explicitly separated and articulated the enclosed 'private functions' of
living on a ground-floor pedestal, thus separating them from the open social functions
in the modular pavilion above. But even here the building becomes a diagram of an
oversimplified program for living – an abstract theory of either-or. Where simplicity cannot
work, simpleness results. Blatant simplification means bland architecture. Less is a bore. …

Contradictory Levels: The Phenomenon of 'Both-And' in Architecture

… Cleanth Brooks refers to Donne's art as 'having it both ways' but, says, 'most of us in this
latter day, cannot.[v] We are disciplined in the tradition either-or, and lack the mental agility

---

iii   Ludwig Mies van der Rohe (1886–1969), German architect, one of the leaders of the modern
      International Style and director of the Bauhaus school.
iv   Two buildings by contemporary American architect Philip Johnson in New Canaan, Connecticut.
v   The great English poet John Donne (1572–1631).

– to say nothing of the maturity of attitude – which would allow us to indulge in the finer distinctions and the more subtle reservations permitted by the tradition of both-and.'[7] The tradition 'either-or' has characterized orthodox modern architecture: a sun screen is probably nothing else; a support is seldom an enclosure; a wall is not violated by window penetrations but is totally interrupted by glass; program functions are exaggeratedly articulated into wings or segregated separate pavilions. Even 'flowing space' has implied being outside when inside, and inside when outside, rather than both at the same time. Such manifestations of articulation and clarity are foreign to an architecture of complexity and contradiction, which tends to include 'both-and' rather than exclude 'either-or'.

If the source of the both-and phenomenon is contradiction, its basis is hierarchy, which yields several levels of meanings among elements with varying values. It can include elements that are both good and awkward, big and little, closed and open, continuous and articulated, round and square, structural and spatial. An architecture which includes varying levels of meaning breeds ambiguity and tension.

Most of the examples will be difficult to 'read', but abstruse architecture is valid when it reflects the complexities and contradictions of content and meaning. Simultaneous perception of a multiplicity of levels involves struggles and hesitations for the observer, and makes his perception more vivid. …

Conventional elements in architecture represent one stage in an evolutionary development, and they contain in their changed use and expression some of their past meaning as well as their new meaning. What can be called the vestigial element parallels the double-functioning element. It is distinct from a superfluous element because it contains a double meaning. This is the result of a more or less ambiguous combination of the old meaning, called up by associations, with a new meaning created by the modified or new function, structural or programmatic, and the new context. The vestigial element discourages clarity of meaning; it promotes richness of meaning instead. It is a basis for change and growth in the city as manifest in remodeling which involves old buildings with new uses both programmatic and symbolic (like palazzi which become museums or embassies), and old street patterns with new uses and scales of movement. The paths of medieval fortification walls in European cities became boulevards in the 19th century; a section of Broadway is a piazza and a symbol rather than an artery to upper New York state. The ghost of Dock Street in Philadelphia's Society Hill, however, is a meaningless vestige rather than a working element resulting from a valid transition between the old and the new. I shall later refer to the vestigial element as it appears in Michelangelo's architecture and in what might be called Pop architecture.

The rhetorical element, like the double-functioning element, is infrequent in recent architecture. If the latter offends through its inherent ambiguity, rhetoric offends orthodox Modern architecture's cult of the minimum. But the rhetorical element is justified as a valid if outmoded means of expression. An element can seem rhetorical from one point of view, but if it is valid, at another level it enriches meaning by underscoring. In the project for a gateway at Bourneville by Ledoux, the columns in the arch are structurally rhetorical if not redundant.[vi] Expressively, however, they underscore the abstractness of the opening as a semicircle more than an arch, and they further define the opening as a gateway. ... the stairway at the Pennsylvania Academy of the Fine Arts by Furness is too big in its immediate context, but appropriate as a gesture towards the outside scale and a sense of entry.[vii] The classical portico is a rhetorical entrance. The stairs, columns and pediment are juxtaposed upon the other-scale, real entrance behind. Paul Rudolph's entrance in the Art and Architecture Building at Yale is at the scale of the city; most people use the little door at the side in the stair tower.[viii]

Much of the function of ornament is rhetorical – like the use of Baroque pilasters for rhythm, and Vanbrugh's disengaged pilasters at the entrance to the kitchen court at Blenheim which are an architectural fanfare.[ix] The rhetorical element which is also structural is rare in Modern architecture, although Mies has used the rhetorical I-beam with an assurance that would make Bernini envious.[x]

Accommodation and the Limitations of Order: The Conventional Element

In short, that contradictions must be accepted.[8]

A valid order accommodates the circumstantial contradictions of a complex reality. It accommodates as well as imposes. It thereby admits 'control *and* spontaneity', 'correctness *and* ease' – improvisation within the whole. It tolerates qualifications and compromise. There are no fixed laws in architecture, but not everything will work in a building or a city. The architect must decide, and these subtle evaluations are among his principal functions. He must determine what must be made to work and what it is possible to compromise with, what will give in, and where and how. He does not ignore or exclude inconsistencies of program and structure within the order.

I have emphasized that aspect of complexity and contradiction which grows out of the medium more than the program of the building. Now I shall emphasize the complexity and contradiction that develops from the program and reflects the inherent complexities and contradictions of living. It is obvious that in actual practice the two must be interrelated. Contradictions can represent the exceptional inconsistency that modifies the otherwise consistent order, or they can represent inconsistencies throughout the order as a whole. In the first case, the relationship between inconsistency and order accommodates circumstantial exceptions to the order, or it juxtaposes particular with general elements of order. Here you build an order up and then break it down, but break it from strength rather than from weakness. I have described this relationship as 'contradiction accommodated'.

---

vi   Gateway in Bourneville, France, by French architect Claude-Nicolas Ledoux (1736–1806).

vii American architect Frank Furness's (1839–1912) work on Pennsylvania Academy of Fine Arts, Philadelphia.

viii Contemporary American architect Paul Rudolph.

ix   English architect John Vanbrugh's (1664–1726) work on Blenheim Palace in Oxfordshire, England.

x   Gian Lorenzo Bernini (1598–1680), great Italian Renaissance sculptor.

The relationship of inconsistency within the whole I consider a manifestation of 'the difficult whole', which is discussed in the last chapter.

Mies refers to a need to 'create order out of the desperate confusion of our times'. But Kahn has said 'by order I do not mean orderliness'.[xi] Should we not resist bemoaning confusion? Should we not look for meaning in the complexities and contradictions of our times and acknowledge the limitations of systems? These, I think, are the two justifications for breaking order: the recognition of variety and confusion inside and outside, in program and environment, indeed, at all levels of experience; and the ultimate limitation of all orders composed by man. When circumstances defy order, order should bend or break: anomalies and uncertainties give validity to architecture.

Meaning can be enhanced by breaking the order; the exception points up the rule. A building with no 'imperfect' part can have no perfect part, because contrast supports meaning. An artful discord gives vitality to architecture. You can allow for contingencies all over, but they cannot prevail all over. If order without expediency breeds Formalism, expediency without order, of course, means chaos. Order must exist before it can be broken. No artist can belittle the role of order as a way of seeing a whole relevant to its own characteristics and context. 'There is no work of art without a system' is Le Corbusier's dictum. ...

Ironic convention is relevant both for the individual building and the townscape. It recognizes the real condition of our architecture and its status in our culture. Industry promotes expensive industrial and electronic research but not architectural experiments, and the federal government diverts subsidies toward air transportation, communication and the vast enterprises of war or, as they call it, national security, rather than toward the forces for the direct enhancement of life. The practicing architect must admit this. In simple terms, the budgets, techniques and programs for his buildings must relate more to 1866 than 1966. Architects should accept their modest role rather than disguise it and risk what might be called an electronic Expressionism which might parallel the industrial Expressionism of early Modern architecture. The architect who would accept his role as combiner of significant old clichés – valid banalities – in new contexts as his condition within a society that directs its best efforts, its big money and its elegant technologies elsewhere, can ironically express in this indirect way a true concern for society's inverted scale of values.

... honky-tonk elements in our architecture and townscape are here to stay, especially in the important short-term view, ... such a fate should be acceptable. Pop art has demonstrated that these commonplace elements are often the main source of the occasional variety and vitality of our cities, and that it is not their banality or vulgarity as elements which make for the banality or vulgarity of the whole scene, but rather their contextual relationships of space and scale.

Another significant implication from Pop art involves method in city planning. Architects and planners who peevishly denounce the conventional townscape for its

---

xi   American architect Louis Kahn (1901–74).

vulgarity or banality promote elaborate methods for abolishing or disguising honky-tonk elements in the existing landscapes, or for excluding them from the vocabulary of their new townscapes. But they largely fail either to enhance or to provide a substitute for the existing scene because they attempt the impossible. By attempting too much they flaunt their impotence and risk their continuing influence as supposed experts. Cannot the architect and planner, by slight adjustments to conventional elements of the townscape, existing or proposed, promote significant effects? By modifying or adding conventional elements to still other conventional elements they can, by a twist of context, gain a maximum of effect through a minimum of means. They can make us see the same things in a different way.

Finally, standardization, like convention, can be another manifestation of the strong order. But unlike convention it has been accepted in Modern architecture as an enriching product of our technology, yet dreaded for its potential domination and brutality. But is it not standardization that is without circumstantial accommodation and without a creative use of context that is to be feared more than standardization itself? The ideas of order and circumstance, convention and context – of employing standardization in an unstandard way – apply to our continuing problem of standardization versus variety. Giedion has written of Aalto's[xii] unique 'combination of standardization with irrationality so that standardization is no longer master but servant'.[9] I prefer to think of Aalto's art as contradictory rather than irrational – an artful recognition of the circumstantial and the contextual and of the inevitable limits of the order of standardization.

The Obligation Toward the Difficult Whole

… Toledo [Ohio] was very beautiful.[10]

An architecture of complexity and accommodation does not forsake the whole. In fact, I have referred to a special obligation toward the whole because the whole is difficult to achieve. And I have emphasized the goal of unity rather than of simplification in an art 'whose … truth [is] in its totality'.[11] It is the difficult unity through inclusion rather than the easy unity through exclusion. Gestalt psychology considers a perceptual whole the result of, and yet more than, the sum of its parts. The whole is dependent on the position, number and inherent characteristics of the parts. A complex system in Herbert A Simon's definition includes 'a large number of parts that interact in a non-simple way'.[12] The difficult whole in an architecture of complexity and contradiction includes multiplicity and diversity of elements in relationships that are inconsistent or among the weaker kinds perceptually. …

Inherent in an architecture of opposites is the inclusive whole. The unity of the interior of the Imatra church or the complex at Wolfsburg is achieved not through suppression or

---

xii   Finnish architect Alvar Aalto (1898–1976).

exclusion but through the dramatic inclusion of contradictory or circumstantial parts.[xiii] Aalto's architecture acknowledges the difficult and subtle conditions of program, while 'serene' architecture, on the other hand, works simplifications.

However, the obligation toward the whole in an architecture of complexity and contradiction does not preclude the building which is unresolved. Poets and playwrights acknowledge dilemmas without solutions. The validity of the questions and vividness of the meaning are what make their works art more than philosophy. A goal of poetry can be unity of expression over resolution of content. Contemporary sculpture is often fragmentary, and today we appreciate Michelangelo's unfinished *Pietàs* more than his early work, because their content is suggested, their expression more immediate, and their forms are completed beyond themselves. A building can also be more or less incompleted in the expression of its program and its form.

The Gothic cathedral, like Beauvais, for instance, of which only the enormous choir was built, is frequently unfinished in relation to its program, yet it is complete in the effect of its form because of the motival consistency of its many parts.[xiv] The complex program which is a process, continually changing and growing in time yet at each stage at some level related to a whole, should be recognized as essential at the scale of city planning. The incomplete program is valid for a complex single building as well.

Each of the fragmental twin churches on the Piazza del Popolo,[xv] however, is complete at the level of program but incomplete in the expression of form. The uniquely assymmetrically placed tower ... inflects each building toward a greater whole outside itself. The very complex building, which in its open form is incomplete, in itself relates to Maki's 'group form': it is the antithesis of the 'perfect single building'[13] or the closed pavilion. As a fragment of a greater whole in a greater context this kind of building relates again to the scope of city planning as a means of increasing the unity of the complex whole. An architecture that can simultaneously recognize contradictory levels should be able to admit the paradox of the whole fragment: the building which is a whole at one level and a fragment of a greater whole at another level.

In *God's Own Junkyard* Peter Blake has compared the chaos of commercial Main Street with the orderliness of the University of Virginia.[xvi] Besides the irrelevancy of the comparison, is not Main Street almost all right? Indeed, is not the commercial strip of a Route 66 almost all right? As I have said, our question is: what slight twist of context will make them all right? Perhaps more signs more contained. Illustrations in *God's Own Junkyard* of Times Square and roadtown are compared with illustrations of New England villages and arcadian countrysides. But the pictures in this book that are supposed to

---

xiii Two projects by Aalto: Vooksenniska church in Imatra, Finland, and the Cultural Centre, Wolfsburg, Germany.

xiv Gothic cathedral in Beauvais, France.

xv In Rome.

xvi Peter Blake, *God's Own Junkyard: The Planned Deterioration of America's Landscape*, Holt, Rinehart & Winston (New York), 1964.

Thomas Jefferson, University of Virginia, Charlottesville. © Charles Jencks.

Typical Main Street, USA. © Charles Jencks.

be bad are often good. The seemingly chaotic juxtapositions of honky-tonk elements express an intriguing kind of vitality and validity, and they produce an unexpected approach to unity as well.

It is true that an ironic interpretation such as this results partly from the change in scale of the subject matter in photographic form and the change in context within the frames of the photographs. But in some of these compositions there is an inherent sense of unity not far from the surface. It is not the obvious or easy unity derived from the dominant binder or the motival order of simpler, less contradictory compositions, but that derived from a complex and illusive order of the difficult whole. It is the taut composition which contains contrapuntal relationships, equal combinations, inflected fragments and acknowledged dualities. It is the unity which 'maintains, but only just maintains, a control over the clashing elements which compose it. Chaos is very near; its nearness, but its avoidance, gives … force.'[14] In the validly complex building or cityscape, the eye does not want to be too easily or too quickly satisfied in its search for unity within a whole.

Some of the vivid lessons of Pop art, involving contradictions of scale and context, should have awakened architects from prim dreams of pure order, which, unfortunately, are imposed in the easy Gestalt unities of the urban renewal projects of establishment Modern architecture and yet, fortunately are really impossible to achieve at any great scope. And it is perhaps from the everyday landscape, vulgar and disdained, that we can draw the complex and contradictory order that is valid and vital for our architecture as an urbanistic whole.

Notes

1 Frank Lloyd Wright, *An American Architecture*, ed Edgar Kaufmann, Horizon Press (New York), 1955, p 207.
2 Le Corbusier, *Towards a New Architecture*, Architectural Press (London), 1927, p 31.
3 Christopher Alexander, *Notes on the Synthesis of Form*, Harvard University Press (Cambridge, MA), 1964, p 4.
4 August Heckscher, *The Public Happiness*, Atheneum Publishers (New York), 1962, p 102.
5 Paul Rudolph, *Perspecta 7, The Yale Architectural Journal* (New Haven), 1961, p 51.
6 Kenneth Burke, *Permanence and Change*, Hermes Publications (Los Altos), 1954, p 107.
7 Cleanth Brooks, *The Well Wrought Urn*, Harcourt, Brace and World (New York), 1947, p 81.
8 David Jones, *Epoch and Artist*, Chilmark Press (New York), 1959.
9 Sigfried Giedion, *Space, Time and Architecture*, Harvard University Press (Cambridge), 1963, p 565.
10 Gertrude Stein, *Gertrude Stein's America*, eds Gilbert A Harrison and Robert B Luce (Washington, DC), 1965.
11 August Heckscher, *The Public Happiness*, p 287.
12 Herbert A Simon, *Proceedings of the American Philosophical Society*, 106, no 6, December 12, 1962, p 468.
13 Fumihiko Maki, *Investigations in Collective Form*, Special Publication No 2, Washington University (St Louis), 1964, p 5.
14 August Heckscher, *The Public Happiness*, p 289.

From Robert Venturi, *Complexity and Contradiction in Architecture*, Museum of Modern Art (New York), 1966. © 1966 The Museum of Modern Art (New York).

The Language of Post-Modern Architecture and the Complexity Paradigm

Charles Jencks

These excerpts from Jencks's statements on Post-Modernism start with the now famous metaphor of the death of Modern Architecture: the blowing up of Minoru Yamasaki's Pruitt-Igoe scheme in St Louis, Missouri, in 1972. Modern Architecture, Jencks explains, is characterised by univalence: 'an architecture created around one (or a few) simplified values' and using only a 'few materials and a single, right-angled geometry', an architecture that paid little respect to the codes of the inhabitants. Countering this is a multivalent architecture often based on multiple metaphors. These have been used to recode Modern Architecture with other languages. He claims: 'the more the metaphors, the greater the drama, and the more they are slightly suggestive, the greater the mystery.' Following the importance of language and multiple codes in architecture, Jencks concludes in the third part of his text, that the basis of this new post-modern complexity paradigm is the 'new way of constructing architecture and conceiving cities'. Drawing upon his evolutionary charts, Jencks explains how the new paradigm grew out of the 1960s counterculture to eventually embrace the pluralism of global cultures.

Charles Jencks (1939–) is an American-born architectural critic and landscape architect, particularly known for his books on the history of Modern, Late- and Post-Modern architecture. *LCS*

The Death of Modernism

Happily, we can date the death of Modern Architecture to a precise moment in time. Unlike the legal death of a person, which is becoming a complex affair of brain waves versus heartbeats, Modern Architecture went out with a bang. That many people didn't notice, and no one was seen to mourn, does not make the sudden extinction any less of a fact, and that many designers are still trying to administer the kiss of life does not mean that it has been miraculously resurrected. No, it expired finally and completely in 1972, after having been flogged to death remorselessly for 10 years by critics such as Jane Jacobs; and the fact that many so-called Modern architects still go around practising a trade as if it were alive can be taken as one of the great curiosities of our age (like the British monarchy giving life-prolonging drugs to the Royal Company of Archers or the Extra Women of the Bedchamber).

Modern Architecture died in St Louis, Missouri on 15 July 1972 at 3.32 pm (or thereabouts) when the infamous Pruitt-Igoe scheme, or rather several of its slab blocks, were given the final *coup de grâce* by dynamite. Previously it had been vandalised, mutilated and defaced by its black inhabitants, and although millions of dollars were pumped back, trying to keep it alive (fixing the broken elevators, repairing smashed windows, repainting), it was finally put out of its misery. Boom, boom, boom.

Without doubt, the ruins should be kept, the remains should have a preservation order slapped on them, so that we keep a live memory of this failure in planning and architecture. Like the folly or artificial ruin – constructed on the estate of an 18th-century English eccentric to provide him with instructive reminders of former vanities and glories – we should learn to value and protect our former disasters. As Oscar Wilde said, 'experience is the name we give to our mistakes', and there is a certain health in leaving them judiciously scattered around the landscape as continual lessons.

Pruitt-Igoe was constructed according to the most progressive ideals of CIAM (the Congress of International Modern Architects) and it won an award from the American Institute of Architects when it was designed in 1951. Why? Because it carried out the major doctrines of modern city planning. It consisted of elegant slab blocks 14 storeys high with rational 'streets in the air' (which were safe from cars, but as it turned out, not safe from crime); 'sun, space and greenery', which Le Corbusier called the 'three essential joys of urbanism' (instead of conventional streets, gardens and semiprivate space, which he banished). It had a separation of pedestrian and vehicular traffic, the provision of play space and local amenities such as laundries, crèches and gossip centres – all rational substitutes for traditional patterns. Moreover, its Purist style, its clean, salubrious hospital metaphor, was meant to instil, by good example, corresponding virtues in the inhabitants. Good form was to lead to good content, or at least good conduct; the intelligent planning of abstract space was to promote healthy behaviour.

Alas, such simplistic ideas, taken over from the philosophies of Rationalism, Behaviourism and Pragmatism proved as irrational as the philosophies themselves. Modern Architecture, as the son of the Enlightenment, was an heir to its congenital naivetes, too great and awe-inspiring to warrant refutation in a book on mere building.
* * *

Univalence/Multivalence

For the general aspect of an architecture created around one (or a few) simplified values, I will use the term univalence. No doubt in terms of expression the architecture of Mies van der Rohe and his followers is one of the most univalent formal systems, because it makes use of few materials and a single, right-angled geometry. Minimalism was the style he preferred, after 1925, and the slogans of an architecture were 'less is more' and the building is 'almost nothing'. Although it can be relevant in some contexts this reduced style was justified as generally rational (when it was often uneconomic), and universal (when it fitted only a few functions). As a result of his persuasive arguments, and example, the glass-and-steel box has become the single most used type in Modern Architecture, and it signifies throughout the world 'office building'.

Yet in the hands of Mies and his disciples this system has also become fetishised to the point where it dominates all other concerns, just as the leather boot dominates the shoe

1. Minoru Yamasaki, Pruitt-Igoe Housing, St Louis, 1952–5 being dynamited in 1972. Photos and films of this were reproduced around the world.

fetishist and distracts him from more relevant parts of the body. The architectural fetishist is typically obsessed by materials, or a consistent geometry, and sublimates further issues to this central concern. Are beams and plate glass appropriate to the home? That is a question Mies would dismiss as irrelevant, or at least secondary to visual consistency. Surprisingly, his first, classic use of the curtain wall was on housing, not for an office, and it was used because he was interested in perfecting certain formal problems. In this case, on Lake Shore Drive in Chicago, he concentrated on the proportion of the I-beam to the infill panels, the setbacks, glass area, supporting column and articulating lines. He kept full-scale details of these members close to his draughting board so he would never lose sight of the elements he loved.

A larger question thus did not arise: what if housing looked like offices, or what if the two functions were indistinguishable? Clearly the result would diminish and compromise both functions by equating them: working and living would become interchangeable on the most banal level, and the particular virtue of each would be obscured. The psychic overtones to these two very different activities would remain unexplored or accidental.

Another masterpiece of the Modern Movement, the Chicago Civic Center designed by a follower of Mies, shows similar confusions in communicating the diversity of its content. The long horizontal spans and dark corten steel express 'office building', 'power', 'purity', while the variations in surface express 'mechanical equipment'. All this is as intended, as far as it goes, but the primitive (and occasionally mistaken) meanings do not express anything deep or complex about working in the city. On a literal level the building does not communicate its important civic functions, nor the social and psychological meanings of this significant building task (a meeting place for the citizens of Chicago).

How could an architect justify such inarticulate building? The answer lies in an ideology that celebrates process, which symbolises only the changes in technology and building material. The Modern Movement revered the means of production, the Machine Aesthetic and metaphors such as Le Corbusier's: 'the house is a machine for living.' In one of those cryptic aphorisms, too delirious to overlook, Mies gave expression to this fetish: 'I see in industrialization the central problem of building in our time. If we succeed in carrying out this industrialization, the social, economic, technical and also artistic problems will be readily solved.'(1924)[1]
* * *

Double-Coding

Such contradictions between statement and result have reached impressive proportions in Modern Architecture, and one can speak of a credibility gap that parallels the loss of trust in politicians. One cause of this, I believe, stems from the kind of language architecture is. As something rooted in peoples' childhood experience of crawling around on flat floors and perceiving such normal elements as vertical doors, it is by necessity partly tradition and slow changing. But also it is partly rooted in a fast-changing society, with its new functional tasks, new materials, new technologies and ideologies. On the one hand, architecture is as conservative as spoken language (we can still understand Renaissance English); and, on the other, as revolutionary and esoteric as modern art and science. The

2. Mies van der Rohe, Seagram Building corners and I-beams, New York, 1958. The anonymous office was turned into the sign of housing and other building types as the aesthetic of production became the signifier for Modern architects. © Charles Jencks.

result is that architecture is *radically schizophrenic*, and this fact leads directly to the post-modern strategy of double-coding. As we will see, PMs design buildings with mixed languages that recognise the basic duality. [...]

Arata Isozaki designed a country club in Japan, with a Roman barrel vault that ends in a Palladian motif and round green dot. The ensemble forms a giant question mark, posing the metaphysical (and social) question: 'why do the Japanese play golf?' Indeed, why? Implied answer: 'because, like the classical quotes, they help settle deals with the West.'

Quotation and irony, the ability to send two opposite meanings at once, became the PM approach. Umberto Eco argued that this generic double-coding stemmed from the condition of living in an age of lost innocence, when everything had already been said. He explains our plight with an amusing example:

> I think of the postmodern attitude as that of a man who loves a very cultivated woman and knows he cannot say to her, 'I love you madly', because he knows that she knows (and that she knows that he knows) that these words have already been written by Barbara Cartland. Still there is a solution. He can say, 'As Barbara Cartland would put it, I love you madly.' At this point, having avoided false innocence, having said clearly that it is no longer possible to speak innocently, he will nevertheless have said what he wanted to say to the woman: that he loves her; but he loves her in an age of lost innocence.[2]

In other words, to labour the point, if architects are going to use past conventions, as they must do in order to communicate, then they have to signal the already said. This signalling gives their forms and ornament a subversive meaning counter to the revivalists, that is, it subverts tradition from within it.

* * *

Metaphor and Code

People invariably see one building in terms of another, or in terms of a similar object; in short, as a metaphor. The more unfamiliar a modern building is, the more they will compare it metaphorically to what they know. This matching of one experience to another is a property of all thought, particularly that which is creative. Thus, when precast concrete grilles were first used on buildings in the late 1950s, they were seen as 'cheese-graters', 'beehives', 'chain-link fences', while 10 years later, when these forms became a norm in a certain building type, they were seen in functional terms: 'this looks like a parking garage.' From metaphor to cliché, from neologism through constant usage to architectural sign, this is the continual route travelled by new and successful forms and technics.

Typical negative metaphors used by the public and by critics such as Lewis Mumford to condemn Modern Architecture were 'cardboard box, shoe-box, egg-crate, filing cabinet, grid-paper'. These comparisons were sought not only for their pejorative, mechanistic overtones, but also because they were strongly *coded* in a culture that had become sensitised to the spectre of 1984. This obvious point has some curious implications, as we shall see.

3. Kisho Kurokawa, Nakagin Capsule Building, Tokyo, 1972. Forty mass-produced boxes stacked 'like sugar cubes, or bricks' was the metaphor of industrial housing for Modernists since Walter Gropius, but they carry other meanings, depending on local codes. © Charles Jencks.

169 The Language of Post-Modern Architecture and the Complexity Paradigm

4. The Duck–Rabbit illusion is first read by unconscious codes, but one can make it flip back and forth between readings on second glance, and then even force third and fourth possible meanings. Unconscious and conscious codes guide perception and meaning. © Charles Jencks.

One implication became apparent when I was visiting Japan and the architect Kisho Kurokawa in 1972. We went to see his new apartment tower in Tokyo, made from stacked shipping containers, which had a most unusual overall shape. They looked like stacked sugar cubes, or even more, like superimposed washing machines, because the white cubes all had round windows in their centre. When I said this metaphor had unfortunate overtones for living, Kurokawa evinced surprise. 'They aren't washing machines, they're bird cages. You see, in Japan we build concrete-box bird nests with round holes and place them in the trees. I've built these bird nests for itinerant businessmen who visit Tokyo, for bachelors who fly in every so often with their birds.' A witty answer, perhaps made up on the spot, but one which underscored very nicely a difference in our visual codes.

The basic point is that codes of perception underlie the way we see architecture and value it. A well-known visual illusion brings this out: the famous 'duck–rabbit figure', which will be seen first one way then the other. Since we all have well-learned visual codes for *both* animals, and even probably now a code for the hybrid monster with two heads, we can see it three ways. One view may predominate, according to either the strength of the code or according to the direction from which we see the figure at first. To get further readings ('bellows' or 'keyhole' etc) is harder because these codes are less strong for this figure, they map less well than the primary ones — at least in our culture. The general point is that code restrictions, based on personal learning and background culture, guide a reading of architecture. In a global civilisation there are multiple codes, some of which may be in conflict and this presents the basic starting point for the post-modern architect: how to deal with this plurality? How to balance conflicting meaning, which codes to prefer, which to suppress?

In very general terms, there are two large subcultures: one with the contemporary code based on the training and ideology of Modern architects, and another with the traditional or local code based on everyone's experience of normalised architectural elements. As I have already mentioned, there are compelling reasons why these codes may be at odds and architecture may be radically schizophrenic, both in its creation and interpretation. Since some buildings incorporate various codes, they can become mixed metaphors with opposing meanings: eg 'the pure volume' of the Modern architect becomes the 'shoe-box' or 'filing cabinet' to the public.

One building just on the cusp between Modernism and Post-Modernism, the Sydney Opera House, provoked an abundance of metaphorical response, both in the popular and professional press. The reasons are, again, that the forms are both unfamiliar to architecture and reminiscent of other visual objects. Most of the metaphors are organic: thus the architect, Jørn Utzon, showed how the shells of the building related to the surface of a sphere (like 'orange segments') and the wings of a bird in flight. They also relate, obviously, to white seashells, and it is this metaphor, plus the comparison to the white sails bobbing around in Sydney Harbour, that have become journalistic clichés. This raises another obvious point with unexpected implications: the interpretation of architectural metaphor is more elastic and dependent on local codes than the interpretation of metaphor in spoken or written language. Local context guides the reading, limits the metaphors to travel along certain routes, although very wide ones.

* * *

In any case, the Sydney Opera House does pose essential questions that have become particularly relevant to post-modernism, especially in its complexity phase today. While the organic metaphors are suitable analogues for a culture centre, they are not reinforced by conventional signs that spring from the Australian vernacular, and therefore their initial meaning is erratic and Surrealist. Like a Magritte painting — the apple that expands to fill a whole room — their reference is striking but enigmatic, evasive but suggestive. Clearly by piling on evocative connotations *our emotions are being heightened* but there is no exact goal towards which all the overtones – shells, sails, nun's cowls, orange peels, etc – converge. They float around in our mind to pick up connections where they can, like a luxuriant dream following too much cheese and wine.

They do however prove a general point about communication: the more the metaphors, the greater the drama, and the more they are slightly suggestive, the greater the mystery. A mixed metaphor is strong, as every student of Shakespeare knows, but a suggested and mixed one is powerful. [...]

Here [with Eero Saarinen's TWA Building] the imaginative meanings add up in an appropriate and calculated way, pointing towards a common metaphor of flight — the mutual interaction of these meanings produces a multivalent work of architecture, a true symbolic architecture and one of the first post-modern buildings.

The most effective use of *suggested* metaphor that I can think of in Modern Architecture is Le Corbusier's chapel at Ronchamp in northeastern France. This, because of its suggestiveness, is a good candidate for the first PM building. It has been compared to all

5. Sydney Opera House, cartoon by architectural students on the occasion of the Queen's opening. 'Turtles Making Love' was their wry response to 'orange segments' and 'white sails' etc. © Charles Jencks.

sorts of things, varying from the white houses of Mykonos to Swiss cheese. Part of its power is this suggestiveness — to mean many different things at once, to set the mind off on a wild goose chase where it actually catches the goose, among other animals. For instance a duck (once again this famous character of Modern Architecture) is vaguely suggested in the south elevation (see illustration 6). But so too is a ship and, appropriately, praying hands. The visual codes, which here take in both elitist and popular meanings, are working mostly on an unconscious level, unlike the hot dog stand. We read the metaphors immediately without bothering to name or draw them (as is done here) and clearly the skill of the architect is dependent on his ability to call up our rich storehouse of visual images without our being aware of it. Perhaps it is also a somewhat unconscious process for the designer. Le Corbusier only admitted to two metaphors, both of which are esoteric: the 'visual acoustics' of the curving walls which shape the four horizons as if they were 'sounds' (responding in antiphony), and the 'crab shell' form of the roof. But the building conveys many more metaphors than two; so many, in fact, that it is overcoded, saturated with possible interpretations.

This overcoding explains why British critics such as Nikolaus Pevsner and James Stirling have found the building so upsetting, but also why others have found it so enigmatic. It seems to suggest precise ritualistic meanings, it looks like the temple of some very complicated sect which reached a high degree of metaphysical sophistication; whereas we *know* it is simply a pilgrimage chapel created by someone who believed in a natural religion, a pantheism. Put another way, the Ronchamp Chapel has all the fascination of the discovery of a new archaic language. We stumble upon this Rosetta stone, this fragment of a lost civilisation, and every attempt to decode its surface yields yet another coherent meaning which we know does not refer to any precise social practice, as it appears to do. Le Corbusier has so overcoded his building with metaphor, and so precisely related part to part, that the meanings seem as if they had been fixed by countless generations engaged in ritual: something as rich as the delicate patterns of Islam, the exact iconography of Shinto, is suggested. How frustrating, how enjoyable it is to experience this game of signification, which we know rests mostly on imaginative brilliance. Frank Gehry has used the same enigmatic overcoding ... with his Disney Hall in Los Angeles and this type of symbolic building has become the standard way a post-modernist handles the monument in a pluralist culture. It suggests, and heightens, perception allowing different taste-cultures to read their own meanings. Over time this multivalence provokes yet more interpretation, keeps the building alive, turns it into a classic. Thus Ronchamp has become the first open-ended, enigmatic signifier of our time.
* * *

The New Paradigm

My argument is that we are at the *beginning* of a new way of constructing architecture and conceiving cities, that it has grown out of the post-modern movement in the sciences and elsewhere, but that it has not yet grown up [...]

[...] in the sciences and in architecture itself a new way of thinking has indeed started. It stresses self-organising systems rather than mechanistic ones. It favours fractal

6. Le Corbusier's Ronchamp Chapel, 1955, one of the first Post-Modern buildings that was conceived as a multiple metaphor, could be read in several different ways, as a ship, nun's cowl, praying hands, a mother embracing her children, etc. Some of these visual codes were understood by the priests and public, but they certainly provoked a reaction from doctrinaire modernists. With the prevalence of iconic buildings, 50 years later, this became a conscious tradition. © Charles Jencks.

forms, self-similar ones, over those that are endlessly repeated. It looks to the notions of emergence, complexity and chaos science more than to the linear, predictable and mechanistic sciences. In more technical terms it is based on nonlinear dynamics, and a new worldview coming from contemporary cosmology. From this perspective it sees our place in a universe that is continuously emerging, as a single creative unfolding event. [...]

* * *

What are the characteristics of the new architecture? It is committed to pluralism, the heterogeneity of our cities and global culture, and it acknowledges the variety of taste-cultures and visual codes of the users. From participatory architecture to close consultation with the client is the route travelled. It insists on the wider ecological and urban tissue in which buildings are placed even if it cannot do much about these large issues on a global scale. It is fractal in form and closer to nature and the nature of perception than highly repetitive architecture. It may employ non-Euclidean geometries – curves, blobs, folds, crinkles, twists or scattered patterns. It sends complex messages, ones that often carry ironic, dissenting or critical meanings, those that challenge the status quo. It may be explicitly based on complexity theory, and emerge as a surprise to the designer from the belly of a computer.

Need I say that no single building fits this compound definition. There has never been an architect who was totally Gothic, Baroque or Modern. A virtue of the new thinking is that it critiques totalisations, it allows statistical and fuzzy categories, ones of more or less, and it is obvious that the architects I will be following sometimes are post-modern, and other times not.

Let me therefore clarify some terms. Post-Modernism is a broad category that includes a diverse set of architects shown in the evolutionary chart on page 176. It is a historical formation that grows out of the 1960s counterculture; not only Jane Jacobs, Robert Venturi and their complexity theories, but Rachel Carson, the student movement, post-industrial society, the electronic revolution, contextualism, adhocism, metabolism and more 'isms' than one cares to remember. It is thus a rainbow coalition that resists the excesses of modernism – a *critical*, not anti-modernism. Let us make no mistake. As I will point out many times, some of the best PMs are former modernists critical of their own tradition. To clarify this idea let me give as an example an architect whom everyone perceives as *the* Modernist, Norman Foster.

* * *

An incredible irony of this book is that the post-modernism it describes was started in the early 1970s, when Minoru Yamasaki's housing in St Louis was dynamited by the authorities, and it comes to an end after his twin towers were blown up by terrorists. The problem of architectural symbolism still remains the one I pointed out above, of univalent content. What can an architect symbolise in a commercial era that devotes its extra money not to publicly credible functions but to monopolies, big business, world fairs, great engineering feats and shopping? Some major changes have occurred in the West since that question was asked in 1977. Ecological issues have become more pressing, the global market has deregulated somewhat, shopping has become in Koolhaas's phrase 'the

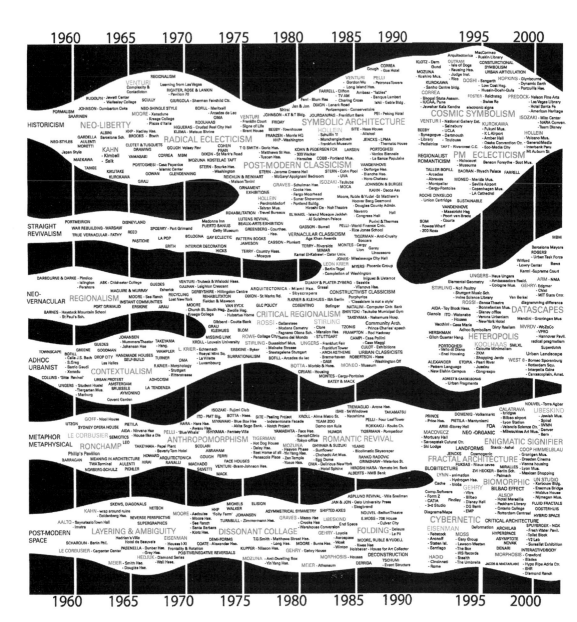

7. Post-Modern Evolutionary Tree, 1960–2000. Pluralism of competing traditions is the keynote of the Post-Modern movement, but these six coherent strands show some of the common threads that continue over 40 years. Some of the major foci and keywords are in red, the major figures in green. © Charles Jencks.

terminal condition of man', and the museum has emerged as *the* public building type of the time. Art, science and cultural centres are far preferable as civic expressions of pride and democracy than the corporate monument to the global market. The twin towers of the World Trade Center were not only arrogant, as Goldberger wrote, but confused as symbols. Their aetiolated Gothic neither had the confidence of the Woolworth skyscraper, the Cathedral to Commerce of 1914, nor the strength of a Modern Purist tower, such as Eero Saarinen's CBS (New York City) of 1961. Its confusion partly stemmed from the very ambivalence of its content. How can a skyscraper express world trade without becoming a triumphalist assertion of American dominance? Yamasaki did not face the ambiguities and complexities of this task, a supremely architectural one.

Notes

1   See Mies van der Rohe, *Industrialized Building*, originally printed in *G* magazine, Berlin, 1924, and reprinted in Ulrich Conrad's, *Programmes and Manifestos on 20th-Century Architecture*, London, 1970, p 81.

2   Umberto Eco, *Postscript to the Name of the Rose*, Harcourt Brace Jovanovitch (New York and London), pp 67–8.

Charles Jencks, 'The Language of Post-Modern Architecture and the Complexity Paradigm' originally appeared in *The New Paradigm in Architecture*, Yale University Press (New Haven and London), 2002 (the seventh revised edition of *The Language of Post-Modern Architecture*, 1977, 1978, 1981, 1984, 1987, 1991, published by Academy Editions). © Charles Jencks.

What Is the Postmodern?

Paolo Portoghesi

In this essay, Portoghesi contends that postmodern architects are part of a heterogeneous group that 'arises from a common dissatisfaction with ... modernity'. But before postmodernism, says Portoghesi, there was a widespread postmodern condition, characterised by a growing interest in history, folkloric costumes and tradition as well as a need for contemplative experiences and a contact with nature. Hence a postmodern building is a construction that speaks on at least at two levels at once, as a re-emergence of archetypes and as a communicative image. Portoghesi also stresses here the 'return to the study of the city as a complex phenomenon'.

Paolo Portoghesi (1931–) is an Italian architectural historian of Roman Baroque, an architect and a professor of architecture. He was appointed curator of the First Architecture Biennale in Venice (1980), and led its first exhibition, which travelled on to Paris and then San Francisco. These became key moments in the dissemination of the Postmodern movement. *LCS*

'A spectre is roaming through Europe: the Postmodern'. A columnist from *Le Monde* gave this title to an article on the most passion-stirring event to occur in the world of culture in the past several years. This phenomenon exploded in America at the end of the last decade, but its roots are especially deep in Europe, where it has found the most fertile ground for theoretical debate.

But what exactly is the Postmodern? Is it possible to give a single definition to such a paradoxical and irritating word? I feel that it is indeed possible. But we must first stop thinking of it as a label designating homogeneous and convergent things. Its usefulness lies, rather, in its having allowed us temporarily to put together and compare different things arising from a common dissatisfaction with that group of equally heterogeneous things called modernity. To put it another way, the Postmodern is a refusal, a rupture, a renouncement, much more than a simple change of direction. To define it poetically, we could borrow the celebrated verses of Montale: 'Do not ask us for the key that cannot open ... Only this we can tell you today, what we are not, and what we do not want.' And exactly what many of us do not want any more today is the antiquated Modern, that set of formulas which, in the second decade of this century, acquired the rigidity and clarity of a sort of statute in which general laws are collected that must be obeyed. This statute has never come up for discussion again, even though taste has changed more than once since then. Its main article was precisely an annihilation of tradition, the obligation towards renewal, the theology of the new, and the difference as an autonomous value.

This perverse guarantee of perpetual renewal has given modernity the appearance of an elusive shadow, difficult to contend with because of its readiness to assume ever changing forms and strategies. But in the end, a sense of uneasiness upset even the certainties of the Modern: the discomfort of men of culture when evaluating its products. Sixty years comprise a man's life, and just as a man of this age looks back (and just as the others tend to judge him), the trial against the Modern has been outlined as a physiological necessity, as an unpostponable goal for the new generations, at least since 1968. Therefore, a trial against the Modern and its consequences, but not only this; the Postmodern is a rebellion originating in the realisation that in the past 60 years everything has changed in the world of social relationships and production; that industry has undergone radical transformations, and the energy crisis has once more uncovered problems that had been thought to be solved for some time.

The statute of modernity had been custom-made for a society in which the revolution of information that has profoundly shaken all the structures of our world had not yet occurred. Before a Postmodern culture, there previously existed a 'postmodern condition', the product of 'post-industrial' society. It was inevitable that sooner or later this creeping, underground revolution would end up changing the direction of artistic research. What was less foreseeable was that instead of developing in the Futurist-mechanical sense, in the '2000' style, as many had imagined, art steered its course towards Ithaca. It made its way towards the recovery of certain aspects of tradition, and reopened the discussion, the impassable embankment erected by the avant-garde between present and past, and went back to mix the waters with creative results. This recovery of memory, after the forced amnesia of a half century, is manifest in customs, dress (folk, casual and the various revivals), in the mass diffusion of an interest in history and its products, in the ever vaster need for contemplative experiences and contact with nature that seemed antithetical to the civilisation of machines.

Architecture was one of the first disciplines to go into crisis when faced with the new needs and desires of postmodern society. The reason for this precociousness is simple. Given its direct incidence on daily life, architecture could not elude the practical verification of its users. Modern architecture has thus been judged by its natural product: the modern city, the suburbs without quality, the urban environment devoid of collective values that has become an asphalt jungle and a dormitory; the loss of local character, of the connection with the place: the terrible homologation that has made the outskirts of the cities of the whole world similar to one another, and whose inhabitants have a hard time recognising an identity of their own.

The architects of the new generations have made the city, the mechanisms of the production and reproduction of the city, their preferred field of study. They have discovered that the perpetual invention of and search for the new at all costs, the breaking off of environmental equilibria, perspective decomposition, abstract volumetric play, and all the ingredients of modern architectural cuisine were equally toxic to the physiological regimen of urban growth. They have discovered that the imitation of types is more important than linguistic invention. They also realise that it is once again necessary to learn modesty and the knowledge of rules and canons produced over centuries of experiences and errors, that the character of a place is a patrimony to use and not to mindlessly squander. A kind of new Renaissance is thus being outlined which intends to recover certain aspects of the past, not to interrupt history, but to arrest its paralysis. And whoever objects that we are in a time of economic and moral crisis hardly fit for a Renaissance should be reminded that Brunelleschi's and Leonardo's times were just as dark.

As always, when change is desired, the Postmoderns have also been the target of the arrows of the new conservatives, of those guardians of modernity at any cost, who refuse to relinquish their privileges and power. Unable to refute the radical criticisms of the tradition of the new, they speak of an incomplete project of modernity that must be continued; they pretend to ignore the fact that in order to really change the essential premises of the modern project, and not its last consequences, must be debated once more. And they refuse to admit that continuity with the great tradition of modern art lies today more in the courage to break with the past (which in this case is precisely what was modern yesterday), than in keeping its surviving traces on ice.

In Italy, the harshest and most subtle attack came from the old exponents of the '63 group, which 20 years ago raised the banner of the neo-avant-garde and experimentalism. Precursors of the Postmodern in many marginal aspects of research (the use of the historical quotation, the new-antique corruption, the semiological and linguistic approach), they refuse the products of this new attitude without even analysing them, making a handy image of these products in order to destroy them with the old weapon of irony. An old system already used once by the enemies of the Modern when it deserved the name. History repeats itself, even if there will always be those who confuse it with a straight line. That postmodern theses have deep roots in the present human condition is confirmed today in the document on architecture issued by the Polish union Solidarity. This text accuses the modern city of being the product of an alliance between bureaucracy and totalitarianism, and singles out the great error of modern architecture in the break of historical continuity. Solidarity's words should be meditated upon, especially by those who have confused a great movement of collective consciousness with a passing fashion.

A New Renaissance

> Zoroaster wants to lose nothing of humanity's past, and wants to throw everything into the crucible. (Nietzsche)

During the last decade, the adjective postmodern has made a journey of varying success through humanistic disciplines. Used systematically for the first time in 1971 by Ihab Hassan in relation to literature, it then made its way into the social sciences, into semiology and philosophy. In architecture, the adjective postmodern found fertile cultural ground, priming a process which started out from criticism and historiography, and finally became the unifying label of a series of trends, theoretical propositions and concrete experiences.

It is worth our while today to reflect upon the unforeseeable fortune of this word in architecture, in order to try to clear up many misunderstandings, and to establish just how useful it can be in relating parallel phenomena taking place in very different areas. In the field of architecture, the term has been used to designate a plurality of tendencies directed towards an escape from the crisis of the Modern Movement with a radical refusal of its logic of development. In the last several decades, this development had led to a chaotic labyrinth, or to the anachronistic attempt to restore the orthodoxy of the golden age of Functionalism; the age, of course, of the Bauhaus and CIAM.

The Postmodern has signalled, therefore, the way out of a movement that had for some time stopped 'moving ahead', that had transformed itself into a gaudy bazaar of inventions motivated only by personal ambition and by the alibi of technological experimentation. The critics who first put into focus the vast and contradictory phenomenon of an exit from orthodoxy tried to control it by putting it into traditional categories. They also tried to simplify it and make it more comprehensible; but in the end, the neutrality of a word like postmodern is tantamount to an absurd definition based on difference more than on identity. With regard to didactic simplification, the same critics finally surrendered to pluralism and complexity. Charles Jencks, the most able of the announcers of this new show, proposed that its specificity can in fact be grasped, since it is the product of architects particularly mindful of the aspects of architecture understood as a language, as a means of communication:

> A Postmodern building is, if a short definition is needed, one which speaks on at least two levels at once: to other architects and a concerned minority who care about specifically architectural meanings, and to the public at large, or the local inhabitants, who care about other issues concerned with comfort, traditional building and a way of life. Thus Postmodern architecture looks hybrid and, if a visual definition is needed, rather like the front of a classical Greek temple. The latter is a geometric architecture of elegantly fluted columns below, and a riotous billboard of struggling giants above, a pediment painted in deep reds and blues. The architects can read the implicit metaphors and subtle meanings of the column drums, whereas the public can respond to the explicit metaphors and messages of the sculptors. Of course everyone responds somewhat to both codes of meaning, as they do in a Postmodern building, but certainly with different intensity and understanding, and it is this discontinuity in taste cultures which creates both the theoretical base and 'dual-coding' of Postmodernism.[1]

This definition certainly covers the unifying aspect of many of the most significant works realised in the last decade which have overcome the ideological crisis of the Modern Movement. It fails, however, to satisfy the historical need of relating the shift carried out by architectural culture to the profound changes in society, and risks confining the phenomenon to an area completely within the private realm of the architect, therefore remaining more of a psychological than an historico-critical definition. It is more correct, in my view, to try to get to the specificity of the phenomenon by revealing the substantial differences with modernity, from which it wishes to distinguish itself, in what are its most typical aspects. And since modernity coincides in Western architectural culture with the progressive rigorous detachment from everything traditional, it should be pointed out that in the field of architecture, the postmodern means that explicit, conscious abolition of the dam carefully built around the pure language elaborated *in vitro* on the basis of the rationalist statute. This language is put into contact again with the universe of the architectural debate, with the entire historical series of its past experiences, with no more distinctions between the periods before or after the first industrial revolution. With the barrier torn down, old and new waters have mixed together. The resulting product is before our eyes, paradoxical and ambiguous but vital, a preparatory moment of something different that can only be imagined: reintegration in architecture of a vast quantity of values, layers, semitones, which the homologation of the International Style had unpardonably dispersed.

The return of architecture to the womb of its history has just begun, but the proportions of this operation are quite different from those which orthodox critics suppose. This reversion to history would always be a laboratory experiment if it were not also the most convincing answer given thus far by architectural culture to the profound transformations of society and culture, to the growth of a 'postmodern condition' following from the development of post-industrial society. To convince ourselves, a synthetic review of the historical symptoms of this condition should suffice.

The Age of Information

No technical revolution has thus far produced such great and lasting transformations as the quantification and elaboration of information, made possible by the new electronic technology. Our age has seen the world of the machine, with its working systems and its rhythms, miss the impact of novelty. It has watched a new artificial universe move ahead, composed of wires and circuits, which resemble more organic material than something really mechanical. Information and communication have therefore become terms of comparison with which to redefine and reinterpret the role of all disciplines. And at that moment when the semiotic aspect of architecture and that of the transmission of information, along with its productive and stylistic aspects, was put into focus, it was inevitable that the constrictive and utopian character of the revolution which took place beginning with the 1920s, with the worldwide diffusion of the paradigms of the avant-garde, would be evident. In fact, renouncing the systems of conventions through which it had developed uninterruptedly, since the ancient world (the structural principle of the order, base, column, capital, trabeation, and so on), architecture had lost its specificity and had become, on the one hand, an autonomous figurative art, on the same level as painting, or, on the other hand, had reduced itself to pure material production.

Architecture, instead, seen in the area of the different civilisation of man, reveals a much more complex nature and role. It is an instrument of the production and transmission of communicative models, which have for a particular society a value analogous to that of laws and other civil institutions, models whose roots lie in the appropriation and transformation of the places of the earth, and which have for centuries played the part of confirming and developing the identity of places (of cities) and of communities.

The result of the discovery of the sudden impoverishment produced in architecture by the adoption of technologies and morphologies separated from places and traditions has been the re-emergence of architectonic archetypes as precious instruments of communication. These archetypes are elementary institutions of the language and practice of architecture that live on in the daily life and collective memory of man. These differ greatly depending on the places where we live and where our spatial experiences were formed. The Postmodern in architecture can therefore be read overall as a re-emergence of archetypes, or as a reintegration of architectonic conventions, and thus as a premise to the creation of an *architecture of communication*, an architecture of the image for a civilisation of the image.

The Fall of Centred Systems

Another aspect of the postmodern condition is the progressive dismantling of the bases of the critical theory of bourgeois society. The sharp polarity of social classes, faith in the redeeming capabilities of the socialisation of the means of production, and the analogy of the intricate processes of industrial society in capitalist and socialist countries have placed a profoundly changed reality on guard against the sterility of the dogmatisms and the incapability to explore, with the old tools of consecrated and sclerotic theories.

It should not surprise us that, together with the much more serious and proven ideological scaffolding, even the Modern Movement is in crisis: a variable and undefined container, within which quite different and often divergent phenomena were placed. This was an attempt to construct a linear function of architectural progress, in regard to which it would be possible at all times to distinguish good from evil, decree annexations and impulsions as in a political party. The Modern Movement proposed to change society for the better, avoiding (according to Le Corbusier) the revolution, or carrying it out, as the Russian Constructivists believed. Among its great tasks, the most important was that of teaching man to become modern, to change his way of life according to a model capable of avoiding waste. Today, this undertaking hardly seems valid for a colonialist programme, while the real problem is one of understanding what postmodern man wants, and how he lives. He is not an animal to be programmed in a laboratory, but an already existing species which has almost reached maturity, while architects were still trying to realise their obsolete project of modernity.

The great intellectual work done in the past 20 years on the concept and structures of power has put another drifting mine beneath the fragile and suspect structure of the Modern Movement. Separating the idea of power from the relationships of work and property 'in which,' as Alain Touraine has written, 'it seemed to be totally incarnated', even the role of the architectural avant-gardes has been able to be analysed in different terms, recognising its responsibilities and inadequacies, and putting in crisis the theory that stripped them of responsibility. They attributed all blame to the 'design of capital'.

The history of architecture of the past 30 years could, therefore, be written as the history of a 'way out' of the Modern Movement according to a direction already experimented by the masters in the last years of their lives, at the beginning of the 1950s.

The crisis of theoretical legitimation, which Jean-François Lyotard calls the 'scarce credibility of the great *Récits'*, and the fact that today we must confront the problem of the meaning 'without having the possibility of responding with the hope of the emancipation of Mankind, as in the school of the Enlightenment, of the Spirit, as in the school of German Idealism, or of the Proletariat, by means of the establishment of a transparent society', has unhinged the fundamental principles of architectural modernity, consisting of a series of equations which have never been verified except through insignificant small samples. These are the equations: useful=beautiful, structural truth=aesthetic prestige, and the dogmatic assertions of the Functionalist statute: 'form follows function', 'architecture must coincide with construction', 'ornament is crime', and so on. The truth of architecture as a simple coincidence of appearance and substance contradicts what is greatest and most lasting among the architectural institutions, from the Greek temple to the cathedral; and even what the Modern Movement built under the banner of truth often has its worth in an 'appearance' that has little to do with constructive truth. The great moral tale that hoped to grasp the human aspect of architecture, theorising its function and 'sincerity', by this time has the distant prestige of a fable.

In place of faith in the great centred designs, and the anxious pursuits of salvation, the postmodern condition is gradually substituting the concreteness of small circumstantiated struggles with its precise objectives capable of having a great effect because they change systems of relations.

The Crisis of Resources and the City–Country Relationship

The postmodern condition has put into crisis even that discipline that the Modern Movement had placed beside architecture, as a theoretical guarantee of its socialisation: city planning understood as the science of territorial transformations. From the time when city planning, abandoning the tradition of 19th-century urban rhetoric, had become that strange mixture of ineffectual sociological analyses and implacable zoning, the city seemed to have lost the very principle of its reproduction, growing from the addition of fatty or cancerous tissue, lacking essential urban features, as in the great peripheral areas.

The most obvious symptom of the change in direction of architectural research was a return to the study of the city as a complex phenomenon in which building typologies play a role comparable to that of institutions, and profoundly condition the production and change of the urban face. The analytical study of the city has skipped over the Functionalist logic of the building block, reproposing instead the theme of the continuity of the urban fabric, and of the fundamental importance of enclosed spaces, actual component cells of the urban environment. The study of collective behaviour divided the criterion of the dismemberment of the urban body into its monofunctioning parts, the standard which informs ideal cities, proposed as models by the masters of modern architecture.

The energy crisis, on the other hand, and the crisis of the governability of the great metropolitan administrations has focused once again on the problem of the alternatives to the indefinite growth of the large cities, and on the necessity of correcting the relationship of exploitation still characterising the city in relation to small centres and the region. The great myth of the double equation, city=progress, development=well-being has given way to the theory of limit and of controlled development. With regard to a postmodern urbanism, an institutional reformism is beginning to be considered that would give new competitive strength to smaller centres through federative initiatives (in Italy, a process of this kind is going on in the Vallo di Diano, under the aegis of Socialist administrators). Ecological problems and the energy crisis have led to the self-criticism of the acritical propensity towards the new technologies that have substituted old ones, often with no advantage whatsoever for the life span of the product, the absorption of manpower and aesthetic quality. A change of direction is inevitable if we do not want to further aggravate economic and social problems. To realise the importance of these programmes, it is sufficient to reflect upon the fact that the energy consumption of a plastic panel is 20 times that needed for the construction of a brick wall of the same area, or that the progressive disappearance of certain trades because of the abandonment of certain techniques would render us, for a lack of skilled workers, unable to restore historic monuments and ancient cities, whose integral preservation seems to have been, at least on paper, one of the great cultural conquests of our time.

The truth is that the postmodern condition has reversed the theoretical scaffolding of so-called modernity. Those who are amazed that, among the most apparent results of the new culture in its infancy, there is also a certain superficial feeling for a 'return to the antique', seem to forget that in every serious mixture, the artificial order of chronology is one of the first structures to be discussed and then dismissed. Just as grandchildren often resemble their grandparents, and certain features of the family reappear after centuries, the world now emerging is searching freely in memory, because it knows how to find its own 'difference' in the removed repetition and utilisation of the entire past. Recently in Japan, sailboats have been built whose sails are manoeuvred not by hundreds of sailors, but by complicated and extremely fast electronic devices. These ships, equipped also with conventional engines, allow for a great saving in fuel. Postmodern architecture, whose naive manifestations of a precocious childhood we see today, will probably resemble these ships that have brought the imaginary even into the world of the machine.

Note

1   Charles Jencks, *The Language of Post-Modern Architecture*, Academy (London), 1981.

From Paolo Portoghesi, *Postmodern: The Architecture of the Postindustrial Society*, Rizzoli (New York), 1983. © Used with permission from Rizzoli International Publications, Inc.

PART 3 Sociology, Economics, Feminism, Science

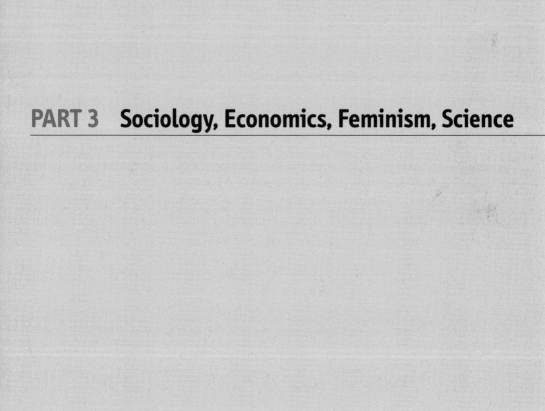

ATLAS Detector at CERN measures the meaning of ultimate particles. © Charles Jencks.

Is There a Postmodern Sociology?

Zygmunt Bauman

According to Bauman, the concept of 'postmodernity' relates particularly to the experience of intellectuals. Characteristically in the modern era, intellectuals considered the Western world as superior, and in so doing they extensively underwrote the consumer society and repression, the kind of panoptical power described by Michel Foucault. In other words, for Bauman postmodernity is really a concept invented by intellectuals to describe their feelings of anxiety as well as their loss of power and direction as a result of subsequent developments. He suggests new directions in sociology by articulating how intellectuals are now part of a society that is dominated by market dependency, techniques of seduction, plurality and consumption of information. Interestingly this text, written in 1988, predicts the coming advances in information technology. He writes: 'It will turn the consumption of information into a pleasurable, entertaining pastime. Education will become just one of the many variants of self-amusement.' In this reading, such technology (known today as the Internet) will become a good example of a weapon of seduction and repression, perhaps eventually causing the anxiety and loss of direction that Bauman describes.

Zygmunt Bauman (1925–) is a Polish-born sociologist and emeritus Professor of Sociology at the University of Leeds. Best known for his analyses of the links between modernity and the Holocaust, and of postmodern consumerism, Bauman has published more than 50 books and well over 100 articles. *LCS*

Why do we need the concept of 'postmodernity'? On the face of it, this concept is redundant. In so far as it purports to capture and articulate what is novel at the present stage of Western history, it legitimizes itself in terms of a job which has been already performed by other, better established concepts – like those of the 'post-capitalist' or 'post-industrial' society. Concepts which have served the purpose well: they sharpened our attention to what is new and discontinuous, and offered a reference point for counter-arguments in favour of continuity.

Is, therefore, the advent of the 'postmodernity' idea an invitation to rehash or simply replay an old debate? Does it merely signify an all-too-natural fatigue, which a protracted and inconclusive debate must generate? Is it merely an attempt to inject new excitement into an increasingly tedious pastime (as Gordon Allport once said, we social scientists never solve problems; we only get bored with them)? If this is the case, then the idea of 'postmodernity' is hardly worth a second thought, and this is exactly what many a seasoned social scientist suggests.

Appearances are, however, misleading (and the advocates and the detractors of the idea of 'postmodernity' share the blame for confusion). The concept of 'postmodernity' may well capture and articulate a quite different sort of novelty than those the older, apparently similar concepts accommodated and theorized. It can legitimize its right to exist – its cognitive value – only if it does exactly this: if it generates a social-scientific discourse which theorizes different aspects of contemporary experience, or theorizes them in a different way.

I propose that the concept of 'postmodernity' has a value entirely of its own in so far as it purports to capture and articulate the novel experience of just one, but crucial social category of contemporary society: the intellectuals. Their novel experience – that is, their confidence of the West and its spokesmen has been built. Superiority of the West over the rest remained self-evident for almost three centuries. It was not, as it were, a matter of idle comparison. The era of modernity had been marked by an active superiority: part of the world constituted the rest as inferior – either as a crude, still unprocessed 'raw material' in need of cleaning and refinement, or a temporarily extant relic of the past. Whatever could not be brought up to the superior standards, was clearly destined for the existence of subordination. Western practices defined the rest as a pliable or malleable substance still to be given shape. This active superiority meant the right of the superior to proselytyze, to design the suitable form of life for the others, to refuse to grant authority to the ways of life which did not fit that design.

Such superiority could remain self-evident as long as the denied authority showed no signs of reasserting itself, and the designs seemed irresistible. A historical domination could interpret itself as universal and absolute, as long as it could believe that the future would prove it such; the universality of the Western mode (the absoluteness of Western domination) seemed indeed merely a matter of time. The grounds for certainty and self-confidence could not be stronger. Human reality indeed seemed subject to unshakeable laws and stronger ('progressive') values looked set to supersede or eradicate the weaker ('retrograde', ignorant, superstitious) ones. It was this historically given certainty, grounded in the unchallenged superiority of forces aimed at universal domination, which had been articulated, from the perspective of the intellectual mode, as universality of the standards of truth, judgment and taste. The strategy such articulation legitimated was to supply the forces, bent on universal and active domination, with designs dictated by universal science, ethics and aesthetics.

The certitude of yesteryear is now at best ridiculed as naivety, at worst castigated as ethnocentric. Nobody but the most rabid of the die-hards believes today that the Western mode of life, either the actual one or one idealized ('utopianized') in the intellectual mode, has more than a sporting chance of ever becoming universal. No social force is in sight (including those which, arguably, are today aiming at global domination) bent on making it universal. The search for universal standards has suddenly become gratuitous; there is no credible 'historical agent' to which the findings could be addressed and entrusted. Impracticality erodes interest. The task of establishing universal standards of truth, morality, taste does not seem that much important. Unsupported by will, it appears now misguided and irreal.

Secondly – even the localized powers, devoid of ecumenical ambitions, seem less receptive to the products of intellectual discourse. The time modern intellectuals were born was one of the great 'shake-up': everything solid melted into air, everything sacred was profaned … The newborn absolutist state did not face the task of wrenching power from old and jaded hands; it had to create an entirely new kind of social power, capable of carrying the burden of *societal* integration. The task involved the crushing of those mechanisms of social reproduction which had been based in communal traditions. Its performance took the form of a 'cultural crusade'; that is, practical destruction of communal bases of social power, and theoretical delegitimation of their authority. Faced with such tasks, the state badly needed 'legitimation' (this is the name given to intellectual discourse when considered from the vantage point of its power-oriented, political application).

Mais où sont les croisades d'autant? The present-day political domination can reproduce itself using means more efficient and less costly than 'legitimation'. Weber's 'legal–rational legitimation' – the point much too seldom made – is, in its essence, a declaration of the redundancy of legitimation. The modern state is effective without authority; or, rather, its effectivity depends to a large extent on rendering authority irrelevant. It does not matter any more, for the effectivity of state power, and for the reproduction of political domination in general, whether the social area under domination is culturally unified and uniform, and how idiosyncratic are the values sectors of this area may uphold.

The weapon of legitimation has been replaced with two mutually complementary weapons: this of *seduction* and that of *repression*. Both need intellectually trained experts, and indeed both siphon off, accommodate and domesticate an ever growing section of educated elite. Neither has a need, or a room, for those 'hard-core' intellectuals whose expertise is 'legitimation', ie supplying proof that what is being done is universally correct and absolutely true, moral and beautiful.

Seduction is the paramount tool of integration (of the reproduction of domination) in a consumer society. It is made possible once the market succeeds in making the consumers dependent on itself. Market dependency is achieved through the destruction of such skills (technical, social, psychological, existential) which do not entail the use of marketable commodities; the more complete the destruction, the more necessary become new skills which point organically to market-supplied implements. Market dependency is guaranteed and self-perpetuating once men and women, now consumers, cannot proceed with the business of life without tuning themselves to the logic of the market. Much debated 'needs creation' by the market means ultimately creation of the need of the market. New technical, social, psychological and existential skills of the consumers are such as to be practicable only in conjunction with marketable commodities; rationality comes to mean the ability to make right purchasing decisions, while the craving for certainty is gratified by conviction that the decisions made have been, indeed, right.

Repression stands for 'panoptical' power, best described by Foucault (1977). It employs surveillance, it is aimed at regimentation of the body, and is diffused (made invisible) in the numerous institutionalizations of knowledge-based expertise. Repression as a tool of domination-reproduction has not been abandoned with the advent of seduction. Its time is not over and the end of its usefulness is not in sight, however overpowering and effective seduction may become. It is the continuous, tangible presence of repression as a viable alternative that makes seduction unchallengeable. In addition, repression is indispensable to reach the areas seduction cannot, and is not meant to, reach: it remains the paramount tool of subordination of the considerable margin of society which cannot be absorbed by market dependency and hence, in market terms, consists of 'non-consumers'. Such 'non-consumers' are people reduced to the satisfaction of their elementary needs; people whose business of life does not transcend the horizon of survival. Goods serving the latter purpose are not, as a rule, attractive as potential merchandise; they serve the needs over which the market has no control and thus undermine, rather than boost, market dependency. Repression reforges the market unattractiveness of non-consumer existence into the unattractiveness of alternatives to market dependency.

Seduction and repression between them, make 'legitimation' redundant. The structure of domination can now be reproduced, ever more effectively, without recourse to legitimation; and thus without recourse to such intellectuals as make the legitimation discourse their speciality. Habermas's (1976) 'legitimation crisis' makes sense, in the final account, as the intellectual perception of 'crisis' caused by the ever more evident irrelevance of legitimation.

The growing irrelevance of legitimation has coincided with the growing freedom of intellectual debate. One suspects more than coincidence. It is indifference on the part of political power which makes freedom of intellectual work possible. Indifference, in its turn, arises from the lack of interest. Intellectual freedom is possible as political power has freed itself from its former dependence on legitimation. This is why freedom, coming as it does in a package deal with irrelevance, is not received by the intellectuals with unqualified enthusiasm. All the more so as the past political patronage made a considerable part of intellectual work grow in a way which rendered it dependent on the continuation of such a patronage.

What, however, more than anything else prevents the intellectuals from rejoicing is the realization that the withdrawal of the government troops does not necessarily mean that the vacated territory will become now their uncontested domain. What the state has relinquished, is most likely to be taken over by the powers on which the intellectuals have even less hold than they ever enjoyed in their romance with politics.

The territory in question is that of culture. Culture is one area of social life which is defined (cut out) in such a way as to reassert the social function claimed by the intellectuals. One cannot even explain the meaning of the concept without reference to human 'incompleteness', to the need of teachers and, in general, of 'people in the know' to make up for this incompleteness, and to a vision of society as a continuous 'teach-in' session. The idea of culture, in other words, establishes knowledge in the role of power, and simultaneously supplies legitimation of such power. Culture connotes power of the educated elite and knowledge as power; it denotes institutionalized mechanisms of such power – science, education, arts.

Some of these mechanisms, or some areas of their application, remain relevant to the repressive functions of the state, or to the tasks resulting from the state role in the reproduction of consumer society (reproduction of conditions for the integration-through-seduction). As far as this is the case, the state acts as the protector-cum-censor, providing funds but reserving the right to decide on the tasks and the value of their results. The mixed role of the state rebounds in a mixed reaction of the educated elite. The calls for more state resources intermingle with the protests against bureaucratic interference. There is no shortage of the educated willing to serve; neither is there a shortage of criticisms of servility.

Some other mechanisms, or some other areas of their application, do not have such relevance. They are, as a rule, 'underfunded', but otherwise suffer little political interference. They are free. Even the most iconoclastic of their products fail to arouse the intended wrath of the dominant classes and in most cases are received with devastating equanimity. Challenging the capitalist values stirs little commotion in as far as the capitalist domination does not depend on the acceptance of its values. And yet freedom *from* political interference does not result in freedom *for* intellectual creativity. A new protector-cum-censor fills the vacuum left by the withdrawal of the state: the market.

This is the third respect in which the intellectual status is perceived as undermined. Whatever their other ambitions, modern intellectuals always saw culture as their private property; they made it, they lived in it, they even gave it its name. Expropriation of this particular plot hurts most. Or has it been, in fact, an expropriation? Certainly intellectuals never controlled 'popular' consumption of cultural products. Once they felt firmly in the saddle, they saw themselves as members of the circle of 'culture consumers', which, in the sense they would have recognized, was probably significant, if small. It is only now that the circle of people eager to join the culture consumption game has grown to unheard of proportions – has become truly 'massive'. What hurts, therefore, is not so much an expropriation, but the fact that the intellectuals are not invited to stand at the helm of this breathtaking expansion. Instead, it is gallery owners, publishers, TV managers and other 'capitalists' or 'bureaucrats' who are in control. The idea has been wrested out of the intellectual heads and in a truly sorcerer's apprentice's manner, put to action in which the sages have no power.

In another sense, however, what has happened is truly an expropriation, and not just 'stealing the profits'. In the early modern era, intellectual forces had been mobilized (or self-mobilized) for the gigantic job of conversion – the culture crusade which involved a thorough revamping or uprooting of the totality of heretofore autonomously reproduced forms of life. The project was geared to the growth of the modern absolutist state and its acute need of legitimation. For reasons mentioned before, this is not the case any more. Native forms of life have not, however, returned to autonomous reproduction; there are others who manage it – agents of the market, this time, and not the academia. No wonder the old gamekeepers view the new ones as poachers. Once bent on the annihilation of 'crude, superstitious, ignorant, bestial' folkways, they now bewail the enforced transformation of the 'true folk culture' into a 'mass' one. Mass culture debate has been the lament of expropriated gamekeepers.

The future does not promise improvement either; the strength of the market forces continues to grow, their appetite seems to grow even faster, and for an increasing sector of the educated elite the strategy 'if you cannot beat them, join them' gains in popularity. Even the areas of intellectual domain still left outside the reach of the market forces are now felt to be under threat. It was the intellectuals who impressed upon the once incredulous population the need for education and the value of information. Here as well their success turns into their downfall. The market is only too eager to satisfy the need and to supply the value. With the new DIY (electronic) technology to offer, the market will reap the rich crop of the popular belief that education is human duty and (any) information is useful. The market will thereby achieve what the intellectual educators struggled to attain in vain: it will turn the consumption of information into a pleasurable, entertaining pastime. Education will become just one of the many variants of self-amusement. It will reach the peak of its popularity and the bottom of its value as measured by original intellectual-made standards.

The three developments discussed above go some way, if not all the way, towards explaining this feeling of anxiety, out-of-placeness, loss of direction which, as I propose, constitutes the true referent of the concept of 'postmodernity'. As a rule, however, intellectuals tend to articulate their own societal situation and the problems it creates as a situation of the society at large, and its, systemic or social, problems. The way in which the passage from 'modernity' to 'postmodernity' has been articulated is not an exception. This time, however, those who articulate it do not hide as thoroughly as in the past behind the role of 'organic intellectuals' of other classes; and the fact that they act as 'organic intellectuals of themselves' is either evident or much easier to discover. Definitions of both 'modernity' and 'postmodernity' refer overtly to such features of respective social situations which have direct and crucial importance for the intellectual status, role and strategy.

The main feature ascribed to 'postmodernity' is thus the permanent and irreducible *pluralism* of cultures, communal traditions, ideologies, 'forms of life' or 'language games' (choice of items which are 'plural' varies with theoretical allegiance); or the awareness and recognition of such pluralism. Things which are plural in the postmodern world cannot be arranged in an evolutionary time sequence, seen as each other's inferior or superior stages; neither can they be classified as 'right' or 'wrong' solutions to common problems. No knowledge can be assessed outside the context of culture, tradition, language game etc which makes it possible and endows it with meaning. Hence no criteria of validation are available which could be themselves justified 'out of context'. Without universal standards, the problem of the postmodern world is not how to globalize superior culture, but how to secure communication and mutual understanding between cultures.

Seen from this 'later' perspective, 'modernity' seems in retrospect a time when pluralism was not yet a foregone conclusion; or a time when the ineradicability of pluralism was not duly recognized. Hence the substitution of one, 'supra-communal', standard of truth, judgment and taste for the diversity of local, and therefore inferior, standards, could be contemplated and strived for as a viable prospect. Relativism of knowledge could be perceived as a nuisance, and as a temporary one at that. Means could be sought – in theory and in practice – to exorcize the ghost of relativism once and for all. The end to parochialism of human opinions and ways of life was nigh. This could be a chance – once real, then lost. Or this could be an illusion from the start. In the first case, postmodernity means the failure of modernity. In the second case, it means a step forward. In both cases, it means opening our eyes to the futility of modern dreams of universalism.

* * *

Less philosophical, more empirically inclined varieties of traditional social studies are even less fortunate. Modern empirical sociology developed in response to the demand of the modern state aiming at the 'total administration' of society. With capital engaging the rest of the society in their roles of labour, and the state responsible for the task of 'recommodifying' both capital and labour, and thus ensuring the continuation of such an engagement – the state needed a huge apparatus of 'social management' and a huge supply of expert social-management knowledge. Methods and skills of empirical sociology were geared to this demand and to the opportunities stemming from it. The social-managerial tasks were large scale, and so were the funds allotted to their performance. Sociology specialized therefore in developing the skills of use in mass, statistical research; in collecting information about 'massive trends' and administrative measures likely to redirect, intensify or constrain such trends. Once institutionalised, the skills at the disposal of empirical sociologists have defined the kind of research they are capable of designing and conducting. Whatever else this kind of research is, it invariably requires huge funds – and thus a rich bureaucratic institution wishing to provide them. Progressive disengagement of capital from labour, falling significance of the 'recommodification' task, gradual substitution of 'seduction' for 'repression' as the paramount weapon of social integration, shifting of the responsibility for integration from the state bureaucracy to the market – all this spells trouble for traditional empirical research, as state bureaucracies lose interest in financing it.

The widely debated 'crisis of (empirical) sociology' is, therefore, genuine. Empirical sociology faces today the choice between seeking a new social application of its skills or seeking new skills. Interests of state bureaucracy are likely to taper to the management of 'law and order', ie a task aimed selectively at the part of the population which cannot be regulated by the mechanism of seduction. And there are private bureaucracies, in charge of the seduction management, who may or may not need the skill of empirical sociology, depending on the extent in which the latter are able, and willing, to reorient and readjust their professional know-how to the new, as yet not fully fathomed, demand.

To sum up: if the radical manifestoes proclaiming the end of sociology and social philosophy 'as we know them' seem unfounded – equally unconvincing are the pretensions that nothing of importance has happened and that there is nothing to stop 'business as usual'. The form acquired by sociology and social philosophy in the course of what is now, retrospectively, described as 'modernity' is indeed experiencing at the moment an unprecedented challenge. While in no way doomed, it must adjust itself to new conditions in order to self-reproduce.

I will turn now to those actual, or likely, developments in sociology which do admit (overtly or implicitly) the novelty of the situation and the need for a radical reorientation of the tasks and the strategies of social study.

One development is already much in evidence. Its direction is clearly shown by the consistently expanding assimilation of Heideggerian, Wittgensteinian, Gadamerian and other 'hermeneutical' themes and inspirations. This development points in the direction of sociology as, above all, the skill of interpretation. Whatever articulable experience there is which may become the object of social study – it is embodied in its own 'life-world', 'communal tradition', 'positive ideology', 'form of life', 'language game'. The names for that 'something' in which the experience is embedded are many and different, but what truly counts are not names but the inherent pluralism of that 'something' which all the names emphasize more than anything else. Thus there are *many* 'life-worlds', *many* 'traditions' and *many* 'language games'. No external point of view is conceivable to reduce this variety. The only reasonable cognitive strategy is therefore one best expressed in Geertz's (1973) idea of 'thick description': recovery of the meaning of the alien experience through fathoming the tradition (form of life, life-world etc) which constitutes it, and then translating it, with as little damage as possible, into a form assimilable by one's own tradition (form of life, life-world, etc). Rather than proselytizing, which would be the task of a cross-cultural encounter in the context of 'orthodox' social science, it is the expected 'enrichment' of one's own tradition, through incorporating other, heretofore inaccessible, experiences, which is the meaning bestowed upon the exercise by the project of 'interpreting sociology'.

As interpreters, sociologists are no more concerned with ascertaining the 'truth' of the experience they interpret – and thus the principle of 'ethnomethodological indifference' may well turn from the shocking heresy it once was into a new orthodoxy. The only concern which distinguishes sociologists-turned-interpreters as professionals is the correctness of interpretation; it is here that the professional credentials as experts (ie holders of skills inaccessible to lay and untrained public) are re-established. Assuming that the world is irreducibly pluralist, rendering the messages mutually communicable is its major problem. Expertise in the rules of correct interpretation is what it needs most. It is badly needed even by such powers that are not any more bent on total domination and do not entertain universalistic ambitions; they still need this expertise for their sheer survival. Potential uses are clear; the users, so far, less so – but one may hope they can be found.

As all positions, this one has also its radical extreme. The admission of pluralism does not have to result in the interest in interpretation and translation, or for that matter in any 'social' services sociology may offer. Release from the often burdensome social duty sociology had to carry in the era of modernity may be seen by some with relief – as the advent of true freedom of intellectual pursuits. It is, indeed, an advent of freedom – though freedom coupled with irrelevance: freedom *from* cumbersome and obtrusive interference on the part of powers that be, won at the price of resigning the freedom to influence their actions and their results. If what sociology does does not matter, it can do whatever it likes. This is a tempting possibility: to immerse oneself fully in one's own specialized discourse inside which one feels comfortably at home, to savour the subtleties of distinction and discretion such discourse demands and renders possible, to take the very disinterestedness of one's pursuits for the sign of their supreme value, to take pride in keeping alive, against the odds, a precious endeavour for which the rest, the polluted or corrupted part of the world, has (temporarily – one would add, seeking the comfort of hope) no use. It is one's own community, tradition, form of life, etc which commands first loyalty; however small, it provides the only site wherein the intrinsic value of the discourse can be tended to, cultivated – and enjoyed. After all, the recognition of futility of universal standards, brought along by postmodernity, allows that self-centred concerns treat lightly everything outside criticism. There is nothing to stop one from coming as close as possible to the sociological equivalent of *l'art pour l'art* (the cynic would comment: nothing, but the next round of education cuts).

The two postmodern strategies for sociology and social philosophy, discussed so far, are – each in its own way – internally consistent and viable. Looked at from inside, they both seem invulnerable. Given their institutional entrenchment, they have a sensible chance of survival and of virtually infinite self-reproduction (again, barring the circumstances referred to by the cynic). Whatever critique of these strategies may be contemplated, it may only come from outside, and thus cut little ice with the insiders.

Such a critique would have to admit its allegiance to ends the insiders are not obliged to share. It would have to cite an understanding of the role of sociology the insiders have every reason to reject, and no reason to embrace. In particular, such a critique would have to declare its own value preference, remarkable above all for the supreme position allotted to the *social relevance* of sociological discourse.

The critique under consideration may be launched in other words only from the intention to preserve the hopes and ambitions of modernity in the age of postmodernity. The hopes and ambitions in question refer to the possibility of a reason-led improvement of the human condition; an improvement measured in the last instance by the degree of human emancipation. For better or worse, modernity was about increasing the volume of human autonomy, but not autonomy which, for the absence of solidarity, results in loneliness; and about increasing the intensity of human solidarity, but not solidarity which, for the absence of autonomy, results in oppression. The alternative strategy for a postmodern sociology would have to take as its assumption that the two-pronged ambition of modernity is still a viable possibility, and one certainly worth promoting.

What makes a strategy which refuses to renounce its modern ('pre-postmodern'?) commitments a 'postmodern' one, is the bluntness with which its premises are recognized as assumptions; in a truly 'postmodern' vein, such a strategy refers to values rather than laws; to assumptions instead of foundations; to purposes, and not to 'groundings'. And it is determined to do without the comfort it once derived from the belief that 'history was on its side', and that the inevitability of its ultimate success had been guaranteed beforehand by inexorable laws of nature (a pleonasm: 'nature' *is* inexorable laws).

* * *

I suggest that a sociology bent on the continuation of modern concerns under postmodern conditions would be distinguished not by new procedures and purposes of sociological work, as other postmodern strategies suggest – but by a new *object* of investigation. As far as this strategy is concerned, what matters is that the society (its object) has changed; it does not necessarily admit that its own earlier pursuits were misguided and wasted, and that the crucial novelty in the situation is the dismissal of the old ways of doing sociology and 'discovery' of new ways of doing it. Thus to describe a sociology pursuing the strategy under discussion one would speak, say, of a 'post-full-employment' sociology, or a 'sociology of the consumer society', rather than of a 'post-Wittgensteinian' or 'post-Gadamerian' sociology. In other words, this strategy points toward a sociology of postmodernity, rather than a postmodern sociology.

There are a number of specifically 'postmodern' phenomena which await sociological study. There is a process of an accelerating emancipation of capital from labour; instead of engaging the rest of society in the role of producers, capital tends to engage them in the role of consumers. This means in its turn that the task of reproducing the capital-dominated society does not consist, as before, in the 'recommodification of labour', and that the nonproducers of today are not a 'reserve army of labour', to be tended to and groomed for the return to the labour market. This crucial fact of their life is still concealed in their own consciousness, in the consciousness of their political tutors, and of the sociologists who study them, by a historical memory of society which is no more and will not return. The new poor are not socially, culturally or systemically an equivalent of the old poor; the present 'depression', manifested in the massive and stable unemployment, is not a later day edition of the 1930s (one hears about the poor losing their jobs, but one does not hear of the rich jumping out of their windows). 'The two nations' society, mark two, cannot be truly understood by squeezing it into the model of mark one.

'The two nations, mark two' society is constituted by the opposition between 'seduction' and 'repression' as a means of social control, integration and the reproduction of domination. The first is grounded in 'market dependency': replacement of old life skills by the new ones which cannot be effectively employed without the mediation of the market; in the shifting of the disaffection and conflict from the area of political struggle to the area of commodities and entertainment; in the appropriate redirecting of the needs for rationality and security; and in the growing comprehensiveness, the market-centred world, so that it can accommodate the totality of life business, making the other aspects of systemic context invisible and subjectively irrelevant. The second is grounded in a normative regulation pushed to the extreme, penetration of the 'private' sphere to an ever growing degree, disempowering of the objects normative regulation as autonomous agents. It is important to know how these two means of social control combine and support each other; and the effects their duality is likely to have on the tendencies of political power, democratic institutions and citizenship.

One may guess – pending further research – that while control-through-repression destroys autonomy and solidarity, control-through-seduction generates marketable means serving the pursuit (if not the attainment) of both, and thus effectively displaces the pressures such a pursuit exerts from the political sphere, at the same time redeploying them in the reproduction of capital domination. Thus the opposite alternatives which determine the horizon and the trajectory of life strategies in the postmodern society neutralize the possible threat to systemic reproduction which might emanate from the unsatisfied ambitions of autonomy and solidarity.

Those alternatives, therefore, need to be explored by any sociology wishing seriously to come to grips with the phenomenon of postmodernity. Conscious of the postmodern condition it explores, such a sociology would not pretend that its preoccupations, however skilfully pursued, would offer it the centrality in the 'historic process' to which it once aspired. On the contrary, the problematic sketched above is likely to annoy rather than entice the managers of law and order; it will appear incomprehensible to the seduced, and alluring yet nebulous to the repressed. A sociology determined to tread this path would have to brace itself for the uneasy plight of unpopularity. Yet the alternative is irrelevance. This seems to be the choice sociology is facing in the era of postmodernity.

References
Foucault, Michel, *Discipline and Punish*, Allen Lane (Harmondsworth), 1977.
Geertz, Clifford, *The Interpretation of Culture*, Basic Books (New York), 1973.
Gramsci, Antonio, *Selections from the Prison Notebooks*, Lawrence & Wishart (London), 1971.
Habermas, Jürgen, *Legitimation Crisis*, Heinemann (London), 1976.
Mills, C Wright, *The Sociological Imagination*, Oxford University Press (Oxford), 1959.
Williams, Raymond, *The Country and the City*, Paladin (St Albans), 1975.

Abbreviated version, Zygmunt Bauman, 'Is There a Postmodern Sociology?' from *Theory, Culture & Society*, vol 5, numbers 2–3, SAGE Publications (Newbury Park), June 1988. © Reproduced by permission of SAGE Publications Ltd, Los Angeles, New Delhi, Singapore and Washington DC.

The Condition of Postmodernity

David Harvey

David Harvey dates the beginning of postmodernity to 1972, just before the oil crisis of that decade. According to him, the so-called postmodern is more than a shift in architectural style and is due to contradictions within capitalism itself and major changes in the quality of urban life. Taking on McLuhan's ideas on the time–space compression of the global village, he explains how, in the beginning of the 1970s we experienced 'the emergence of more flexible modes of capital accumulation'. Harvey is proposing a portrait of the new reality which he pictures as much more complex than a simple binary polarisation between modern and postmodern (although he accepts Ihab Hassan's 'incomplete' binary schema). Harvey also reminds us that postmodernism is not an autonomous artistic current. He writes: 'Its rootedness in daily life is one of its most patently transparent features.'

David Harvey (1935–) is a distinguished Professor of Anthropology at the Graduate Center of the City University of New York (CUNY). *LCS*

The Argument

There has been a sea change in cultural as well as in political-economic practices since around 1972.

This sea change is bound up with the emergence of new dominant ways in which we experience space and time.

While simultaneity in the shifting dimensions of time and space is no proof of necessary or causal connection, strong a priori grounds can be adduced for the proposition that there is some kind of necessary relation between the rise of postmodernist cultural forms, the emergence of more flexible modes of capital accumulation, and a new round of 'time–space compression' in the organisation of capitalism. But these changes, when set against the basic rules of capitalistic accumulation, appear more as shifts in surface appearance rather than as signs of the emergence of some entirely new post-capitalist or even post-industrial society …

Introduction

I was recently reminded of Raban's evocative descriptions while visiting an exhibition of Cindy Sherman's photographs. The photographs depict seemingly different women drawn from many walks of life. It takes a little while to realise, with a certain shock, that these are portraits of the same woman in different guises. Only the catalogue tells you that it is the artist herself who is that woman. The parallel with Raban's insistence upon the plasticity of human personality through the malleability of appearances and surfaces is striking, as is the self-referential positioning of the authors to themselves as subject. Cindy Sherman is considered a major figure in the postmodern movement.

So what is the postmodern of which many now speak? Has social life so changed since the early 1970s that we can reasonably talk about living in a postmodern culture, a postmodern age? Or is it simply that trends in high culture have taken, as their wont, yet another twist, and that academic fashions have also changed with scarcely a ripple of effect or an echo of correspondence in the daily life of ordinary citizens? Raban's book suggests that there is more to matters than the latest intellectual fad imported from Paris or the latest twirl in the New York art market. There is more to it, too, than the shift in architectural style that Jencks records,[1] though here we approach a realm that has the potential to bring high cultural concerns closer to daily life through the production of built form. Major changes have indeed occurred in the qualities of urban life since 1970 or so. But whether such drifts deserve the appellation of 'postmodern' is another question. The answer depends rather directly, of course, on exactly what we might mean by that term. And here we do have to grapple with the latest intellectual fads imported from Paris and twists in the New York art market, because it is out of those ferments that the concept of the 'postmodern' has emerged. No one exactly agrees as to what is meant by the term, except, perhaps, that 'postmodernism' represents some kind of reaction to, or departure from, 'modernism'. Since the meaning of modernism is also very confused, the reaction or departure known as 'postmodernism' is doubly so. The literary critic Terry Eagleton tries to define the term as follows:

> There is perhaps, a degree of consensus that the typical postmodernist artefact is playful, self-ironising and even schizoid; and that it reacts to the austere autonomy of high modernism by impudently embracing the language of commerce and the commodity. Its stance towards cultural tradition is one of irreverent pastiche, and its contrived depthlessness undermines all metaphysical solemnities, sometimes by a brutal aesthetics of squalor and shock.[2]

In more positive vein, the editors of the architectural journal *PRECIS* see postmodernism as a legitimate reaction to the 'monotony' of universal modernism's vision of the world. 'Generally perceived as positivistic, technocentric, and rationalistic, universal modernism has been identified with the belief in linear progress, absolute truths, the rational planning of ideal social orders and the standardisation of knowledge and production.'[3] Postmodernism by way of contrast, privileges 'heterogeneity and difference as liberative forces in the redefinition of cultural discourse'. Fragmentation, indeterminacy, and intense distrust of all universal or 'totalising' discourses (to use the favoured phrase) are the hallmark of postmodernist thought. The rediscovery of pragmatism in philosophy,[4] the shift of ideas about the philosophy of science wrought by Kuhn and Feyerabend,[5] Foucault's emphasis upon discontinuity and difference in history and his privileging of 'polymorphous correlations in place of simple or complex causality', new developments in mathematics emphasising indeterminacy (catastrophe and chaos theory, fractal geometry), the re-emergence of concern in ethics, politics and anthropology for the validity and dignity of 'the other', all indicate a widespread and profound shift in 'the structure of feeling'. What all these examples have in common is a rejection of 'metanarratives' (large-scale theoretical interpretations purportedly of universal application), which leads Eagleton to complete his description of postmodernism thus:

> Post-modernism signals the death of such 'meta-narratives' whose secretly terroristic function was to ground and legitimate the illusion of a 'universal' human history. We are now in the process of wakening from the nightmare of modernity, with its manipulative reason and fetish of the totality, into the laid-back pluralism of the post-modern, that heterogeneous range of life-styles and language games which has renounced the nostalgic urge to totalise and legitimate itself … Science and philosophy must jettison their grandiose metaphysical claims and view themselves more modestly as just another set of narratives.

If these depictions are correct, then it would certainly seem as if Raban's *Soft City* is suffused with postmodernist sentiment. But the real import of that has still to be established. Since the only agreed point of departure for understanding the postmodern is in its purported relation to the modern …

Postmodernism

Over the last two decades 'postmodernism' has become a concept to be wrestled with, and such a battleground of conflicting opinions and political forces that it can no longer be ignored. 'The culture of the advanced capitalist societist,' announce the editors of *PRECIS*, 'has undergone a profound shift in the structure of feeling'. Most, I think, would now agree with Huyssen's more cautious statement:

> What appears on one level as the latest fad, advertising pitch and hollow spectacle is part of a slowly emerging cultural transformation in Western societies, a change in sensibility for which the term 'post-modern' is actually, at least for now, wholly adequate. The nature and depth of that transformation are debatable, but transformation it is. I don't want to be misunderstood as claiming that there is a wholesale paradigm shift of the cultural, social, and economic orders; any such claim clearly would be overblown. But in an important sector of our culture there is a noticeable shift in sensibility, practices and discourse formations which distinguishes a post-modern set of assumptions, experiences and proportions from that of a preceding period.[6]

With respect to architecture, for example, Charles Jencks dates the symbolic end of modernism and the passage to the postmodern as 3.32 pm on 15 July 1972, when the Pruitt-Igoe housing development in St Louis (a prize-winning version of Le Corbusier's 'machine for modern living') was dynamited as an uninhabitable environment for the low-income people it housed. Thereafter, the ideas of the CIAM, Le Corbusier and the other apostles of 'high modernism' increasingly gave way before an onslaught of diverse possibilities, of which those set forth in the influential *Learning from Las Vegas* by Venturi, Scott Brown and Izenour (also published in 1972) proved to be but one powerful cutting edge. The point of that work, as its title implies, was to insist that architects had more to learn from the study of popular and vernacular landscapes (such as those of suburbs and commercial strips) than from the pursuit of some abstract, theoretical and doctrinaire ideals. It was time, they said, to build for people rather than for Man. The glass towers, concrete blocks and steel slabs that seemed set fair to steamroller over every urban landscape from Paris to Tokyo and from Rio to Montreal, denouncing all ornament as crime, all individualism as sentimentality, all romanticism as kitsch, have progressively given way to ornamented tower blocks, imitation medieval squares and fishing villages, custom-designed or vernacular housing, renovated factories and warehouses and rehabilitated landscapes of all kinds, all in the name of procuring some more 'satisfying' urban environment. So popular has this quest become that no less a figure than Prince Charles has weighed in with vigorous denunciations of the errors of postwar urban redevelopment and the developer destruction that has done more to wreck London, he claims, than the Luftwaffe's attacks in the Second World War.

In planning circles we can track a similar evolution. Douglas Lee's influential article 'Requiem for large-scale planning models' appeared in a 1973 issue of the *Journal of the American Institute of Planners* and correctly predicted the demise of what he saw as the futile efforts of the 1960s to develop large-scale, comprehensive, and integrated planning models (many of them specified with all the rigour that computerised mathematical modelling could then command) for metropolitan regions. Shortly thereafter, *The New York Times* (13 June 1976) described as 'mainstream' the radical planners (inspired by Jane Jacobs) who had mounted such a violent attack upon the soulless sins of modernist urban planning in the 1960s. It is nowadays the norm to seek out 'pluralistic' and 'organic' strategies for approaching urban development as a 'collage' of highly differentiated spaces and mixtures, rather than pursuing grandiose plans based on functional zoning of different activities. 'Collage city' is now the theme and 'urban revitalisation' has replaced the vilified 'urban renewal' as the key buzz-word in the planners' lexicon. 'Make no little plans,' Daniel Burnham wrote in the first wave of modernist planning euphoria at the end of the 19th century, to which a postmodernist like Aldo Rossi can now more modestly reply: 'To what, then, could I have aspired in my craft? Certainly to small things, having seen that the possibility of great ones was historically precluded.'

Shifts of this sort can be documented across a whole range of diverse fields. The postmodern novel, McHale argues, is characterised by a shift from an 'epistemological' to an 'ontological' dominant.[7] By this he means a shift from the kind of perspectivism that allowed the modernist to get a better bearing on the meaning of a complex but nevertheless singular reality, to the foregrounding of questions as to how radically different realities may coexist, collide and interpenetrate. The boundary between fiction and science fiction has, as a consequence, effectively dissolved, while postmodernist characters often seem confused as to which world they are in, and how they should act with respect to it. Even to reduce the problem of perspective to autobiography, says one of Borges's characters, is to enter the labyrinth: 'Who was I? Today's self, bewildered, yesterday's, forgotten; tomorrow's, unpredictable?' The question marks tell it all.

In philosophy, the intermingling of a revived American pragmatism with the post-Marxist and poststructuralist wave that struck Paris after 1968 produced what Bernstein calls 'a rage against humanism and the Enlightenment legacy'.[8] This spilled over into vigorous denunciation of abstract reason and a deep aversion to any project that sought universal human emancipation through mobilisation of the powers of technology, science and reason. Here, also, no less a person than Pope John Paul II has entered the fray on the side of the postmodern. The pope 'does not attack Marxism or liberal secularism because they are the wave of the future,' says Rocco Buttiglione, a theologian close to the pope, but because the 'philosophies of the twentieth century have lost their appeal their time has already passed'. The moral crisis of our time is a crisis of Enlightenment thought. For while the latter may indeed have allowed man to emancipate himself 'from community and tradition of the Middle Ages in which his individual freedom was submerged', the Enlightenment affirmation of 'self without God' in the end negated itself because reason, a means, was left, in the absence of God's truth, without any spiritual or moral goal. If lust and power are 'the only values that don't need the light of reason to be discovered', then reason had to become a mere instrument to subjugate others.[9] The postmodern theological project is to reaffirm God's truth without abandoning the powers of reason.

With such illustrious (and centrist) figures as the Prince of Wales and Pope John Paul II resorting to postmodernist rhetoric and argumentation, there can be little doubt as to the breadth of change that has occurred in 'the structure of feeling' in the 1980s. Yet there is still abundant confusion as to what the new 'structure of feeling' might entail. Modernist sentiments may have been undermined, deconstructed, surpassed or bypassed, but there is little certitude as to the coherence or meaning of the systems of thought that may have replaced them. Such uncertainty makes it peculiarly difficult to evaluate, interpret and explain the shift that everyone agrees has occurred.

Does postmodernism, for example, represent a radical break with modernism, or is it simply a revolt within modernism against a certain form of 'high modernism' as represented, say, in the architecture of Mies van der Rohe and the blank surfaces of minimalist Abstract Expressionist painting? Is postmodernism a style (in which case we can reasonably trace its precursors back to Dada, Nietzsche, or even, as Kroker and Cook prefer,[10] to St Augustine's *Confessions* in the 4th century) or should we view it strictly as a periodising concept (in which case we debate whether it originated in the 1950s, 1960s or 1970s)? Does it have a revolutionary potential by virtue of its opposition to all forms of metanarratives (including Marxism, Freudianism and all forms of Enlightenment reason) and its close attention to 'other worlds' and to 'other voices' that have for too long been silenced (women, gays, blacks, colonised peoples with their own histories)? Or is it simply the commercialisation and domestication of modernism, and a reduction of the latter's already tarnished aspirations to a *laissez-faire*, 'anything goes' market eclecticism? Does it, therefore, undermine or integrate with neo-conservative politics? And do we attach its rise to some radical restructuring of capitalism, the emergence of some 'post-industrial' society, view it, even, as the 'art of an inflationary era' or as the 'cultural logic of late capitalism' (as Newman and Jameson have proposed)?

We can, I think, begin to get to grips on these difficult questions by casting an eye over the schematic differences between modernism and postmodernism as laid out by Hassan; see Table). Hassan sets up a series of stylistic oppositions in order to capture the ways in which postmodernism might be portrayed as a reaction to the modern. I say 'might' because I think it dangerous (as does Hassan) to depict complex relations as simple polarisations, when almost certainly the true state of sensibility, the real 'structure of feeling' in both the modern and postmodern periods lies in the manner in which these stylistic oppositions are synthesised. Nevertheless, I think Hassan's tabular schema provides a useful starting point.

There is much to contemplate in this schema, drawing as it does on fields as diverse as linguistics, anthropology, philosophy, rhetoric, political science and theology. Hassan is quick to point out how the dichotomies are themselves insecure, equivocal. Yet there is much here that captures a sense of what the differences might be. 'Modernist' town planners, for example, do tend to look for 'mastery' of the metropolis as a 'totality' by deliberately designing a 'closed form', whereas postmodernists tend to view the urban process as uncontrollable and 'chaotic', one in which 'anarchy' and 'change' can 'play' in entirely 'open' situations. 'Modernist' literary critics do tend to look at works as examples of a 'genre' and to judge them by the 'master code' that prevails within the 'boundary' of the genre, whereas the 'postmodern' style is simply to view a work as a 'text' with its own particular 'rhetoric' and 'idiolect', but which can in principle be compared with any other text of no matter what sort. Hassan's oppositions may be caricatures, but there is scarcely an arena of present intellectual practice where we cannot spot some of them at work. In what follows I shall try and take up a few of them in the richer detail they deserve.

I begin with what appears to be the most startling fact about postmodernism: its total acceptance of the ephemerality, fragmentation, discontinuity and the chaotic that formed the one half of Baudelaire's conception of modernity. But postmodernism responds to the fact of that in a very particular way. It does not try to transcend it, counteract it, or even to define the 'eternal and immutable' elements that might lie within it. Postmodernism swims, even wallows, in the fragmentary and the chaotic currents of change as that is all there is. Foucault instructs us, for example, to 'develop action, thought, and desires by proliferation, juxtaposition, and disjunction', and 'to prefer what is positive and multiple, difference over uniformity, flows over unities, mobile arrangements over systems. Believe that what is production is not sedentary but nomadic.' To the degree that it does try to legitimate itself by reference to the past, therefore, postmodernism typically harks back to that wing of thought, Nietzsche in particular, that emphasises the deep chaos of modern life and its intractability before rational thought. This does not imply, however, that postmodernism is simply a version of modernism; real revolutions in sensibility can occur when latent and dominated ideas in one period become explicit and dominant in another. Nevertheless, the continuity of the condition of fragmentation, ephemerality, discontinuity and chaotic change in both modernist and postmodernist thought is important. I shall make much of it in what follows.

TABLE
Schematic Differences Between Modernism and Postmodernism

modernism	postmodernism
Romanticism/Symbolism	paraphysics/Dadaism
form (conjunctive, closed)	anti-form (disjunctive, open)
purpose	play
design	chance
hierarchy	anarchy
mastery/logos	exhaustion/silence
art object/finished work	process/performance/happening
distance	participation
creation/totalisation/synthesis	decreation/deconstruction/antithesis
presence	absence
centring	dispersal
genre/boundary	text/intertext
semantics	rhetoric
paradigm	syntagm
hypotaxis	parataxis
metaphor	metonymy
selection	combination
root/depth	rhizome/surface
interpretation/reading	against interpretation/misreading
signified	signifier
lisible (readerly)	scriptable (writable)
narrative/*grande histoire*	anti-narrative/*petite histoire*
master code	idiolect
symptom	desire
type	mutant
genital/phallic	polymorphous/androgynous
paranoia	schizophrenia
origin/cause	difference-difference/trace
God the Father	The Holy Ghost
metaphysics	irony
determinacy	indeterminacy
transcendence	immanence

Source: Ihab Hassan, *Paracriticisms: Seven Speculations of the Times*, Urbana, IL, 1985, pp 123–4

Embracing the fragmentation and ephemerality in an affirmative fashion implies a whole host of consequences that bear directly on Hassan's oppositions. To begin with, we find writers like Foucault and Lyotard explicitly attacking any notion that there might be a metalanguage, metanarrative or metatheory through which all things can be connected or represented. Universal and eternal truths, if they exist at all, cannot be specified. Condemning metanarratives (broad interpretative schemes like those deployed by Marx or Freud) as 'totalising', they insist upon the plurality of 'power-discourse' formations (Foucault), or of 'language games' (Lyotard). Lyotard in fact defines the postmodern simply as 'incredulity towards metanarratives'.

Foucault's ideas – particularly as developed in his early works – deserve attention since they have been a fecund source for postmodernist argument. The relation between power and knowledge is there a central theme. But Foucault breaks with the notion that power is ultimately located within the state, and abjures us to 'conduct an *ascending* analysis of power, starting that is from its infinitesimal mechanisms, which each have their own history, their own trajectory, their own techniques and tactics, and then see how these mechanisms of power have been – and continue to be – invested, colonised, utilised, involuted, transformed, displaced, extended, etc by ever more general mechanisms and by forms of global domination.'[11] Close scrutiny of the micropolitics of power relations in different localities, contexts and social situations leads him to conclude that there is an intimate relation between the systems of knowledge ('discourses') which codify techniques and practices for the exercise of social control and domination within particular localised contexts. The prison, the asylum, the hospital, the university, the school, the psychiatrist's office, are all examples of sites where a dispersed and piecemeal organisation of power is built up independently of any systematic strategy of class domination. What happens at each site cannot be understood by appeal to some overarching general theory. Indeed the only irreducible in Foucault's scheme of things is the human body, for that is the 'site' at which all forms of repression are ultimately registered. So while there are, in Foucault's celebrated dictum, 'no relations of power without resistances' he equally insists that no utopian scheme can ever hope to escape the power-knowledge relation in nonrepressive ways. He here echoes Max Weber's pessimism as to our ability to avoid the 'iron cage' of repressive bureaucratic-technical rationality. More particularly, he interprets Soviet repression as the inevitable outcome of a utopian revolutionary theory (Marxism) which appealed to the same techniques and knowledge systems as those embedded in the capitalist system it sought to replace. The only way open to 'eliminate the fascism in our heads' is to explore and build upon the open qualities of human discourse, and thereby intervene in the way knowledge is produced and constituted at the particular sites where a localised power-discourse prevails. Foucault's work with homosexuals and prisoners was not aimed at producing reforms in state practices, but dedicated to the cultivation and enhancement of localised resistance to the institutions, techniques and discourses of organised repression.

Foucault evidently believed that it was only through such a multifaceted and pluralistic attack upon localised practices of repression that any global challenge to capitalism might be mounted without replicating all the multiple repressions of capitalism in a new form.

His ideas appeal to the various social movements that sprang into existence during the 1960s (feminists, gays, ethnic and religious groupings, regional autonomists, etc) as well as to those disillusioned with the practices of communism and the politics of communist parties. Yet it leaves open, particularly so in the deliberate rejection of any holistic theory of capitalism, the question of the path whereby such localised struggles might add up to a progressive, rather than regressive, attack upon the central forms of capitalist exploitation and repression. Localised struggles of the sort that Foucault appears to encourage have not generally had the effect of challenging capitalism, though Foucault might reasonably respond that only struggles fought in such a way as to challenge all forms of power-discourse might have such a result.

Lyotard, for his part, puts a similar argument, though on a rather different basis. He takes the modernist preoccupation with language and pushes it to extremes of dispersal. While 'the social bond is linguistic,' he argues, it 'is not woven with a single thread' but by an 'indeterminate number' of 'language games'. Each of us lives 'at the intersection of many of these' and we do not necessarily establish 'stable language combinations and the properties of the ones we do establish are not necessarily communicable'. As a consequence, 'the social subject itself seems to dissolve in this dissemination of language games'. Interestingly, Lyotard here employs a lengthy metaphor of Wittgenstein's (the pioneer of the theory of language games), to illuminate the condition of postmodern knowledge: 'Our language can be seen as an ancient city; a maze of little streets and squares, of old and new houses, and of houses with additions from different periods; and this surrounded by a multitude of new boroughs with straight regular streets and uniform houses.'

The 'atomisation of the social into flexible networks of language games' suggests that each of us may resort to a quite different set of codes depending upon the situation in which we find ourselves (at home, at work, at church, in the street or pub, at a memorial service, etc). To the degree that Lyotard (like Foucault) accepts that 'knowledge is the principal force of production' these days, so the problem is to define the locus of that power when it is evidently 'dispersed in clouds of narrative elements' within a heterogeneity of language games. Lyotard (again like Foucault) accepts the potential open qualities of ordinary conversations in which rules can bend and shift so as 'to encourage the greatest flexibility of utterance'. He makes much of the seeming contradiction between this openness and the rigidities with which institutions (Foucault's 'non-discursive domains') circumscribe what is or is not admissible within their boundaries. The realms of law, of the academy, of science and bureaucratic government, of military and political control, of electoral politics and corporate power, all circumscribe what can be said and how it can be said in important ways. But the 'limits the institution imposes on potential language "moves" are never established one and for all', they are 'themselves the stakes and provisional results of language strategies, within the institution and without'. We ought not, therefore, to reify institutions prematurely, but to recognise how the differentiated performance of language games creates institutional languages and powers in the first place. If 'there are many different language games – a heterogeneity of elements' we have then also to recognise that they can 'only give rise to institutions in patches – local determinism'.

Such 'local determinisms' have been understood by others[12] as 'interpretative communities', made up of both producers and consumers of particular kinds of knowledge, of texts, often operating within a particular institutional context (such as the university, the legal system, religious groupings), within particular divisions of cultural labour (such as architecture, painting, theatre, dance) or within particular places (neighbourhoods, nations, etc). Individuals and groups are held to control mutually within these domains what they consider to be valid knowledge.

To the degree that multiple sources of oppression in society and multiple foci of resistance to domination can be identified, so this kind of thinking has been taken up in radical politics, even imported into the heart of Marxism itself. We thus find Aronowitz arguing in *The Crisis of Historical Materialism* that 'the multiple, local, autonomous struggles for liberation occurring throughout the postmodern world make all incarnations of master discourses absolutely illegitimate'.[13] Aronowitz is here seduced, I suspect, by the most liberative and therefore most appealing aspect of postmodern thought – its concern with 'otherness'. Huyssen (1984) particularly castigates the imperialism of an enlightened modernity that presumed to speak for others (colonised peoples, blacks and minorities, religious groups, women, the working class) with a unified voice. The very title of Carol Gilligan's *In a Different Voice* – a feminist work which challenges the male bias in setting out fixed stages in the moral development of personality – illustrates a process of counterattack upon such universalising presumptions.[14] The idea that all groups have a right to speak for themselves, in their own voice, and have that voice accepted as authentic and legitimate is essential to the pluralistic stance of postmodernism. Foucault's work with marginal and interstitial groups has influenced a whole host of researchers, in fields as diverse as criminology and anthropology, into new ways to reconstruct and represent the voices and experiences of their subjects. Huyssen, for his part, emphasises the opening given in postmodernism to understanding difference and otherness, as well as the liberatory potential it offers for a whole host of new social movements (women, gays, blacks, ecologists, regional autonomists, etc). Curiously, most movements of this sort, though they have definitely helped change 'the structure of feeling', pay scant attention to postmodernist arguments, and some feminists are hostile ... [15]

Interestingly, we can detect this same preoccupation with 'otherness' and 'other worlds' in postmodernist fiction. McHale, in emphasising the pluralism of worlds that coexist within postmodernist fiction, finds Foucault's concept of a heterotopia a perfectly appropriate image to capture what that fiction is striving to depict. By heterotopia, Foucault means the coexistence in 'an impossible space' of a 'large number of fragmentary possible words' or, more simply, juxtaposed or superimposed upon each other. Characters no longer contemplate how they can unravel or unmask a central mystery, but are forced to ask, 'Which world is this? What is to be done in it? Which of myselves is to do it?' instead. The same shift can be detected in the cinema. In a modernist classic like *Citizen Kane* a reporter seeks to unravel the mystery of Kane's life and character by collecting multiple reminiscences and perspectives from those who had known him. In a more postmodernist format of the contemporary cinema we find, in a film like *Blue Velvet*, the central character revolving between two quite incongruous worlds – that of a conventional 1950s small-town America with its high school, drugstore culture, and a bizarre, violent, sex-crazed underworld of drugs, dementia and sexual perversion. It seems impossible that these two worlds should exist in the same space, and the central character moves between them, unsure which is the true reality, until the two worlds collide in a terrible denouement. A postmodernist painter like David Salle likewise tends to 'collage together incompatible source materials as an alternative to choosing between them'.[16] Pfeil even goes so far as to depict the total field of postmodernism as 'a distilled representation of the whole antagonistic, voracious world of otherness.'[17]

But to accept the fragmentation, the pluralism and the authenticity of other voices and other worlds poses the acute problem of communication and the means of exercising power through command thereof. Most postmodernist thinkers are fascinated by the new possibilities for information and knowledge production, analysis and transfer. Lyotard for example, firmly locates his arguments in the context of new technologies of communication and, drawing upon Bell's and Touraine's theses of the passage to a 'post-industrial' information-based society, situates the rise of postmodern thought in the heart of what he sees as a dramatic social and political transition in the languages of communication in advanced capitalist societies.[18] He looks closely at the new technologies for the production, dissemination and use of that knowledge as a 'principal force of production'. The problem, however, is that knowledge can now be coded in all kinds of ways, some of which are more accessible than others. There is more than a hint in Lyotard's work, therefore, that modernism has changed because the technical and social conditions of communication have changed.

Postmodernists tend to accept, also, a rather different theory as to what language and communication are all about. Whereas modernists had presupposed that there was a tight and identifiable relation between what was being said (the signified or 'message') and how it was being said (the signifier or 'medium'), poststructuralist thinking sees these as 'continually breaking apart and re-attaching in new combinations'. 'Deconstructionism' (a movement initiated by Derrida's reading of Martin Heidegger in the late 1960s) here enters the picture as a powerful stimulus to postmodernist ways of thought. Deconstructionism is less a philosophical position than a way of thinking about and 'reading' texts. Writers who create texts or use words do so on the basis of other texts and words they have encountered, while readers deal with them in the same way. Cultural life is then viewed as a series of texts intersecting with other texts, producing more texts (including that of the literary critic, who aims to produce another piece of literature in which texts under consideration are intersecting freely with other texts that happen to have affected his or her thinking). This intertextual weaving has a life of its own. Whatever we write conveys meanings we do not or could not possibly intend, and our words cannot say what we mean. It is vain to try and master a text because the perpetual interweaving of texts and meanings is beyond our control. Language works through us. Recognising that, the Deconstructionist impulse is to look inside one text for another, dissolve one text into another, or build one text into another.

Derrida considers, therefore, collage/montage as the primary form of postmodern discourse. The inherent heterogeneity of that (be it in painting, writing, architecture) stimulates us, the receivers of the text or image, 'to produce a signification which could be neither univocal nor stable'. Both producers and consumers of 'texts' (cultural artefacts) participate in the production of significations and meanings (hence Hassan's emphasis upon 'process', 'performance', 'happening' and 'participation' in the postmodernist style). Minimising the authority of the cultural producer creates the opportunity for popular participation and democratic determinations of cultural values, but at the price of a certain incoherence or, more problematic, vulnerability to mass-market manipulation. However this may be, the cultural producer merely creates raw materials (fragments and elements), leaving it open to consumers to recombine those elements in any way they wish. The effect is to break (deconstruct) the power of the author to impose meanings or offer a continuous narrative. Each cited element says Derrida, 'breaks the continuity or the linearity of discourse and leads necessarily to a double reading: that of the fragment perceived in relation to its text of origin; that of the fragment as incorporated into a new whole, a different totality'. Continuity is given only in 'the trace' of the fragment as it moves from production to consumption. The effect is to call into question all the illusions of fixed systems of representation.[19]

There is more than a hint of this sort of thinking within the modernist tradition (directly from Surrealism, for example) and there is a danger here of thinking of the metanarratives in the Enlightenment tradition as more fixed and stable than they truly were. Marx, as Ollman observes,[20] deployed his concepts relationally, so that terms like value, labour, capital, are 'continually breaking apart and re-attaching in new combinations' in an open-ended struggle to come to terms with the totalising processes of capitalism. Benjamin, a complex thinker in the Marxist tradition, worked the idea of collage/montage to perfection, in order to try and capture the many-layered and fragmented relations between economy, politics and culture without ever abandoning the standpoint of a totality of practices that constitute capitalism. Taylor likewise concludes, after reviewing the historical evidence of its use (particularly by Picasso), that collage is a far from adequate indicator of difference between modernist and postmodernist painting.[21]

But if, as the postmodernists insist, we cannot aspire to any unified representation of the world, or picture it as a totality full of connections and differentiations rather than as perpetually shifting fragments, then how can we possibly aspire to act coherently with respect to the world? The simple postmodernist answer is that since coherent representation and action are either repressive or illusionary (and therefore doomed to be self-dissolving and self-defeating), we should not even try to engage in some global project. Pragmatism (of the Dewey sort) then becomes the only possible philosophy of action. We thus find Rorty, one of the major US philosophers in the postmodern movement, dismissing 'the canonical sequence of philosophers from Descartes to Nietzsche as a distraction from the history of concrete social engineering which made the contemporary North American culture what it is now, with all its glories and all its dangers'.[22] Action can be conceived of and decided only within the confines of some local determinism, some interpretative community, and its purported meanings and anticipated effects are bound to break down when taken out of these isolated domains, even when coherent within them. We similarly find Lyotard arguing that 'consensus has become an outmoded and suspect value' but then adding, rather surprisingly, that since 'justice as a value is nether outmoded nor suspect' (how it could remain such a universal, untouched by the diversity of language games, he does not tell us), we 'must arrive at an idea and practice of justice that is not linked to that of consensus'.[23]

It is precisely this kind of relativism and defeatism that Habermas seeks to combat in his defence of the Enlightenment project. While Habermas is more than willing to admit what he calls 'the deformed realisation of reason in history' and the dangers that attach to the simplified imposition of some metanarrative on complex relations and events, he also insists that 'theory can locate a gentle, but obstinate, a never silent although seldom redeemed claim to reason, a claim that must be recognised de facto whenever and wherever there is to be consensual action'. He, too, turns to the question of language, and in *The Theory of Communicative Action* insists upon the dialogical qualities of human communication in which speaker and hearer are necessarily oriented to the task of reciprocal understanding. Out of this, Habermas argues, consensual and normative statements do arise, thus grounding the role of universalising reason in daily life. It is this that allows 'communication reason' to operate 'in history as an avenging force'. Habermas's critics are, however, more numerous than his defenders.

The portrait of postmodernism I have so far sketched in seems to depend for its validity upon a particular way of experiencing, interpreting and being in the world. This brings us to what is, perhaps, the most problematic facet of postmodernism, its psychological presuppositions with respect to personality, motivation and behaviour. Preoccupation with the fragmentation and instability of language and discourse carries over directly, for example, into a certain conception of personality. Encapsulated, this conception focuses on schizophrenia (not, it should be emphasised, in its narrow clinical sense), rather than on alienation and paranoia (see Hassan's schema). Jameson explores this theme to very telling effect. He uses Lacan's description of schizophrenia as a linguistic disorder, as a breakdown in the signifying chain of meaning that creates a simple sentence. When the signifying chain snaps, then 'we have schizophrenia in the form of a rubble of distinct and unrelated signifiers'. If personal identity is forged through 'a certain temporal unification of the past and future with the present before me', and if sentences move through the same trajectory, then an inability to unify past, present and future in the sentence betokens a similar inability to 'unify the past, present, and future of our own biographical experience or psychic life'. This fits, of course, with postmodernism's preoccupation with the signifier rather than the signified, with participation, performance and happening rather than with an authoritative and finished art object, with surface appearances rather than roots (again, see Hassan's schema). The effect of such a breakdown in the signifying chain is to reduce experience to 'a series of pure and unrelated presents in time'. Offering no counterweight, Derrida's conception of language colludes in the production of a certain schizophrenic effect, thus, perhaps, explaining Eagleton's and Hassan's characterisation of the typical postmodernist artefact as schizoid. Deleuze and Guattari,[24] in their supposedly playful exposition *Anti-Oedipus*, hypothesise a relationship between schizophrenia and capitalism that prevails 'at the deepest level of one and the same economy, one and the same production process', concluding that 'our society produces schizos the same way it produces Prell shampoo or Ford cars, the only difference being that the schizos are not saleable'.

A number of consequences follow from the domination of this motif in postmodernist thought. We can no longer conceive of the individual as alienated in the classical Marxist sense, because to be alienated presupposes a coherent rather than a fragmented sense of self from which to be alienated. It is only in terms of such a centred sense of personal identity that individuals can pursue projects over time, or think cogently about the production of a future significantly better than time present and time past. Modernism was very much about the pursuit of better futures, even if perpetual frustration of that aim was conducive to paranoia. But postmodernism typically strips away that possibility by concentrating upon the schizophrenic circumstances induced by fragmentation and all those instabilities (including those of language) that prevent us even picturing coherently, let alone devising strategies to produce some radically different future. Modernism, of course, was not without its schizoid moments – particularly when it sought to combine myth with heroic modernity – and there has been a sufficient history of the 'deformation of reason' and of 'reactionary modernisms' to suggest that the schizophrenic circumstance, though for the most part dominated, was always latent within the modernist movement. Nevertheless, there is good reason to believe that 'alienation of the subject is displaced by fragmentation of the subject' in postmodern aesthetics.[25] If, as Marx insisted, it takes the alienated individual to pursue the Enlightenment project with a tenacity and coherence sufficient to bring us to some better future, then loss of the alienated subject would seem to preclude the conscious construction of alternative social futures.

The reduction of experience to 'a pure and unrelated present' further implies that the 'experience of the present becomes powerfully, overwhelmingly vivid and "material": the world comes before the schizophrenic with heightened intensity, bearing the mysterious and oppressive charge of affect, glowing with hallucinatory energy'.[26] The image, the appearance, the spectacle can all be experienced with an intensity (joy or terror) made possible only by their appreciation as pure and unrelated presents in time. So what does it matter 'if the world thereby momentarily loses its depth and threatens to become a glossy skin, a stereoscopic illusion, a rush of filmic images without density?'[27] The immediacy of events, the sensationalism of the spectacle (political, scientific, military, as well as those of entertainment), become the stuff of which consciousness is forged.

Such a breakdown of the temporal order of things also gives rise to a peculiar treatment of the past. Eschewing the idea of progress, postmodernism abandons all sense of historical continuity and memory, while simultaneously developing an incredible ability to plunder history and absorb whatever it finds there as some aspect of the present. Postmodernist architecture, for example, takes bits and pieces from the past quite eclectically and mixes them together at will. Another example, taken from painting, is given by Crimp.[28] Manet's *Olympia*, one of the seminal paintings of the early modernist movement, was modelled on Titian's *Venus*. But the manner of its modelling signalled a self-conscious break between modernity and tradition, and the active intervention of the artist in that transition.[29] Rauschenberg, one of the pioneers of the postmodernist movement, deployed images of Velazquez's *Rokeby Venus* and Rubens's *Venus at her Toilet* in a series of paintings in the 1960s. But he uses these images in a very different way, simply silk-screening a photographic original onto a surface that contains all kinds of other features (trucks, helicopters, car keys). Rauschenberg simply *reproduces*, whereas Manet *produces*, and it is this move, says Crimp, 'that requires us to think of Rauschenberg as a post-modernist'. The modernist 'aura' of the artist as producer is dispensed with. 'The fiction of the creating subject gives way to frank confiscation, quotation, excerption, accumulation and repetition of already existing images.'

This sort of shift carries over into all other fields with powerful implications. Given the evaporation of any sense of historical continuity and memory, and the rejection of metanarratives, the only role left for the historian, for example, is to become, as Foucault insisted, an archaeologist of the past, digging up its remnants as Borges does in his fiction, and assembling them, side by side, in the museum of modern knowledge. Rorty, in attacking the idea that philosophy can ever hope to define some permanent epistemological framework for enquiry, likewise ends up insisting that the only role of the philosopher, in the midst of the cacophony of cross-cutting conversations that comprise a culture, is to 'decry the notion of having a view while avoiding having a view about having views'.[30] 'The essential trope of fiction', we are told by the post-modernist writers of it, is a 'technique that requires suspension of belief as well as of disbelief'.[31] There is in postmodernism, little overt attempt to sustain continuity of values, beliefs or even disbeliefs.

This loss of historical continuity in values and beliefs, taken together with the reduction of the work of art to a text stressing discontinuity and allegory, poses all kinds of problems for aesthetic and critical judgement. Refusing (and actively 'deconstructing') all authoritative or supposedly immutable standards of aesthetic judgment, postmodernism can judge the spectacle only in terms of how spectacular it is. Barthes proposes a particularly sophisticated version of that strategy. He distinguishes between *pleasure* and *'jouissance'* (perhaps best translated as 'sublime physical and mental bliss') and suggests we strive to realise the second, more orgasmic effect (note the connection to Jameson's description of schizophrenia) through a particular mode of encounter with the otherwise lifeless cultural artefacts that litter our social landscape. Since most of us are not schizoid in the clinical sense, Barthes defines a kind of 'mandarin practice' that allows us to achieve *'jouissance'* and to use that experience as a basis for aesthetic and critical judgements. This means identification with the act of writing (creation) rather than reading (reception). Huyssen reserves his sharpest irony for Barthes, however, arguing that he reinstitutes one of the tiredest modernist and bourgeois distinctions: that 'there are lower pleasures for the rabble, ie mass culture, and then there is *nouvelle cuisine* of the pleasure of the text, *jouissance'*.[32] This reintroduction of the highbrow/lowbrow disjunction avoids the whole problem of the potential debasement of modern cultural forms by their assimilation to Pop culture through Pop art. 'The euphoric American appropriation of Barthes's *jouissance* is predicated on ignoring such problems and on enjoying, not unlike the 1984 yuppies, the pleasures of writerly connoisseurism and textual gentrification. Huyssen's image, as Raban's descriptions in *Soft City* suggest, may be more than a little appropriate.

The other side to the loss of temporality and the search for instantaneous impact is a parallel loss of depth. Jameson has been particularly emphatic as to the 'depthlessness' of much of contemporary cultural production, its fixation with appearances, surfaces and instant impacts that have no sustaining power over time.[33] The image sequences of Sherman's photographs are of exactly that quality, and as Charles Newman remarked in a *New York Times* review on the state of the American novel (17 July 1987):

> The fact of the matter is that a sense of diminishing control, loss of individual autonomy and generalised helplessness has never been so instantaneously recognisable in our literature – the flattest possible characters in the flattest possible landscapes rendered in the flattest possible diction. The presumption seems to be that America is a vast fibrous desert in which a few laconic weeds nevertheless manage to sprout in the cracks.

'Contrived depthlessness' is how Jameson describes postmodern architecture, and it is hard not to give credence to this sensibility as *the* overwhelming motif in postmodernism, offset only by Barthes's attempts to help us to the moment of *jouissance*. Attention to surfaces has, of course, always been important to modernist thought and practice (particularly since the Cubists), but it has always been paralleled by the kind of question that Raban posed about urban life: how can we build, represent and attend to these surfaces with the requisite sympathy and seriousness in order to get behind them and identify essential meanings? Postmodernism, with its resignation to bottomless fragmentation and ephemerality, generally refuses to contemplate that question.

The collapse of time horizons and the preoccupation with instantaneity have in part arisen through the contemporary emphasis in cultural production on events, spectacles, happenings and media images. Cultural producers have learned to explore and use new technologies, the media and ultimately multimedia possibilities. The effect, however, has been to re-emphasise the fleeting qualities of modern life and even to celebrate them. But it has also permitted a *rapprochement*, in spite of Barthes's interventions, between popular culture and what once remained isolated as 'high culture'. Such a *rapprochement* has been sought before, though nearly always in a more revolutionary mode, as movements like Dada and early Surrealism, Constructivism and Expressionism tried to bring their art to the people as part and parcel of a modernist project of social transformation. Such avant-gardist movements possessed a strong faith in their own aims as well as immense faith in new technologies. The closing of the gap between popular culture and cultural production in the contemporary period, while strongly dependent on new technologies of communication, seems to lack any avant-gardist or revolutionary impulse, leading many to accuse postmodernism of a simple and direct surrender to commodification, commercialisation and the market.[34] However this may be, much of postmodernism is consciously anti-auratic and anti-avant-garde and seeks to explore media and cultural arenas open to all. It is no accident that Sherman, for example, uses photography and evokes Pop images as if from film stills in the poses she assumes.

This raises the most difficult of all questions about the postmodern movement, namely its relationship with, and integration into, the culture of daily life. Although much of the discussion of it proceeds in the abstract, and therefore in the not very accessible terms that I have been forced to use here, there are innumerable points of contact between producers of cultural artefacts and the public: architecture, advertising, fashion, films, staging of multimedia events, grand spectacles, political campaigns, as well as the ubiquitous television. It is not always clear who is influencing whom in this process.

Venturi et al recommend that we learn our architectural aesthetics from the Las Vegas strip or from much-maligned suburbs like Levittown, simply because people evidently like such environments.[35] 'One does not have to agree with hard hat politics,' they go on to say, 'to support the rights of the middle-middle class to their own architectural aesthetics, and we have found that Levittown-type aesthetics are shared by most members of the middle-middle class, black as well as white, liberal as well as conservative.' There is absolutely nothing wrong, they insist, with giving people what they want, and Venturi himself was even quoted in *The New York Times* (22 October 1972), in an article fittingly entitled 'Mickey Mouse Teaches the Architects', saying 'Disney World is nearer to what people want than what architects have ever given them'. Disneyland, he asserts, is 'the symbolic American utopia'.

There are those, however, who see such a concession of high culture to Disneyland aesthetics as a matter of necessity rather than choice. Daniel Bell, for example, depicts postmodernism as the exhaustion of modernism through the institutionalisation of creative and rebellious impulses by what he calls 'the cultural mass' (the millions of people working in broadcast media, films, theatre, universities, publishing houses, advertising and communications industries, etc who process and influence the reception of serious cultural products and produce the popular materials for the wider mass-culture audience).[36] The degeneration of highbrow authority over cultural taste in the 1960s, and its replacement by Pop art, Pop culture, ephemeral fashion and mass taste is seen as a sign of the mindless hedonism of capitalist consumerism.

Iain Chambers interprets a similar process rather differently.[37] Working-class youth in Britain found enough money in their pockets during the postwar boom to participate in the capitalist consumer culture, and actively used fashion to construct a sense of their own public identities, even defined their own Pop-art forms, in the face of a fashion industry that sought to impose taste through advertising and media pressures. The consequent democratisation of taste across a variety of subcultures (from inner-city macho male to college campuses) is interpreted as the outcome of a vital struggle that pitched the rights of even the relatively underprivileged to shape their own identities in the face of a powerfully organised commercialism. The urban-based cultural ferments that began in the early 1960s and continue to this very day lie, in Chambers's view at the root of the postmodern turn:

Post modernism, whatever form its intellectualising might take, has been fundamentally anticipated in the metropolitan cultures of the last twenty years: among the electronic signifiers of cinema, television and video, in recording studios and record players, in fashion and youth styles, in all those sounds, images and diverse histories that are daily mixed, recycled and 'scratched' together on that giant screen which is the contemporary city.

It is hard, also, not to attribute some kind of shaping role to the proliferation of television use. After all, the average American is now reputed to watch television for more than seven hours a day, and television and video ownership (the latter now covering at least half all US households) is now so widespread throughout the capitalist world that some effects must surely be registered. Postmodernist concerns with surface, for example, can be traced to the necessary format of television images. Television is also, as Taylor points out, 'the first cultural medium in the whole of history to present the artistic achievements of the past as a stitched-together collage of equi-important and simultaneously existing phenomena, largely divorced from geography and material history and transported to the living rooms and studios of the West in a more or less uninterrupted flow.'[38] It posits a viewer, furthermore, 'who shares the medium's own perception of history as an endless reserve of equal events'. It is hardly surprising that the artist's relation to history (the peculiar historicism we have already noted) has shifted, that in the era of mass television there has emerged an attachment to surfaces rather than roots, to collage rather than in-depth work, to superimposed quoted images rather than worked surfaces, to a collapsed sense of time and space rather than solidly achieved cultural artefact. And these are all vital aspects of artistic practice in the postmodern condition.

To point to the potency of such a force in shaping culture as a total way of life is not necessarily to lapse, however, into a simple-minded technological determinism of the 'television causes post-modernism' variety. For television is itself a product of late capitalism and, as such, has to be seen in the context of the promotion of a culture of consumerism. This directs our attention to the production of needs and wants, the mobilisation of desire and fantasy, of the politics of distraction as part and parcel of the push to sustain sufficient buoyancy of demand in consumer markets to keep capitalist production profitable. Charles Newman sees much of the postmodernist aesthetic as a response to the inflationary surge of late capitalism.[39] 'Inflation,' he argues, 'affects the ideas exchange just as surely as it does commercial markets.' Thus 'we are witness to continual internecine warfare and spasmodic change in fashion, the simultaneous display of all past styles in their infinite mutations, and the continuous circulation of diverse and contradictory intellectual elites, which signal the reign of the cult of creativity in all areas of behaviours, an unprecedented non-judgmental receptivity to Art, a tolerance which finally amounts to indifference.' From this standpoint, Newman concludes, 'the vaunted fragmentation of art is no longer an aesthetic choice: it is simply a cultural aspect of the economic and social fabric'.

This would certainly go some way to explain the postmodernist thrust to integrate into popular culture though the kind of frank, even crass, commercialisation that modernists tended to eschew by their deep resistance to the idea (though never quite the fact) of commodification of their production. There are those however, who attribute the exhaustion of high modernism precisely to its absorption as the formal aesthetics of corporate capitalism and the bureaucratic state. Postmodernism then signals nothing more than a logical extension of the power of the market over the whole range of cultural production. Crimp waxes quite acerbic on this point:

> What we have seen in the last several years is the virtual takeover of art by big corporate interests. For whatever role capital played in the art of modernism, the current phenomenon is new precisely because of its scope. Corporations have become the major patrons of art in every respect. They form huge collections. They fund every major museum exhibition. ... Auction houses have become lending institutions, giving a completely new value to art as collateral. And all of this affects not only the inflation of value of old masters but art production itself. ... [The corporations] are buying cheap and in quantity, counting on the escalation of the value of young artists. ... The return to painting and sculpture of a traditional cast is the return to commodity production, and I would suggest that, whereas traditionally art had an ambiguous commodity status, it now has a thoroughly unambiguous one.[40]

The growth of a museum culture (in Britain a museum opens every three weeks, and in Japan over 500 have opened up in the last 15 years) and a burgeoning 'heritage industry' that took off in the early 1970s, add another populist (though this time very middle class) twist to the commercialisation of history and cultural forms. 'Post-modernism and the heritage industry are linked', says Hewison, since 'both conspire to create a shallow screen that intervenes between our present lives and our history.'[41] History becomes a 'contemporary creation, more costume drama and re-enactment than critical discourse'. We are, he concludes, quoting Jameson, condemned to seek History by way of our own Pop images and simulacra of that history which itself remains for ever out of reach. 'The house is viewed no longer as a machine but as an antique for living in.'

The invocation of Jameson brings us, finally, to his daring thesis that postmodernism is nothing more than the cultural logic of late capitalism. Following Mandel, he argues that we have moved into a new era since the early 1960s in which the production of culture 'has become integrated into commodity production generally: the frantic urgency of producing fresh waves of ever more novel seeming goods (from clothes to airplanes), at ever greater rates of turnover, now assigns an increasingly essential structural function to aesthetic innovation and experimentation.' The struggles that were once exclusively waged in the arena of production have, as a consequence, now spilled outwards to make of cultural production an arena of fierce social conflict. Such a shift entails a definite change in consumer habits and attitudes as well as a new role for aesthetic definitions and interventions. While some would argue that the countercultural movements of the 1960s created an environment of unfulfilled needs and repressed desires that postmodernist popular cultural production has merely set out to satisfy as best it can in commodity form, others would suggest that capitalism, in order to sustain its markets, has been forced to produce desire and so titillate individual sensibilities as to create a new aesthetic over and against traditional forms of high culture. In either case, I think it important to accept the proposition that the cultural evolution which has taken place since the early 1960s, and which asserted itself as hegemonic in the early 1970s, has not occurred in a social, economic or political vacuum. The deployment of advertising as 'the official art of capitalism' brings advertising strategies into art, and art into advertising strategies. It is interesting, therefore, to ruminate upon the stylistic shift that Hassan sets up in relation to the forces that emanate from mass-consumer culture: the mobilisation of fashion, Pop art, television and other forms of media image, and the variety of urban lifestyles that have become part and parcel of daily life under capitalism. Whatever else we do with the concept, we should not read postmodernism as some autonomous artistic current. Its rootedness in daily life is one of its most patently transparent features.

The portrait of postmodernism I have here constructed, with the help of Hassan's schema, is certainly incomplete. It is equally certainly rendered fragmentary and ephemeral by the sheer plurality and elusiveness of cultural forms wrapped in the mysteries of rapid flux and change. But I think I have said enough as to what constitute the general frame of that 'profound shift in the structure of feeling' that separates modernity from postmodernity to begin upon the task of unravelling its origins and speculatively constructing an interpretation of what it might betoken for our future.

Notes

1   C Jencks, *The Language of Post-Modern Architecture* (London), 1984.
2   T Eagleton, 'Awakening from Modernity', *Times Literary Supplement*, 20 February 1987.
3   *PRECIS* 6, *The Culture of Fragments*, Columbia University Graduate School of Architecture (New York), 1987.
4   Eg Richard Rorty, *Philosophy and the Mirror of Nature* (Princeton, NJ), 1979.
5   T Kuhn, *The Structure of Scientific Revolutions* (Chicago), 1962; P Feyerabend, *Against Method* (London), 1975.
6   A Huyssen, 'Mapping the Post-Modern', *New German Critique* 33, pp 5–52.
7   B McHale, *Postmodernist Fiction* (London), 1987.
8   R Bernstein (ed), *Habermas and Modernity* (Oxford), 1985.
9   *Baltimore Sun*, 9 September 1987.
10   A Kroker and D Cook, *The Postmodern Scene: Excremental Culture and Hyper-Aesthetics* (New York), 1986.
11   M Foucault, *Power/Knowledge* (New York), 1972.
12   Eg S Fish, *Is there a Text in this Class? The Authority of Interpretive Communities* (Cambridge, MA), 1980.
13   P Bove, 'The Ineluctability of Difference: Scientific Pluralism and the Critical Intelligence', *Postmodernism and Politics*, ed J Arac (Manchester), 1986, p 18.
14   C Gilligan, *In a Different Voice: Psychological Theory and Women's Development* (Cambridge, MA), 1982.
15   Eg N Hartsock, 'Rethinking Modernism: Minority Versus Majority Theories', *Cultural Critique* 7, 1987, pp 187–206.
16   B Taylor, *Modernism, Postmodernism, Realism: A Critical Perspective for Art* (Winchester), 1987.
17   F Pfeil, 'Postmodernism as a "Structure of Feeling"', *Marxism and the Interpretation of Culture*, eds C Nelson and L Grossberg (Urbana, IL), 1988.
18   J-F Lyotard, *The Postmodern Condition* (Manchester), 1984.

19 H Foster (ed), *The Anti-Aesthetic: Essays on Postmodern Culture* (Port Townsend, WA), 1983.
20 B Ollman, *Alienation* (Cambridge), 1971.
21 B Taylor, *Modernism, Postmodernism, Realism,* pp 53–65.
22 R Rorty, 'Habermas and Lyotard on Postmodernity', *Habermas and Modernity*, ed Bernstein, p 173.
23 J-F Lyotard, *The Postmodern Condition* (Manchester), 1984, p 66.
24 G Deleuze and F Guattari, *Anti-Oedipus: Capitalism and Schizophrenia* (London), 1984.
25 F Jameson, 'The Politics of Theory: Ideological Positions in the Post-Modernism Debate', *New German Critique* 33, p 120.
26 F Jameson, 'Postmodernism and the Cultural Logic of Late Capitalism', *New Left Review* 146, 1984, p 120.
27 Ibid.
28 D Crimp, 'On the Museum's Ruins', *Anti-Aesthetic*, ed H Foster, pp 44–5.
29 TJ Clark, *The Painting of Modern Life: Paris in the Art of Manet and his Followers* (New York), 1983.
30 R Rorty, *Philosophy and the Mirror of Nature*, p 371.
31 B McHale, *Postmodernist Fiction*, pp 27–33.
32 A Huyssen, 'Mapping the Post-Modern', *New German Critique* 33, pp 38–45.
33 F Jameson, 'Politics of Theory'; idem, 'Cultural Logic'.
34 H Foster, *Recordings: Art, Spectacle, Cultural Politics* (Port Townsend, WA), 1985.
35 R Venturi, D Scott Brown and S Izenour, *Learning from Las Vegas* (Cambridge, MA), 1972.
36 D Bell, *The Cultural Contradictions of Capitalism* (New York), 1978.
37 I Chambers, *Popular Culture: The Metropolitan Experience* (London), 1986; idem, 'Maps for the Metropolis: A Possible Guide to the Present', *Cultural Studies* 1, 1987, pp 1–22.
38 B Taylor, *Modernism, Post-Modernism, Realism,* pp 103–5.
39 C Newman, 'The Postmodern Aura: The Act of Fiction in an Age of Inflation', *Salmagundi* 63–4, 1984, pp 3–199.
40 D Crimp, 'Art in the 80s: The Myth of Autonomy', *PRECIS* 6, p 85.
41 R Hewison, *The Heritage Industry* (London), 1987, p 135.

From David Harvey, *The Condition of Postmodernity*, Basil Blackwell Inc (Cambridge, MA) and Basil Blackwell (Oxford), 1989. © John Wiley & Sons Ltd.

Fordism and Post-Fordism

Robin Murray

> Looking at the changes of the 1980s through the lens of economics, Robin
> Murray explains how in post-industrial society, the production processes of
> Fordism – the large-scale factory system – have been supplemented by post-
> Fordism – the small fast-moving group system networked by computers,
> with designers often the real producers of innovation. Murray asserts that
> important aspects of the post-Fordist system are consumption, flexibility
> and customisation, all of which are achieved through various information
> technologies. For Murray, the consequences of the post-Fordist economy
> include a new type of time management, job insecurity and a wider 'split
> between core and periphery in the labour market and the welfare system'.
> Finally, his text calls for a new solution: we must find a new model for the
> public economy: a decentralised system, an heir of Fordism yet adapted to
> a post-Fordist age.
>
> **Robin Murray (1940–) is an industrial economist. He was educated at Balliol
> College, Oxford, and at the London School of Economics. He joined the
> London Business School, where he lectured in economics, and then moved
> to the Institute of Development Studies, the national centre for the study
> and teaching of development at the University of Sussex, where he was a
> fellow for 20 years.** *LCS*

During the first two centuries of the industrial revolution, the focus of employment
shifted from the farm to the factory. It is now shifting once more, from the factory
to the office and the shop. A third of Britain's paid labour force now works in offices.
A third of the value of national output is in the distribution sector. Meanwhile 2.5
million jobs have been lost in British manufacturing since 1960. If the Ford plants at
Halewood and Dagenham represented late industrialism, Centrepoint and Habitat are
the symbols of a new age.

The Right portrayed the growth of services as a portent of a post-industrial society
with growing individualism, a weakened state and a multiplicity of markets. I want to
argue that it reflects a deeper change in the production process. It is one that affects
manufacturing and agriculture as well as services, and has implications for the way in
which we think about socialist alternatives. I see this as a shift from the dominant form of
20th-century production, known as Fordism, to a new form, post-Fordism.

Fordism is an industrial era whose secret is to be found in the mass-production
systems pioneered by Henry Ford. These systems were based on four principles from
which all else followed:

a) products were standardised; this meant that each part and each task could also be standardised. Unlike craft production – where each part had to be specially designed, made and fitted – for a run of mass-produced cars, the same headlight could be fitted to the same model in the same way.
b) if tasks are the same, then some can be mechanised; thus mass-production plants developed special-purpose machinery for each model, much of which could not be switched from product to product.
c) those tasks which remained were subject to scientific management or Taylorism, whereby any task was broken down into its component parts, redesigned by work-study specialists on time-and-motion principles, who then instructed manual workers on how the job should be done.
d) flowline replaced nodal assembly, so that instead of workers moving to and from the product (the node), the product flowed past the workers.

Ford did not invent these principles. What he did was to combine them in the production of a complex commodity, which undercut craft-made cars as decisively as the handloom weavers had been undercut in the 1830s. Ford's Model T sold for less than a 10th of the price of a craft-built car in the US in 1916, and he took 50 per cent of the market.

This revolutionary production system was to transform sector after sector during the 20th century, from processed food to furniture, clothes, cookers, and even ships after the Second World War. The economies came from the scale of production, for although mass-production might be more costly to set because of the purpose-built machinery, once in place the cost of an extra unit was discontinuously cheap.

Many of the structures of Fordism followed from this tension between high fixed costs and low variable ones, and the consequent drive for volume. First, as Ford himself emphasised, mass-production presupposes mass consumption. Consumers must be willing to buy standardised products. Mass advertising played a central part in establishing a mass consumption norm. So did the provision of the infrastructure of consumption – housing and roads. To ensure that the road system dominated over rail, General Motors, Standard Oil and Firestone Tyres bought up and then dismantled the electric trolley and transit systems in 44 urban areas.

Second, Fordism was linked to a system of protected national markets, which allowed the mass-producers to recoup their fixed costs at home and compete on the basis of marginal costs on the world market, or through the replication of existing models via foreign investment.

Third, mass-producers were particularly vulnerable to sudden falls in demand. Ford unsuccessfully tried to offset the effect of the 1930s depression by raising wages. Instalment credit, Keynesian demand and monetary management, and new wage and welfare systems were all more effective in stabilising the markets for mass-producers in the postwar period. HP and the dole cheque became as much the symbols of the Fordist age as the tower block and the motorway.

The mass-producers not only faced the hazard of changes in consumption. With production concentrated in large factories, they were also vulnerable to the new 'mass worker' they had created. Like Taylorism, mass-production had taken the skill out of work, it fragmented tasks into a set of repetitive movements, and erected a rigid division between mental and manual labour. It treated human beings as interchangeable parts of a machine, paid according to the job they did rather than who they were.

The result was high labour turnover, shop-floor resistance and strikes. The mass-producers in turn sought constant new reservoirs of labour, particularly from groups facing discrimination, from rural areas and from less developed regions abroad. The contractual core of Taylorism – higher wages in return for managerial control of production – still applied, and a system of industrial unions grew up to bargain over these wage levels. In the USA, and to an extent the UK, a national system of wage bargaining developed in the postwar period, centred on high-profile car industry negotiations, that linked wage rises to productivity growth, and then set wage standards for other large-scale producers and the state. It was a system of collective bargaining that has been described as implementing a Keynesian incomes policy without a Keynesian state. As long as the new labour reservoirs could be tapped, it was a system that held together the distinct wage relation of Fordism.

Taylorism was also characteristic of the structure of management and supplier relations. Fordist bureaucracies are fiercely hierarchical with links between the divisions and departments being made through the centre rather than at the base. Planning is done by specialists; rule books and guidelines are issued for lower management to carry out. If you enter a Ford factory in any part of the world, you will find its layout, materials, even the position of its Coca-Cola machines, all similar, set up as they are on the basis of a massive construction manual drawn up in Detroit. Managers themselves complain of de-skilling and the lack of room for initiative, as do suppliers who are confined to producing blueprints at a low margin price.

These threads – of production and consumption, of the semiskilled worker and collective bargaining, of a managed national market and centralised organisation – together make up the fabric of Fordism. They have given rise to an economic culture which extends beyond the complex assembly industries, to agriculture, the service industries and parts of the state. It is marked by its commitment to scale and the standard product (whether it is a Mars Bar or an episode of *Dallas*); by a competitive strategy based on cost reduction; by authoritarian relations, centralised planning and a rigid organisation built round exclusive job descriptions.

These structures and their culture are often equated with industrialism, and regarded as an inevitable part of the modern age. I am suggesting that they are linked to a particular form of industrialism, one that developed in the late 19th century and reached its most dynamic expression in the postwar boom. Its impact can be felt not just in the economy, but in politics (in the mass party) and in much broader cultural fields – whether American football or classical ballet (Diaghilev was a Taylorist in dance), industrial design or modern architecture. The technological hubris of this outlook, its Faustian bargain of dictatorship in production in exchange for mass consumption, and above all its destructiveness in the name of progress and the economy of time, all this places Fordism at the centre of modernism.

Why we need to understand these deep structures of Fordism is that they are embedded, too, in traditional socialist economies. Soviet-type planning is the apogee of Fordism. Lenin embraced Taylor and the stopwatch. Soviet industrialisation was centred on the construction of giant plants, the majority of them based on Western mass-production technology. So deep is the idea of scale burnt into Soviet economies that there is a hairdresser's in Moscow with 120 barbers' chairs. The focus of Soviet production is on volume and because of its lack of consumer discipline it has caricatured certain features of Western mass-production, notably a hoarding of stocks, and inadequate quality control.

In social-democratic thinking, state planning has a more modest place. But in the writings of Fabian economists in the 1930s, as in the Morrisonian model of the public corporation, and Labour's postwar policies, we see the same emphasis on centralist planning, scale, Taylorist technology and hierarchical organisation. The image of planning was the railway timetable, the goal of planning was stable demand and cost reduction. In the welfare state, the idea of the standard product was given a democratic interpretation as the universal service to meet basic needs, and although in Thatcher's Britain this formulation is still important, it effectively forecloses the issue of varied public services and user choice. The shadow of Fordism haunts us even in the terms in which we oppose it.

The Break-Up of Fordism

Fordism as a vision – both left and right – had always been challenged, on the shop floor, in the political party, the seminar room and the studio. In 1968 this challenge exploded in Europe and the USA. It was a cultural as much as an industrial revolt, attacking the central principles of Fordism, its definitions of work and consumption, its shaping of towns and its overriding of nature.

From that time we can see a fracturing of the foundations of predictability on which Fordism was based. Demand became more volatile and fragmented. Productivity growth fell as the result of workplace resistance. The decline in profit drove down investment. Exchange rates were fluctuating, oil prices rose and in 1974 came the greatest slump the West had had since the 1930s.

The consensus response was a Keynesian one, to restore profitability through a managed increase in demand and an incomes policy. For monetarism the route to profitability went through the weakening of labour, a cut in state spending and a reclaiming of the public sector for private accumulation. Economists and politicians were refighting the battles of the last slump. Private capital on the other hand was dealing with the present one. It was using new technology and new production principles to make Fordism flexible, and in doing so stood much of the old culture on its head.

In Britain, the groundwork for the new system was laid not in manufacturing but in retailing. Since the 1950s, retailers had been using computers to transform the distribution system. All mass-producers have the problem of forecasting demand. If they produce too little they lose market share. If they produce too much, they are left with stocks, which are costly to hold, or have to be sold at a discount. Retailers face this problem not just for a few products, but for thousands. Their answer has been to develop information and supply systems which allow them to order supplies to coincide with demand. Every evening Sainsbury's receives details of the sales of all 12,000 lines from each of its shops; these are turned into orders for warehouse deliveries for the coming night, and replacement production for the following day. With computerised control of stocks in the shop, transport networks, automatic loading and unloading, Sainsbury's flow line make-to-order system has conquered the Fordist problem of stocks.

They have also overcome the limits of the mass-product. For, in contrast to the discount stores which are confined to a few, fast-selling items, Sainsbury's, like the new wave of high street shops, can handle ranges of products geared to segments of the market. Market niching has become the slogan of the high street. Market researchers break down market by age (youth, young adults, 'grey power'), by household types (dinkies, single-gender couples, one-parent families), by income, occupation, housing and increasingly, by locality. They analyse 'lifestyles', correlating consumption patterns across commodities, from food to clothing, and health to holidays.

The point of this new anthropology of consumption is to target both product and shops to particular segments. Burton's – once a mass-producer with generalised retail outlets – has changed in the 1980s to being a niche-market retailer with a team of anthropologists, a group of segmented stores – Top Shop, Top Man, Dorothy Perkins, Principles and Burton's itself – and now has no manufacturing plants of its own. Conran's Storehouse group – Habitat, Heals, Mothercare, Richards and BHS – all geared to different groups, offers not only clothes, but furniture and furnishings, in other words entire lifestyles. At the heart of Conran's organisation in London is what amounts to a factory of 150 designers, with collages of different lifestyles on the wall, Bold Primary, Orchid, mid-Atlantic and the Cottage Garden.

In all these shops the emphasis has shifted from the manufacturer's economies of scale to the retailer's economies of scope. The economies come from offering an integrated range from which customers choose their own basket of products. There is also an economy of innovation, for the modern retail systems allow new product ideas to be tested in practice, through shop sales, and the successful ones then to be ordered for wider distribution. Innovation has become a leading edge of the new competition. Product life has become shorter, for fashion goods and consumer durables.

A centerpiece of this new retailing is design. Designers produce the innovations. They shape the lifestyles. They design the shops, which are described as 'stages' for the act of shopping. There are now 29,000 people working in design consultancies in the UK, which have sales of £1,600 million per annum. They are the engineers of designer capitalism. With market researchers they have steered the high street from being retailers of goods to retailers of style.

These changes are a response to, and a means of shaping, the shift from mass consumption. Instead of keeping up with the Joneses there has been a move to be different from the Joneses. Many of these differences are vertical, intended to confirm status and class. But some are horizontal and centred round group identities, linked to age, or region or ethnicity. In spite of the fact that basic needs are still unmet, the high street does offer a new variety and creativity in consumption which the Left's puritan tradition should also address. Whatever our responses, the revolution in retailing reflects new principles of production, a new pluralism of products and a new importance for innovation. As such it marks a shift to a post-Fordist age.

There have been parallel shifts in manufacturing, not least in response to the retailers' just-in-time system of ordering. In some sectors where the manufacturers are little more than subcontractors to the retailers, their flexibility has been achieved at the expense of labour. In others, capital itself has suffered, as furniture retailers like MFI squeeze their suppliers, driving down prices, limiting design, and thereby destroying much of the mass-production furniture industry during the downturns.

But the most successful manufacturing regions have been ones which have linked flexible manufacturing systems with innovative organisation and an emphasis on 'customisation' design and quality. Part of the flexibility has been achieved through new technology, and the introduction of programmable machines which can switch from product to product with little manual resetting and downtime. Benetton's automatic dyeing plant, for example, allows it to change its colours in time with demand. In the car industry, whereas General Motors took nine hours to change the dyes on its presses in the early 1980s, Toyota have lowered the time to two minutes, and have cut the average lot size of body parts from 5,000 to 500 in the process. The line, in short, has become flexible. Instead of using purpose-built machines to make standard products, flexible automation uses general-purpose machines to produce a variety of products.

Japanisation

Manufacturers have also been adopting the retailers' answer to stocks. The pioneer is Toyota which stands to the new era as Ford did to the old. [Kiichiro] Toyoda, the founder of Toyota, inspired by a visit to an American supermarket, applied the just-in-time system to his component suppliers, ordering on the basis of his daily production plans, and getting the components delivered right beside the line. Most of Toyota's components are still produced on the same day as they are assembled.

Toyoda's prime principle of the elimination of wasteful practices meant going beyond the problem of stocks. His firm has used design and materials technology to simplify complex elements, cutting down the number of parts and operations. It adopted a zero-defect policy, developing machines which stopped automatically when a fault occurred, as well as statistical quality control techniques. As in retailing, the complex web of processes, inside and outside the plant, were coordinated through computers, a process that economists have called systemation (in contrast to automation). The result of these practices is a discontinuous speed-up in what Marx called the circulation of capital. Toyota turns over its materials and products 10 times more quickly than Western car producers, saving material and energy in the process.

The key point about the Toyota system, however, is not so much that it speeds up the making of a car. It is in order to make these changes that it has adopted quite different methods of labour control and organisation. Toyota saw that traditional Taylorism did not work. Central management had no access to all the information needed for continuous innovation. Quality could not be achieved with de-skilled manual workers. Taylorism wasted what they called 'the gold in workers' heads'.

Toyota, and the Japanese more generally, having broken the industrial unions in the 1950s, have developed a core of multiskilled workers whose tasks include not only manufacture and maintenance, but the improvement of the products and processes under their control. Each breakdown is seen as a chance for improvement. Even hourly-paid workers are trained in statistical techniques and monitoring, and register and interpret statistics to identify deviations from a norm – tasks customarily reserved for management in Fordism. Quality circles are a further way of tapping the ideas of the workforce. In post-Fordism, the worker is designed to act as a computer as well as a machine.

As a consequence the Taylorist contract changes. Workers are no longer interchangeable. They gather experience. The Japanese job-for-life and corporate welfare system provides security. For the firm it secures an asset. Continuous training, payment by seniority, a breakdown of job demarcations, are all part of the Japanese core wage relation. The EETPU's lead in embracing private pension schemes, BUPA, internal flexibility, union-organised training and single-company unions are all consistent with this path of post-Fordist industrial relations.

Not the least of the dangers of this path is that it further hardens the divisions between the core and the peripheral workforce. The cost of employing lifetime workers means an incentive to subcontract all jobs not essential to the core. The other side of the Japanese jobs-for-life is a majority of low-paid, fragmented peripheral workers, facing an underfunded and inadequate welfare state. The duality in the labour market, and in the welfare economy, could be taken as a description of Thatcherism. The point is that neither the EETPU's policy nor that of Mrs Thatcher should [be] read as purely political. There is a material basis to both, rooted in changes in production.

There are parallel changes in corporate organisation. With the revision of Taylorism, a layer of management has been stripped away. Greater central control has allowed the decentralisation of work. Day-to-day autonomy has been given to work groups and plant managers. Teams linking departments horizontally have replaced the rigid verticality of Fordist bureaucracies.

It is only a short step from here to subcontracting and franchising. This is often simply a means of labour control. But in engineering and light consumer industries networks and semi-independent firms have often proved more innovative than vertically integrated producers. A mark of post-Fordism is close two-way relations between customer and supplier, and between specialised producers in the same industry. Cooperative competition replaces the competition of the jungle. These new relationships within and between enterprises and on the shop floor have made least headway in the countries in which Fordism took fullest root, the USA and the UK. Here firms have tried to match continental and Japanese flexibility through automation while retaining Fordist shop floor, managerial and competitive relations.

Yet in spite of this we can see in this country a culture of post-Fordist capitalism emerging. Consumption has a new place. As for production the keyword is flexibility – of plant and machinery, as of products and labour. Emphasis shifts from scale to scope, and from cost to quality. Organisations are geared to respond to rather than regulate markets. They are seen as frameworks for learning as much as instruments of control. Their hierarchies are flatter and their structures more open. The guerrilla force takes over from the standing army. All this has liberated the centre from the tyranny of the immediate. Its task shifts from planning to strategy, and to the promotion of the instruments of post-Fordist control – systems, software, corporate culture and cash.

On the book shelf, Peters and Waterman replace FW Taylor. In the theatre the audience is served lentils by the actors. At home Channel 4 takes its place beside ITV. Majorities are transformed into minorities, as we enter the age of proportional representation. And under the shadow of Chernobyl even Fordism's scientific modernism is being brought to book, as we realise there is more than one way up the technological mountain.

Not all these can be read off from the new production systems. Some are rooted in the popular opposition to Fordism. They represent an alternative version of post-Fordism, which flowered after 1968 in the community movements and the new craft trade unionism of alternative plans. Their organisational forms – networks, workplace democracy, cooperatives, the dissolving of the platform speaker into meetings in the round have echoes in the new textbooks of management, indeed capital has been quick to take up progressive innovations for its own purposes. There are then many sources and contested versions of post-Fordist culture. What they share is a break with the era of Ford.

Post-Fordism is being introduced under the sway of the market and in accordance with the requirements of capital accumulation. It validates only what can command a place in the market; it cuts the labour force in two, and leaves large numbers without any work at all. Its prodigious productivity gains are ploughed back into yet further accumulation and the quickening consumption of symbols in the Post-Modern marketplace. In the UK, Thatcherism has strengthened the prevailing wind of the commodity economy, liberating the power of private purses and so fragmenting the social sphere.

To judge from Kamata's celebrated account, working for Toyota is hardly a step forward from working for Ford. As one British worker in a Japanese factory in the north-east of England put it, 'they want us to live for work, where we want to work to live'. Japanisation has no place in any modern *News from Nowhere*.

Yet post-Fordism has shaken the kaleidoscope of the economy, and exposed an old politics. We have to respond to its challenges and draw lessons from its systems.

Political Consequences of Post-Fordism

Firstly, there is the question of consumption. How reluctant the Left has been to take this on, in spite of the fact that it is a sphere of unpaid production, and, as Gorz insists, one of creative activity. Which local council pays as much attention to its users, as does the market research industry on behalf of commodities? Which bus or railway service cuts queues and speeds the traveller with as much care as retailers show to their just-in-time stocks? The perspective of consumption – so central to the early socialist movement – is emerging from under the tarpaulin of production: the effects of food additives and low-level radiation, of the air we breathe and surroundings we live in, the availability of childcare and community centres, or access to privatised city centres and transport geared to particular needs. These are issues of consumption, where the social and the human have been threatened by the market. In each case the market solutions have been contested by popular movements. Yet their causes and the relations of consumption have been given only walk-on parts in party programmes. They should now come to the centre of the stage.

Secondly, there is labour. Post-Fordism sees labour as the key asset of modern production. Rank Xerox is trying to change its accounting system so that machinery becomes a cost, and labour its fixed asset. The Japanese emphasise labour and learning. The Left should widen this reversal of Taylorism, and promote a discontinuous expansion of adult education inside and outside the workplace.

They should also provide an alternative to the new management of time. The conservative sociologist Daniel Bell sees the management of time as the key issue of post-industrial society. Post-Fordist capital is restructuring working time for its own convenience: with new shifts, split shifts, rostering, weekend working and the regulation of labour, through part-time and casual contracts, to the daily and weekly cycles of work. Computer systems allow Tesco to manage more than 130 different types of labour contract in its large stores. These systems of employment and welfare legislation should be moulded for the benefit not the detriment of labour. The length of the working day, of the working week, and year, and lifetime, should be shaped to accommodate the many responsibilities and needs away from work.

The most pressing danger from post-Fordism, however, is the way it is widening the split between core and periphery in the labour market and the welfare system. The EETPU's building a fortress round the core is as divisive as Thatcherism itself. We need bridges across the divide, with trades unions representing core workers using their power to extend benefits to all, as IG Metall have been doing in Germany. A priority for any Labour government would be to put a floor under the labour market, and remove the discriminations faced by the low paid. The Liberals pursued such a policy in late 19th-century London. Labour should reintroduce it in late 20th-century Britain.

Underlying this split is the post-Fordist bargain which offers security in return for flexibility. Because of its cost, Japanese capital restricts this bargain to the core; in the peripheral workforce, flexibility is achieved through insecurity. Sweden has tried to widen the core bargain to the whole population with a policy of full employment, minimum incomes, extensive retraining programmes, and egalitarian income distribution. These are the two options, and Thatcherism favours the first.

Could Labour deliver the second? How real is a policy of full employment when the speed of technical change destroys jobs as rapidly as growth creates them? The question – as Sweden has shown – is one of distribution. There is the distribution of working time: the campaign for the 35-hour week and the redistribution of overtime should be at the centre of Labour policy in the 1990s. There is also the distribution of income and the incidence of tax. Lafontaine's idea of shifting tax from labour to energy is an interesting one. Equally important is the need to tax heavily the speculative gains from property, the rent from oil, and unearned and inherited income. Finally taxes will need to be raised on higher incomes, and should be argued for not only in terms of full employment, but in terms of the improvements to the caring services, the environment and the social economy which the market of the 1980s has done so much to destroy. Full employment is possible. It should be based on detailed local plans, decentralised public services and full employment centres. It cannot be delivered from Westminster alone.

Thirdly, we need to learn from post-Fordism's organisational innovations, and apply them within our own public and political structures. Representative democracy within Fordist bureaucracies is not enough. What matters is the structure of the bureaucracy and its external relations. In the state this means redefining its role as strategist, as innovator, coordinator and supporter of producers. In some cases the span of coordination needs to be extended (notably in integrating public transport and the movement of freight): in others production should be decentralised and the drive for scale reversed (the electricity industry, education and health have all suffered from overcentralised operations). Public services should move beyond the universal to the differentiated service. Nothing has been more outrageous than the attack on local government as loony leftist, when councils have sought to shape policies to the needs of groups facing discrimination. Capitalist retailers and market researchers make these distinctions in the pursuit of sales, and socialists should match them in pursuit of service. If greater user control and internal democracy were added to this, then we would be some way towards the dismantling of mass-produced administration, and the creation of a progressive and flexible state.

Lastly, there is private industry. In many sectors both industry and public policy are frozen in Fordism, even as the leading edge of competition has shifted from scale to product, and from costs to strategy. In spite of the restructuring that has taken place in the 1980s, largely at the expense of labour, manufacturing competitiveness continues to decline. By 1984 only five out of 34 major manufacturing sectors did not have a negative trade balance.

The Left's response to this decline has been couched largely in terms of macro policy: devaluing the pound, controlling wage levels and expanding investment. Industrial policy has taken second place, and centred on amalgamations and scale and the encouragement of new technology. This has been Labour's version of modernisation.

The fact remains that size has not secured competitiveness. Neither has a declining exchange rate with the yen, nor wage levels which have made the UK one of the cheap labour havens of Europe. The changes are much deeper than this.

An alternative needs to start not from plans but from strategies. Strategic capacity within British industry is thin and even thinner in the state and the labour movement. Sector and enterprise strategies need to take on board the nature of the new competition, the centrality of skilled labour, the need for specialisation and quality, and for continuous innovation.

What public policy should do is to find ways of ensuring that the resultant restructuring takes account of social priorities: labour and educational reform is one part of this; industrial democracy another; environmental and energy saving a third; user concerns about quality and variety a fourth. Some of these will require new laws; others incentive schemes; others collective bargaining. They all need to be a part of strategic restructuring.

In each sector there will be giants barring the path towards such a programme. One will be the stock market. A priority for a Labour government will be to reduce the stock market's power to undermine long-term strategic investment (in this we need to follow the example of the Japanese). Another will be multinationals which dominate so many industrial and service sectors in the economy. The urgent task here is to form coalitions of states, unions and municipalities across the European Community to press for common strategic alternatives at the European level. A third will be the retailers. In some cases retailers will be important allies in restructuring industry progressively (the co-op has a role here); in others the conduct of retailers is destructive, and a Labour government should take direct measures against them.

At the same time, Labour needs to develop a network of social industrial institutions, decentralised, innovative and entrepreneurial. For each sector and area there should be established one or more enterprise boards. They would be channels for long-term funds for new technology, for strategic support across a sector, for common services, and for initiatives and advice on the social priorities.

Public purchasing should be coordinated and used not just to provide protection in the old manner, but as supporters of the sectoral programme, as contributors to the improvement of quality, and as sources of ideas. New technology networks should also be set up, linking universities and polytechnics with the sectors and unions (this is an effective part of Dukakis's Massachusetts programme).

In short we need a new model of the public economy made up of a honeycomb of decentralised, yet synthetic institutions, integrated by a common strategy, and intervening in the economy at the level of production rather than trying vainly to plan all from on high. The success of the Italian consortia and the German industrial regions has been centrally dependent on such a network of municipal and regional government support.

A key role in taking forward this industrial programme should be played by the unions. Restructuring has put them on the defensive. They have found their power weakened and their position isolated. Few have had the resources to develop alternative strategies and build coalitions of communities and users around them. Yet this is now a priority if unions are to reclaim their position as spokespeople of an alternative economy rather than defenders of a sectional interest. Research departments should be expanded, and commissions given to external researchers. There should be joint commissions of members, and users and other related groups, as well as supportive local authorities. The production of the policy would itself be a form of democratic politics.

Mrs Thatcher has led an attack on the key institutions of Fordism: on manufacturing, on the centralised state, on industrial unions and on the national economy. She has opened up Britain to one version of post-Fordism, one that has strengthened the control of finance and international capital, has increased inequality and destroyed whole areas of collective life.

There is an alternative. It has grown up in the new movements, in the trades unions, and in local government over the past 20 years. It has broken through the bounds of the Left's Fordist inheritance, in culture, structure and economics. From it can develop – as is already happening in Europe – an alternative socialism adequate to the post-Fordist age.

Robin Murray, 'Fordism and Post-Fordism' from *New Times: The Changing Face of Politics in the 1990s*, edited by Stuart Hall and Martin Jacques, Lawrence and Wishart (London), 1989. © Robin Murray.

9/15 – The Birthpangs of Post-Modern Economics?

Anatole Kaletsky

Anatole Kaletsky takes the financial meltdown of 2007–9 as a point of departure from which to analyse the history of modern economics and discuss why the system failed so catastrophically. He explains that rationality was at the basis of modern economics, but by the turn of the century it became clear that this system of *Homo Economicus,* which calculated optimum trading strategies for maximum consumption, was unable to cope with the social and economic upheaval of the early 20th century with its wars, revolutions and the Great Depression. A different model was needed and the field divided into microeconomics which continued the rational approach, and macroeconomics which dealt with labour, capital and money, factors much more susceptible to instability and fluctuation. Macroeconomics was a major challenge to previous thinking and paralleled many post-modern concepts such as nonlinear complex feedback. After the Second World War this was replaced by the neoclassical synthesis (NCS), a new model based on the earlier rationalist thinking but which challenged the role of the government within the macroeconomic balancing act. The principles that underpinned this move back into microeconomics were called rational expectations hypothesis (REH) and efficient market hypothesis (EMH). The system of thinking was even more streamlined with Reagan and Thatcher's mantra that 'the market is always right' where financial blips were smoothed over. This one-size-fits-all approach eventually proved itself woefully inadequate and Kaletsky concludes that if economics is to prevail as an academic subject, the field will have to change drastically, opening itself to other disciplines and embracing rather than suppressing the implicit complexities of a post-modern world.

Anatole Kaletsky is editor at large of *The Times* in London with a weekly column on economics, politics and international relations. He has also written for the *Financial Times* and *The Economist.* In 1998 he expanded his activities in 1998 to include economic forecasting and financial consulting, and has received many awards and distinctions for his contributions to the field of economics. He was born in 1952 in Moscow and was educated at Cambridge and Harvard. *EB*

The Death of Modern Economics

The bankruptcy of Lehman Brothers on 15 September, 2008 blew up the ideology of modern economics in the same way that the demolition of Pruitt-Igoe refuted modern architecture; or the attack on the Twin Towers exploded modern diplomacy. In fact, with hindsight 9/15 could turn out to have been an even more important date than 9/11.

The economic doctrines discredited on that day were actually more fundamental to the structure of the modern world than even US military hegemony. And the disintegration of these doctrines alongside the great financial institutions which had symbolised their dominance, created an evolutionary break in the nature of global capitalism. Like an asteroid transforming the environment by wiping out a dominant species, the 2007–9 financial crisis extinguished 30 years of market fundamentalism and created the conditions for a new species of capitalism to emerge.

Capitalism was not destroyed, as many on both Left and Right predicted, by the implosion of the world financial system and its government-led reconstruction. Far from it. Instead a new, and possibly stronger, form is gradually rising to fill the gap. This newly dominant species is clearly from the same genus as the last one, just as the market fundamentalism of the late 20th century was from the same genus as the social democratic Keynesian capitalism that rose in the 1930s. But these varieties of capitalism also vary widely; they are as different and as similar as the tiger, leopard and lion.

If Modern Capitalism can be dated to 1776, and the near-simultaneous publication of Adam Smith's *Wealth of Nations* and the US Declaration of Independence, then this would be the third example of what biologists call an 'extinction event' followed by 'sudden evolution'. The first such great transformation was the social democratic and Keynesian reform movement from the 1930s onwards. The second was the Thatcher–Reagan monetarist counter revolution of the 1980s. These two events reflected the conflicting visions of modernity that struggled for dominance throughout the 20th century: the collectivist rationalism of the just and omniscient state versus the individualist rationalism of the impartial and 'efficient' market. Among the most interesting intellectual questions of the 21st century, which will have a major influence on the political development of the new version of capitalism, is whether the ideology that underpins the next transformation of the politico-economic system will move beyond the mechanistic assumptions about social behaviour – perfect information, atomistic agents and stable equilibrium – that took over and eventually monopolised academic economics during the market fundamentalist phase.

In order to keep up with the evolution of the capitalist system, economics will have to move both forwards and backwards – in a characteristically post-modern dance. It would hark back to Keynes, Hayek, Schumpeter and other great economists of the mid-20th century. These pioneers can be viewed as early post-modernists in their rejection of mechanistic determinism and their embrace of rich and ambiguous concepts such as reflexive expectations, inconsistent preferences, fallacies of composition and positive feedbacks. But also it would look forward to new social science methodologies and numerical techniques that can cope with indeterminacy, multiple equilibrium and the emergent properties of complex systems. There are good signs that just such a back-and-forth movement may result from 9/15.

An intellectual revolution can be expected in economics for positive and negative reasons. The negative motives are obvious enough. The events that followed 9/15 discredited the dominating paradigm of 'efficient markets' and 'rational expectations'. The positive reason is the reinvention of methodologies that incorporate the complexities which the ultra-rationalist economics of the late 20th century deliberately tried to suppress: intrinsic uncertainty, socially conditioned behaviour, conflicting viewpoints, positive feedbacks and so on. If these new approaches develop, economics will again become a fertile field of academic study, especially if it finds enrichment from related post-modern movements. If, on the other hand, economics fails to deliver useful insights, it will disappear as an independent academic subject, merging instead with accountancy, market research and mathematical statistics. It will migrate entirely from universities to management schools.

Since post-modern economics is still an emerging paradigm, I will focus here more on the demise of the previous one. In the last section, however, some of the most promising research programmes will be briefly described. An ironic word of warning, however. The reader should be wary of the salad of acronyms that litters the economic menu, and keeps mixing it up with stale modernist ingredients: such theories termed REH and EMH, and the first modern brand, the 19th-century *Homo Economicus* or HE. Unfortunately, in order to improve on this unpalatable fare, one has to sample the ingredients raw with, we hope, the promise of a better meal in the future.

Modern Theories and the 'Efficient' Market Hypothesis (EMH)

Academic economics was revealed as an emperor with no clothes after 9/15 not so much because it had failed to foresee the 2007–8 financial crisis, but because it was unable to offer any useful guidance on what to do at the moment of greatest need. The failure of analysis was much more embarrassing than the failure of prediction because not even the most complacent of mechanical modernists ever claimed economics to be a strictly predictive science. What they did claim, however, was an ability to *explain* economic reality and to *guide* policy makers in responding to unexpected events. In this respect they abjectly failed. One of the dirty little secrets of modern academic economics, for example, is that the computer models used by central banks and finance ministries to guide them in setting interest rates and regulating financial institutions do not contain any equations at all relating to the behaviour or financial condition of banks.

On first inspection, this looks absurd. The methodological assumptions imposed by the theory of rational expectations mean these models must assume that all debts are repaid in full at the end of each period and that money is 'neutral' in the sense that changes in credit availability have no effect on real variables such as jobs and output. What this academic jargon means in practice is politicians and central bankers who turned to the models designed for them by academic economists, were essentially told, 'The situation you now have to deal with is impossible – our theories have proved that it simply cannot happen.'

Why, then, did modern economics fail so badly? And what does this suggest about its evolution in the new phase of capitalism that lies ahead? Economics as a discipline has suffered grievously from its pretensions to mathematical rigour and its preference for logical consistency over social and psychological realism. In effect, this was a deliberate decision to fight against the intellectual currents of the post-modern world.

In the years before the crisis, almost all academic economists agreed on one thing. The greatest triumph of their subject, sometimes described as the 'apotheosis of 20th-century social science', was a mechanistic and ultra-rationalist programme. This intellectually modernist, but ideologically conservative movement was built around the two related 'hypotheses' of rational expectations and efficient markets. For a combination of ideological and methodological reasons it became completely dominant in American universities from the early 1980s onwards. Having taken hold of 'high theory' it colonised central banks, finance ministries and the global institutions of the 'Washington consensus', typically the IMF, OECD and World Bank. Over time, this movement established a near-monopoly on economic thinking, crushing dissent through its control of academic publications, appointments and funding purse-strings. Ironically, an intellectual movement that glorified unfettered competition as the greatest social achievement, proved as ruthlessly monopolistic as John D Rockefeller in suppressing competition from other economic ideas.

In this case, modern economics was not so much a specific theory as a mindset. With a characteristic combination of false modesty and pseudoscientific pretension, the central tenets were described not as theories or conclusions, but merely as 'hypotheses'. The movement's grand ambitions were emphasised, however, by its adjectives and acronyms, capitalised like all religious explanations: Rational Expectations Hypothesis (REH) and the Efficient Market Hypothesis (EMH).

To understand the ideological significance of these two ideas, some history is required. The concept of 'rationality', as an emergent property that naturally evolves out of a competitive economic system, has a long and influential history, going back to Adam Smith, David Hume and ultimately to Aristotle and Plato. After Smith's discovery of the 'invisible hand' of competitive markets and especially after the 'marginal revolution' of the English Utilitarians in the 1870s, economic theory came to be dominated by the 'rationality' of *Homo Economicus*, the human calculating-machine invented by John Stuart Mill in 1871. *Homo Economicus* (*HE* for short) was supposed to spend his entire life computing optimum trading strategies that maximised his own consumption. Importantly for Adam Smith and moralists of the system, through the magic of perfectly competitive markets, HE also achieved the greatest possible utility for society as a whole. This quintessential product of the industrial revolution was, for obvious reasons, a wonderful ideological construct, helping to explain and legitimise an age of social upheaval and extreme inequality. HE suffered, however, from two fatal weaknesses. Firstly, HE was unable to explain why the poverty, inequality and class struggle identified by Marx and various brands of utopian and Christian socialists was an even more characteristic product of the capitalist system than optimal utility. Secondly, there was the concept of a 'general equilibrium' in which perfectly competitive markets in everything and anything HE could imagine, both now and in the future, kept everything in perfect balance and every able-bodied worker fully employed. This glorious self-confident Victorian concept was unable to cope, either in theory or in practice, with the upheavals of the First World War, the Russian Revolution and the Great Depression.

Keynes the First Post-Modernist?

Under the combined pressures of Marxist theory and the political realities of communism and mass unemployment, the capitalist system nearly broke down and classical economics was forced to subdivide into two separate branches. The traditional branch, now described as microeconomics, continued to use the tools of 19th-century economics to analyse the behaviour of profit-maximising individuals in competitive markets for ordinary commodities such as coal, steel or tomatoes. It continued to assume equilibrium between supply and demand in these markets, which generally speaking did prevail. The new branch, called macroeconomics, was essentially invented from scratch in the 1930s by Keynes. It focused not on ordinary goods but on the basic factors of production – labour, capital and money – especially on the two-way interdependence between the instabilities of these factors and the dynamics of the 'macro' economy as a whole. And it challenged the static, determinist classical economics with what might now be described as post-modern concepts: an unknowable future, inconsistent expectations, intrinsic but unpredictable cyclicality and emergent properties of a complex system. As we now know from the complexity sciences, the behaviour of complex systems governed by such forces cannot be inferred from aggregating the individual behaviour of atomistic components.

Keynes, incidentally, could in many ways be seen as an early post-modernist, not only in his intellectual focus on unpredictability, fallacies of composition, divergent viewpoints and the two-way interaction between reality and observation. In his personal, political and cultural life he was also fascinated with ambiguities and creative contradictions, ranging from his sexuality to his attitudes to Britain's political parties. He was, in these respects, a quintessential member of Britain's Bloomsbury set and the complex reinterpretations of modernity, social reality and psychology reflected in his economics could be seen as a parallel to the literary experimentation of Virginia Woolf.

What Keynes realised was that the markets for labour, capital and money were not driven by the same dynamics as markets for ordinary goods such as coal. When businesses see prices and wages falling in a recession, they do not treat this as a reason to invest more and create jobs. In fact, they generally do the opposite, because investment is *motivated* by expectations of future sales and profits, not by the price of money and capital today. Consumers, meanwhile, respond to signs of economic slowdown by trying to increase their savings. Thus savings rise in a recession, while the willingness to use those savings for business investment declines. The result is insufficient demand in the economy and rising unemployment. That, in turn, makes the situation worse by depressing wages and consumer spending, doing even more damage to business expectations and leading to even higher unemployment. Expectation about the future, not present demand, is therefore what determines investment and employment decisions, and this has radical implications.

For, if the future economy is inherently unpredictable, as we know now it is, then there is no way for business and investors to make fully rational decisions. Moreover the expectations of one business affect the reality faced by others. If one major business decides to fire its workers or cut their wages, this lowers the purchasing power of the whole economy and thereby puts pressure on other businesses to follow suit. It is like highly contagious diseases.

Similar momentum effects among investors in shares, currencies and bond markets can be even more extreme. For Keynes, this inconsistency of expectations between savers and investors is aggravated by the divide between macro- and microeconomics. Actions that seem rational for individuals become dangerously counterproductive when undertaken by millions of people acting at once. It leads to a great contradiction, and the most important is called Keynes's 'paradox of thrift'. When one household saves more this money flows directly into investment and increases both personal and social wealth; but when millions simultaneously decide to save more, this can reduce investment, employment and economic activity. Thus an increase in *planned* or *ex ante* savings can end up reducing achieved or *ex post* savings and diminish society's total wealth.

Keynes focused on this cognitive dissonance – firstly, between perceptions about the present and expectations about the future and secondly between individual and collective objectives – and was thus able to identify positive feedback in the economy. It pushes a faltering economy further and further away from equilibrium, an outcome that the classical equilibrium theory could neither predict nor analyse. From the late 1930s onwards, the 'macroeconomics' of social aggregates and dynamic instability emerged as a separate – and ultimately dominant – field partly because of Keynes's intellectual breakthroughs. Of course, political events certified the shift. Mass unemployment of the 1930s created demands for government to take responsibility for macroeconomic management in ways that had never been conceivable. This changed the methodology in economics. Instead of viewing general equilibrium as a natural, God-given property of the capitalist system (or a secular, but divinely ordained 'hidden hand'), economists now assumed that a wise government bureaucracy would intervene as required to balance aggregate supply and demand. And the public followed suit.

But even as Keynes's policy recommendations were broadly adopted, his most interesting post-modern insights were overwhelmed by the return to a mechanistic rationalism. The Keynesian view that capitalist economies could suffer depressions because of inconsistent expectations, destabilising feedbacks and fallacies of composition was gradually replaced by the so-called 'neo-classical synthesis', a quintessentially modernist reinterpretation. This brought back the idea of equilibrium as the economy's natural state, and argued that depressions were simply a function of market 'imperfections'. The alleged culprit was a 'stickiness' in prices and wages, which fail to adjust quickly enough to changes in economic conditions. Ponder the symmetries here. Keynesian economics viewed stable equilibrium as an implausible, special case; but the neo-classical synthesis reversed this thinking. It restored the 19th-century modernist idea of a perfectly competitive equilibrium as the theoretical norm, and depression and unemployment as the dysfunctional, special case.

For ideological reasons, however, the neo-classical synthesis (NCS) prevailed. During the early Cold War years especially, there were obvious attractions in a description of capitalism as a collection of independent, atomistic individuals who cooperate voluntarily as cogs in a vast Fordist social machine. Better still, the NCS made room for the post-Depression political realities of safety nets and active demand management. They justified stabilising the business cycle, and explained why the Fordist economic machine needed occasional lubrication: 'pump-priming' and 'kick-starting' became the mantra of a benign, pro-business government. Thus, while conservative economists were able to describe the new orthodoxy of the 1950s as the neo-classical synthesis, progressives like Paul Samuelson could call it neo-Keynesian economics. In this process of accommodation to the postwar ideological consensus, however, the most important post-modern insight of macroeconomics was lost. Economic and financial instability were no longer recognised as natural consequences of indeterminacy about the future; dynamic instability was now merely an aberration caused by market 'imperfections' which could, at least in theory, be somehow ironed out.

As the unprecedented prosperity of the 1950s and 1960s – the neo-Keynesian 'Golden Age' of benign government intervention – degenerated into the social conflicts and economic upheavals of the 1970s, the residue of post-modern thinking in the prevailing economic thinking came under further intellectual and political attack. The target now was the government's role in macroeconomic stabilisation, the main point on which the Keynesians and the neo-classicals had agreed.

From the mid-1960s onwards conservative economists, many of them based at the University of Chicago, started claiming that macroeconomics had no intellectual basis and could only be taken as seriously as a scientific study if rebuilt on proper 'micro-foundations'. In other words, economists were falling into precisely the trap of aggregating the individual parts of a complex system which post-modern mathematics had just exposed. And to carry out this quixotic programme, economists disinterred the all-knowing and ever-calculating *Homo Economicus* who was buried in the 1930s. And to make matters worse, they reinforced HE with two even more outlandish 'hypotheses', which were actually treated as unquestionable axioms by the newly dominant Chicago paradigm. The Rational Expectations Hypothesis (REH) asserted that all 'rational' economic actors, because they had access to all possible knowledge, must therefore have identical expectations about the future. The Efficient Market Hypothesis (EMH) built on this assumption by stating that competitive financial markets would always incorporate the best possible analysis of all publicly available information. The implication was that occasional financial crises were just random fluctuations, as meaningless and ultimately as predictable as the takings of a well-run casino.

For conservative politicians, the pseudoscientific objectivism of the new theories was equally attractive. The mathematical technicalities of 'rational' and 'efficient' markets were quickly simplified by Margaret Thatcher and Ronald Reagan into their favourite slogans: 'You can't buck the market' and 'The market is always right.' The triumph of these theories was as much a testament to the Orwellian power of language as to Keynes's famous comment that, 'madmen in authority, who hear voices in the air, are distilling their frenzy from some academic scribbler of a few years back'. Imagine if rational expectations had instead been called 'consistent expectations', as some of its proponents originally suggested. An adequate refutation might then have been Ralph Waldo Emerson's acerbic comment that 'a foolish consistency is the hobgoblin of little minds'. Or suppose that the efficient market hypothesis had been renamed the 'casino-banking hypothesis'. The bankers and regulators whose faith in efficient markets wrecked the global economy after 9/15 might then have heeded Keynes's famous dictum that 'when the capital development of a country becomes a by-product of the activities of a casino, the job is likely to be ill-done'.

Chaos, Complexity and Emergent Post-Modernism

So what is to be done? Can economics escape from this intellectual blind alley? More importantly, is there a prospect that capitalism can save itself from the public outrage about rewarding fraud and failure, especially when the costs of doing this are imposed on middle-class taxpayers, not to mention the poor, the sick and the old.

The broader political question about the evolution of a new species of capitalism, based on different relationships between the market and government, is a huge subject well beyond the scope of the present discussion, but one salient factor is worth noting. The new balance which will have to be struck between the principles of one-man-one vote and one-dollar-one-vote, will have to reflect some very post-modern concepts, such as intrinsic uncertainty, ambiguity and fuzzy logic. The first phase of capitalism, from 1776 until the 1920s, assumed that economics and politics were two distinct spheres of human activity, which were either simultaneously improving (in the Whig view of history) or simultaneously doomed to failure (in the Marxist view). The second phase, from the 1930s until the 1970s, assumed that markets were short-sighted and prone to failure, but governments were omniscient and just. The third phase, from the 1980s until 9/15, assumed the opposite – that markets were always right, while government was always wrong. In the next phase of capitalism, if there is to be one, it will have to be recognised that markets and government are *both* prone to be wrong. Capitalists, politicians and voters will have to accept that most socioeconomic questions have no clear-cut answers and the best way to maintain progress is through competition of ideas and experimentation, rather than rationalist grand plans.

For economics as a discipline this post-modern worldview implies two options. Either academic economics will be abandoned and become a mere appendage to the collection of industrial and social statistics. Or it will undergo an intellectual revolution. The dominant research programmes will have to be recognised as failures and for what they are: the substitute of mathematical models for a more complex reality. However, if we assume a positive response, then economists will have to reopen their subject to a wide diversity of speculative approaches, drawing insights from history, psychology and sociology, and applying the methods of historians, political theorists and even journalists.

Many such approaches have been attempted. The most recently publicised has come from history and psychology, the behavioural economics popularised by Robert Shiller, the Yale professor. His bestselling book, *Irrational Exuberance*, published first in 2000, is said to have predicted the dotcom crash while the second edition, of 2005, predicted the subprime crisis of 2008. Whether or not this is true, behavioural economics considers a world in which investors and businesses are motivated by crowd psychology rather than the careful calculation of rational expectation. This model is, however, the least radical of the alternative approaches and does not challenge the methodology of REH, even if it weakens the strict 'rationality' assumptions. Partly because of its compatibility with the reigning modernist approach, academic economics has not found it difficult to embrace the behavioural approach. Indeed, there has been much brilliant work contradicting 'rational' economics, but close enough in its methods to be rewarded with Nobel prizes: for example, the ideas of 'bounded rationality' and 'satisficing' (as opposed to optimising) pioneered by Herbert Simon; the use of game theory by Vernon Smith; the 'experimental economics' of behavioural psychologists such as Daniel Kahneman, and the mathematical analysis of asymmetrical information (essentially 'cheating') by George Akerloff and Joe Stiglitz.

More radical extensions of behavioural and experimental economics involve neuro-physiology, anthropology and even Freudian analysis. The last-mentioned is the subject of a paper written in 2007 by David Tuckett and Richard Taffler of the psychoanalysis unit at University College, London. It explains financial boom–bust cycles in terms of Freudian theories of 'phantastic objects', psychological 'splitting' and 'wish-fulfilment'. Most of this work, however, only scratches the surface of a post-modern economics, and few of these efforts have tried to incorporate their ideas into macroeconomic models. Ironically, macroeconomics is now even more dominated than microeconomics by the rational expectations approach.

More challenging to the orthodoxy is the mathematical work in chaos theory and advanced control engineering which shows that many of the mathematical techniques used in modern economics have been simply wrong-headed. Brian Arthur, previous director of the Santa Fe Institute, where complexity theory was formulated, has spent a lifetime developing the mathematics of nonlinear complex systems for economics. Using models with positive feedback and the idea of 'increasing returns', he has come up with results impressively divergent from those of conventional modern economics. As opposed to the notion of just one solution to a given economic situation, deterministic chaos in the environment leads to *many different* outcomes. This can be proven. Yet so far, none of these ideas have been integrated into macroeconomics where they are most obviously required. Working in the same tradition of complexity theory and fractals, Benoît Mandelbrot, one of the great mathematicians of the 20th century, has also made a devastating critique of reigning models. He describes, in *The Misbehaviour of Markets*, 2004, how economists ignored 40 years of progress in the study of complex systems, that is the research into earthquakes, weather, ecology and other nonlinear behaviour. Mandelbrot explains how the standard objection from economists was that non-Gaussian statistics, fractal geometry and nonlinear numerical modelling used to study chaos did not offer the precise answers provided by EMH. The fact that the 'precise' answers given by EMH were demonstrably wrong was no deterrent to 'scientific' economists. It's as if weather forecasters denied the rain falling on their head because it was not confirmed by theory.

Roman Frydman and Michael D Goldberg provide other striking examples of such cognitive dissonance in their *Imperfect Knowledge Economics* of 2007. IKE, as the authors ironically call their research programme (as if they were beating up the

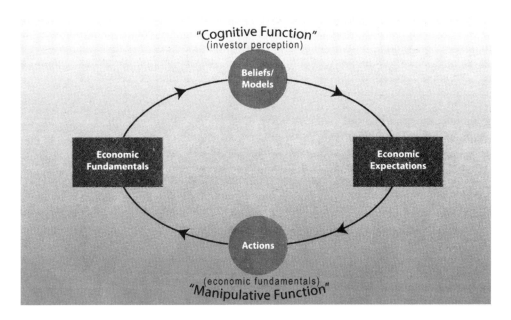

"Cognitive Function"
(investor perception)

Beliefs/
Models

Economic
Fundamentals

Economic
Expectations

Actions

(economic fundamentals)
"Manipulative Function"

After John Cassidy, 'He Saw the End of an Era', *New York Review of Books*, 23 October 2008; diagram modified by Charles Jencks. © Charles Jencks.

modernist acronyms with Ike Eisenhower) explicitly challenges the assumption of rational expectations. Like Brian Arthur they argue that, at least in theory, there is no 'right' model of how the economy works. Instead IKE draws on the insights of Keynes and Hayek that the fundamental problems of macroeconomics all derive ultimately from one ineluctable reality. Even if markets are perfectly efficient, the capitalist economy is far too complex for any of its participants to have exact knowledge, especially about future events. This means that businesses and investors will quite rationally operate on a wide variety of different assumptions. And far from this being irrational, as suggested by behavioural economics, such divergent behaviour is *the* essential ingredient of capitalism: it is the one that makes entrepreneurship and financial markets work. IKE builds on the concept of 'reflexivity' popularised by George Soros, that market expectations that initially appear false can actually change reality and become self-fulfilling prophecies, examples of the Oedipus Effect (the effect of predictive theories on the outcome of events). IKE discusses a world in which market participants with diverse views about the laws of economics change macroeconomic conditions by changing these views. By formalising such insights, IKE generates 'qualitative' forecasts of currency movements. The point of these post-modern theories, and their 'fuzzy' numbers, is that they turn out to be much closer to actual movements in exchange rates than the 'sharp' predictions of rational expectations models. The latter are indeed precise, but invariably precisely wrong.

All the post-modern approaches I have been mentioning have two features in common: they address such issues as unstable perceptions and expectations, positive feedbacks and emergent fluctuations. They also move away from the stifling demand that economic insights must be expressed in internally consistent mathematical formulae. The main purpose of mathematics in any intellectual inquiry is to guarantee internal consistency, to eliminate ambiguity and to simplify reality into clear chains of inference with one-way logical causation. But social scientists working outside economics have long recognised that reality can be logically inconsistent, ambiguous and multicausal. As Keynes once said it is better to be roughly right than precisely wrong. It is even more important to be able to ask questions with ambiguous answers and to make qualitative judgements about causes and effects, to take into account complex feedback. To operate with a methodology that denies ambiguity and multiple causation is to give up on political economy.

Economics today is a discipline that will either die or undergo a paradigm shift; and for the latter it must become both more broadminded, and more modest. It must broaden its horizons to recognise the insights of other social sciences and historical studies and return to its roots. Smith, Keynes, Hayek, Schumpeter and all the other truly great economists were interested in economic reality. They studied real human behaviour in markets that actually existed. Their insights came from historical knowledge, psychological intuition and political understanding. Their main analytical tools were concepts and words, not mathematics. They persuaded with eloquence and wit, not just formal logic. It must address the vexed question of moral hazard, wrestle with the dilemma that is on everybody's mind – why continue rewarding bankers for cheating? – and try to show how 'the system' instead rewards virtue and effort. That is what Adam Smith tried to do. One can see why many of today's academics may fear such a return of economics to its philosophical, moral and literary roots.

Academic establishments fight hard to resist such paradigm shifts, as Thomas Kuhn showed. Such a shift will not be easy, despite the obvious failure of academic economics. But economists do spend a lot of time understanding incentives and therefore they may be inspired to break the monopoly of mechanistic economics. If not they may well lose public funding, have to give up their lucrative consultancies and tarnish their old Nobels gathering dust on the top shelf. Max Planck observed, in the context of the post-modern revolution of the 1900s, that 'science progresses one funeral at a time'. But economics cannot afford to wait for the passing of a whole academic generation. Either it must act quickly to reform itself after 9/15, or the funeral will be for the discipline as a whole.

Adapted from Anatole Kaletsky, *Capitalism 4.0: Economics, Politics and Markets after the Crisis*, PublicAffairs (New York), 2010. © 2010 Anatole Kaletsky.

Feminism and Postmodernism
A Question of Politics

Susan Rubin Suleiman

This text is unusual in that it does not attempt a definition of postmodernism. Instead, Suleiman discusses the relevance of postmodernism in terms of what it does and its effect on various discourses, rather than seeking to grasp its divergent characteristics. Challenging Jameson's critique that it is an irrelevant form of pastiche, she contends that it is the politics surrounding the subject, not the thing itself, that is relevant. Gender is key, and Suleiman positions the female protagonists she cites alongside their male colleagues at the core of the debate. The plethora of citations also suggests that feminism has been integrated within intellectual discourse at large.

Susan Suleiman was born in Hungary in 1940 and emigrated to the USA with her parents when she was 11. She is Professor of Comparative Literature at Harvard University and is known for her interdisciplinary research on memory, trauma, testimony, forgetting and forgiveness. *EB*

... and to this day young authors sally forth in fiction like majestic – indeed, divinely ordained! – picaros to discover, again and again, their manhood.
(Robert Coover)

To write a quality cliché you have to come up with something new. (Jenny Holzer)

Contrary to what some recent commentators on postmodernism seem to think, there was life before Jean-François Lyotard.[1] The term 'postmodernism', designating a cultural sequel and/or challenge to modernism (however one defined that term) existed well before the publication of *La Condition postmoderne* (1979).[2] It is ironic that Lyotard's book, or rather its English translation, *The Postmodern Condition* (1981), should have become the required starting point for all current discussions of postmodernism by American and English critics, when Lyotard himself, in what I have called elsewhere a 'rare instance of "reverse importation" in the French-American theoretical marketplace', credited his use of the term to American critics, notably to Ihab Hassan.[3]

One would not be altogether wrong to see in this displacement, whereby the French philosopher 'takes the place of' all his American predecessors, a sign of what Fredric Jameson diagnosed as the absence of historical consciousness in postmodern culture – as if the memory of those who discuss postmodernism in the 1980s did not extend beyond the confines of the decade itself; or perhaps, more ironically, to see in it a sign of the snob appeal of 'genuine French imports' (or what are mistakenly thought to be such) in a certain sector of American intellectual life. But if this view would not be altogether wrong it would not be altogether right either, for although Lyotard's book did not initiate the discourse on postmodernism, it did place it on a new theoretical and philosophical footing. Most notably, it articulated the links between French poststructuralist philosophy and postmodern cultural practices ('culture' being understood to include science and everyday life as well as the arts), so that the latter could be seen – at least in the ideal sketched by Lyotard – as an instantiation of the former.

All of the concepts Lyotard invoked to define the innovative aspects of postmodern knowledge – the crisis of legitimation and the refusal of 'grand narratives', the choice of models of dissent and heterogeneity over models of consensus and systemic totality, the view of cultural practices as overlapping language games with constantly shifting rules and players – are concepts grounded in poststructuralist thought, as the latter was elaborated in France in the 1960s and 1970s by Lyotard, Derrida, Foucault and others. *The Postmodern Condition* can thus be read as a poststructuralist manifesto or 'manifesto of decentred subjectivities', expressing the optimism for the future that the manifesto genre requires. Although Lyotard is aware of the nightmarish possibilities offered by the 'computerisation of society' (his model of postmodern knowledge invokes and seeks to generalise the new technologies and conceptualisations – such as Mandelbrot's fractals – made possible by the computer), he emphasises instead its potentialities as a positive dream. The dream is of a society in which knowledge would consist of language games that would be 'non-zero-sum games', where there would be no losers or winners, only players in a constantly evolving process; where openness would be the rule, with information and data banks available to all; where instability and 'temporary contracts' would lead neither to alienation nor to anarchy, but to 'a politics that would respect both the desire for justice and the desire for the unknown'.[4]

In short, a utopian – or cautiously utopian, if such a thing is possible – version of Babel, a positive counter-argument to the pessimistic views being elaborated, during the same post-1968 decade, by Jean Baudrillard. Lyotard was seeing the same things as Baudrillard, but interpreting them differently: what to Baudrillard appeared as the increasingly horrifying world of simulacra evacuating the real, indeed evacuating the very concept of a difference between the simulacrum and the real, appeared to Lyotard – at least potentially – as a world of increasing possibilities for innovation, brought about precisely by the breakdown of stable categories like 'the real'. Where Baudrillard saw the 'postmodern condition' (a term he did not use) as the end of all possibility for (real) action, community, resistance or change, Lyotard saw it as potentially a whole new game, whose possibilities remained open.[5]

That difference marked one of the stakes in what was soon to become, with the entry of Jürgen Habermas into the fray, the best-known version of the 'modernism–postmodernism debate.'[6] Since then, the debate has shifted again: What is now in question is not so much whether postmodernism constitutes a totally new development or 'break' in relation to modernism (most people, it seems to me, have now accepted that as a given, even if they don't agree on all the details of why and how), but rather the current significance and future direction of the new development as such. What does all this have to do with women or feminism? And with earlier American discourses about postmodernism, which I accused other recent commentators of ignoring and then proceeded to ignore myself? Obviously, this is not the place to undertake a full-scale history of discourses on the postmodern.[7] Suffice it to say that, like a number of other important 'isms', (Romanticism, modernism, classicism), postmodernism has functioned as both a formal/stylistic category and a broadly cultural category. From the start, the most provocative discussions have been those that linked the formal or stylistic to the broadly cultural. Irving Howe's 1959 essay, for example, 'Mass Society and Postmodern Fiction', which is generally credited with first use of the term 'postmodern' in its current sense, saw in the emergence of a new kind of American fiction (roughly, that of the Beat generation) both a stylistic sequel to modernism – exemplified by Joyce, Mann and Kafka as well as Hemingway and Fitzgerald – and a cultural symptom of the transformations that had occurred in Western countries after the Second World War.[8] A similar argument, although adopting a different, more positive judgement on these transformations and on the literature that accompanied them, was made by Leslie Fiedler a few years later; it was also suggested, again in positive terms, by Robert Venturi and Denise Scott Brown around the same time regarding architecture, in the essay that was to become the basis for their famous (or infamous) manifesto of postmodern architecture, *Learning from Las Vegas*.[9]

A few years ago, I argued that as far as literature was concerned, it made no sense to try and establish clear-cut formal differences between the 'modernist' and the 'postmodernist', for such an attempt invariably involved oversimplification and flattening out of both categories.[10] Although I would now want to change some of the premises of that earlier argument, I still believe that the effort to define postmodernism chiefly as a formal (or even as a formal and thematic) category and to oppose it as such to modernism is, even when successful, of limited interest.[11] If postmodernist practice in the arts has provoked controversy and debate, it is because of what it 'does' (or does not do), not because of what it 'is'. In other words, it is as an object 'to be read', an intervention in the sense of an action or a statement requiring a response, rather than as an object of descriptive poetics, that postmodernism, whether in literature or in the other arts, strikes me as significant today.

This position, whether explicitly stated or not, seems to me to be shared by all those who are currently involved in the 'postmodernism debate'. Where is postmodernist practice going? Can it be political? – should it be? Does it offer possibilities for opposition, critique, resistance to dominant ideologies? Or is it irremediably compromised by its complicity with the market, with mass culture, capitalism, commercialism? Familiar questions, questions that have been asked in one form or another, at one time or another, about every avant-garde movement and experimental practice since Impressionism. Which does not make them less significant when asked about postmodernism, though it suggests that no definitive answers may be forthcoming.

And women? And feminism?

Discourses on the Postmodern and the Emergence of Feminist Postmodernism

It should come as no surprise, knowing what we know about earlier avant-garde movements and their historians, to learn that the first writings about postmodernism made absolutely no mention of the work of women. One could argue that if early commentators like Irving Howe and Leslie Fiedler, whose prime examples of the postmodern were the Beats (Fiedler also mentioned Pop art in the visual arts), did not mention women's work, it was because there was little or no such work around to be mentioned at the time. This would mean that the Beats and the Pop artists were male avant-gardes similar to certain earlier movements like Surrealism, excluding women during their most dynamic period.[12] In fact, there were some women, active in both movements, if not at the very beginning, then close enough to it (Diane Di Prima among the writers, Marisol among the painters). Still, as in the case of Surrealism, one can ascribe the early critics' silence not only to ordinary sexism ('not seeing' women who are there), but also to a real scarcity of women's work in those movements.

Critics who started to write about postmodernism in the 1970s or 1980s had less of an excuse for excluding the work of women; for in what I take to be a genuinely *new* (*inédit*, as they say on book covers in Paris) historical development, women's participation in experimental literary and visual work during those two decades reached a level, both in terms of quantity and quality, that could no longer be ignored. Some critics, of course, even among the most brilliant, managed to ignore it, as late as the mid-1980s others, less brilliant, went so far as to theorise its absence. (A few years ago, I received a letter from a European doctoral student who asked whether I agreed with her professor that 'women have not produced any postmodernist fiction', and if so, to what I attributed that lack. I replied that the lack may have been in the beholder rather than in the object.)

In the 1980s women's work began to be mentioned, and even featured, in academic discussions of postmodernism, especially in the visual arts. Rosalind Krauss's important 1981 article, 'The Originality of the Avant-Garde: A Postmodernist Repetition', which made a strong, polemically 'pro-postmodernist' case for the difference between postmodernism and its modernist or historical avant-garde predecessors (the difference residing, according to Krauss, in postmodernism's 'radical questioning of the concept of origin ... and originality'), cited as exemplary postmodernist works the photographs of Sherrie Levine; two years earlier, in the pages of the same journal, Douglas Crimp had argued for the innovativeness (originality?) of postmodernist 'pictures' and cited, among other examples, the photographs of Levine and Cindy Sherman.[13]

To discuss the work of women as part of a new movement, trend or cultural paradigm one is defending is undoubtedly a desirable thing. As Renato Poggioli showed, every avant-garde has its critical defenders and explicators;[14] their work, in turn, becomes a basis on which the movement, once it goes beyond its 'scandalous' phase, is integrated into the standard literary and cultural histories. It is quite another thing, however, to take into account not only the existence of women's work, but also its (possibly) feminine or feminist specificity; and to raise, furthermore, the question of how the specificity, whether sexual or political, of women's work within a larger movement affects one's understanding of the movement itself.

In his 1983 essay, 'The Discourse of Others: Feminists and Postmodernism', Craig Owens made one of those conceptual leaps that later turn out to have initiated a whole new train of thought. Simply, what Owens did was to theorise the political implications of the intersection between the 'feminist critique of patriarchy and the postmodernist critique of representation'.[15] He was not the first to suggest the political potential of poststructuralism (which, in the preceding sentence and in Owens's argument, is virtually interchangeable with postmodernism); the ideological critique of the 'unified bourgeois subject' and of classical representation had been a continuing theme in French poststructuralist writing from the late 1960s on, and had been part of the political platform of *Tel Quel* in its most revolutionary period.[16] Nor was the linking of the feminist critique of patriarchy with poststructuralism surprising, since French feminist theory had from the beginning acknowledged its linking to deconstruction, and even proclaimed it in its famous portmanteau word, 'phallogocentrism'. The novelty, indeed the path-breaking quality of Owens's essay was that it placed the feminist issue at the centre of the debate on postmodernism (which was also, if one wishes, a debate on poststructuralism), as that debate was unfolding in the United States (and, with a bit of delay, in England) after the publication of Lyotard's *The Postmodern Condition*.[17]

On the one hand, Owens quite rightly criticised the major players in the debate for ignoring both the 'insistent feminist voice' in postmodern culture and the whole issue of sexual difference in their discussions of postmodernist practices: thus even those critics who, like Crimp, Krauss and Hal Foster (and Owens himself, in an earlier essay), discussed women's work as an important part of postmodernist art, could be faulted for ignoring the specifically feminist – or even 'feminine' – meanings of that work.[18] On the other hand, Owens suggested that if the feminist/critical aspect of postmodernist work was taken into account, there would result a new and more politically sharpened view of postmodernism itself – for feminism, after all, is not only a theory or an aesthetics, it is also a politics.

By linking feminist politics with postmodernist artistic practice, Owens provided the pro-postmodernists in the debate with a precious argument, whose advantages they were quick to grasp. Feminism provided for postmodernism a concrete political edge, or wedge, that could be used to counter the accusatory pessimism of a Baudrillard or a Jameson: for if there existed a genuinely feminist postmodernist practice, then postmodernism could no longer be seen only as the expression of a fragmented, exhausted culture steeped in nostalgia for a lost centre. Indeed, such a view of postmodernism, with its sense of irremediable decline and loss, could now itself be shown to be implicated in the Western, patriarchal logic of the 'grand narratives' – the very logic that feminism, and feminist postmodernism, contested. As Hal Foster, in a 1984 essay that I read as a response to and development of Owens's argument, eloquently noted:

Here, then we begin to see what is at stake in [the] so-called dispersal of the subject. For what is this subject that, threatened by loss, is so bemoaned? For some, for many, this may indeed be a great loss, a loss which leads to narcissistic laments and hysterical disavowals of the end of art, of culture, of the west. But for others, precisely for Others, it is no great loss at all.[19]

Andreas Huyssen, around the same time, was arguing that feminism and the women's movement, together with anti-imperialism, the ecology movement and the growing awareness of 'other cultures, non-European, non-Western cultures', had created a new 'postmodernism of resistance' that would 'satisfy the needs of the political and those of the aesthetic'.[20] Most recently, following up on these arguments, Linda Hutcheon has spoken of the overlapping agendas between postmodernism and 'ex-centrics': blacks, women and other traditionally marginalised groups.[21]

In short, feminism brings to postmodernism the political guarantee postmodernism needs in order to feel respectable as an avant-garde practice. Postmodernism, in turn, brings feminism into a certain kind of 'high theoretical' discourse on the frontiers of culture, traditionally an exclusively male domain.[22]

If this summary sounds cynical, the effect is only partly intended. There is, I believe, an element of mutual opportunism in the alliance of feminists and postmodernists, but it is not necessarily a bad thing. The opportunism operates not so much, or perhaps not at all, in the actual practice of feminist postmodernist artists, but rather in the public discourse about that practice: influential critics who write about the work of feminist postmodernists, especially in the realm of the visual arts, are both advancing their own reputations as 'high theorists' and contributing to – or even creating – the market value of those artists' work, while other, less fashionable feminist work may go unnoticed. And once it becomes valuable on the market, the feminist postmodernist work may lose its critical edge.

This is not a new problem, as I have already suggested and will suggest again. In a world in which everything, even the discourse of high postmodernist theory, has an exchange value, should one reject the advantages of the feminist–postmodernist alliance for the sake of an ideal of aesthetic or intellectual purity? If every avant-garde has its public defenders and promoters, why not feminist postmodernism?

Oh dear oh dear, now I do sound excessively cynical. Let me therefore quickly affirm that I take the theoretical arguments advanced by Owens, Foster, Huyssen and Hutcheon in favour of the feminism/postmodernism alliance extremely seriously, and indeed subscribe to them (mostly); that I believe it is important to look for the critical and political possibilities of avant-garde practices in general, and of postmodernism in particular; and that I think women and feminists rightfully belong in the centre of such discussions and practices – in the middle of the margin, as it were.[23] As I said earlier, with postmodernism we have arrived at a totally new situation for women artists: for the first time in the history of avant-gardes (or in history *tout court*), there exists a critical mass of outstanding, innovative work by women, both in the visual arts and in literature.[24] Simone de Beauvoir's complaint, in *The Second Sex*, that women artists lacked genius – that is, the audacity to take real risks and to carry 'the weight of the world on their shoulders' – is no longer true, if it ever was. Today, thanks in part to the existence of predecessors like Beauvoir, there are women artists who possess genius in her sense – and who are aware at the same time that 'genius', like every other abstract universal category, is determined by particulars: race, sex, nationality, religion, history. As Christine Brooke-Rose has recently noted, 'genius' has the same Indo-European root as gender, genre and genesis.[25]

Still, it would be unwise to celebrate postmodernism, even more so feminist postmodernism, without keeping one's ears open to dissenting voices, or without acknowledging things that don't 'fit'. Feminist postmodernism, like postmodernism in general, must confront anew some of the dilemmas that have plagued every successful avant-garde for the past century or more: the dilemma of political effectiveness versus stylistic indirection and innovation, numbingly familiar to students of the 1930s; or the dilemma of the market and the avant-garde's relation to mass culture, which dominated, as Andreas Huyssen has shown, the 'Greenberg and Adorno decades' after the Second World War. In addition, feminist postmodernism must confront the specific questions and challenges posed to it from within the feminist movement, notably as concerns the political status of the 'de-centred subject'.

Not a short order, in sum. Enough to fill a whole book, in fact. But I shall fill only a few more pages, with thoughts and notes for future reflection and work, whether by me or others.

Opposition in Babel? The Political Status of (Postmodern, Ironic) Intertextuality

> Then I shall enter with my hypotheses and sweep the detritus of civilisation. (Christine Brooke-Rose, *Amalgamemnon*)

> The vital thing is to have an alternative so that people will realise that there's no such thing as a true story. (Jeanette Winterson, *Boating for Beginners*)

The appropriation, misappropriation, montage, collage, hybridization and general mixing up of visual and verbal texts and discourses, from all periods of the past as well as from the multiple social and linguistic fields of the present, is probably the most characteristic feature of what can be called the 'postmodern style'. The question, as it has emerged in the debate on postmodernism, is: Does this style have a critical political meaning or effect, or is it – in Fredric Jameson's words – merely 'blank parody', a 'neutral practice' devoid of any critical impulse or historical consciousness?[26]

There is not much point in looking for a single 'right' answer to that question, since it is precisely the object of the debate. One can, however, try to refine and clarify the question; and one must, sooner or later, state one's own position on it. What, then, does it mean to talk about the political effect of a novel or painting or photograph? If one means that in a particular historical circumstance an artwork can be used for political ends, well and good: Picasso's *Guernica*, exhibited in major European and American capitals between 1937 and 1939, earned a lot of sympathy as well as material support for the Spanish Republic before coming to rest for a few decades in the Museum of Modern Art. If one means that the work elicits a political response, whether in the form of public commentaries or private reactions, including the production of other artworks that build on it (*Guernica* is again a good example), that is also well and good.[27] What seems to me wrong-headed, or at the very least problematic, is to talk about the political effect or meaning of a work – especially of a self-conscious, insistently intertextual, often multiply ironic work – as if that meaning were clear, immutable and immanent to the 'text', rather than determined by its interpretive context.

Political readings – indeed, all interpretations – tend to speak of works as if their meanings and effects were immanent; in order to convince someone else of the validity of one's reading, one has to claim, or at least imply, that it is the best reading, the reading most closely corresponding to the 'work itself'. When Jameson made his often quoted claim that postmodern pastiche 'is a neutral practice of ... mimicry, without any of parody's ulterior motives, amputated of the 'satiric impulse, devoid of laughter and of any conviction that ... some healthy linguistic normality still exists', implicit in the claim (which was used to support his general argument that postmodernism lacked authentic historical awareness) was the assumption that works of art determine their own meaning and reading. Linda Hutcheon, who strongly criticises Jameson for not citing any examples, and offers many examples of her own to show that postmodern parody does not lack the satiric impulse and is not apolitical or ahistorical, is no doubt justified in her critique; but as the very act of citing counterexamples shows, she shares Jameson's assumption that political meanings reside in works, not in their readings.

As the by now familiar theories of 'reader-oriented criticism' have shown, however, this assumption is extremely problematic, and probably downright wrong. Stanley Fish and others have argued that every reading of a text, no matter how personal or 'quirky', can be shown to be part of a collective discourse and analysed historically and ideologically as characteristic of a group, or what Fish has called an interpretive community.[28] It is a matter of having learned, in the classroom or through scholarly exchange, or through more informal modes of communication, certain shared ways of approaching a text: asking certain questions of it, and elaborating a language and an interpretive 'strategy' for answering those questions.

Displacing the political effect from the work to its reading has the advantage of moving the debate from the question of what postmodernism 'is' to the question of what it does – in a particular place, for a particular public (which can be a public of one, but as I have just suggested, every individual is part of a larger interpretive community) at a particular time. That displacement does not, however, alter the basic questions about the politics of intertextuality or of irony, or more generally about the relation between symbolic action and 'real' action in the world. It merely ... displaces them, from the work to its readings and readers.

Jameson, reading postmodernist intertextuality as an expression of advanced capitalism 'a field of stylistic and discursive heterogeneity without a norm', calls it 'blank parody, a statue with blind eyeballs'.[29] But postmodernist intertextuality (is it the 'same' one?) can also be thought, for example in the British artist Mary Kelly's terms, as a sign of critical commitment to the contemporary world. According to Kelly, this commitment distinguished British postmodernist art of the 1970s and early 1980s from its American counterpart: whereas the Americans merely 'purloined' previous images and 'pilfered' the contemporary world's 'cultural estate', the British were 'exploring its boundaries, deconstructing its centre, proposing the decolonisation of its visual codes and of language itself'.[30]

It is not clear from Kelly's comparison how one can distinguish, objectively, 'mere pilfering' from political deconstruction and decolonisation. Similarly, Jameson's recent attempt to distinguish the 'ahistorical' postmodernism he deplores from its 'homeopathic critique' in the works of EL Doctorow, works he admires and finds salutary, strikes me as dubitable at best.[31] So, for that matter, do all the other attempts that have been made to distinguish a 'good' postmodernism (of resistance) from a 'bad' postmodernism (what Lyotard calls the 'anything goes' variety).[32]

It seems a good bet that almost any given work can be shown to belong to either of those categories, depending on how one reads it. Cindy Sherman's early work, the series of *Untitled Film Stills* from nonexistent Hollywood films, which the artist interprets as being 'about the fakeness of role playing as well as contempt for the domineering "male" audience who would read the images as sexy',[33] and which some critics have read in those terms as a form of feminist ironic critique, have been read by other critics as works that play up to the 'male gaze' for the usual profit: 'the work seems a slicked-up version of the original, a new commodity. In fact, much of this work has proved quite salable, easy to show, easy to write about, easy to sell.'[34] Even the 'Third World' and 'women of colour', those brave new banners under which (together with feminism) the postmodernism of resistance has sought its political credentials, can be shown, if one is so inclined, to be caught up in the logic of the simulacrum and in the economics of multinational capitalism. In today's world, one can argue, there are no more places outside: the Third World too is part of the society of the spectacle.

Perhaps it all comes down, in the end, to how one understands Christine Brooke-Rose's evocative phrase about 'sweeping the detritus of civilisation'. Does (can?) the sweeper hope to clear the detritus, or is she merely making new patterns with it and thus adding to the heap? And if the latter, should the sweeper put away her broom?

Yet another twist: If postmodernist intertextuality can be read both ways, that fact itself is open to interpretation. For Linda Hutcheon, it proves that postmodernist works are ambivalent and contradictory, 'doubly encoded', and that they therefore constitute not a 'break' but a 'challenge to culture from within'.[35] For Craig Owens, it proves that postmodernism is the true art of deconstruction, for it recognises the 'unavoidable necessity of participating in the very activity that is being denounced precisely in order to denounce it'.[36] On the other hand, one could call this apology for postmodernism itself part of a strategy of 'anything goes', with the added proviso: 'as long as I recognise that I am not innocent'. This was already, in an ethical and existential perspective, the strategy of Camus's 'penitent judge' in *La Chute* (1956). Clamence is more than willing to admit his own guilt, as long as it allows him to denounce everyone else. But Clamence is not exactly an admirable character. ...

And so it goes – the twists may be unending.
Does that mean we should no longer play?

Martha Rosler, who calls her work 'didactic' but not 'hortatory', and whom critics consider a political postmodernist, worries that if the ironic work is not 'derived from a process of politicisation, although it claims a politics', it will simply end up in the art-critical establishment, where even feminist work – which has been affiliated with a politics – may become no more than 'just a competing style of the sixties and seventies ... outdated by fashion.'[37] I recognise in Rosler's worry the outlines of two old but apparently inexhaustible arguments: can art which claims an oppositional edge take the risk of entering a museum? Can it afford to be negative and individualistic, rather than offering a positive, collective 'alternative vision' of 'how things might be different'?[38]

Related to these arguments is the question of the symbolic versus the real. Meaghan Morris recently criticised the facile uses that apologists for postmodernism have made of the verb 'appropriate':

> it outrages humanist commitments, adds a little frisson of impropriety and risk by romanticising as violation the intertextual *sine qua non* of all cultural activity, and semantically guarantees a politics to practitioners by installing predation as the universal rule of cultural exchange. ... All energies become seizures and we all get a piece of the action.[39]

Morris's critique is both humorous and apt: it is too easy to endow metaphorical appropriation with the power of real takeovers, and one *should* look for connections between 'the politics of culture and the politics of politics'.[40] One should also, however, not belittle the value of symbolic interventions in the field of the real. Is it necessary to belabour the fact that language is part of the world (the 'real world') and plays a non-negligible part in shaping both our perceptions of it and our actions in it?

And then there are those who believe only a certain kind of 'real' can be political. Laura Kipnis, who identifies herself as a video artist and critic, dismisses all 'first-world' writing that is not concerned with immediate political action – for example, French feminist theory – as an elitist luxury: 'real shifts in world power and economic distribution have little to do with jouissance, the pre-Oedipal, or "fluids"', she notes sarcastically.[41] (Sarcasm, as we know, is not to be confused, with 'blank' postmodern pastiche.) For Kipnis, if I read her right, the true postmodernist critique is an act of international terrorism in which 'retaliation is taken, as has been announced, for "American arrogance"'and a truly new form of political struggle, which the West in its blindness has not recognised, is one 'in which civilian tourists are held responsible for the actions of their governments'.[42]

This position, for all its hard-nosed charm, strikes me as too close for comfort to the murderous anti-intellectualism of commissars, and other ayatollahs – or, since Kipnis is neither, to the traditional self-hatred of intellectuals who dream of getting their hands dirty.

Jeanette Winterson's *Boating for Beginners* is an outrageously blasphemous rewriting of the Flood story from Genesis. It is also very funny. Has it escaped the censorious eyes of those who picket Scorsese's *Last Temptation of Christ* because it is 'only a novel', by an author who is not a household name? Or because it is not 'serious'? And yet, what could be more serious than the realisation (if indeed it is true) that 'there is no such thing as a true story'?

Postmodernism for postmodernism, politics for politics, I'd rather be an ironist than a terrorist.

To Market, to Market: Oppositional Art in Mass Culture

> The whole world is constrained to pass through the filter of the culture industry.
> (Max Horkheimer and Theodor Adorno, *Dialectic of Enlightenment*)

Horkheimer and Adorno's pessimistic analysis of the power of the culture industry has become so much a part of contemporary intellectual discourse (to the point that it is almost itself a cliché, part of an anonymous 'general wisdom') that one may wonder whether there is any new way to conceptualise the relation between authentic art and degraded entertainment, or between genuine thought and the manipulated thought-control of advertising and the mass media.[43] It is not that their argument hasn't been criticised for its elitism – it has been, most recently by Andreas Huyssen. Furthermore, it can be criticised as a 'grand narrative', explaining all of contemporary culture in terms of a single paradigm: the culture industry, in their analysis, appears to be a monolithic mechanism whose effects are omnipresent and inescapable.

Yet, the argument still has power; it is hard to get around. One possible conclusion to which their analysis leads has been stated by Thomas Crow, concerning the deep logic of innovative art since the mid-19th century: 'the avant-garde serves as a kind of research and development arm of the culture industry.'[44] According to Crow (whose rich and complex argument would be worth following in detail), there exists a predictable pattern from Impressionism on, in which the avant-garde 'appropriates' certain dynamic oppositional practices from 'below', from marginal groups or subcultures (here Crow differs significantly from Horkheimer and Adorno); these practices, transformed into avant-garde invention, become, after a moment of productive tension between the 'high' and the 'low' (or between the oppositional and the institutional), simply a part of 'high' art, but are eventually recuperated by the culture industry and returned to the lower zone of mass culture – in a form, however, where the avant-garde invention is 'drained of its original force and integrity'.[45] This cycle, alternating between 'moments of negation and an ultimately overwhelming recuperative inertia',[46] accounts for the chronically problematic status of avant-garde art movements, which claim to want to have a real effect in the world but are always, in the end, 'domesticated'.

What hope is there for postmodernism, and specifically for feminist postmodernism, as an oppositional avant-garde practice? Quite possibly, not much – or not more than for previous avant-gardes. But that does not mean that the attempt is not worth making. Rozsika Parker and Griselda Pollock suggest that 'feminism explores the pleasures of resistance, of deconstruction, of discovery, of defining, of fragmenting, of redefining'.[47]

Is it possible that such pleasures can be experienced by more than a privileged few and still maintain their critical charge? I think it is significant that a number of politically motivated experimental women artists working today have found some unexpected ways to use technologies associated with the culture industry.[48] Jenny Holzer's use of electronic signs in airports and other public places – such as the Spectacolor Board in Times Square, which flashed her message in huge letters (part of a series titled *Truisms*): PRIVATE PROPERTY CREATED CRIME – is one well-known example; Barbara Kruger, who has used billboards to display some of her photomontages has also used the Spectacolor Board, to display the message: I AM NOT TRYING TO SELL YOU ANYTHING.

In an interview in 1985, Holzer explained: 'My work has been designed to be stumbled across in the course of a person's daily life. I think it has the most impact when someone is just walking along, not thinking about anything in particular, and then finds these unusual statements either on a poster or on a sign.'[49] In the same interview, Holzer mentioned her discovery that 'television is not prohibitively expensive. ... You can buy thirty seconds in the middle of "Laverne & Shirley" for about seventy-five dollars, or you can enhance the CBS Morning News for a few hundred dollars. The audience is all of Connecticut and a little bit of New York and Massachusetts, which is enough people.'[50] Barbara Kruger has expressed a similar view. While harbouring no illusions about the alienating effects of television ('TV is an industry that manufactures blind eyes'), Kruger, like Holzer, seeks new ways to use it: for Kruger it is in the very 'site of the stereotype', characteristic of TV representations, that 'the rules of the game can be changed and subtle reformations can be enacted'.[51]

The hope expressed in such statements is that it is possible to find openings even in the monolithic mechanism of the culture industry; that it is possible for innovative, critical work to reach a large audience without passing through the 'upward and downward' cycle analysed by Crow, where what reaches the mass public is always already 'evacuated cultural goods', deprived of force and integrity. I am sure there must exist arguments to deflate this hope. But I will not look for them here.

Of Cyborgs and (Other) 'Women': The Political Status of Decentred Subjects

> What kind of politics could embrace partial, contradictory, permanently unclosed constructions of personal and collective selves and still be faithful, effective – and, ironically, socialist feminist? (Donna Haraway, 'A Manifesto for Cyborgs')

The question asked by Donna Haraway sums up, as well as any could, what is at stake in the feminist embrace, but also in the feminist suspicion, of postmodernism.[52] Haraway, proposing the technological cyborg as an 'ironic political myth' to take the place of earlier, naturalistic myths of the goddess, celebrates the postmodernist model of 'identity out of otherness and difference'; she proclaims herself anti-essentialist, anti-naturalist, anti-dualist, anti-maternal, utopically 'for a monstrous world without gender'.[53] All of this ironically, and politically to boot.

Next to such inventiveness, those feminists who want to hang on to a notion of feminine specificity may look (in Naomi Schor's ironic self-characterisation) like 'wallflowers at the carnival of plural sexualities'.[54] But the differences between worshippers of the goddess and celebrants of the cyborg may themselves need to be put into question.

'If authenticity is relational, there can be no essence except as a political, cultural invention, a local tactic', writes James Clifford.[55] Which makes me think that sometimes it is politic to 'be' a goddess, at other times a cyborg – and at still other times, a laughing mother[56] or an 'alone-standing woman'[57] who sweeps the detritus of civilisation.

Julia Kristeva's recent book, an exploration of what it means to be 'foreign', reached the best-seller list in France – a country, Kristeva writes, which is both the best and the worst place to be an *étranger*. It is the worst, because the French consider everything that is not French 'an unpardonable offence to universal taste';[58] it is the best, because (as Kristeva, being herself one, knows) in France a foreigner is a constant object of fascination, loved or hated, never ignored.

Of course it makes a difference (nor would Kristeva suggest otherwise) whether one feels loved or hated. It also makes a difference if one is actively persecuted for being 'different'. Still, for yet another ironic myth, I feel much drawn to her evocation of the 'happy cosmopolitan', foreign not to others but to him or herself, harbouring not an essence but a 'pulverised origin'. Such a person 'transmutes into games what for some is a misfortune and for others an untouchable void'.[59] Which may not be a bad description of a feminist postmodernist.

As for politics, I don't hesitate to make my own ('appropriate' is the word) a message I recently found on a card sold at the Centre Georges Pompidou. The card is by Jamie Reid, the British artist whose work appeared on posters and jacket covers for the short-lived punk rock group the Sex Pistols. I bought it at the Paris opening (February 1989) of the exhibition on Situationism, a revolutionary movement of the 1960s that spurned museums (their chief spokesman was Guy Debord – he was not at the opening). Some of Reid's other work, ironic and anti-Thatcher, is shown in the exhibit.

The card is quite expensive, as cards go, and comes wrapped in cellophane; it is sold only in the museum. The picture on the cover shows Delacroix's *Liberty Leading the People*, against a background formed by four tilted modernist skyscrapers. The message reads (not exactly in this order): 'Live in the Present. Learn from the Past. Look to the Future.'

Notes

1. This essay is a shortened version of the last chapter of my book, *Subversive Intent: Gender, Politics and the Avant-Garde*, Harvard University Press (Cambridge, MA), 1990. Besides the people I mention in specific notes, I wish to thank Ingeborg Hoesterey and Mary Russo for their careful reading and very useful suggestions regarding this essay.

2. Jean-François Lyotard, *La Condition postmoderne: rapport sur le savoir*, Editions de Minuit (Paris), 1979. English translation: *The Postmodern Condition: A Report on Knowledge*, trans Geoff Bennington and Brian Massumi, University of Minnesota Press (Minneapolis), 1981.

3. Susan Suleiman, 'Naming and Difference: Reflections on "Modernism versus Postmodernism" in Literature', *Approaching Postmodernism*, eds Douwe Fokkema and Hans Bertens, John Benjamins (Amsterdam and Philadelphia), 1986, p 255. As I note in that essay, the first footnote in Lyotard's book cites Hassan, *The Dismemberment of Orpheus: Toward a Postmodern Literature*, Oxford

University Press (New York), 1971, as a source for his use of the term 'postmodern'; in the introduction to his book, Lyotard justifies his choice of 'postmodern' to characterise 'the condition of knowledge in the most highly developed societies', by noting that 'the word is in current use on the American continent among sociologists and critics' (*The Postmodern Condition*, p xxiii). Recent works on postmodernism that use Lyotard as an obligatory reference and make virtually no mention of any work before his on the subject include: *Universal Abandon? The Politics of Postmodernism*, ed Andrew Ross, University of Minnesota Press (Minneapolis), 1988; *Postmodernism and Its Discontents*, ed E Ann Kaplan, Verso (London), 1988; 'Modernity and Modernism, Postmodernity and Postmodernism', special issue of *Cultural Critique* 5, Winter 1986–7; 'Postmodernism', special issue of *Social Text* 18, Winter 1987–8. This may be a specifically American, or Anglo-American phenomenon, I should add; Richard Martin informs me that in Germany, where he teaches, Lyotard's book is known but Hassan's work remains the starting reference. I wish to thank Richard Martin for his careful reading and very useful criticisms of this essay.

4   Lyotard, *Postmodern Condition*, p 67.

5   Lyotard situates himself explicitly in opposition to Baudrillard early on in *The Postmodern Condition*, when he notes that the 'breaking up of the grand Narratives … leads to what some authors analyse in terms of the dissolution of the social bond and the disintegration of social aggregates into a mass of individual atoms thrown into the absurdity of Brownian motion. Nothing of the kind is happening: this point of view, it seems to me, is haunted by the paradisiac representation of a lost "organic" society' (p 15). Although he does not name Baudrillard in the text, Lyotard footnotes Baudrillard's 1978 book, *A l'ombre des majorités silencieuses*, as the one example of the analyses he is contesting here. Baudrillard's theory of the simulacrum, to which I referred, dates from 1975: *L'échange symbolique et la mort*, Gallimard (Paris). This theory is much indebted to Debord's theory of the 'society of the spectacle', which dates from just before 1968. (Guy Debord, *La société du spectacle*, Buchet-Chastel (Paris), 1967). In 1988, Debord published a short commentary on his earlier book, which reiterates and reinforces his earlier pessimistic analyses. See his *Commentaires sur la société du spectacle*, Gerard Lebovici (Paris), 1988.

6   Habermas's contribution to the debate was the now famous essay, 'Modernity – An Incomplete Project' (1981), reprinted in *The Anti-Aesthetic: Essays on Postmodern Culture*, ed Hal Foster, Bay Press, WA (1986), pp 3–15. Habermas criticised all those, including the French poststructuralists (whom he called 'anti-modernist young conservatives'), who argued for a 'break' with the 'modernist' project of the Enlightenment. Habermas does not seem to have been responding here to Lyotard's book (the essay does not mentioin Lyotard), and he did not link postmodernism to poststructuralism. Lyotard, however, responded to Habermas in his 1982 essay, 'Réponse à la question: qu'est-ce que le postmoderne?' which appears in English as an appendix to *The Postmodern Condition*. It was after that essay that the version of the 'modernism–postmodernism' debate associated with the names of Lyotard and Habermas reached full swing. There are other versions of the debate as well. For an American response specifically to this debate, see Richard Rorty, 'Habermas and Lyotard on Postmodernity', reprinted in *Zeitgeist in Babel*, ed Ingeborg Hoesterey, Indiana University Press (Bloomington), 1991.

7   For a somewhat useful historical overview (as of about 1985), see Hans Bertens, 'The Postmodern *Weltanschauung* and Its Relation with Modernism: An Introductory Survey', *Approaching Postmodernism*, pp 9–51. My essay in the same volume, 'Naming and Difference', distinguishes various discourses on the postmodern in terms of their founding impulse: ideological, diagnostic or classificatory.

8   Irving Howe, 'Mass Society and Postmodern Fiction', *The Decline of the New*, Harcourt, Brace and World (New York), 1970; first published in *Partisan Review* in 1959 The term *postmodernismo* was, it appears, already used in Spain by Federico de Onis in 1934; however, its meaning was quite different. See John Barth, 'Postmodernism Revisited', *The Review of Contemporary Fiction* 8, no 3, Fall 1988, p 8.

9   Leslie Fiedler, 'The New Mutants' (1965), reprinted in *Collected Essays*, vol 2, Stein and Day (New York), 1971, pp 379–400; Robert Venturi, Denise Scott Brown, and Steven Izenour, *Learning from Las Vegas: The Forgotten Symbolism of Architectual Form*, revised edition, MIT Press (Cambridge, MA), 1988 (original ed 1977). In the preface to the first edition, Brown and Venturi cite their 1968 article, 'A Significance for A&P Parking Lots, or, Learning from Las Vegas', as the basis for the book.

10 Suleiman, 'Naming and Difference'.

11 The most successful effort of this kind so far, I believe, is Brian McHale's *Postmodernist Fiction*, Methuen (New York and London), 1987. Describing his work as an example of 'descriptive poetics', McHale makes no attempt to link postmodernist fiction to any contemporary or cultural issues – indeed, he concludes that postmodernist fiction, like all scientific literature, treats the eternal themes of love and death. Within its self-imposed Formalist parameters, I find McHale's criterion for distinguishing modernist from postmodernist fiction (the former being dominated by epistemological issues, the latter by ontological ones) extremely interesting, and his detailed reading of postmodernist works in terms of the ontological criterion suggestive and persuasive.

12 I develop the argument about Surrealism and analyse the place of women in that movement's history (which, I suggest, differs in significant ways from the place of women in the history of Anglo-American modernism) in chapter 1 of my book, *Subversive Intent*.

13 Rosalind Krauss, 'The Originality of the Avant-Garde: A Postmodernist Repetition' (1981), reprinted in *Zeitgeist in Babel*, ed Hoesterey; Douglas Crimp, 'Pictures', *October* 8, Spring 1979, pp 75–88, both reprinted in *Art after Modernism: Rethinking Representation*, ed Brian Wallis, The New Museum of Contemporary Art, New York and David R Godine (Boston), 1984. Among literary critics, Brian McHale has included some discussion of the work of women, notably Angela Carter and Christine Brooke-Rose, in his *Postmodernist Fiction*, without, however, raising the question of sexual difference. Ihab Hassan, in the new postface to the second edition of *The Dismemberment of Orpheus,* cites Brooke-Rose's name in some of his postmodernist lists (she was not cited in the first edition, 1971). The only general study of postmodernist writing to date which discusses women's work (along with that of other marginal groups) and also makes some attempt to take into account its political specificity is Linda Hutcheon, *A Poetics of Postmodernism: History, Theory, Fiction*, Routledge (New York and London), 1988.

14 Renato Poggioli, *The Theory of the Avant-Garde*, Harvard University Press (Cambridge, MA), 1968, chaps 5, 8.

15 Craig Owens, 'The Discourse of Others: Feminists and Postmodern', *Anti-Aesthetic*, ed Foster, p 59.

16 I discuss the politics of *Tel Quel* as an avant-garde movement in my essay, 'As Is', *A New History of French Literature*, Denis Hollier et al (eds), Harvard University Press (Cambridge, MA), 1989.

17 See note 6 above. The most explicit linking of postmodernism and poststructuralism in the debate was made by Terry Eagleton, in his highly negative Marxist critique, 'Capitalism, Modernism and Postmodernism', *New Left Review* 152, 1985, pp 60–73.

18 Owens. 'Discourse of Others', pp 73–7.

19 Hal Foster, '(Post) Modern Polemics', *Recordings: Art, Spectacle, Cultural Politics*, Bay Press (Seattle, WA), 1985, p 136.

20 Andreas Huyssen, 'Mapping the Postmodern', *After the Great Divide: Modernism, Mass Culture, Postmodernism*, Indiana University Press (Bloomington), 1986, pp 219–21.

21 Hutcheon, *A Poetics of Postmodernism*, chap 4.

22 It is true, as Richard Martin reminds me, that some feminists are critical of this 'high theoretical' discourse (or of any theoretical discourse closely associated with a male tradition) and would just as soon not participate in it. That raises a whole number of other questions regarding alliances and dialogue between men and women, which I will not attempt to develop here. My own favouring of dialogue and 'complication' over separatist and binarist positions is explicitly argued in chaps 4, 6 and 7 of *Subversive Intent*.

23 The same argument can be made (as Linda Hutcheon's grouping together of 'ex-centrics' and Huyssen's and Foster's use of the concept 'Others' shows) for the alliance between postmodernism and Third World minorities or Afro-American writers, male and female. Many black American critics (Henry Louis Gates comes especially to mind) have recognised the similarity of concerns and of analytic concepts between feminist criticism and Afro-American criticism. The links between Afro-American writing and postmodernism have also been recognised, notably in the novels of Ishmael Reed. Black women writers, however, have rarely been called postmodernists, and even less feminist postmodernists. A case can be made for considering Toni Morrison and Ntozate Shange (among others) 'black women feminist postmodernists'. But the question of priorities (race or gender) remains.

24 To be sure, there were a number of important women writers and artists associated with Anglo-American modernism and other earlier movements who were ignored or belittled by male critics, as recent feminist scholarship has shown. (See, for example, Sandra Gilbert and Susan Gubar, *No Man's*

Land, vol 1, *The War of the Words*, Yale University Press (New Haven), 1987. And as I have argued elsewhere, there are significant historical and national differences that must be taken into account when discussing the participation of women in avant-garde movements. My sense is, however, that none of the early movements had the *critical mass of outstanding, innovative work by women, both in the visual arts and in literature* (the phrase is worth restating and underlining) that exists today. Is naming names necessary? Here, for the doubtful, is a partial list of outstanding English and American women artists working today, who can be (and at some time or other have been) called feminist postmodernists: In performance, Joanne Akalaitis, Laurie Anderson, Karen Finley, Suzanne Lacy, Meredith Monk, Carolee Schneemann; in film and video, Lizzie Borden, Cecilia Condit, Laura Mulvey, Sally Potter, Yvonne Rainer, Martha Rosler; in photography and visual arts, Jenny Holzer, Mary Kelly, Barbara Kruger, Sherrie Levine, Cindy Sherman, Nancy Spero: in fiction, Kathy Acker, Christine Brooke-Rose, Angela Carter, Rikki Ducornet, Emily Prager, Jeanette Winterson. (See also note 23.) I thank Elinor Fuchs and Judith Piper for sharing their expertise with me about women in postmodern performance. For more on contemporary women performers and visual artists, see the exhibition catalogue (which bears out my point about critical mass), *Making Their Mark: Women Artists Move into the Mainstream, 1970–1985*, Abbeville Press (New York), 1989.

25   Christine Brooke-Rose, 'Illiterations', *Breaking the Sequence: Women's Experimental Fiction*, eds Ellen G Friedman and Miriam Fuchs, Princeton University Press, 1989, p 59.

26   Fredric Jameson, 'Postmodernism, or the Cultural Logic of Late Capitalism', *New Left Review* 146, July–August 1984, pp 53–92.

27   For an excellent collection of responses to *Guernica* and clear exposition of its history as a 'political' painting, see *Picasso's Guernica: Illustrations, Introductory Essay, Documents, Poetry, Criticism, Analysis*, ed Ellen C Oppler, Norton (New York), 1988.

28   Stanley Fish, *Is There a Text in This Class?* Harvard University Press (Cambridge, MA), 1980. For an overview of theories of reading, see my introductory essay, 'Varieties of Reader-Oriented Criticism', *The Reader in the Text: Essays on Audience and Interpretation*, eds Susan R Suleiman and Inge K Crosman, Princeton University Press, 1980, pp 3–45.

29   Jameson, 'Cultural Logic', p 65.

30   Mary Kelly, 'Beyond the Purloined Image' (essay on a 1983 London exhibition with the same title, curated by Kelly), quoted in Rozsika Parker and Griselda Pollock, 'Fifteen Years of Feminist Action: From Practical Strategies to Strategic Practices', *Framing Feminism: Art and the Women's Movement 1970–85*, Pandora Press (London and New York), 1987, p 53. Aside from the excellent introductory essays by Parker and Pollock, this book offers a rich selection of written and visual work by women involved in various British feminist avant-garde art movements of the 1970s and early 1980s.

31   See Anders Stephanson, 'Regarding Postmodernism – A Conversation with Fredric Jameson', *Universal Abandon? The Politics of Postmodernism*, pp 3–30. Jameson suggests that Doctorow's works offer the possibility 'to undo postmodernism homeopathically by the methods of postmodernism to work at dissolving the pastiche by using all the instruments of pastiche itself, to reconquer some genuine historical sense by using instruments of what I have called substitutes for history' (p 17). The question Jameson does not answer (or raise) is: How does one tell the 'fake' (homeopathic) postmodernist pastiche from the 'real' one – which is itself a 'fake', a substitute for history? The play of mirrors here may strike one as quite postmodernist.

32   Lyotard, 'Answering the Question: What is Postmodernism?' trans Regis Durand, *The Postmodern Condition*, p 77. Huyssen picks up the distinction in *Mapping the Postmodern*, p 220. See also Foster, '(Post)Modern Polemics', *Recodings*.

33   See Sherman's interview with Jeanne Siegel, *Artwords 2: Discourse on the Early 80's*, ed Jeanne Siegel, Ann Arbor and UMI Research Press (London), 1988, p 272.

34   Martha Rosler, 'Notes on Quotes', *Wedge* 2; Fall 1982, p 71. Rosler does not refer to anyone by name, but her critique here appears clearly to be directed at the work of Kruger, Levine and Sherman.

35   Hutcheon, *Poetics of Postmodernism*, p xiii and passim.

36   Craig Owens, 'The Allegorical Impulse: Towards a Theory of Postmodernism', *Art After Modernism*, ed Wallis, p 235.

37   Rosler, 'Notes on Quotes', pp 72, 73. Rosler's characterisation of her work as didactic but not hortatory is in an interview with Jane Weinstock, 17 October, Summer 1981, p 78.

38   Ibid, p 72.

39 Meaghan Morris, 'Tooth and Claw: Tales of Survival and Crocodile Dundee', *Universal Abandon?* p 123.

40 Ibid, p 125.

41 Laura Kipnis, 'Feminism: The Political Conscience of Postmodernism?' *Universal Abandon?* p 162.

42 Ibid, p 13.

43 Max Horkheimer and Theodor W Adorno, 'The Culture Industry: Enlightenment As Mass Deception', *Dialectic of Enlightenment*, trans John Cumming, Continuum (New York), 1982, pp 120–67.

44 Thomas Crow, 'Modernism and Mass Culture in the Visual Arts', *Pollock and After*, p 257. I wish to thank Bernard Gendron for bringing Crow's essay, in particular the remark I have quoted about the avant-garde and the culture industry, to my attention; and for his thoughtful reading and criticism of my own essay.

45 Ibid, p 258.

46 Ibid, p 259.

47 Rozsika Parker and Griselda Pollock, 'Fifteen years of feminist action: from practical strategies to strategic practices', *Framing Feminism*, p 54.

48 Women postmodernists are not the only ones to have practised a kind of public intervention, of course; among men doing comparable things, Hans Haacke and Daniel Buren come to mind (though Buren's work questions more the politics of museums than the 'politics of politics'). Nor is all of the political work by women exclusively feminist. These considerations do not invalidate my general point; rather, they enlarge it.

49 Interview with Jeanne Siegel. 'Jenny Holzer's Language Games', *Artwords* 2, p 286. See also, in the same volume, the interview with Barbara Kruger, where Kruger refers to her use of billboards and of the Times Square Spectacolor Board, pp 299–311.

50 Ibid, p 297.

51 Barbara Kruger, interview with Jeanne Siegel, *Artwords* 2, p 304.

52 Donna Haraway, 'A Manifesto for Cyborgs: Science, Technology, and Socialist Feminism in the 1980s', *Socialist Review* 50, 1984 p 75.

53 Ibid, p 100.

54 Naomi Schor, 'Dreaming Dissymetry', *Men in Feminism*, eds Alice Jardine and Paul Smith, Methuen (New York and London), 1987, p 109.

55 James Clifford, *The Predicament of Culture*, Harvard University Press (Cambridge, MA), 1988, p 12.

56 On the figure of the 'laughing mother', see Suleiman, *Subversive Intent*.

57 On the figure of the 'alone-standing woman' – a fictional creation of Christine Brooke-Rose – as an emblem of postmodernity, see my essay on Brooke-Rose's novel *Between:* 'Living Between, or the Lone(love)liness of the alleinstehende Frau', *The Review of Contemporary Fiction*, Fall 1989, pp 124–7.

58 Julia Kristeva, *Etrangers à nous-mêmes*, Fayard (Paris), 1988, p 58, my translation.

59 Ibid, p 57.

The Discourse of Others
Feminists and Postmodernism

Craig Owens

In this article feminist practice is located within the postmodern condition. Owens discusses female exclusion as arising from modernist representation, particularly the dominant male gaze, but also from woman being turned into a symbol for that which is unrepresentable and unspeakable such as Nature, Truth and the Sublime – the Other. He contends that women's insistence on difference coincides with postmodern thought, not as a binary opposition to the male but in allowing for plural alternatives. Following this he identifies feminist practice as the ability to concentrate on multiple activities, often bringing together theory and practice as a postmodern phenomenon.

Craig Owens (1950–90) was a postmodern art critic. He taught as a professor of art history at Yale University and Barnard College, and became senior editor of *Art in America*. His research focused on photography, feminism, psychoanalysis and gay politics. *EB*

Postmodern knowledge (*le savoir postmoderne*) is not simply an instrument of power. It refines our sensitivity to differences and increases our tolerance of incommensurability. (J-F Lyotard, *La Condition postmoderne*)

Decentred, allegorical, schizophrenic – however we choose to diagnose its symptoms, postmodernism is usually treated, by its protagonists and antagonists alike, as a crisis of cultural authority, specifically of the authority vested in Western European culture and its institutions. That the hegemony of European civilisation is drawing to a close is hardly a new perception; since the mid-1950s, at least, we have recognised the necessity of encountering different cultures by means other than the shock of domination and conquest. Among the relevant texts are Arnold Toynbee's discussion, in the eighth volume of his monumental *A Study in History*, of the end of the modern age (an age that began, Toynbee contends, in the late 15th century when Europe began to exert its influence over vast land areas and populations not its own) and the beginning of a new, properly postmodern age characterised by the coexistence of different cultures. Claude Lévi-Strauss's critique of Western ethnocentrism could also be cited in this context, as well as Jacques Derrida's critique of this critique in *Of Grammatology*. But perhaps the most eloquent testimony to the end of Western sovereignty has been that of Paul Ricoeur, who wrote in 1962 that 'the discovery of the plurality of cultures is never a harmless experience.'

When we discover that there are several cultures instead of just one and consequently at the time when we acknowledge the end of a sort of cultural monopoly, be it illusory or real, we are threatened with the destruction of our own discovery. Suddenly it becomes possible that there are just *others*, that we ourselves are an 'other' among others. All meaning and every goal having disappeared, it becomes possible to wander through civilisations as if through vestiges and ruins. The whole of mankind becomes an imaginary museum: where shall we go this weekend – visit the Angkor ruins or take a stroll in the Tivoli of Copenhagen? We can very easily imagine a time close at hand when any fairly well-to-do person will be able to leave his country indefinitely in order to taste his own national death in an interminable, aimless voyage.[1]

Lately, we have come to regard this condition as postmodern. Indeed, Ricoeur's account of the more dispiriting effects of our culture's recent loss of mastery anticipates both the melancholia and the eclecticism that pervade current cultural production – not to mention its much-touted pluralism. Pluralism, however, reduces us to being an other among others; it is not a recognition, but a reduction to difference to absolute indifference, equivalence, interchangeability (what Jean Baudrillard calls 'implosion'). What is at stake, then, is not only the hegemony of Western culture, but also (our sense of) our identity as a culture. These two stakes, however, are so inextricably intertwined (as Foucault has taught us, the positing of an Other is a necessary moment in the consolidation, the incorporation of any cultural body) that it is possible to speculate that what has toppled our claims to sovereignty is actually the realisation that our culture is neither as homogeneous nor as monolithic as we once believed it to be. In other words, the causes of modernity's demise – at least as Ricoeur describes its effects – lie as much within as without. Ricoeur, however, deals only with the difference without. What about the difference within?

In the modern period the authority of the work of art, its claim to represent some authentic vision of the world, did not reside in its uniqueness or singularity, as is often said; rather, that authority was based on the universality modern aesthetics attributed to the *forms* utilised for the representation of vision, over and above differences in content due to the production of works in concrete historical circumstances.[2] (For example, Kant's demand that the judgement of taste be universal – ie, universally communicable – that it derive from 'grounds deep-seated and shared alike by all men, underlying their agreement in estimating the forms under which objects are given to them'.) Not only does the postmodernist work claim no such authority, it also actively seeks to undermine all such claims; hence, its generally deconstructive thrust. As recent analyses of the 'enunciative apparatus' of visual representation – its poles of emission and reception – confirm, the representational systems of the West admit only one vision – that of the constitutive male subject – or, rather, they posit the subject of representation as absolutely centred, unitary, masculine.[3]

The postmodernist work attempts to upset the reassuring stability of that mastering position. This same project has, of course, been attributed by writers like Julia Kristeva and Roland Barthes to the *modernist* avant-garde, which through the introduction of heterogeneity, discontinuity, glossolalia, etc, supposedly put the subject of representation in crisis. But the avant-garde sought to transcend representation in favour of presence and immediacy; it proclaimed the autonomy of the signifier, its liberation from the 'tyranny of the signified'; postmodernists instead expose the tyranny of the *signifier*, the violence of its law.[4] (Lacan spoke of the necessity of submitting to the 'defiles' of the signifier; should we not ask rather who in our culture is defiled by the signifier?) Recently, Derrida has cautioned against a wholesale condemnation of representation, not only because such a condemnation may appear to advocate a rehabilitation of presence and immediacy and thereby serve the interests of the most reactionary political tendencies, but more importantly, perhaps, because that which exceeds, 'transgresses the figure of all possible representation', may ultimately be none other than … the law. Which obliges us, Derrida concludes, 'to thinking altogether *differently*'.[5]

It is precisely at the legislative frontier between what can be represented and what cannot that the postmodernist operation is being staged – not in order to transcend representation, but in order to expose that system of power that authorises certain representations while blocking, prohibiting or invalidating others. Among those prohibited from Western representation, whose representations are denied all legitimacy, are women. Excluded from representation by its very structure, they return within it as a figure for – a representation of – the unrepresentable (Nature, Truth, the Sublime, etc). This prohibition bears primarily on woman as the subject, and rarely as the object of representation, for there is certainly no shortage of images of women. Yet in being represented by, women have been rendered an absence within the dominant culture as Michèle Montrelay proposes when she asks 'whether psychoanalysis was not articulated precisely in order to repress femininity (in the sense of producing its symbolic representation)'.[6] In order to speak, to represent herself, a woman assumes a masculine position; perhaps this is why femininity is frequently associated with masquerade, with false representation, with simulation and seduction. Montrelay, in fact, identifies women as the 'ruin of representation': not only have they nothing to lose; their exteriority to Western representation exposes its limits.

Here, we arrive at an apparent crossing of the feminist critique of patriarchy and the postmodernist critique of representation; this essay is a provisional attempt to explore the implications of that intersection. My intention is not to posit identity between these two critiques; nor is it to place them in a relation of antagonism or opposition. Rather, if I have chosen to negotiate the treacherous course between postmodernism and feminism, it is in order to introduce the issue of sexual difference into the modernism/postmodernism debate – a debate which has until now been scandalously in-different.[7]

'A Remarkable Oversight'[8]

Several years ago I began the second of two essays devoted to an allegorical impulse in contemporary art – an impulse that I identified as postmodernist – with a discussion of Laurie Anderson's multimedia performance *Americans on the Move*.[9] Addressed to transportation as a metaphor for communication – the transfer of meaning from one place to another – *Americans on the Move* proceeded primarily as verbal commentary on visual images projected on a screen behind the performers. Near the beginning Anderson introduced the schematic image of a nude man and woman, the former's right arm raised in greeting, that had been emblazoned on the Pioneer spacecraft. Here is what she had to say about this picture; significantly, it was spoken by a distinctly male voice (Anderson's own processed through a harmoniser, which dropped it an octave – a kind of electronic vocal transvestism):

> In our country, we send pictures of our sign language into outer space. They are speaking our sign language in these pictures. Do you think they will think his hand is permanently attached that way? Or do you think they will read our signs? In our country, goodbye looks just like hello.

Here is my commentary on this passage:

> Two alternatives: either the extraterrestrial recipient of this message will assume that it is simply a picture, that is, an analogical likeness of the human figure, in which case he might logically conclude that male inhabitants of Earth walk around with their right arms permanently raised. Or he will somehow divine that this gesture is addressed to him and attempt to read it, in which case he will be stymied, since a single gesture signifies both greeting and farewell, and any reading of it must oscillate between these two extremes. The same gesture could also mean 'Halt!' or represent the taking of an oath, but if Anderson's text does not consider these two alternatives that is because it is not concerned with ambiguity, with multiple meanings engendered by a single sign; rather, two *clearly defined but mutually incompatible* readings are engaged in blind confrontation in such a way that it is impossible to choose between them.

This analysis strikes me as a case of gross critical negligence. For in my eagerness to rewrite Anderson's text in terms of the debate over determinate versus indeterminate meaning, I had overlooked something – something that is so obvious, so 'natural' that it may at the time have seemed unworthy of comment. It does not seem that way to me today. For this is, of course, an image of sexual difference or, rather, of sexual differentiation according to the distribution of the phallus – as it is marked and then re-marked by the man's right arm, which appears less to have been raised than erected in greeting. I was, however, close to the 'truth' of the image when I suggested that men on Earth might walk around with something permanently raised – close perhaps, but no cigar. (Would my reading have been different – or less in-different – had I known then that, earlier in her career, Anderson had executed a work which consisted of photographs of men who had accosted her in the street?)[10] Like all representations of sexual difference that our culture produces, this is an image not simply of anatomical difference, but of the values assigned to it. Here, the phallus is a signifier (that is, it represents the subject for another signifier);

it is, in fact, the privileged signifier, the signifier of privilege, of the power and prestige that accrue to the male in our society. As such, it designates the effects of signification in general. For in this (Lacanian) image, chosen to represent the inhabitants of Earth for the extraterrestrial Other, it is the man who speaks, who represents mankind. The woman is only represented; she is (as always) already spoken for.

If I return to this passage here, it is not simply to correct my own remarkable oversight, but more importantly to indicate a blind spot in our discussions of postmodernism in general: our failure to address the issue of sexual difference – not only in the objects we discuss, but in our own enunciation as well.[11] However restricted its field of inquiry may be, every discourse on postmodernism – at least insofar as it seeks to account for certain recent mutations within that field – aspires to the status of a general theory of contemporary culture. Among the most significant developments of the past decade – it may well turn out to have been *the* most significant – has been the emergence, in nearly every area of cultural activity, of a specifically feminist practice. A great deal of effort has been devoted to the recovery and revaluation of previously marginalised or underestimated work; everywhere this project has been accompanied by energetic new production. As one engaged in these activities – Martha Rosler – observes, they have contributed significantly to debunking the privileged status modernism claimed for the work of art: 'The interpretation of the meaning and social origin and rootedness of those (earlier) forms helped undermine the modernist tenet of the separateness of the aesthetic from the rest of human life, and an analysis of the oppressiveness of the seemingly unmotivated forms of high culture was companion to this work.'[12]

Still, if one of the most salient aspects of our postmodern culture is the presence of an insistent feminist voice (and I use the terms *presence* and *voice* advisedly), theories of postmodernism have tended either to neglect or to repress that voice. The absence of discussions of sexual difference in writings about postmodernism, as well as the fact that few women have engaged in the modernism/postmodernism debate, suggest that postmodernism may be another masculine invention engineered to exclude women. I would like to propose, however, that women's insistence on difference and incommensurability may not only be compatible with, but also an instance of postmodern thought. Postmodern thought is no longer binary thought (as Lyotard observes when he writes, 'Thinking by means of oppositions does not correspond to the liveliest modes of postmodern knowledge [*le savoir postmoderne*]').[13] The critique of binarism is sometimes dismissed as intellectual fashion; it is, however, an intellectual imperative, since the hierarchical opposition of marked and unmarked terms (the decisive/divisive presence/absence of the phallus) is the dominant form both of representing difference and justifying its subordination in our society. What we must learn, then, is how to conceive difference without opposition.

Although sympathetic male critics respect feminism (an old theme: respect for women)[14] and wish it well, they have in general declined the dialogue in which their female colleagues are trying to engage them. Sometimes feminists are accused of going too far, at others, not far enough.[15] The feminist voice is usually regarded as one among many, its insistence on difference as testimony to the pluralism of the times. Thus, feminism is rapidly assimilated to a whole string of liberation or self-determination movements. Here is one recent list, by a prominent male critic: 'ethnic groups, neighborhood movements, feminism, various "countercultural" or alternative life-style groups, rank-and-file labour dissidence, student movements, single-issue movements'. Not only does this forced coalition treat feminism itself as monolithic, thereby suppressing its multiple internal differences (essentialist, culturalist, linguistic, Freudian, anti-Freudian …); it also posits a vast, undifferentiated category, 'Difference', to which all marginalised or oppressed groups can be assimilated, and for which women can then stand as an emblem, a *pars totalis* (another old theme: woman is incomplete, not whole). But the specificity of the feminist critique of patriarchy is thereby denied, along with that of all other forms of opposition to sexual, racial and class discrimination. (Rosler warns against using woman as 'a token for all markers of difference', observing that 'appreciation of the work of women whose subject is oppression exhausts consideration of all oppressions'.)

Moreover, men appear unwilling to address the issues placed on the critical agenda by women unless those issues have first been neut(e)ralised – although this, too, is a problem of assimilation: to the already known, the already written. In *The Political Unconscious*, to take but one example, Fredric Jameson calls for the 'reaudition of the oppositional voices of black and ethnic cultures, women's or gay literature, "naïve" or marginalised folk art *and the like*' (thus, women's cultural production is anachronistically identified as folk art), but he immediately modifies this petition: 'The affirmation of such non hegemonic cultural voices remains ineffective', he argues, if they are not first *rewritten* in terms of their proper place in 'the dialogical system of the social classes'.[16] Certainly, the class determinants of sexuality – and of sexual oppression – are too often overlooked. But sexual inequality cannot be reduced to an instance of economic exploitation – the exchange of women among men – and explained in terms of class struggle alone; to invert Rosler's statement, exclusive attention to economic oppression can exhaust consideration of other forms of oppression.

To claim that the division of the sexes is irreducible to the division of labour is to risk polarising feminism and Marxism; this danger is real, given the latter's fundamentally patriarchal bias. Marxism privileges the characteristically masculine activity of production as the *definitively human* activity (Marx: men begin to distinguish themselves from animals as soon as they begin to produce their means of subsistence');[17] women historically consigned to the spheres of nonproductive or reproductive labour, are thereby situated outside the society of male producers, in a state of nature. (As Lyotard has written, 'The frontier passing between the sexes does not separate two parts of the same social entity.'[18]) What is at issue, however, is not simply the oppressiveness of Marxist discourse, but its totalising ambitions, its claim to account for every form of social experience. But this claim is characteristic of all theoretical discourse, which is one reason women frequently condemn it as phallocratic.[19] It is not always theory per se that women repudiate, nor simply, as Lyotard has suggested, the priority men have granted to it, its rigid opposition to practical experience. Rather, what they challenge is the distance it maintains between itself and its objects – a distance which objectifies and masters.

Because of the tremendous effort of reconceptualisation necessary to prevent a phallologic relapse in their own discourse, many feminist artists have, in fact, forged a new (or renewed) alliance with theory – most profitably, perhaps, with the writing of women influenced by Lacanian psychoanalysis (Luce Irigaray, Hélène Cixous, Montrelay …). Many of these artists have themselves made major theoretical contributions: film maker Laura Mulvey's 1975 essay on 'Visual Pleasure and Narrative Cinema', for example, has generated a great deal of critical discussion on the masculinity of the cinematic gaze.[20] Whether influenced by psychoanalysis or not, feminist artists often regard critical or theoretical writing as an important arena of strategic intervention: Martha Rosler's critical texts on the documentary tradition in photography – among the best in the field – are a crucial part of her activity *as an artist*. Many modernist artists, of course, produced texts about their own production, but writing was almost always considered supplementary to their primary work as painters, sculptors, photographers, etc,[21] whereas the kind of simultaneous activity on multiple fronts that characterises many feminist practices is a postmodern phenomenon. And one of the things it challenges is modernism's rigid opposition of artistic practice and theory.

At the same time, postmodern feminist practice may question theory – and not only *aesthetic* theory. Consider Mary Kelly's *Post-Partum Document* (1973–9), a six-part, 165-piece artwork (plus footnotes) that utilises multiple representational modes (literary, scientific, psychoanalytic, linguistic, archaeological and so forth) to chronicle the first six years of her son's life. Part archive, part exhibition, part case history, the *Post-Partum Document* is also a contribution to as well as a critique of Lacanian theory. Beginning as it does with a series of diagrams taken from *Ecrits* (diagrams which Kelly presents as *pictures*), the work might be (mis)read as a straightforward application or illustration of psychoanalysis. It is, rather, a mother's interrogation of Lacan, an interrogation that ultimately reveals a remarkable oversight within the Lacanian narrative of the child's relation to the mother – the construction of the mother's fantasies vis-à-vis the child. Thus, the *Post-Partum Document* has proven to be a controversial work, for it appears to offer evidence of *female* fetishism (the various substitutes the mother invests in order to disavow separation from the child); Kelly thereby exposes a lack within the theory of fetishism, a perversion heretofore reserved for the male. Kelly's work is not anti-theory; rather, as her use of multiple representational systems testifies, it demonstrates that no one narrative can possibly account for all aspects of human experience. Or as the artist herself has said, 'There's no single theoretical discourse which is going to offer an explanation for all forms of social relations or for every mode of political practice.'[22]

A la Recherche du Récit Perdu

'No single theoretical discourse …' – this feminist position is also a postmodern condition. In fact, Lyotard diagnoses *the* postmodern condition as one in which the *grands récits* of modernity – the dialectic of Spirit, the emancipation of the worker, the accumulation of wealth, the classless society – have all lost credibility. Lyotard defines a discourse as modern when it appeals to one or another of these *grands récits* for its legitimacy;

the advent of postmodernity, then, signals a crisis in narrative's legitimising function, its ability to compel consensus. Narrative, he argues, is out of its element(s) – 'the great dangers, the great journeys, the great goal'. Instead, 'it is dispersed into clouds of linguistic particles – narrative ones, but also denotative, prescriptive, descriptive, etc – each with its own pragmatic valence. Today, each of us lives in the vicinity of many of these. We do not necessarily form stable linguistic communities, and the properties of those we do form are not necessarily communicable.'[23]

Lyotard does not, however, mourn modernity's passing, even though his own activity as a philosopher is at stake. 'For most people,' he writes, 'nostalgia for the lost narrative (*le récit perdu*) is a thing of the past'.[24] 'Most people' does not include Fredric Jameson, although he diagnoses the postmodern condition in similar terms (as a loss of narrative's social function) and distinguishes between modernist and postmodernist works according to their different relations to the '"truth- content" of art, its claim to possess some truth or epistemological value'. His description of a crisis in modernist literature stands metonymically for the crisis in modernity itself:

> At its most vital, the experience of modernism was not one of a single historical movement or process, but of a 'shock of discovery, a commitment and an adherence to its individual forms through a series of religious conversions'. One did not simply read DH Lawrence or Rilke, see Jean Renoir or Hitchcock, or listen to Stravinsky as distinct manifestations of what we now term modernism. Rather one read all the works of a particular writer, learned a style and a phenomenological world, to which one converted. … This meant, however, that the experience of one form of modernism was incompatible with another, so that one entered one world only at the price of abandoning another. … The crisis of modernism came, then, when it suddenly became clear that 'DH Lawrence' was not an absolute after all, not the final achieved figuration of the truth of the world, but only one art-language among others, only one shelf of works in a whole dizzying library.[25]

Although a reader of Foucault might locate this realisation at the origin of modernism (Flaubert, Manet) rather than at its conclusion,[26] Jameson's account of the crisis of modernity strikes me as both persuasive and problematic – problematic because persuasive. Like Lyotard, he plunges us into a radical Nietzschean perspectivism: each *oeuvre* represents not simply a different view of the same world, but corresponds to an entirely different world. Unlike Lyotard, however, he does so only in order to extricate us from it. For Jameson, the loss of narrative is equivalent to the loss of our ability to locate ourselves historically; hence, his diagnosis of postmodernism as 'schizophrenic', meaning that it is characterised by a collapsed sense of temporality.[27] Thus, in *The Political Unconscious* he urges the resurrection not simply of narrative – as a 'socially symbolic act' – but specifically of what he identifies as the Marxist 'master narrative' – the story of mankind's 'collective struggle to wrest a realm of Freedom from a realm of Necessity'.[28]

Master narrative – how else to translate Lyotard's *grand récit*? And in this translation we glimpse the terms of another analysis of modernity's demise, one that speaks not of the incompatibility of the various modern narratives, but instead of their fundamental solidarity. For what made the *grands récits* of modernity master narratives if not the fact that they were all narratives of mastery, of man seeking his *telos* in the conquest of nature? What function did these narratives play other than to legitimize Western man's self-appointed mission of transforming the entire planet in his own image. And what form did this mission take if not that of man's placing of his stamp on everything that exists – that is, the transformation of the world into a representation, with man as its subject? In this respect, however, the phrase *master narrative* seems tautologous, since all narrative, by virtue of 'its power to master the dispiriting effects of the corrosive force of the temporal process',[29] may be narrative of mastery.[30]

What is at stake, then, is not only the status of narrative, but of representation itself. For the modern age was not only the age of the master narrative, it was also the age of representation—at least this is what Martin Heidegger proposed in a 1938 lecture delivered in Freiburg im Breisgau, but not published until 1952 as 'The Age of the World Picture' (*Die Zeit die Weltbildes*).[31] According to Heidegger, the transition to modernity was not accomplished by the replacement of a medieval by a modern world picture, 'but rather the fact that the world becomes a picture at all is what distinguishes the essence of the modern age'. For modern man, everything that exists does so only in and through representation. To claim this is also to claim that the world exists only in and through a subject who believes that he is producing the world in producing its representation:

> The fundamental event of the modern age is the conquest of the world as picture. The word 'picture' (*Bild*) now means the structured image (*Gebild*) that is the creature of man's producing which represents and sets before. In such producing, man contends for the position in which he can be that particular being who gives the measure and draws up the guidelines for everything that is.

Thus, with the 'interweaving of these two events' – the transformation of the world into a picture and man into a subject – 'there begins that way of being human which mans the realm of human capability given over to measuring and executing, for the purpose of gaining mastery of that which is as a whole.' For what is representation if not a 'laying hold and grasping' (appropriation), a 'making-stand-over-against, an objectifying that goes forward and masters'?[32] Thus, when in a recent interview Jameson calls for 'the *reconquest* of certain forms of representation' (which he equates with narrative: '"Narrative"', he argues, 'is, I think, generally what people have in mind when they rehearse the usual post-structuralist "critique of representation"'),[33] he is in fact calling for the rehabilitation of the entire social project of modernity itself. Since the Marxist master narrative is only one version among many of the modern narrative of mastery (for what is the 'collective struggle to wrest a realm of Freedom from a realm of Necessity' if not mankind's progressive exploitation of the Earth?), Jameson's desire to resurrect (this) narrative is a modern desire, a desire *for* modernity. It is one symptom of our postmodern condition, which is experienced everywhere today as a tremendous loss of mastery and thereby gives rise to therapeutic programmes, from both the Left and the Right, for recuperating that loss. Although Lyotard warns – correctly, I believe – against explaining transformations in modern/postmodern culture primarily as effects of social transformations (the hypothetical advent of a post-industrial society, for example),[34] it is clear that what has been lost is not primarily a cultural mastery, but an economic, technical and political one. For what if not the emergence of Third World nations, the 'revolt of nature' and the women's movement – that is, the voices of the conquered – has challenged the West's desire for ever-greater domination and control?

Symptoms of our recent loss of mastery are everywhere apparent in cultural activity today – nowhere more so than in the visual arts. The modernist project of joining forces with science and technology for the transformation of the environment after rational principles of function and utility (Productivism, the Bauhaus) has long since been abandoned; what we witness in its place is a desperate, often hysterical attempt to recover some sense of mastery via the resurrection of heroic large-scale easel painting and monumental cast-bronze sculpture – mediums themselves identified with the cultural hegemony of western Europe. Yet contemporary artists are able at best to *simulate* mastery, to manipulate its signs; since in the modern period mastery was invariably associated with human labour, aesthetic production has degenerated today into a massive deployment of the signs of artistic labour – violent, 'impassioned' brushwork, for example. Such simulacra of mastery testify, however, only to its loss; in fact, contemporary artists seem engaged in a collective act of disavowal – and disavowal always pertains to a loss ... of virility, masculinity, potency.[35]

This contingent of artists is accompanied by another which refuses the simulation of mastery in favour of melancholic contemplation of its loss. One such artist speaks of 'the impossibility of passion in a culture that has institutionalised self-expression'; another, of 'the aesthetic as something which is really about longing and loss rather than completion'. A painter unearths the discarded genre of landscape painting only to borrow for his own canvases, through an implicit equation between their ravaged surfaces and the barren fields he depicts, something of the exhaustion of the Earth itself (which is thereby glamourised); another dramatises his anxieties through the most conventional figure men have conceived for the threat of castration – Woman ... aloof, remote, unapproachable. Whether they disavow or advertise their own powerlessness, pose as heroes or as victims, these artists have, needless to say, been warmly received by a society unwilling to admit that it has been driven from its position of centrality; theirs is an 'official' art which, like the culture that produced it, has yet to come to terms with its own impoverishment.

Postmodernist artists speak of impoverishment – but in a very different way. Sometimes the postmodernist work testifies to a deliberate refusal of mastery, for example, Martha Rosler's *The Bowery in Two Inadequate Descriptive Systems* (1974–5), in which photographs of Bowery storefronts alternate with clusters of typewritten words signifying inebriety. Although her photographs are intentionally flat-footed, Rosler's refusal of mastery in this work is more than technical. On the one hand, she denies the caption/text its conventional function of supplying the image with something it lacks; instead, her juxtaposition of two representational systems, visual and verbal, is calculated (as the title suggests) to 'undermine' rather than 'underline' the truth value of each.[36] More importantly, Rosler has refused to photograph the inhabitants of Skid Row, to speak on their behalf, to illuminate them from a safe distance (photography as social work in the tradition of Jacob Riis). For 'concerned' or what Rosler calls 'victim' photography overlooks the constitutive role of its own activity, which is held to be merely representative (the 'myth' of photographic transparency and objectivity). Despite his or her benevolence in representing those who have been denied access to the means of representation, the photographer inevitably functions as an agent of the system of power that silenced these people in the first place. Thus, they are twice victimised: first by society, and then by the photographer who presumes the right to speak on their behalf. In fact, in such photography it is the photographer rather than the 'subject' who poses – as the subject's consciousness, indeed, as conscience itself. Although Rosler may not, in this work, have initiated a counterdiscourse of drunkenness – which would consist of the drunks' own theories about their conditions of existence – she has nevertheless pointed negatively to the crucial issue of a politically motivated art practice today: 'the indignity of speaking for others'.[37]

Rosler's position poses a challenge to criticism as well, specifically, to the critic's substitution of his own discourse for the work of art. At this point in my text, then, my own voice must yield to the artist's; in the essay 'in, around and afterthoughts (on documentary photography)' which accompanies The Bowery ..., Rosler writes:

> If impoverishment is a subject here, it is more certainly the impoverishment of representational strategies tottering about alone than that of a mode of surviving. The photographs are powerless to *deal with* the reality that is yet totally comprehended-in-advance by ideology, and they are as diversionary as the word formations – which at least are closer to being located within the culture of drunkenness rather than being framed on it from without.[38]

The Visible and the Invisible

A work like The Bowery in Two Inadequate Descriptive Systems not only exposes the 'myths' of photographic objectivity and transparency; it also upsets the (modern) belief in vision as a privileged means of access to certainty and truth ('Seeing is believing'). Modern aesthetics claimed that vision was superior to the other senses because of its detachment from its objects: 'Vision', Hegel tells us in his Lectures on Aesthetics, 'finds itself in a purely theoretical relationship with objects, through the intermediary of light, that immaterial matter which truly leaves objects their freedom, lighting and illuminating them without consuming them.'[39] Postmodernist artists do not deny this detachment, but neither do they celebrate it. Rather, they investigate the particular interests it serves. For vision is hardly disinterested; nor is it indifferent, as Luce Irigaray has observed:

'Investment in the look is not privileged in women as in men. More than the other senses, the eye objectifies and masters. It sets at a distance, maintains the distance. In our culture, the predominance of the look over smell, taste, touch, hearing, has brought about an impoverishment of bodily relations. ... The moment the look dominates, the body loses its materiality.'[40] That is, it is transformed into an image.

That the priority our culture grants to vision is a sensory impoverishment is hardly a new perception; the feminist critique, however, links the privileging of vision with sexual privilege. Freud identified the transition from a matriarchal to a patriarchal society with the simultaneous devaluation of an olfactory sexuality and promotion of a more mediated, sublimated visual sexuality.[41] What is more, in the Freudian scenario it is by looking that the child discovers sexual difference, the presence or absence of the phallus according to which the child's sexual identity will be assumed. As Jane Gallop reminds us in her recent book *Feminism and Psychoanalysis: The Daughter's Seduction*, 'Freud articulated the "discovery of castration" around a sight: sight of a phallic presence in the boy, sight of a phallic absence in the girl, ultimately sight of a phallic absence in the mother. *Sexual difference takes its decisive significance from a sighting.*'[42] Is it not because the phallus is the most visible sign of sexual difference that it has become the 'privileged signifier'? However, it is not only the discovery of difference, but also its denial that hinges upon vision (although the reduction of difference to a common measure – woman judged according to the man's standard and found lacking – is already a denial). As Freud proposed in his 1926 paper on 'Fetishism', the male child often takes the last visual impression prior to the 'traumatic' sighting as a substitute for the mother's 'missing' penis:

> Thus the foot or the shoe owes its attraction as a fetish, or part of it, to the circumstance that the inquisitive boy used to peer up at the woman's legs towards her genitals. Velvet and fur reproduce – as has long been suspected – the sight of the pubic hair which ought to have revealed the longed-for penis; the underlinen so often adopted as a fetish reproduces the scene of undressing, the last moment in which the woman could still be regarded as phallic.[43]

What can be said about the visual arts in a patriarchal order that privileges vision over the other senses? Can we not expect them to be a domain of masculine privilege – as their histories indeed prove them to be – a means, perhaps, of mastering through representation the 'threat' posed by the female? In recent years there has emerged a visual arts practice informed by feminist theory and addressed, more or less explicitly, to the issue of representation and sexuality – both masculine and feminine. Male artists have tended to investigate the social construction of masculinity (Mike Glier, Eric Bogosian, the early work of Richard Prince); women have begun the long-overdue process of deconstructing femininity. Few have produced new, 'positive' images of a revised femininity; to do so would simply supply and thereby prolong the life of the existing representational apparatus. Some refuse to represent women at all, believing that no representation of the female body in our culture can be free from phallic prejudice. Most of these artists, however, work with the existing repertory of cultural imagery – not because they either lack originality or criticise it – but because their subject, feminine sexuality, is always constituted in and as representation, a representation of difference. It must be emphasised that these artists are not primarily interested in what representations say about women; rather, they investigate what representation *does* to women (for example, the way it invariably positions them as objects of the male gaze). For, as Lacan wrote, 'Images and symbols *for* the woman cannot be isolated from images and symbols *of* the woman. ... It is representation, the representation of feminine sexuality whether repressed or not, which conditions how it comes into play.'[44]

Critical discussions of this work have, however, assiduously avoided – skirted – the issue of gender. Because of its generally deconstructive ambition, this practice is sometimes assimilated to the modernist tradition of demystification. (Thus, the critique of representation in this work is collapsed into ideological critique.) In an essay devoted (again) to allegorical procedures in contemporary art, Benjamin Buchloh discusses the work of six women artists – Dara Birnbaum, Jenny Holzer, Barbara Kruger, Louise Lawler, Sherrie Levine, Martha Rosler – claiming them for the model of 'secondary mythification' elaborated in Roland Barthes's 1957 *Mythologies*. Buchloh does not acknowledge the fact that Barthes later repudiated this methodology – a repudiation that must be seen as part of his increasing refusal of mastery from *The Pleasure of the Text* on.[45] Nor does Buchloh grant any particular significance to the fact that all these artists are women; instead, he provides them with a distinctly male genealogy in the Dada tradition of collage and montage. Thus, all six artists are said to manipulate the languages of popular culture – television, advertising, photography – in such a way that 'their ideological functions and effects become *transparent*'; or again, in their work, 'the minute and seemingly inextricable interaction of behaviour and ideology' supposedly becomes an '*observable* pattern'.[46]

But what does it mean to claim that these artists render the invisible visible, especially in a culture in which visibility is always on the side of the male, invisibility on the side of the female? And what is the critic really saying when he states that these artists reveal, expose, 'unveil' (this last word is used throughout Buchloh's text) hidden ideological agendas in mass-cultural imagery? Consider, for the moment, Buchloh's discussion of the work of Dara Birnbaum, a video artist who re-edits footage taped directly from broadcast television. Of Birnbaum's *Technology/Transformation: Wonder Woman* (1978–9), based on the popular television series of the same name, Buchloh writes that it 'unveils the puberty fantasy of Wonder Woman'. Yet, like all of Birnbaum's work, this tape is dealing not simply with mass-cultural imagery, but with mass-cultural *images of women*. Are not the activities of unveiling, stripping, laying bare in relation to a female body unmistakably male prerogatives?[47] Moreover, the women Birnbaum represents are usually athletes and performers absorbed in the display of their own physical perfection. They are without defect, without lack, and therefore with neither history nor desire. (Wonder Woman is the perfect embodiment of the phallic mother.)

What we recognise in her work is the Freudian trope of the narcissistic woman, or the Lacanian 'theme' of femininity as contained spectacle, which exists only as a representation of masculine desire.[48]

The deconstructive impulse that animates this work has also suggested affinities with poststructuralist textual strategies, and much of the critical writing about these artists – including my own – has tended simply to translate their work into French. Certainly, Foucault's discussion of the West's strategies of marginalisation and exclusion, Derrida's charges of 'phallocentrism', Deleuze and Guattari's 'body without organs' would all seem to be congenial to a feminist perspective. (As Irigaray has observed, is not the 'body without organs' the historical condition of woman?[49]). Still, the affinities between poststructuralist theories and postmodernist practice can blind a critic to the fact that, when women are concerned, similar techniques have very different meanings. Thus, when Sherrie Levine appropriates – literally takes – Walker Evans's photographs of the rural poor or, perhaps more pertinently, Edward Weston's photographs of his *son* Neil posed as a classical Greek torso, is she simply dramatising the diminished possibilities for creativity in an image-saturated culture, as is often repeated? Or is her refusal of authorship not in fact a refusal of the role of creator as 'father' of his work, of the paternal rights assigned to the Author by law?[50] (This reading of Levine's strategies is supported by the fact that the images she appropriates are invariably images of the Other: women, nature, children, the poor, the insane …)[51] Levine's disrespect for paternal authority suggests that her activity is less one of appropriation – a laying hold and grasping – and more one of expropriation: she expropriates the appropriators.

Sometimes Levine collaborates with Louise Lawler under the collective title 'A Picture is No Substitute for Anything' – an unequivocal critique of representation as traditionally defined. (EH Gombrich: 'All art is image-making, and all image-making is the creation of substitutes.') Does not their collaboration move us to ask what the picture is supposedly a substitute for, what it replaces, what absence it conceals? And when Lawler shows 'A Movie without the Picture', as she did in 1979 in Los Angeles and again in 1983 in New York, is she simply soliciting the spectator as a collaborator in the production of the image? Or is she not also denying the viewer the kind of visual pleasure which cinema customarily provides – a pleasure that has been linked with the masculine perversions voyeurism and scopophilia?[52] It seems fitting, then, that in Los Angeles she screened (or didn't screen) *The Misfits* – Marilyn Monroe's last completed film. So that what Lawler withdrew was not simply a picture, but the archetypal image of feminine desirability.

When Cindy Sherman, in her untitled black-and-white studies for film stills (made in the late 1970s and early 1980s), first costumed herself to resemble heroines of grade-B Hollywood films of the late 1950s and early 1960s and then photographed herself in situations suggesting some immanent danger lurking just beyond the frame, was she simply attacking the rhetoric of 'auteurism by equating the known artifice of the actress in front of the camera with the supposed authenticity of the director behind it'?[53] Or was her play-acting not also an acting out of the psychoanalytic notion of femininity as masquerade, that is, as a representation of male desire? As Hélène Cixous has written,

'One is always in representation, and when a woman is asked to take place in this representation, she is, of course, asked to represent man's desire'[54] Indeed, Sherman's photographs themselves function as mirror-masks that reflect back at the viewer his own desire (and the spectator posited by this work is invariably male) specifically, the masculine desire to fix the woman in a stable and stabilising identity. But this is precisely what Sherman's work denies: for while her photographs are always self-portraits, in them the artist never appears to be the same, indeed, not even the same model; while we can presume to recognise the same person, we are forced at the same time to recognise a trembling around the edges of that identity.[55] In a subsequent series of works, Sherman abandoned the film-still format for that of the magazine centrefold, opening herself to charges that she was an accomplice in her own objectification, reinforcing the image of the woman bound by the frame.[56] This may be true; but while Sherman may pose as a pin-up, she still cannot be pinned down.

Finally, when Barbara Kruger collages the words 'Your gaze hits the side of my face' over an image culled from a 1950s photo-annual of a female bust, is she simply 'making an equation … between aesthetic reflection and the alienation of the gaze: both reify'? Or is she not speaking instead of the *masculinity* of the look; the ways in which it objectifies and masters? Or when the words 'You invest in the divinity of the masterpiece' appear over a blown-up detail of the creation scene from the Sistine ceiling, is she simply parodying our reverence for works of art, or is this not a commentary on artistic production as a contract between fathers and sons? The address of Kruger's work is always gender-specific; her point, however, is not that masculinity and femininity are fixed positions assigned in advance by the representational apparatus. Rather, Kruger uses a term with no fixed content, the linguistic shifter ('I/you'), in order to demonstrate that masculine and feminine themselves are not stable identities, but subject to ex-change.

There is irony in the fact that all these practices, as well as the theoretical work that sustains them, have emerged in a historical situation supposedly characterised by its complete indifference. In the visual arts we have witnessed the gradual dissolution of once fundamental distinctions – original/copy, authentic/inauthentic, function/ornament. Each term now seems to contain its opposite, and this indeterminacy brings with it an impossibility of choice or, rather, the absolute equivalence and hence interchangeability of choices. Or so it is said. The existence of feminism, with its insistence on difference, forces us to reconsider. For in our country goodbye may look just like hello, but only from a masculine position. Women have learned – perhaps they have always known – how to recognise the difference.

Notes

1   Paul Ricoeur, 'Civilization and National Cultures,' *History and Truth*, trans Chas A Kelbley, Northwestern University Press (Evanston), 1965, p 278.
2   Hayden White, 'Getting Out of History,' *diacritics* 12, 3, Fall 1982, p 3. Nowhere does White acknowledge that it is precisely this universality that is in question today.
3   See, for example, Louis Marin, 'Toward a Theory of Reading in the Visual Arts: Poussin's *The Arcadian Shepherds*', *The Reader in the Text*, eds S Suleiman and I Crosman, Princeton University Press, 1980, pp 293–324. This essay reiterates the main points of the first section of Marin's

Détruire le peinture, Galilée (Paris), 1977. See also Christian Metz's discussion of the enunciative apparatus of cinematic representation in his 'History Discourse: A Note on Two Voyeurisms', *The Imaginary Signifier*, trans Britton, Williams, Brewster and Guzzetti, Indiana University Press (Bloomington), 1982. And for a general survey of these analyses, see my 'Representation, Appropriation & Power', *Art in America* 70, 5, May 1982, pp 9–21.

4   Hence Kristeva's problematic identification of avant-garde practice as feminine – problematic because it appears to act in complicity with all those discourses which exclude women from the order of representation, associating them instead with the presymbolic (Nature, the Unconscious, the body, etc).

5   Jacques Derrida, 'Sending: On Representation', trans P and MA Caws, *Social Research* 49, 2, Summer 1982, pp 325, 326, italics added. (In this essay Derrida is discussing Heidegger's 'The Age of the World Picture', a text to which I will return.) 'Today there is a great deal of thought against representation', Derrida writes. 'In a more or less articulated or rigorous way, this judgment is easily arrived at: representation is bad … And yet, whatever the strength and the obscurity of this dominant current, the authority of representation constrains us, imposing itself on our thought through a whole dense, enigmatic, and heavily stratified history. It programmes us and precedes us and warns us too severely for us to make a mere object of it, a representation, an object of representation confronting us, before us like a theme' (p 304). Thus, Derrida concludes that 'the essence of representation is not a representation, it is not representable, *there is no representation of representation*' (p 314, italics added).

6   Michèle Montrelay, 'Recherches sur la femininité', *Critique* 278, July 1970; trans Parveen Adams as 'Inquiry into Femininity', m/f 1, 1978; reprinted in *Semiotext(e)* 10, 1981), p 232.

7   Many of the issues treated in the following pages – the critique of binary thought, for example, or the privileging of vision over the other senses – have had long careers in the history of philosophy. I am interested, however, in the ways in which feminist theory articulates them onto the issue of sexual privilege. Thus, issues frequently condemned as merely epistemological turn out to be political as well. (For an example of this kind of condemnation, see Andreas Huyssens, 'Critical Theory and Modernity', *New German Critique* 26, Spring/Summer 1982, pp 3–11.) In fact, feminism demonstrates the impossibility of maintaining the split between the two.

8   'What is unquestionably involved here is a conceptual foregrounding of the sexuality of the woman, which brings to our attention a remarkable oversight.' Jacques Lacan, 'Guiding Remarks for a Congress on Feminine Sexuality', *Feminine Sexuality*, eds J Mitchell and J Rose, Norton and Pantheon (New York), 1982, p 87.

9   See my 'The Allegorical Impulse: Toward a Theory of Postmodernism' (part 2), *October* 13, Summer 1980, pp 59–80. *Americans on the Move* was first performed at The Kitchen Centre for Video, Music, and Dance in New York City in April 1979; it has since been revised and incorporated into Anderson's two-evening work *United States, Parts I–IV*, first seen in its entirety in February 1983 at the Brooklyn Academy of Music.

10 This project was brought to my attention by Rosalyn Deutsche.

11 As Stephen Heath writes, 'Any discourse which fails to take account of the problem of sexual difference in its own enunciation and address will be, within a patriarchal order, precisely indifferent, a reflection of male domination.' 'Difference', *Screen* 19, 4, Winter 1978–9, p 53.

12 Martha Rosler, 'Notes on Quotes', *Wedge*, 2, Fall 1982, p 69.

13 Jean-François Lyotard, *La Condition postmoderne*, Minuit (Paris), 1979, p 29.

14 See Sarah Kofman, *Le Respect des femmes*, Galilée (Paris), 1982. A partial English translation appears as 'The Economy of Respect: Kant and Respect for Women', trans N Fisher, *Social Research*, 49, 2 Summer 1982, pp 383–404.

15 Why is it always a question of *distance*? For example, Edward Saïd writes, 'Nearly everyone producing literary or cultural studies makes no allowance for the truth that all intellectual or cultural work occurs somewhere, at some times, on some very precisely mapped-out and permissible terrain, which is ultimately contained by the State. Feminist critics have opened this question part of the way, *but they have not gone the whole distance*.' 'American "Left" Literary Criticism', *The World, the Text, and the Critic*, Harvard University Press (Cambridge, MA), 1983, p 169. Italics added.

16 Fredric Jameson, *The Political Unconscious*, Cornell University Press (Ithaca), 1981, p 84.

17 Marx and Engels, *The German Ideology*, International Publishers (New York), 1970, p 42. One of the things that feminism has exposed is Marxism's scandalous blindness to sexual inequality. Both

Marx and Engels viewed patriarchy as part of a precapitalist mode of production, claiming that the transition from a feudal to a capitalist mode of production was a transition from male domination to domination by capital. Thus, in the *Communist Manifesto* they write, 'The bourgeoisie, wherever it has got the upper hand, has put an end to all feudal, patriarchal … relations.' The revisionist attempt (such as Jameson proposes in *The Political Unconscious*) to explain the persistence of patriarchy as survival of a previous mode of production is an inadequate response to the challenge posed by feminism to Marxism. Marxism's difficulty with feminism is not part of an ideological bias inherited from outside; rather, it is a structural effect of its privileging of production as the definitively human activity. On these problems, see Isaac D Balbus, *Marxism and Domination*, Princeton University Press, 1982, esp chap 2, 'Marxist Theories of Patriarchy', and chap 5, 'Neo-Marxist Theories of Patriarchy'. See also Stanley Aronowitz, *The Crisis in Historical Materialism*, JF Bergin (Brooklyn), 1981, esp chap 4, 'The Question of Class.'

18   Lyotard, 'One of the Things at Stake in Women's Struggles', *Substance*, 20, 1978, p 15.
19   Perhaps the most vociferous feminist anti-theoretical statement is Marguerite Duras's: 'The criterion on which men judge intelligence is still the capacity to theorise and in all the movements that one sees now, in whatever area it may be, cinema, theatre, literature, the theoretical sphere is losing influence. It has been under attack for centuries. It ought to be crushed by now, it should lose itself in a reawakening of the senses, blind itself, and be still.' In E Marks and I de Courtivron (eds), *New French Feminisms,* Schocken (New York), 1981, p 111. The implicit connection here between the privilege men grant to theory and that which they grant to vision over the other senses recalls the etymology of *theoria*; see below.

Perhaps it is more accurate to say that most feminists are ambivalent about theory. For example, in Sally Potter's film *Thriller* (1979) – which addresses the question 'Who is responsible for Mimi's death?' in *La Bohème* – the heroine breaks out laughing while reading aloud from Kristeva's introduction to *Théorie d'ensemble*. As a result, Potter's film has been interpreted as an anti-theoretical statement. What seems to be at issue, however, is the inadequacy of currently existing theoretical constructs to account for the specificity of a woman's experience. For as we are told, the heroine of the film is 'searching for a theory that would explain her life and her death'. On *Thriller*, see Jane Weinstock, 'She Who Laughs First Laughs Last', *Camera Obscura* 5, 1980.
20   Published in *Screen* 16, 3, Autumn 1975.
21   See my 'Earthwords', *October* 10, Fall 1979, pp 120–32.
22   'No Essential Femininity: A Conversation between Mary Kelly and Paul Smith', *Parachute* 26, Spring 1982, p 33.
23   Lyotard, *La Condition postmoderne*, p 8.
24   Ibid, p 68.
25   Fredric Jameson, '"In the constructive Element Immerse": Hans-Jürgen Syberberg and Cultural Revolution', *October* 17, Summer 1981, p 113.
26   See, for example, 'Fantasia of the Library', *Language, counter-memory, practice*, ed DF Bouchard, Cornell University Press (Ithaca) 1977, pp 87–109. See also Douglas Crimp, 'On the Museum's Ruins', *The Anti-Aesthetic*, ed Hal Foster, Bay Press (Seattle, WA), 1983.
27   See Jameson, 'Postmodernism and Consumer Society', *Anti-Aesthetic*, ed Foster.
28   Jameson, *Political Unconscious*, p 19.
29   White, 'Getting Out of History', p 3.
30   Thus, the antithesis to narrative may well be allegory, which Angus Fletcher identifies as the 'epitome of counter-narrative'. Condemned by modern aesthetics because it speaks of the inevitable reclamation of the works of man by nature, allegory is also the epitome of the anti-modern, for it views history as an irreversible process of dissolution and decay. The melancholic, contemplative gaze of the allegorist need not, however, be a sign of defeat; it may represent the superior wisdom of one who has relinquished all claims to mastery.
31   Translated by William Lovitt and published in *The Question Concerning Technology*, Harper and Row (New York), 1977, pp 115–54. I have, of course, oversimplified Heidegger's complex and, I believe, extremely important argument.
32   Ibid, p 149–50. Heidegger's definition of the modern age – as the age of representation for the purpose of mastery – coincides with Theodor Adorno and Max Horkheimer's treatment of modernity in their *Dialectic of Enlightenment* (written in exile in 1944, but without real impact until its republication in 1969). 'What men want to learn from nature,' Adorno and Horkheimer write, 'is how to use it in order wholly to dominate it and other men.' And the primary means of realising this

desire is (what Heidegger, at least, would recognise as) representation – the suppression of 'the multitudinous affinities between existents' in favour of 'the single relation between the subject who bestows meaning and the meaningless object'. What seems even more significant, in the context of this essay, is that Adorno and Horkheimer repeatedly identify this operation as 'patriarchal'.

33 Fredric Jameson, 'Interview', *diacritics* 12, 3, Fall 1982, p 87.

34 Lyotard, *La Condition postmoderne*, p 63. Here, Lyotard argues that the *grands récits* of modernity contain the seeds of their own delegitimation.

35 For more on this group of painters, see my 'Honour, Power and the Love of Women', *Art in America* 71, 1, January 1983, pp 7–13.

36 Martha Rosler interviewed by Martha Gever in *Afterimage*, October 1981, p 15. *The Bowery in Two Inadequate Descriptive Systems* has been published in Rosler's book *3 Works*, The Press of The Nova Scotia College of Art and Design (Halifax), 1981.

37 'Intellectuals and Power: A conversation between Michel Foucault and Gilles Deleuze', *Language, counter-memory, practice*, p 209. Deleuze to Foucault: 'In my opinion, you were the first – in your books and in the practical sphere – to teach us something absolutely fundamental: the indignity of speaking for others.' The idea of a counterdiscourse also derives from this conversation, specifically from Foucault's work with the 'Groupe d'information de prisons'. Thus, Foucault: 'When the prisoners began to speak, they possessed an individual theory of prisons, the penal system, and justice. It is this form of discourse which ultimately matters, a discourse against power, the counter-discourse of prisoners and those we call delinquents – and not a theory *about* delinquency.'

38 Martha Rosler, 'in, around, and afterthoughts (on documentary photography)', *3 Works*, p 79.

39 Quoted in Heath, 'Difference', p 84.

40 Interview with Luce Irigaray in M-F Hans and G Lapouge (eds), *Les femmes, la pornographie, l'erotisme* (Paris), 1978, p 50.

41 *Civilization and Its Discontents*, trans J Strachey, Norton (New York), 1962, pp 46–7.

42 Jane Gallop, *Feminism and Psychoanalysis: The Daughter's Seduction*, Cornell University Press (Ithaca), 1982, p 27.

43 'On Fetishism', reprinted in Philip Rieff (ed), *Sexuality and the Psychology of Love*, Collier (New York), 1963, p 217.

44 Lacan, p 90.

45 On Barthes's refusal of mastery, see Paul Smith, 'We Always Fail – Barthes' Last Writings', *Substance* 36, 1982, pp 34–9. Smith is one of the few male critics to have directly engaged the feminist critique of patriarchy without attempting to rewrite it.

46 Benjamin Buchloh, 'Allegorical Procedures: Appropriation and Montage in Contemporary Art', *Artforum* XXI, 1, September 1982, pp 43–56.

47 Lacan's suggestion that 'the phallus can play its role only when veiled' suggests a different inflection of the term 'unveil' – one that is not, however, Buchloh's.

48 On Birnbaum's work, see my 'Phantasmagoria of the Media', *Art in America*, 70, 5, May 1982, pp 98–100.

49 See Alice A Jardine, 'Theories of the Feminine: Kristeva', *enclitic* 4, 2, Fall 1980, pp 5–15.

50 'The author is reputed the father and owner of his work: literary science therefore teaches respect for the manuscript and the author's declared intentions, while society asserts the legality of the relation of author to work (the "*droit d'auteur*" or "copyright", in fact of recent date since it was only really legalised at the time of the French Revolution). As for the Text, it reads without the inscription of the Father.' Roland Barthes, 'From Work to Text', *Image/Music/Text*, trans S Heath, Hill and Wang (New York), 1977, pp 160–1.

51 Levine's first appropriations were images of maternity (women in their natural role) from ladies' magazines. She then took landscape photographs by Eliot Porter and Andreas Feininger, then Weston's portraits of Neil, then Walker Evans's FSA photographs. Her recent work is concerned with Expressionist painting, but the involvement with images of alterity remains: she has exhibited reproductions of Franz Marc's pastoral depictions of animals, and Egon Schiele's self-portraits (madness). On the thematic consistency of Levine's 'work', see my review, 'Sherrie Levine at A&M Artworks', *Art in America* 70, 6, Summer 1982, p 148.

52 See Metz, 'The Imaginary Signifier'.

53 Douglas Crimp, 'Appropriating Appropriation', *Image Scavengers: Photography*, ed Paula Marincola, Institute of Contemporary Art (Philadelphia), 1982, p 34.

54 Hélène Cixous, 'Entretien avec Françoise van Rossum-Guyon', quoted in Heath, 'Difference', p 6.
55 Sherman's shifting identity is reminiscent of the authorial strategies of Eugenie Lemoine-Luccioni as discussed by Jane Gallop; see *Feminism and Psychoanalysis*, p 105: 'Like children, the various productions of an author date from different moments, and cannot strictly be considered to have the same origin, the same author. At least we must avoid the fiction that a person is the same, unchanging throughout time. Lemoine-Luccioni makes the difficulty patent by signing each text with a different name, all of which are ''hers''.'
56 See, for example, Martha Rosler's criticisms in 'Notes on Quotes', p 73: 'Repeating the images of woman bound in the frame will, like Pop, soon be seen as a *confirmation* by the ''post-feminist'' society.'

Craig Owens, 'The Discourse of Others: Feminists and Postmodernism' from Hal Foster (ed), *The Anti-Aesthetic: Essays on Postmodern Culture*, Bay Press (Port Townsend, WA), 1983. © Craig Owens.

Chaos and Complexity

Tito Arecchi

Tito Arecchi describes the emergence of a third revolution in physics, following those of Galileo and Newton, and Einstein. He explains that the limits placed on inquiries within physics were originally necessary for understanding, but that they have become a hindrance to further knowledge because complexities have been bracketed out. Removing these constraints opens up a variety of viewpoints into the emergent sciences of chaos and complexity, such as weather prediction and the actions of the immune system and the brain. Inevitably, these sciences add depth to, and bring into focus, the complexity theories of the 1960s articulated by Jane Jacobs, Robert Venturi and others.

Tito Arecchi is Chair of Physics at the Università di Firenze. His research has contributed to the knowledge of quantum optics, deterministic chaos, pattern formation in complex systems and also to cognitive processes. He was born in Reggio Calabria, Italy, in 1933. *EB*

People now speak of a third revolution in physics, to follow the first one sparked off by Galileo and Newton, and the second, which took place during the first decades of this century and laid the foundations of relativity and quantum mechanics. This third wave may be called the physics of complexity.

The Galilean revolution consisted of choosing one single point of view from which to interpret the world: a quantitative one. We easily agree that reality is much more complex than the words with which we try to capture it. It is therefore clear that – even with the best will in the world – it is possible to talk about the same thing without managing to reach agreement; simply because it is being looked at from different points of view. The essence of the Galilean method is quite simple: using appropriate apparatus, numbers are extrapolated from things. It is possible to reach agreement on the type of measurement to be carried out excluding all possible ambiguity. The numbers are related mathematically, being organised into equations, and the solutions are used to predict the future. Thus, lack of ambiguity and predictability are the two characteristics of this new language. This approach to knowledge imposes limits on itself from the very start and excludes the possibility of answering questions which do not fall within the scope of the point of view selected.

The success of this approach has given rise to the mistaken belief that it is the only way to knowledge. This misunderstanding, which has become an ideology with practical implications, has been called *scientism*. It has permeated our language, influencing all other sciences from biology to anthropology, and has affected our whole culture and even our ethics.

Leaving aside this ideological aspect, the physical sciences developed with the introduction of suggestive suppositions which, at the time, simplified our view of the world, but which subsequently turned out to be superfluous elements, of little relevance to physics. Of this kind were Newton's absolute space and time, which were criticised by Einstein from 1905 onwards. A similar view was taken of the deterministic 'faith' which prompted the Marquis de Laplace to state: 'an intelligence which could at a given moment have knowledge of the position and velocity of all the particles in the universe would be able to predict with certainty the entire future of the universe.' At the level of the microscopic objects studied by microphysics this belief was discredited by Heisenberg's principle of indeterminacy, which established the impossibility of measuring simultaneously and precisely the position and velocity of a particle. Nevertheless determinism seemed to retain its validity at the level of macroscopic objects – those which we can observe normally, using our senses.

The end of this belief in macroscopic determinism came with the idea of so-called 'deterministic chaos'. This seems to be a contradiction in terms. What it means, in essence, is that chaos, or the impossibility of long-term prediction, is not a prerogative of highly complex systems, but rather to be found even in the physics of a small number of objects: it is enough to go from two (Newton's earth–sun system) up to three (earth–sun and any third body in the solar system). The first person to become aware of this was Poincaré in 1890, but the idea of deterministic chaos has only borne experimental fruit in the past few years, now that physics has reached the end of the long period of symmetries and regularity which seemed compatible with Laplace's belief. In other words, in going from a problem involving the trajectory of two heavenly bodies to one involving three, it emerges that, although a trajectory may be unique in starting from certain initial conditions, it is enough for it to have a minimal uncertainty to lose the predictability of its future path. Now these minimal uncertainties are intrinsic to the method of measurement itself. In translating objects into numbers, all we can establish with any accuracy are the rational numbers (relationships between two whole numbers), but by far the majority are irrational numbers (such as the square root of two), which consist of an infinite number of figures. As infinity can neither be encompassed using our systems of measurement nor recorded in our memory, the truncated version of an infinite number introduces a tiny initial uncertainty, the effects of which become enormous when we try to extend our prediction beyond a certain time. We can express in a diagram (Fig 1) how it is possible to deviate from the 'unique' path. Let us compare two equal paths but with different surrounding 'landscapes': the first with a valley floor, the second with the ridge of a hill. The initial 'exact' position A gives the required path; a slightly wrong position B gives a path which in the first case converges with the correct one (time rectifies our error), but in the second diverges (passage of time increases the initial error). Even simple physical systems like Poincaré's problem of three bodies have critical paths which run along a ridge and can give rise to deterministic chaos. This lack of predictability in the long term was rediscovered by the meteorologist E Lorenz in 1963. Similar effects can be observed nowadays in various different situations: chemical reactions, the motion of fluids, lasers, cardiac rhythms, the movements of asteroids, economic and social trends, etc.

The fact is – as René Thom has put it – that the only physical problem with an exact solution is Newton's earth–sun problem. For all others: physicists have limited themselves to looking for situations of stable equilibrium and have only then examined tiny movements around these. Now these tiny movements obey linear dynamics – that is, with a return force towards the point of equilibrium which is proportional to the displacement: 'ut tensio sic vis', as Hooke put it in the 17th century: and these dynamics always produce trajectories with valley floors, that is, ensure future predictability.

Thus it is not the case that nature was more benign prior to Poincaré but rather that the simplified models used to study nature excluded certain pathologies. Nonlinear dynamics – those to which proportionality does not apply – are, however, the way in which nature normally behaves. To enter this domain is to open a Pandora's box – to discover the world of complexity. The fact that one's starting point is never a geometric point from which there emerges a single line into the future (as Laplace believed), but in general a small blob from which there fan out lines in all directions, can be seen as a case of dynamic complexity, that is, as an infringement of the simplicity requirement which forms the basis of the Galilean method. Complexity had indeed 'exploded' in the hands of physicists as a new paradigm which is undermining the very foundations of that method for providing unambiguous knowledge of the world.

But even his belief in the existence of a privileged viewpoint from which to measure the world, on which all physicists could agree, has failed as well. In effect, if problems of this kind did not exist there would be no need to reward scientific creativity. For example, the helical symmetry of proteins and the double helix of DNA would be an obvious consequence of the links between atoms in a molecule, and it would not have been necessary to award the Nobel Prize for discovering the former to Linus Pauling and for the latter to Watson and Crick. The problem is that deductive reasoning, based on what is known about the constituent elements, would require a length of time and intellectual effort beyond the capacity of a human being in order to reconstruct from among a range of possible worlds the one which actually exists. The physicist Phil Anderson, in a stimulating article entitled 'More is different' (which appeared in the journal *Science* in 1972), criticised 'constructionism', or the presumption that one can construct the behaviour of a complex object conceptually on the basis of one's knowledge of its component parts:

> The constructionist hypothesis fails when it is faced with the double problem of scale and complexity. The behaviour of large and complex aggregates of elementary particles cannot be encompassed in terms of a simple extrapolation of the properties of a few small particles. At every level of complexity there appear new properties, and to understand the new behaviour one requires research which in my opinion is just as basic in its nature as that of elementary particles.

Thus, in addition to the dynamic complexity of deterministic chaos, we can see the emergence of a structural complexity which consists of the impossibility of satisfactorily describing a complex object by reducing it to an interplay of its component parts with their

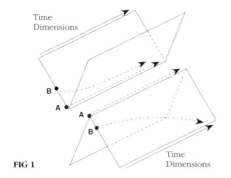

Time
Dimensions

B

A

A

A

B

Time
Dimensions

FIG 1

I *random sequence*
  a o e e a a a o a e

II *regular sequence*
  a e o a e o a e o

III *sequence from the first*
  Canto of the Divine Comedy
  e e o e a o a a
  o a e a e a o a
  e a a a e a a a

FIG 2

elementary laws. In respecting the various, irreducible levels of the description of reality, physics is on the one hand respecting the scientific organisation of other areas of science (from biology to sociology) without trying any longer to reduce these to 'applied physics'; on the other hand it is rehabilitating certain aspects of the Aristotelian 'organicism' for which 'a house is not the sum of its bricks and beams inasmuch as the architect's plan is an integral part of it'.

The two problem areas sketched above, that of deterministic chaos and that of complexity, are beginning to be translated into quantitative parameters. It is precisely the limits on predictability which impose a continual introduction of information if we are to be able to continue to make predictions about the future. The speed with which information is used up is indicated by a parameter K (after the mathematician Kolmogorov, who made an important contribution to this field). Moreover, tentative attempts are being made to portray structural complexity with a parameter C, which indicates the cost of a computer program capable of realising a predefined complex objective. Figure 2 shows three sequences of the letters a, e and o; the first one is random, the second is regular and the third one is derived from the first three lines of the first Canto of Dante's *Divine Comedy*.

Let us agree to define as complexity the cost of the computer program (length of the instructions multiplied by processing time) which enables us to realise one of the three sequences. In the case of sequence I the program is simple: 'write at random a, or e, or o'. For II the instruction is very short; in III there exists no program which would be shorter than the *Divine Comedy* itself. Sequence III we may call complex, the other two simple.

In conclusion, we can classify the limits which physics imposes on itself at present with a diagram C-K (Fig 3). Note the significance of the diagram. Let us start with the horizontal axis: K = 0 means predictable, highly ordered systems (for two reasons: either because they are static and do not change over time, or because they develop according to deterministic laws). A very high K means that the information disappears very rapidly as in the systems with maximum entropy from a thermodynamic point of view (a typical example would be Boltzmann's gas).

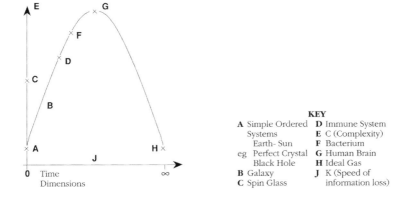

KEY

A Simple Ordered Systems	**D** Immune System
Earth- Sun	**E** C (Complexity)
eg Perfect Crystal	**F** Bacterium
Black Hole	**G** Human Brain
B Galaxy	**H** Ideal Gas
C Spin Glass	**J** K (Speed of information loss)

FIG 3

In the centre, with intermediate amounts of K, there are various dynamic systems affected to a greater or lesser degree by deterministic chaos. While the horizontal axis tells us how things develop in time, it tells us nothing about the structure of the object being studied. The structure is represented by the complexity C. Objects in traditional physics, from the Newtonian system to black holes, are relatively simple. But contrast the 'non-ergodic' systems – a technical term meaning that they allow many possible states of equilibrium – [which] are the objects of more recent study (from the 1970s onwards). These can be regarded like those systems in which the objectives to be achieved are in mutual conflict so that if one is achieved, the others have to be relinquished. We can say, in anthropomorphic terms, that complex systems are those in which choice operates. Obviously all the physics of living organisms finds its natural description in terms of these complex models. Maximum complexity is represented by the human brain. We are very far from being able to measure C or K, not just for the brain, but even for a bacterium. All we know is that they are objects which are much richer (high C) and less predictable (high K) than a galaxy or other objects in conventional physics.

In conclusion, the move from a single viewpoint to a multiplicity of legitimate viewpoints is like the Copernican revolution as compared with the monocentrism of the Ptolemaic system; it rectifies the long-standing disagreements between the 'two cultures', reopening a fertile area of interdisciplinary debate. Before Galileo, Leonardo had tried to investigate complex aspects of nature (clouds, vortices in rivers, the anatomy of animals and plants) in a way which went beyond pure classification. Now his dream is coming true; the physics of complexity is beginning to put forward answers to even these problems – problems which are far more complex than the pendulum or the celestial earth–sun system.

Tito Arecchi, 'Chaos and Complexity' from *Liber 1*, *Times Literary Supplement*, 6 October 1989, trans RG Harrison. © Tito Arecchi.

Evangelical Atheism, Secular Christianity

John Gray

John Gray explains that the public face of religion has changed with recent fundamentalist-inspired terrorism. The more benign mood has been replaced with a feeling of apprehension about religion as a cause of aggression. As a reaction, atheism itself has become somewhat evangelical. It has taken on a proselytising form that paradoxically is similar to that of various faiths. And then there are the parallels in thought between religion and modern secular myths of progress: the search for meaning, the grasp of power, is common to both. Science and its inherent belief in progress is analogous to the Christian belief that things will eventually get better. Neither religion nor science have been immune to exploitation by malevolent agendas of domination. Gray warns of accepting atheism and science as ready-made alternatives to religion. Religion, he says, will never go away, it is hard-wired into humans. Its suppression, however, might well result in its re-emergence in a far more ferocious guise.

John Gray was born in 1948 in South Shields, England. He has held professorships at Oxford and the London School of Economics as well as at Harvard and Yale, but has recently abandoned this impressive academic career for writing. He is the prolific author of many books, including, *Straw Dogs: Thoughts on Humans and Other Animals* (2002), *Al Qaeda and What it Means to be Modern* (2003) and *Black Mass: Apocalyptic Religion and the Death of Utopia* (2007), as well as contributing to the *Guardian*, *Independent* and *Observer*. *EB*

An atmosphere of moral panic surrounds religion. Viewed not so long ago as a relic of superstition whose role in society was steadily declining, it is now demonized as the cause of many of the world's worst evils. As a result, there has been a sudden explosion in the literature of proselytizing atheism. A few years ago, it was difficult to persuade commercial publishers even to think of bringing out books on religion. Today, tracts against religion can be enormous money-spinners, with Richard Dawkins's *The God Delusion* and Christopher Hitchens's *God is Not Great* selling in the hundreds of thousands. For the first time in generations, scientists and philosophers, high-profile novelists and journalists are debating whether religion has a future. The intellectual traffic is not all one way. There have been counterblasts for believers, such as *The Dawkins Delusion?* by the British theologian Alister McGrath and *The Secular Age* by the Canadian Catholic philosopher Charles Taylor. On the whole, however, the anti-God squad has dominated the sales charts, and it is worth asking why.

The abrupt shift in the perception of religion is only partly explained by terrorism. The 9/11 hijackers saw themselves as martyrs in a religious tradition, and Western opinion has accepted their self-image. And there are some who view the rise of Islamic fundamentalism as a danger comparable with the worst that were faced by liberal societies in the 20th century.

For Dawkins and Hitchens, Daniel Dennett and Martin Amis, Michel Onfray, Philip Pullman and others, religion in general is a poison that has fuelled violence and oppression throughout history, right up to the present day. The urgency with which they produce their anti-religious polemics suggests that a change has occurred as significant as the rise of terrorism: the tide of secularization has turned. These writers come from a generation schooled to think of religion as a throwback to an earlier stage of human development, which is bound to dwindle away as knowledge continues to increase. In the 19th century, when the scientific and industrial revolutions were changing society very quickly, this may not have been an unreasonable assumption. Dawkins, Hitchens and the rest may still believe that, over the long run, the advance of science will drive religion to margins of human life, but this is now an article of faith rather than a theory based on evidence.

It is true that religion has declined sharply in a number of countries (Ireland is a recent example) and has not shaped everyday life for most people in Britain for many years. Much of Europe is clearly post-Christian. However, there is nothing to suggest that the move away from religion is irreversible, or that it is potentially universal. The US is no more secular today than it was 150 years ago, when de Tocqueville was amazed and baffled by its all-pervading religiosity. The secular era was in any case partly illusory. The mass political movements of the 20th century were vehicles for myths inherited from religion, and it is no accident that religion is reviving now that these movements have collapsed. The current hostility to religion is a reaction against this turnabout. Secularization is in retreat, and the result is the appearance of an evangelical type of atheism not seen since Victorian times.

As in the past, this is a type of atheism that mirrors the faith it rejects. Philip Pullman's *Northern Lights* – a subtly allusive, multilayered allegory, recently adapted into a Hollywood blockbuster, *The Golden Compass* – is a good example. Pullman's parable concerns far more than the dangers of authoritarianism. The issues it raises are essentially religious, and it is deeply indebted to the faith it attacks. Pullman has stated that his atheism was formed in the Anglican tradition, and there are many echoes of Milton and Blake in his work. His largest debt to this tradition is the notion of free will. The central thread of the story is the assertion of free will against faith. The young heroine Lyra Belacqua sets out to thwart the Magisterium – Pullman's metaphor for Christianity – because it aims to deprive humans of their ability to choose their own course in life, which she believes would destroy what is most human in them. But the idea of free will that informs liberal notions of personal autonomy is biblical in origin (think of the Genesis story). The belief that exercising free will is part of being human is a legacy of faith, and like most varieties of atheism today, Pullman's is a derivative of Christianity.

Proselytizing atheism renews some of the worst features of Christianity and Islam. Just as much as these religions, it is a project of universal conversion. Evangelical atheists never doubt that human life can be transformed if everyone accepts their view of things, and they are certain that one way of living – their own, suitably embellished – is right for everybody. To be sure, atheism need not be a missionary creed of this kind. It is entirely reasonable to have no religious beliefs, and yet be friendly to religion. It is a funny sort of humanism that condemns an impulse that is peculiarly human. Yet that is what evangelical atheists do when they demonize religion.

A curious feature of this kind of atheism is that some of its most fervent missionaries are philosophers. Daniel Dennett's *Breaking the Spell: Religion as a Natural Phenomenon* claims to sketch a general theory of religion. In fact, it is mostly a polemic against American Christianity. This parochial focus is reflected in Dennett's view of religion, which for him means the belief that some kind of supernatural agency (whose approval believers seek) is needed to explain the way things are in the world. For him, religions are efforts at doing something science does better – they are rudimentary or abortive theories, or else nonsense. 'The proposition that God exists.' he writes severely, 'is not even a theory.' But religions do not consist of propositions struggling to become theories. The incomprehensibility of the divine is at the heart of Eastern Christianity, while in Orthodox Judaism practice tends to have priority over doctrine. Buddhism has always recognized that in spiritual matters truth is ineffable, as do Sufi traditions in Islam. Hinduism has never defined itself by anything as simplistic as a creed. It is only some Western Christian traditions, under the influence of Greek philosophy, which have tried to turn religion into an explanatory theory.

The notion that religion is a primitive version of science was popularized in the late 19th century in JG Frazer's survey of the myths of primitive peoples, *The Golden Bough: A Study in Magic and Religion*. For Frazer, religion and magical thinking were closely linked. Rooted in fear and ignorance, they were vestiges of human infancy that would disappear with the advance of knowledge. Dennett's atheism is not much more than a revamped version of Frazer's Positivism. The Positivists believed that with the development of transport and communication – in their day, canals and the telegraph – irrational thinking would wither away, along with the religions of the past. Despite the history of the past century, Dennett believes much the same. In an interview that appears on the website of the Edge Foundation (edge.org) under the title 'The Evaporation of the Powerful Mystique of Religion', he predicts that 'in about 25 years almost all religions will have evolved into very different phenomena, so much so that in most quarters religion will no longer command the awe that it does today'. He is confident that this will come about, he tells us, mainly because of 'the worldwide spread of information technology (not just the internet, but cell phones and portable radios and television)'. The philosopher has evidently not reflected on the ubiquity of mobile phones among the Taliban, or the emergence of a virtual al-Qaeda on the web.

The growth of knowledge is a fact only post-modern relativists deny. Science is the best tool we have for forming reliable beliefs about the world, but it does not differ from religion by revealing a bare truth that religions veil in dreams. Both science and religion are systems of symbols that serve human needs – in the case of science, for prediction and control. Religions have served many purposes, but at bottom they answer to a need for meaning that is met by myth rather than explanation. A great deal of modern thought consists of secular myths – hollowed-out religious narratives translated into pseudo-science. Dennett's notion that new communications technologies will fundamentally alter the way human beings think is just such a myth.

In *The God Delusion*, Dawkins attempts to explain the appeal of religion in terms of the theory of memes, vaguely defined conceptual units that compete with one another in a parody of natural selection. He recognizes that, because humans have a universal tendency to religious belief, it must have had some evolutionary advantage, but today, he argues, it is perpetuated mainly through bad education. From a Darwinian standpoint, the crucial role Dawkins gives to education is puzzling. Human biology has not changed greatly over recorded history, and if religion is hard-wired in the species, it is difficult to see how a different kind of education could alter this. Yet Dawkins seems convinced that, if it were not inculcated in schools and families, religion would die out. This is a view that has more in common with a certain type of fundamentalist theology than with Darwinian theory, and I cannot help being reminded of the evangelical Christian who assured me that children reared in a chaste environment would grow up without illicit sexual impulses.

Dawkins's 'memetic theory of religion' is a classic example of the nonsense that is spawned when Darwinian thinking is applied outside its proper sphere. Along with Dennett, who also holds to a version of the theory, Dawkins maintains that religious ideas survive because they would be able to survive in any 'meme pool', or else because they are part of a 'memeplex' that includes similar memes, such as the idea that, if you die as a martyr, you will enjoy 72 virgins. Unfortunately, the theory of memes is science only in the sense that Intelligent Design is science. Strictly speaking, it is not even a theory. Talk of memes is just the latest in a succession of ill-judged Darwinian metaphors.

Dawkins compares religion to a virus: religious ideas are memes that infect vulnerable minds, especially those of children. Biological metaphors may have their uses – the minds of evangelical atheists seem particularly prone to infection by religious memes, for example. At the same time, analogies of this kind are fraught with peril. Dawkins makes much of the oppression perpetrated by religion, which is real enough. He gives less attention to the fact that some of the worst atrocities of modern times were committed by regimes that claimed scientific sanction for their crimes. Nazi 'scientific racism' and Soviet 'dialectical materialism' reduced the unfathomable complexity of human lives to the deadly simplicity of a scientific formula. In each case, the science was bogus, but it was accepted as genuine at the time, and not only in the regimes in question. Science is as liable to be used for inhumane purposes as any other human institution. Indeed, given the enormous authority science enjoys, the risk of it being used in this way is greater.

Contemporary opponents of religion display a marked lack of interest in the historical record of atheist regimes. In *The End of Faith: Religion, Terror and the Future of Reason*, the American writer Sam Harris argues that religion has been the chief source of violence and oppression in history. He recognizes that secular despots such as Stalin and Mao inflicted terror on a grand scale, but maintains that the oppression they practised had nothing to do with their ideology of 'scientific atheism' – what was wrong with their regimes was that they were tyrannies. But might there not be a connection between the attempt to eradicate religion and the loss of freedom? It is unlikely that Mao, who launched his assault on the people and culture of Tibet with the slogan 'Religion is poison', would have agreed that his atheist worldview had no bearing on his policies. It is true he was worshipped as a semidivine figure – as Stalin was in the Soviet Union. But, in developing these cults, Communist Russia and China were not backsliding from atheism. They were demonstrating what happens when atheism becomes a political project. The invariable result is an ersatz religion that can only be maintained by tyrannical means.

Something like this occurred in Nazi Germany. Dawkins dismisses any suggestion that the crimes of the Nazis could be linked with atheism. 'What matters,' he declares in *The God Delusion*, 'is not whether Hitler and Stalin were atheists, but whether atheism systematically influences people to do bad things. There is not the smallest evidence that it does.' This is simple-minded reasoning. Always a tremendous booster of science, Hitler was much impressed by vulgarized Darwinism and by theories of eugenics that had developed from Enlightenment philosophies of materialism. He used Christian anti-Semitic demonology in his persecution of Jews, and the churches collaborated with him to a horrifying degree. But it was the Nazi belief in race as a scientific category that opened the way to a crime without parallel in history. Hilter's worldview was that of many semiliterate people in interwar Europe, a hotchpotch of counterfeit science and animus towards religion. There can be no reasonable doubt that this was a type of atheism, or that it helped make Nazi crimes possible.

Nowadays most atheists are avowed liberals. What they want – so they will tell you – is not an atheist regime, but a secular state in which religion has no role. They clearly believe that, in a state of this kind, religion will tend to decline. But America's secular constitution has not ensured a secular politics. Christian fundamentalism is more powerful in the US than in any other country, while it has very little influence in Britain, which has an established church. Contemporary critics of religion go much further than demanding disestablishment. It is clear that Dawkins wants to eliminate all traces of religion from public institutions. Awkwardly, many of the concepts he deploys – including the idea of religion itself – have been shaped by monotheism. Lying behind secular fundamentalism is a conception of history that derives from religion.

AC Grayling provides an example of the persistence of religious categories in secular thinking in his *Towards the Light: The Story of the Struggles for Liberty and Rights that Made the Modern West*. As the title indicates, Grayling's book is a type of sermon. Its aim is to reaffirm what he calls 'a Whig view of the history of the modern West', the core of which is that 'the West displays progress'. The Whigs were pious Christians, who believed that divine providence arranged history to culminate in English institutions, and Grayling too believes that history is 'moving in the right direction'. No doubt there have been setbacks – he mentions Nazism and Communism in passing, devoting a few sentences to them. But these disasters were peripheral. They do not reflect on the central tradition of the modern West, which has always been devoted to liberty, and which – Grayling asserts – is inherently antagonistic to religion. 'The history of liberty,' he writes 'is another chapter – and perhaps the most important of all – in the great quarrel between religion and secularism.' The possibility that radical versions of secular thinking may have contributed to the development of Nazism and Communism is not mentioned. More even than the 18th-century Whigs, who were shaken by French Terror, Grayling has no doubt as to the direction of history.

But the belief that history is a directional process is as faith-based as anything in the Christian catechism. Secular thinkers such as Grayling reject the idea of providence, but they continue to think humankind is moving towards a universal goal – a civilization based on science that will eventually encompass the entire species. In pre-Christian Europe, human life was understood as a series of cycles; history was seen as tragic or comic rather than redemptive. With the arrival of Christianity, it came to be believed that history had a predetermined goal, which was human salvation. Though they suppress their religious content, secular humanists continue to cling to similar beliefs. One does not want to deny anyone the consolations of a faith, but it is obvious that the idea of progress in history is a myth created by the need for meaning.

The problem with the secular narrative is not that it assumes progress is inevitable (in many versions, it does not). It is the belief that the sort of advance that has been achieved in science can be reproduced in ethics and politics. In fact, while scientific knowledge increases cumulatively, nothing of the kind happens in society. Slavery was abolished in much of the world during the 19th century, but it returned on a vast scale in Nazism and Communism, and still exists today. Torture was prohibited in international conventions after the Second World War, only to be adopted as an instrument of policy by the world's pre-eminent liberal regime at the beginning of the 21st century. Wealth has increased, but it has been repeatedly destroyed in wars and revolutions. People live longer and kill one another in larger numbers. Knowledge grows, but human beings remain much the same.

Belief in progress is a relic of the Christian view of history as a universal narrative, and an intellectually rigorous atheism would start by questioning it. This is what Nietzsche did when he developed his critique of Christianity in the late 19th century, but almost none of today's secular missionaries have followed his example. One need not be a great fan of Nietzsche to wonder why this is so. The reason, no doubt, is that he did not assume any connection between atheism and liberal values – on the contrary, he viewed liberal values as an offspring of Christianity and condemned them partly for that reason. In contrast, evangelical atheists have positioned themselves as defenders of liberal freedoms – rarely inquiring where these freedoms have come from, and never allowing that religion may have had a part in creating them.

Among contemporary anti-religious polemicists, only the French writer Michel Onfray has taken Nietzsche as his point of departure. In some ways, Onfray's *In Defence of Atheism* is superior to anything English-speaking writers have published on the subject. Refreshingly, he recognizes that evangelical atheism is an unwitting imitation of traditional religion: 'Many militants of the secular cause look astonishingly like clergy. Worse: like caricatures of clergy.' More clearly than his Anglo-Saxon counterparts, Onfray understands the formative influence of religion on secular thinking. Yet he seems not to notice that the liberal values he takes for granted were partly shaped by Christianity and Judaism. The key liberal theorists of toleration are John Locke, who defended religious freedom in explicitly Christian terms, and Benedict Spinoza, a Jewish Rationalist who was also a mystic. Yet Onfray has nothing but contempt for the traditions from which these thinkers emerged – particularly Jewish monotheism: 'We do not possess an official certificate of birth for worship of one God,' he writes. 'But the family line is clear: the Jews invented it to ensure the coherence, cohesion and existence of their small, threatened people.' Here Onfray passes over an important distinction. It may be true that Jews first developed monotheism, but Judaism has never been a missionary faith. In seeking universal conversion, evangelical atheism belongs with Christianity and Islam.

In today's anxiety about religion, it has been forgotten that most of the faith-based violence of the past century was secular in nature. To some extent, this is also true of the current wave of terrorism. Islamism is a patchwork of movements, not all violently jihadist and some strongly opposed to al-Qaeda, most of them partly fundamentalist and aiming to recover the lost purity of Islamic traditions, while at the same time taking some of their guiding ideas from radical secular ideology. There is a deal of fashionable talk of Islamo-Fascism, and Islamist parties have some features in common with interwar Fascist movements, including anti-Semitism. But Islamists owe as much, if not more, to the far Left, and it would be more accurate to describe many of them as Islamo-Leninists. Islamist techniques of terror also have a pedigree in secular revolutionary movements. The executions of hostages in Iraq are copied in exact theatrical detail from European 'revolutionary tribunals' in the 1970s, such as that staged by the Red Brigades when they murdered the former Italian prime minister Aldo Moro in 1978.

The influence of secular revolutionary movements on terrorism extends well beyond Islamists. In *God is Not Great*, Christopher Hitchens notes that, long before Hizbullah and al-Qaeda, the Tamil Tigers of Sri Lanka pioneered what he rightly calls 'the disgusting tactic of suicide murder'. He omits to mention that the Tigers are Marxist-Leninists who, while recruiting mainly from the island's Hindu population, reject religion in all its varieties. Tiger suicide bombers do not go to certain death in the belief that they will be rewarded in any post-mortem paradise. Nor did the suicide bombers who drove American and French forces out of Lebanon in the 1980s, most of whom belonged to organizations of the Left such as the Lebanese Communist Party. These secular terrorists believed they were expediting an historical process from which will come a world better than any that has ever existed. It is a view of things more remote from human realities, and more reliably lethal in its consequences, than most religious myths.

It is not necessary to believe in any narrative of progress to think liberal societies are worth resolutely defending. No one can doubt that they are superior to the tyranny imposed by the Taliban on Afghanistan, for example. The issue is one of proportion. Ridden with conflicts and lacking the industrial base of Communism and Nazism, Islamism is nowhere near a danger of the magnitude of those that were faced down in the 20th century. A greater menace is posed by North Korea, which far surpasses any Islamist regime in its record of repression and clearly does possess some kind of nuclear capability.

Evangelical atheists rarely mention it. Hitchens is an exception, but when he describes his visit to the country it is only to conclude that the regime embodies 'a debased yet refined form of Confucianism and ancestor worship'. As in Russia and China, the noble humanist philosophy of Marxist-Leninism is innocent of any responsibility.

Writing of the Trotskyite-Luxemburgist sect to which he once belonged, Hitchens confesses sadly: 'There are days when I miss my old convictions as if they were an amputated limb.' He need not worry. His record on Iraq shows he has not lost the will to believe. The effect of the American-led invasion has been to deliver most of the country outside the Kurdish zone into the hands of an Islamist elective theocracy, in which women, gays and religious minorities are more oppressed than at any time in Iraq's history. The idea that Iraq could become a secular democracy – which Hitchens ardently promoted – was possible only as an act of faith.

In *The Second Plane*, Martin Amis writes: 'Opposition to religion already occupies the high ground, intellectually and morally.' Amis is sure religion is a bad thing, and that it has no future in the West. In the author of *Koba the Dread: Laughter and the Twenty Million* – a forensic examination of self-delusion in the pro-Soviet Western intelligentsia – such confidence is surprising. The intellectuals whose folly Amis dissects turned to Communism in some sense as a surrogate for religion, and ended up making excuses for Stalin. Are there really no comparable follies today? Some neo-cons – such as Tony Blair, who will soon be teaching religion and politics at Yale – combine their belligerent progressivism with religious belief, though of a kind Augustine and Pascal might find hard to recognize. Most are secular utopians, who justify pre-emptive war and excuse torture as leading to a radiant future in which democracy will be adopted universally. Even on the high ground of the West, messianic politics has not lost its dangerous appeal.

Religion has not gone away. Repressing it is like repressing sex, a self-defeating enterprise. In the 20th century, when it commanded powerful states and mass movements, it helped engender totalitarianism. Today, the result is a climate of hysteria. Not everything in religion is precious or deserving of reverence. There is an inheritance of anthropocentrism, the ugly fantasy that the Earth exists to serve humans, which most secular humanists share. There is the claim of religious authorities, also made by atheist regimes, to decide how people can express their sexuality, control their fertility, and end their lives, which should be rejected categorically. Nobody should be allowed to curtail freedom in these ways, and no religion has the right to break the peace.

The attempt to eradicate religion, however, only leads to it reappearing in grotesque and degraded forms. A credulous belief in world revolution, universal democracy or the occult powers of mobile phones is more offensive to reason than the mysteries of religion, and less likely to survive in years to come. Victorian poet Matthew Arnold wrote of believers being left bereft as the tide of faith ebbs away. Today secular faith is ebbing, and it is the apostles of unbelief who are left stranded on the beach.

The Reenchantment of Science

David Ray Griffin

David Ray Griffin contends that quantum physics, among other sciences, has led to a shift in our worldview, away from materialism and strict thinking in terms of cause and effect. Because quantum physics is removed from everyday reality it is closer to the 'organismic' worldview and Gaia theory than deterministic systems of modernism. It has also forced a re-evaluation of accepted dualities: that between humanity and nature, mind and matter, life and nonlife, subject and object. The lines between these concepts became increasingly blurred as self-determinacy and self-regulation were identified even in the smallest particles. This also required that science concern itself with subjectivity: the aim of analysis, prediction and control was no longer enough. Griffin appeals to a science concerned with the pursuit of ultimate truth.

The process theologian David Ray Griffin was born in 1939 in Oregon, USA. In 1973 he co-founded the Center for Process Studies at the Claremont School of Theology, together with John B Cobb Jr. While much of his research has involved a reconciliation of religion with contemporary science, he is now retired and researching conspiracy theories about September 11th, and the suppression of information by the US government. *EB*

Recent Developments in Science

The move away from the mechanistic, deterministic, reductionistic worldview associated with modern science has been based not only on formal reflections upon the nature of modern science[1] but also on substantive developments within science itself.

Many discussions of this topic focus primarily, if not exclusively, upon quantum physics, seeing it as not only destroying the Cartesian-Newtonian worldview but as also suggesting a new worldview – or a return to an old one, usually a mystical worldview, perhaps Taoist or Buddhist. However, the dominant interpretation of quantum physics, the Copenhagen interpretation, is limited to rules of calculation to predict the content of observations.[2] In other words, it is a nonrealist, phenomenalist interpretation, in which the attempt to describe what is really going on in the world of subatomic entities, independently of human measurement, is eschewed. Most popular accounts of the implications of quantum physics for our worldview neglect this fundamental point. The phenomenalist descriptions are presented as if they tell us something deep about the nature of reality.

A recent interpretation of the significance of quantum physics for the worldview of the founders of quantum theory themselves presents a more sophisticated account. Rejecting the notion that a direct connection exists between quantum theory and mysticism, Ken Wilber argues that quantum theory did nevertheless promote mysticism, but only indirectly. That is, as these physicists became aware that physical theory gave them only shadows and symbols of reality, rather than reality itself, they became freed from the materialistic worldview and hence open to taking their own conscious experience as real and revelatory.[3]

But, regardless of the way the dominant interpretation of quantum physics did in fact loosen the grip of the mechanistic worldview, it does not provide us with the basis for a new worldview. The question remains whether quantum physics, under a different interpretation, might say something more directly helpful about the nature of reality.

There are some physicists, such as David Bohm and Henry Stapp, who have sought to develop a realistic (nonphenomenalist) account of the quantum realm. Bohm has thereby been led to distinguish between the 'explicate' order, upon which physics thus far has focused, and the 'implicate' order, which a more complete physics would describe.[4] In this implicate order, enduring things are not separate from each other, as they appear to be in the explicate order, but are mutually enfolded in each other. Each electron, for example, in some sense enfolds in itself the universe as a whole and hence all its other parts. Accordingly, internal relatedless to other things which we directly experience in our conscious experience is generalised analogically all the way down to the simplest individuals. As Bohm points out, in overcoming the dualism between mind and matter this view implies the transcendence of modern separation between facts and values, truth and virtue. Henry Stapp likewise regards each event as a process of enfoldment: each event enfolds previous events within itself.[5]

This view, that the events of nature are internally constituted by their appropriations from other things, is the central theme of those who are suggesting that the mechanistic paradigm in science be replaced by an ecological one – such as Charles Birch, John Cobb and Frederick Ferré.[6] The term *ecological* most readily suggests biology. But it is important to all of these thinkers that internal relations are characteristic not only of living beings but also of the most elementary physical units. For one thing, only when this view prevails will the current drive to make mechanistic explanations ultimate even in the science of ecology be overcome.

Because internal relatedness is a necessary feature of subjects, the attribution of internal relations to individuals at all levels is one condition for overcoming an ultimate dualism between subjects and objects; *completely* overcoming dualism would involve the attribution of other essential features of subjects, such as feeling, memory and aim or decision, at least in embryonic form: all the way down. Birch refers to Donald Griffin, who is one of several scientists calling for the scientific study of animals to go beyond behaviourism by speaking of subjective experience. Although 'thinking' may occur only in the higher animals, Griffin suggests, the notions of memory and internal imaging seem necessary to understand the behaviour of bats and even bees.[7] Whereas bats and bees are very complex, highly evolved organisms, bacteria are unicellular microorganisms, the simplest form of life, which evidently emerged about four billion years ago, according to the most recent discoveries. Daniel Koshland and his colleagues have provided evidence of rudimentary forms of both 'memory' and 'decision' in bacteria.[8] Going even further down, there is reason now to believe that DNA and RNA macromolecules are not simply passive entities which change as their parts are changed, but that they are active organisms which actively transpose their parts.[9] Going even further, it has been suggested that the Pauli Principle provides reason to think of an atom as a self-regulating whole.[10]

Against the ontological reductionism of the materialistic worldview, according to which all causation runs sideways and upward, from parts to parts and from parts to the whole (with all apparent wholes really being aggregates), there are now developments in science stressing 'downward causation', from the whole to the parts. One of the most striking developments is evidence that the genes which neo-Darwinism considers necessarily impervious to influence from the organism as a purposive whole, are in fact influenced by the organism.[11]

This recognition of downward causation from mind to body is aided if materialism and dualism are transcended. Those positions made it inconceivable that subjective purposes, feelings, decisions and the like could influence the body. But if bodily cells and their components themselves have subjective experience, then downward causation from mind to body is no longer counterintuitive and the recognition of downward as well as upward causation between other levels will be easier.

More inclusive forms of downward causation would be involved in assertions of the influence of the planet as a living organism, and of the universe as a whole, on their parts. Something like the former could be suggested by the 'Gaia hypotheses' of JE Lovelock and Lynn Margulis.[12] The latter is involved in David Bohm's view that every natural unit, as an act of enfoldment, in some sense enfolds the activity of the universe as a whole within it. Because the universe as an active whole can be regarded as divine,[13] Bohm in effect is suggesting that postmodern science, in speaking of the implicate order, would include reference to divine activity. He is thus reversing the dedivinisation of nature bemoaned by Schiller.

The organismic view also overcomes the modern (and premodern) view that, for the world at its most fundamental level, temporality, in the sense of an irreversible distinction between past and future, is unreal. The notion that each electronic or protonic event enfolds past events within itself makes reversibility no more conceivable at the subatomic than at the human level.[14] According to Brian Swimme, we should, instead of regarding the historical evolution of the cosmos as an epiphenomenal development on the surface of the immutable laws of physics, see these laws themselves as products of a temporal development. Accordingly, physics no longer disenchants our stories; physics itself provides us with a new story which can become a common, unifying story underneath our more particular stories. Rupert Sheldrake, agreeing with Swimme that the laws of physics should not be considered changeless,[15] suggests further that they be conceived as habits that have evolved and that continue to evolve. The laws of nature hence become sociological laws, an idea that reduces further the modern dualism between humanity and nature. Rather than seeing mechanisms as fundamental and organisms as derivative phenomena to be explained mechanistically, Sheldrake suggests the opposite: mechanistic phenomena represent the extreme possibility of habit formation on the part of organisms. Sheldrake here restates a major theme of organismic scientists, that while a mechanistic starting point cannot account for genuine oganisms, an organismic starting point can account for all the mechanistic phenomena evident in the world.

Sheldrake's original contribution is his hypothesis about the way such habits could be formed. This hypothesis of morphic resonance, which attributes a cumulative power to the repetition of a similar form, depends not only upon the irreversibility of time, but also upon influence at a distance, that is, over both temporal and spatial gaps. He is thereby bringing back, in a postmodern form, one of the notions that early modern thought most vigorously opposed.[16] That Sheldrake's proposal was condemned by a representative of the modern scientific establishment even prior to its testing is no surprise.[17]

The issue of action at a distance is, of course, central to the controversies about parapsychology. Numerous treatments show that the main difficulty with parapsychological claims, probably even more fundamental than the problem of repeatability, is the fact that 'paranormal claims seem to clash with our twentieth-century presuppositions about reality'.[18] And, as concluded by a recent re-examination of CD Broad's 'basic limiting principles' which paranormal claims seem to violate, the crucial principle is that 'any event that is said to cause another event (the second event being referred to as an "effect") must be related to the effect through some causal chain'.[19] This principle is violated by telepathy, clairvoyance and psychokinesis (and precognition, which also violates the principle that the cause must precede the effect temporally). The author concluded that 'the absence of a specifiable and recognisably causal chain seems to constitute a difficult, if not insurmountable, objection to our giving a coherent account of what it means to make such a claim.'[20] CD Broad himself had suggested that, if there are any well-established facts that are exceptions to these principles, the good thinker 'will want to revise his fundamental concepts and basic limiting principles in such a way as to include the old and new facts in a single coherent system.'[21] The notion that a 'causal chain' of contiguous events or things must exist between a cause and an effect at a distance is part and parcel of the mechanistic worldview and is based on the assumption that the constituents of the world are bits of matter, analogous to billiard balls or parts of a machine, which can only affect each other by contact.[22] But if the basic units of the world are less like cogs or billiard balls than like moments of experience, which enfolds influences from previous moments of experience into themselves, that all influence must come from contiguous events is no longer intuitively self-evident. Hence, in line with their nonmechanistic, organismic views of nature, Bohm and Stapp in physics and Sheldrake in biology point to evidence of nonlocal effects.[23] In this context, the claims of parapsychologists need not be rejected a priori, on the grounds that they clash with the rest of our worldview. In fact, Bohm, Sheldrake and Stapp (as did Whitehead before them) all suggest that events exert two forms of influence on the future, one form on contiguous events, another on noncontiguous ones.[24] They use this nonlocal causation, in which what is normally called *physical energy* is not involved, to explain phenomena that seem inexplicable in terms of causation through chains of contiguous events alone.

These recent developments in the scientific community are reversing the disenchantment of science and its worldview. They are carrying forward what Floyd Matson described in 1964 as 'the affirmative countermovement in postmodern science'.[25]

Reflections on the Relation between Mind and Matter

The main philosophical reason for rejecting the mechanistic, nonanimistic view of nature is that that view makes the relation between mind and matter problematic. Four aspects of this problem can be distinguished: the traditional mind-body problem, the problem of mind as the Great Exception, the problem of emergence, and the problem of where to draw the line.

This mind-body problem is due to the conjunction of a directly known fact, an apparent fact and an inference. The *directly known fact* is that we have, or are, a mind, in the sense of a stream of experiences. As Descartes stressed, if there is one thing I cannot doubt, it is that I am experiencing. The *apparent fact* is that the mind and the body seem to interact; that is, the mind seems to be affected by the body and seems to affect it in return. The *inference* is that the human body is composed of things that are devoid of experience. The resulting problem is: How is it understandable that these two totally unlike things appear to interact? The problem is intensified once we realise that the dualism between nonexperiencing and experiencing things entails a *set* of absolute contrasts, so that the question becomes: How can the impenetrably spatial relate to the nonspatial, the nontemporal to the temporal, the mechanistically caused to the purposively acting, the idea-less to the idea-filled, the purely factual to the value-laden, the externally locomotive to the internally becoming?

Because the founders and early defenders of the dualistic[26] worldview were supernaturalistic theists, they did not find the problem insurmountable. Although they differed in details (with Descartes speaking of an ethereal pineal gland, Malebranche of occasionalism, Leibniz of pre-established harmony or parallelism), they all agreed in essence with Thomas Reid, who simply said that God, being omnipotent, can cause mind and matter to interact, even if such interaction is inconceivable to us.[27] These thinkers thereby illustrated Whitehead's complaint about supernaturalists: having a God who can rise superior to metaphysical difficulties, they did not rethink their metaphysical principles but simply invoked God to prevent those principles from collapsing.[28]

However, as this appeal to God has become unacceptable, dualists are left with no answer. They either ignore the problem or regard it as a mystery we simply must accept. For example, at one time Karl Popper said: 'What we want is to understand how such nonphysical things *as purposes, deliberations, plans, decisions, theories, tensions*, and *values*, can play a part in bringing about physical changes in the physical world.'[29] At a later time, however, he evidently decided that no such understanding was possible. He still confessed to belief in a 'ghost in a machine', but dismissed the question of their interacting with the lame comment that 'complete understanding, like complete knowledge, is unlikely to be achieved'.[30] Materialists use this admitted unintelligibility of dualistic interaction as the basis for equating mind and brain.

The second problem raised against dualism by some materialists is the implausibility of the idea that everything in the universe except human experience can be understood in physicalistic terms. This is the problem of the human mind as the Great Exception. JCC Smart says: 'That everything should be explicable in terms of physics ... except the occurrence of sensations seems to me to be frankly unbelievable.'[31] This problem is lessened somewhat when dualists extend experience to all animals having central nervous systems, as do many dualists; it is lessened even more if experience is attributed all the way down to the lowest forms of life.

However, this solution simply raises the problem of interaction in a new form, resulting in a third problem, the problem of emergence. Whether the ontological gap is located between the human mind and its body or between an experiencing cell and its insentient atoms, the communication across the gap is equally unintelligible. As Smart states: 'How could a nonphysical property or entity suddenly arise in the course of animal evolution? ... What sort of chemical process could lead to the springing into existence of something nonphysical? No enzyme can catalyse the production of a spook!'[32]

A fourth problem for dualists, if they try to solve the first two by extending experience below the human mind, is just *where* to draw the absolute line between sentient and insentient things. Drawing the line with Descartes between the human soul and the rest of nature, so that dogs are simply barking machines, was never very plausible, and it became less so with the theory of evolution. But drawing an absolute line anywhere else seems arbitrary, especially in an evolutionary context. Some vitalists have drawn an absolute line between living and nonliving matter, but the once-clear line between living and nonliving has become vague. Is the cell living and sentient, while its remarkable DNA and RNA macromolecules are insentient mechanisms? Is the bacterium a sentient organism, while the virus is not? Any such line seems arbitrary. For example, while agreeing that crystals and DNA molecules show signs of memory, and that even atoms and elementary particles have 'propensities', Karl Popper refuses to attribute experience any further down than to single-celled animals.[33] The reason Popper cannot attribute experience to atoms and electrons is clear; it is that he, being a modern man, shares 'with old-fashioned materialists the view that ... solid material bodies are the paradigms of reality'.[34]

Given that modern starting point, the only way to avoid the insoluble problems of dualism is to affirm total materialism. Materialists avoid the problem of mind-body dualism by affirming identism, the doctrine that mind and brain are identical. JCC Smart, not being able to believe that experience is 'made of ghost stuff' says that it is 'composed of brain stuff'. In other words: 'Sensations are nothing over and above brain processes.'[35] In DM Armstrong's words, 'mental states are in fact nothing but physical states of the central nervous system.'[36]

Materialism has even more problems than does dualism, because it shares most of the problems of dualism and then adds some of its own. To begin with the problems it shares with dualism: first, it has not really escaped the problem of emergence which it levels against dualism. The identist's claim is that conscious experience is a quality that has 'emerged' in the evolutionary process analogously to the way in which other properties have emerged, such as saltiness, wetness and furriness. Just as saltiness emerged out of a particular configuration of things none of which were by themselves salty, so experience has arisen out of a particular configuration of things (neurons) none of which by themselves had experience. In spite of the initial analogical plausibilitv of this argument, it hinges on a 'category mistake'. All the other emergent properties (saltiness, etc) are properties of things *as they appear* to us from without, ie, to our conscious sensory perception. *But conscious experience itself is not a property of things as they appear to us from without; it is what we are in and for ourselves*. The suggestion that an analogy exists between the other examples of emergent properties and the alleged emergence of sentience out of insentient things confuses two entirely different matters under a single category.[37] All the other examples involve the emergence of one more characteristic of things as they appear to others; *only* in the case of experience is the alleged new property a feature of what the thing is for itself. Surely the question of whether an individual is something for itself is categorically different from the question of what it is for others. Once this is seen, that materialism has the same problem of unintelligibility as does dualism is evident. It equally involves the claim that a thing that is something for itself emerged out of things that are mere objects for others. The fact that the thing in question is called a distinct mind by dualists and a brain by materialists is a secondary matter; an absolutely unique type of causal relation is still being posited. Things that are nothing for themselves are said to causally produce a thing (a brain) that is metaphysically unique in being not only an object for others, but a subject for itself.

Most materialistic identists also share with dualists the implausible idea that experiencing things constitute a Great Exception. For example, after suggesting that mind is strictly identical with matter, so that there is 'only one reality which is represented in two different conceptual systems', ie, physics and phenomenological psychology, Herbert Feigl makes clear that he does not intend panpsychism: 'nothing in the least like a psyche is ascribed to lifeless matter.' Rather, whereas the language of physics applies everywhere, the language of psychology is applicable 'only to an extremely small part of the world'.[38]

The materialist identist also shares the dualist's problem of where to draw the line between things that can be described in physical terms alone, and those to which psychological terms are appropriate. Drawing a line is equally arbitrary whether or not the things with experience are thought to be distinct actualities.

Some identists seek to overcome these problems by denying that psychological language need be used at all, even for our own experience. All language about pains, colours, intentions, emotions and the like would be eliminated. One would talk entirely in physicalistic terms, for example, by talking in terms of certain neuron firings instead of anger, in terms of other neuron firings instead of pain, etc.[39] This so-called eliminative materialism shows the desperate straits to which the mechanistic view of nature can lead.

Besides the problems that identism shares with dualism, it has several of its own. One is that, while claiming to be empirical, it denies the full reality of the directly known in the name of the inferred. That is, the one thing we know from inside, so that we know what it is *in itself*, is our own conscious experience. As almost all modern philosophers have insisted, we do not directly know what objects of sensory perception are in themselves, but only how they appear to us. The idea that these objects are *mere* objects, mere matter, can only be the result of metaphysical speculation. And yet materialists, on the basis of the speculative inference that the human body is composed of 'matter' which is in it*self devoid of experience*, deny that our directly known conscious experience can be a distinct actual thing on the grounds that that hypothesis requires interaction between experiencing and nonexperiencing things.

A second problem unique to materialism is that, in denying the distinction between the mind and the brain, it gives up the hypothesis that had provided the materialistic or mechanistic view of nature its *prima facie* plausibility in the first place. That is, the mechanistic view entailed a distinction between so-called *primary* qualities, which were really attributes of physical things, and *secondary* and *tertiary* qualities, which were only in the mind, although they might falsely appear to be in nature. Hence, nature consisted solely of quantitative factors, locomotion and mechanistic causation; all colour and smells, all pain and pleasure, all good and evil and all purposes and self-motion, resided solely in the mind. By having two types of actual things, dualism could deny that these nonphysical qualities exist in nature without making the counterintuitive assertion that they are wholly unreal. But in materialistic identism the modern worldview has lost its mind and must thereby deny that most of the qualities that are immediately experienced are real. They are illusions created by an illusion.

The materialistic denial that experience plays a causal role in the world also creates a problem of understanding how experience, and then conscious experience, ever emerged. Within an evolutionary framework, especially the neo-Darwinian one presupposed by materialists, the emergence and stabilisation of a new property only can be explained in terms of its enhancement of the chances for survival. But the point of materialistic identism is to deny that experience exerts causal power on the physical world; experience is a concomitant of some physical processes that would by hypothesis interact with the rest of the world in the same way if they were devoid of experience.[40] Hence, by this view, experience cannot enhance an organism's chances of survival. The materialist therefore has no evolutionary explanation as to why any of the things in the world should have experience of any sort, let alone conscious and self-conscious experience.

Adding further to the difficulties of materialistic identism is the fact that, in rejecting the dualism between mind and body, it necessitates a dualism between theory and practice. Whereas dualism said that the mind was the one thing with the power of self-motion, a large part of the motivation for the materialistic denial of nonmaterial mind is to deny that there is any part of the world that is not subject to the deterministic, reductionistic method of modern science. But we all, including the avowed materialists among us, live in practice as if we and other people were partly free from total determination from beyond ourselves. The resulting dualism between theory and practice is at least as vicious as that between mind and matter.

In summary, both dualism and materialism are unintelligible. But if the modern premise that the elementary units of nature are insentient is accepted, dualism and materialism are the only options. This fact suggests that the premise that lies behind the modern disenchantment of the world is false.

Accordingly, a strong philosophical argument converges with recent developments in the philosophy, sociology and history of science, and in science itself, to undermine the basis for the modern disenchantment of the world.

Postmodern Organicism and the Unity of Science

The postmodern organicism has been inspired primarily by the scientist-turned-philosopher Alfred North Whitehead. Without trying to summarise the whole position, I will indicate briefly how it relates to the question of the unity of science, with a focus on the question of causation. I will do this in terms of a contrast of 'paradigms' understood as the basic worldviews presupposed by communities of scientists.

This postmodern organicism can be considered a synthesis of the Aristotelian, Galilean (both forms), and Hermetic paradigms. Aristotelian organicism had a unified science by attributing purposive or final causation to everything, most notoriously saying that a falling stone seeks a state of rest. The Galilean paradigm, in its first form, distinguished absolutely between two types of primary beings: (1) those that exercised purposive or final causation; and (2) those that did not and could consequently be understood completely in terms of receiving and transmitting efficient causation. At first, limiting the beings in the first category to human minds was customary, but that limitation is neither necessary to the dualistic paradigm nor very credible. Many Galilean dualists have accordingly, as mentioned in the previous section, extended final causation further down the animal kingdom: those who are termed *vitalists* see it as arising with the first form of life. Wherever the line was drawn, the drawing of a line between two ontologically different types of primary beings split science into two parts. One science spoke only of efficient causes; the other science (psychology) spoke in terms of final causes or purposes. The second form of the Galilean paradigm tried to restore unity to science by abolishing an internalistic psychology of final causes. Psychology, under the name of *behaviourism*, was transformed into an attempt to describe and explain human and other animal behaviour solely in terms of efficient causes and other externalistic terms. *Eliminative materialism*, mentioned earlier, is the extreme version of this way to achieve unity.

Postmodern organicism holds that all primary individuals are organisms who exercise at least some iota of purposive causation. But it does not hold that all visible objects, such as stones and planets, are primary individuals or even analogous to primary individuals. Rather, it distinguishes between two ways in which primary organisms can be organised: (1) as a compound individual,[41] in which an all-inclusive subject emerges; and (2) as a nonindividuated object, in which no unifying subjectivity is found. Animals belong to the first class; stones to the second. In other words, there is no ontological dualism, but there is an organisational duality which takes account of the important and obvious distinction that the dualists rightly refused to relinquish. Hence, there are (1) things whose behaviour can only be understood in terms of both efficient causes and their own purposive response to these causes, and (2) things whose behaviour can be understood, for most purposes, without any reference to purposive or final causation. In this sense, there is a duality within science.

However, the qualification, f*or most purposes* is important. Whereas the Galilean paradigm maintained that a nonteleological explanation of material things could be adequate for all purposes, including a complete understanding, at least in principle, the postmodern paradigm contends that any explanation devoid of purposive causation will necessarily abstract from concrete facts. *Fully* to understand even the interaction between two billiard balls requires reference to purposive reactions – not indeed of the balls as aggregates, but of their constituents. Because the study of nonindividual objects as well as that of primary individuals and compound individuals requires, at least ultimately, reference to final as well as efficient causes, there is a unity of science.

The relation between final and efficient causation in Whiteheadian postmodern organicism is different from their relation in any previous form of thought, even from other forms of panexperientialism (often called panpsychism), although it was anticipated in Buddhist thought. Other forms of thought that have attributed experience to all individuals, such as that of Gottfried Leibniz and Teilhard de Chardin, have assumed the ultimate constituents of the world to be enduring individuals. An individual was physical from without to others, but conscious or mental from within, for itself. From without, it interacted with other enduring individuals in terms of efficient causation; from within, it lived in terms of purposes or final causation. Given this picture, relating efficient and final causation to each other was difficult. The common view has been that they do not relate, but simply run along parallel to each other. However, as discussed above in relation to materialistic identism, this parallelism raises serious problems. If experience or mentality makes no difference to an individual's interactions with its environment, how can we explain why the higher forms of experience have evolved? And without appeal to a supernatural coordinator, how can we explain the parallelism between inner and outer; eg, why should my brain's signal to my hand to lift a glass follow right after my mental decision to have a drink, if my decision in no way *causes* the appropriate neurons in the brain to fire?

However, if the ultimate individuals of the world are momentary events, rather than enduring individuals, a positive relation can exist between efficient and final causation. Efficient causation still applies to the exterior of an individual and final causation to the interior. But because an enduring individual, such as a proton, neuron or human psyche, is a temporal *society* of momentary events, exterior and interior oscillate and feed into each other rather than running parallel. Each momentary event in an enduring individual originates through the inrush of efficient causation from the past world, ie from previous events, including the previous events that were members of the same enduring individual. The momentary subject then makes a self-determining response to the causal influences; this is the moment of final causation; it is a purposive response to the efficient causes on the event. When this moment of subjective final causation is over, the event becomes an object which exerts efficient causation on future events. Exactly what efficient causation it exerts is a function both of the efficient causes upon it *and* of its own final causation. Hence, the efficient causes of the world do not run along as if there were no mentality with its final causation. An event does not necessarily simply transmit to others what it received; it may do this, but it may also deflect and transform the energy it receives to some degree or other, before passing it on. (*We* do this to the greatest degree when we return good for evil.)

To say that the categories of both final and efficient causation must be employed for the study of all actual beings does *not* imply that the two categories will be *equally* relevant for all beings. Indeed, as already indicated, an appeal to final causation is irrelevant for almost all purposes when studying nonindividuated objects, such as rocks, stars and computers.[42] Even with regard to individuals, the importance of final or purposive causation will vary enormously. In primary individuals, such as photons and electrons (or quarks, if such there be), final causation is minimal. For the most part, the behaviour of these individuals is understandable in terms of efficient causes alone. They mainly just conform to what they have received and pass it on to the future in a predictable way. But not completely: behind the epistemic 'indeterminacy' of quantum physics lies a germ of ontic self-determinacy. The importance of self-determination or final causation increases in compound individuals, especially in those normally called *living*. It becomes increasingly important as the study focuses upon more complex, highly evolved animals; all the evidence suggests that final causation is the most important, on our planet, in determining the experience and behaviour of human beings. The importance of efficient causes, ie of influence from the past, does not diminish as one moves towards the higher individuals; indeed, in a sense higher beings are influenced by *more* past events than are lower ones. But the totality of efficient causes from the past becomes less and less explanatory of experience and behaviour, and the individual's own present self-determination in terms of desired ends becomes more explanatory.

From this perspective we can understand why a mechanistic, reductionist approach has been so spectacularly successful in certain areas and so unsuccessful in others. The modern Galilean paradigm was based on the study of nonindividuated objects, such as stellar masses and steel balls, which exercise *no final causation* either in determining their own behaviour or that of their elementary parts. Absolute predictability and reduction is possible in principle. This paradigm was next applied to very low-grade individuals, in which the final causation is negligible for most purposes except to the most refined observation. With this refinement, the absolute predictability of behaviour broke down with the most elementary individuals; the ideal of predictability could be salvaged only by making it statistical and applying it to large numbers of individuals. With low-grade forms of life, and in particular with their inherited characteristics and certain abstract features of their behaviour, Galilean science has still been very successful, but not completely. Certain features of even low-grade life seemed intractable to this approach, just those features which led to the rise of vitalism. This paradigm has been even less successful with rats than with bacteria. At this level, various problems are virtually ignored, because little chance of success is apparent, and scientists are interested in applying their method where the chances for success are most promising. Finally, the method has been less successful yet with humans than rats. The record of success at this level is so miserable that many scientists and philosophers of science refuse to think of the so-called social or human sciences, such as psychology, sociology, economics and political science, as sciences at all. This pattern of success and failure of the Galilean paradigm fits exactly what the postmodern paradigm predicts. As one leaves nonindividuated objects for individuals, and as one deals with increasingly higher individuals, final causation becomes increasingly important, and regularity and hence predictability become increasingly less possible. Hence, nothing but confusion and unrealistic expectations can result from continuing to regard physics as the paradigmatic science.[43]

This framework can explain why it has been even less possible to discover regularities and attain repeatability in parapsychology than in certain aspects of ordinary psychology. Although every event (by hypothesis) exerts influence directly upon remote as well as spatially and temporally contiguous events, its influence on contiguous events is much more powerful. Hence, the effects of the kind of influence that is exerted upon remote events indirectly via a chain of contiguous events will be much more regular and hence predictable than the effects of the kind of influence that is exerted on remote events directly, without the intervening chain. Accordingly, because sensory perception arises from a chain of contiguous events (photons and neuron firings in vision) connecting the remote object with the psyche, the sensory perception of external objects is much more regular and reliable, hence predictable, than any extrasensory perception of them. Likewise, because effects produced in the external world by the psyche by means of the body are mediated by a chain of contiguous causes, whose reliability, like that of the sensory system, has been perfected over billions of years of evolution, such effects are much more reliable than any psychokinetic effects produced by the direct influence of the psyche upon outer objects without the body's mediation. Additionally, although *unconscious* extrasensory perception and *subtle* and *diffused* psychokinetic action occur continually (by hypothesis), the power to produce *conscious* extrasensory perception and *conspicuous* psychokinetic effects *on specific objects* is – at least for the majority of human beings most of the time – evidently lodged in an unconscious level of experience, which by definition is not under conscious control. Given these assumptions, the fact that parapsychology has attained little repeatability with conspicuous psychokinetic effects and conscious extrasensory perception is what should be expected.[44] In this way, the element of truth in the Hermetic paradigm is coordinated with the elements of truth from the Aristotelian and Galilean paradigms.

What then is science – what constitutes its unity? The anarchistic or relativistic view that 'anything goes', that there is no such thing as a scientific method, is surely too strong. But it serves a useful function, as indeed it was intended,[45] to shake us free from parochial limitations on what counts as science. A description of science for a postmodern world must be much looser than the modern descriptions (which were really prescriptions).

Any activity properly called *science* and any conclusions properly called scientific must, first, be based on an overriding concern to discover truth.[46] Other concerns will of course play a role, but the concern for truth must be overriding, or the activity and its results would be better called by another name, such as *ideology*, or *propaganda*, or politics.[47] Second, science involves demonstration. More particularly, it involves testing hypotheses through data or experiences that are in some sense repeatable and hence open to confirmation or refutation by peers. In sum, science involves the attempt to establish truth through demonstrations open to experiential replication. What is left out of this account of science are (1) limitations to any particular domain, (2) any particular type of repeatability and demonstration, or (3) any particular contingent beliefs.

(1) Science is not restricted to the domain of things assumed to be wholly physical, operating in terms of efficient causes alone, or even to the physical aspects of things, understood as the aspects knowable to sensory perception or instruments designed to magnify the senses.[48] As the impossibility of behaviourism in human and even animal psychology has shown, science must refer to experience and purposes to comprehend (and even to predict) animal behaviour. Although we cannot *see* the purposes motivating our fellow humans or other animals, assuming that such purposes play a causal role is not unscientific, if this hypothesis can be publicly demonstrated to account for the observable behaviour better than the opposite hypothesis. And, once it is explicitly recognised that science *can* deal with subjectivity, there is no reason in principle for it to limit itself to the objective or physical side of other things, if there is good reason to suspect that an experiencing side exercising final causation exists. At the very least, even if we cannot imagine very concretely what the experience of a bacterium or a DNA molecule would be like, we need not try to account for its observable behaviour on the metaphysical assumption that it has no experience and hence no purposes.

Just as the need for experiential replication by peers does not limit science to the physical or objective side of actual things, it does not even limit it to the realm of actuality. Mathematics deals with relationships among ideal entities, and is able to achieve great consensus; geometry was for Descartes of course the paradigmatic science. Therefore, the fact that logic, aesthetics and ethics deal with ideal entities does not, in itself, exclude them from the realm of science.

Furthermore, the domain of scientific study should not be thought to be limited to regularities, or law-like behaviour. There is no reason why the discussion of the origin of laws should not belong to science. If the laws of nature are reconceived as habits, the question of how the habits originated should not be declared off limits.[49] In fact, we should follow Bohm in replacing the language of 'laws' with the more inclusive notion of 'orders', for the reasons Evelyn Fox Keller has suggested: the notion of 'laws of nature' retains the connotation of theological imposition, which is no longer appropriate but continues to sanction unidirectional, hierarchical explanations; it makes the simplicity of classical physics the ideal, so that the study of more complex orders is regarded as 'softer' and less fully scientific; and it implies that nature is dead and 'obedient' rather than generative and resourceful.[50]

(2) While science requires repeatable experiential demonstration, it does not require one particular type of demonstration, such as the laboratory experiment. As Patrick Grim says:

> Field studies, expeditions, and the appearances of comets have played a major role in the history of science. Contemporary reliance on mathematics reflects a willingness to accent a priori deductive as well as inductive demonstration And there are times when the course of science quite properly shifts on the basis of what appear to be almost purely philosophical arguments.[51]

In regard to Grim's last example, I have suggested above that the philosophical difficulties with both dualism and materialistic identism provide a good reason for the scientific community to reconsider the metaphysical-scientific hypothesis that the ultimate constituents of nature are entirely devoid of experience and purpose. More generally, the bias towards the laboratory experiment in the philosophy of science has philosophically reflected the materialistic, nonecological assumption that things are essentially independent of their environments, so that the scientist abstracts from nothing essential in (say) removing cells from the human body or animals from a jungle to study them in a laboratory; it reflects the reductionistic assumption that all complex things are really no more self-determining than the elementary parts in isolation, so that they should be subject to the same kind of strong laboratory repeatability;[52] it reflects the assumption that the main purpose of science is to predict and control repeatable phenomena; and it reflects the assumption that the domain of science is limited to the actual, especially the physical. Recognising the wide domain of science means recognising the necessity and hence appropriateness of diverse types of demonstrations, and the artificiality of holding up one type as the ideal.

(3) Besides not being limited to one domain or one type of demonstration, the scientific pursuit of truth is not tied to any set of contingent beliefs, meaning beliefs that are not inevitably presupposed by human practice, including thought, itself. Science is, therefore, not limited to any particular type of explanation.[53] For example, science is not tied to the belief that the elementary units of nature are devoid of sentience, intrinsic value and internal relations, that time does not exist for these units, that the laws of nature for these units are eternal, that all natural phenomena result from the (currently four) forces rooted in these elementary units, that accordingly all causation is upward and that freedom and purposive or teleological causation are illusory,[54] that ideal entities other than mathematical forms play no role in nature, that there is no influence at a distance,[55] that the universe as a whole is not an organism which influences its parts, or that the universe and its evolution have no inherent meaning.

However, the fact that science as such is not permanently wedded to these contingent beliefs that reigned during the modern period does not mean that there are *no* beliefs that science as such must presuppose. If beliefs exist that are presupposed by human practice, including human thought, as such, then scientific practice and thought must presuppose them. Any theories that verbally deny them should therefore be eschewed on this ground alone. Although any such beliefs would transcend perspectivalism, because they by hypothesis would be common to all people, regardless of their worldview, the questions of whether there are any such beliefs, and if so what they are, are matters not for pontification from some supposedly neutral point of view, because no human point of view is neutral, but for proposals to be subjected to ongoing public discussion among those with diverse worldviews.[56]

To illustrate the types of beliefs intended and to show that they are not limited to innocuous, noncontroversial issues, I propose five principles as candidates. The first three principles relate to the crucial issue of causality. First, every event is causally influenced by other events. This principle rules out, for example, the idea that the universe arose out of absolute nothingness or out of pure possibility![57] Second, neither human experience nor anything analogous to it is wholly determined by external events; rather; every genuine individual is partially self-determining. Incidentally, these first two principles, taken together, provide the basis for a scientific understanding of the activity of scientists themselves in terms of a combination of external and internal causes, which is increasingly seen to be necessary.[58]

Third, every event that exerts causal influence upon another event precedes that event temporally. (Self-determination or self-causation does not fall under this principle, because in it the same event is both cause and effect.) This principle rules out the notion of particles 'going backwards in time' the notion of 'backward causation', and any notion of 'precognition' interpreted to mean that an event affected the knower before it happened or to mean that temporal relations are ultimately unreal.[59]

The final two principles proffered deal with science's concern for truth. These are the traditional principles of correspondence and noncontradiction, which are recovered in a postmodern context.

The idea that truth is a correspondence between statements and objective reality has been subject to a great deal of criticism. Much of this criticism is based upon confusion, inasmuch as the critics, often while verbally rejecting positivism, still presuppose the positivistic equation of the meaning of a statement with the means of its verification. The correspondence notion of truth properly refers only to the *meaning* of 'truth', which is not even identical with the question of knowledge, let alone with the question of the justification of knowledge-claims. Much of the rejection of the relevance of the correspondence notion of truth has conflated truth with knowledge and then assumed that there could be no knowledge, in the sense of justified true belief, in the absence of adequate evidence to defend the knowledge-claim.[60]

However, much of the criticism of the notion of truth as correspondence is valid, especially in relation to naively realistic ideas of a one-to-one correspondence between statements and objective facts. For one thing, our ideas about physical objects, insofar as they are based primarily upon visual and tactile perception, surely involve enormous simplifications, constructions and distortions of the realities existing independently of our perception. For another, language is inherently vague and, in any case, cannot as such 'correspond' in the sense of being similar to nonlinguistic entities. Language aside, the way in which an idea can correspond to a physical object is not self-evident, because an idea can only be similar to another idea. Even many conceptions of truth as the correspondence between one's ideas and the ideas in another mind are held in falsely naive ways, insofar as it is assumed that achieving truth, in the sense of absolute correspondence, is possible. Many critics go on from these valid starting points to argue that the meaning of a statement is exhausted by its relation to other statements, so that language constitutes a closed system, or in some other way argue that our statements can in no meaningful sense correspond to any nonlinguistic entities. Science, in this extreme view, is a linguistic system disconnected from any larger world.

Postmodern organicism rejects this view of language. While language as such does not correspond to anything other than language, it expresses and evokes modes of apprehending nonlinguistic reality that can more or less accurately correspond to features of that reality.[61] Hence, science can lead to ways of thinking about the world that can increasingly approximate to patterns and structures genuinely characteristic of nature.

The other traditional principle involved in science's concern for truth is the principle of noncontradiction. It says that if two statements contradict each other, both cannot be true. This principle has also been subject to much valid criticism. Certainly two statements that appear to contradict each other may not in reality when one or both are more deeply understood. This can be because language is vague and elusive, because various levels of meaning exist, and/or because seemingly contradictory assertions may apply to diverse features of the referent or to different stages of its development. There are yet other objections to simple-minded applications of the principle of noncontradiction. But after all necessary subtleties and qualifications have been added, the principle remains valid and is necessarily presupposed even in attempts to refute it. Accordingly, science must aim for coherence between all its propositions and between its propositions and all those that are inevitably presupposed in human practice and thought in general. (Obtaining such coherence is indeed the primary method of checking for correspondence.)

All of these principles are in harmony with postmodern organicism. Indeed, they are not epistemically neutral principles but ones that are, especially in regard to their exact formulation, suggested by postmodern organicism. However, the claim is made that they are, in fact, implicit in human practice, including human thought (although not, of course, in the content of all the theories produced by human thought). If this claim is sustained through widespread conversation, then this set of beliefs (along with any others that could prove their universality in the same way) should be considered to belong to science as such.[62]

To summarise: Whereas modern science has led to the disenchantment of the world and itself, a number of factors today are converging towards a postmodern organicism in which science and the world are reenchanted. Besides providing a basis for overcoming the distinctive problems of modernity that are due primarily to disenchantment, this postmodern organicism gives science a better basis than it has heretofore had for understanding its own unity.

Notes

1   The prior sections in the essay from which this segment was abstracted dealt with the ways in which modern science led to the disenchantment of the world, then suggested that several converging reasons were reversing this disenchantment. The first of those reasons were a new view of the nature of science, and a new view of the origin of modern science.

2   Henry P Stapp, 'Einstein Time and Process Time', *Physics and Ultimate Significance of Time: Bohm, Prigogine, and Process Philosophy*, ed David Ray Griffin, State University of New York Press (Albany), 1986, pp 264–70, esp 264.

3   'Introduction: Of Shadows and Symbols', *Quantum Questions: Mystical Writings of the World's Great Physicists*, ed Ken Wilber, Shambhala (Boston), 1984, pp 3–29.

4   David Bohm, 'The Implicate Order: A New Order for Physics', *Process Studies* 8/2, ed Dean Fowler, Summer 1978, pp 73–102; *Wholeness and the Implicate Order*, Routledge & Kegan Paul (London), 1980; 'Hidden Variables and the Implicate Order', *Zygon* 20/2, June 1985, pp 111–24; 'Time, the Implicate Order and Pre-Space', *Physics and the Ultimate Significance of Time*, ed David Ray Griffin, pp 177–208.

5   David Bohm, 'Postmodern Science and a Postmodern World', *The Reenchantment of Science: Postmodern Proposals*, ed David R Griffin, State University of New York Press (Albany), 1988, pp 57–68; Henry Stapp, 'Einstein Time and Process Time'; 'Whiteheadian Approach to Quantum Theory and the Generalised Bell's Theorem', *Foundations of Physics* 9/1–2, 1979, pp 1–25.

6   See their essays in *The Reenchantment of Science*, ed David R Griffin.

7   Donald R Griffin, *The Question of Animal Awareness: Evolutionary Continuity of Mental Experience*, Rockefeller University Press (New York), pp 14, 23.

8   A Goldbeter and DE Koshland, Jr, 'Simple Molecular Model for Sensing and Adaptation Based on Receptor Modification with Application to Bacterial Chemotaxis', *Journal of Molecular Biology* 161/3, 1982, pp 395–416; Jess Stock, Greg Kersulis and Daniel E Koshland, Jr, 'Neither Methylating nor Demethylating Enzymes are Required for Bacterial Chemotaxis', *Cell* 42/2, 1985, pp 683–90.

9   John H Campbell, 'Autonomy in Evolution', *Perspectives on Evolution*, ed R Milkman, Sinauer Assoc (Sunderland, MA), 1982, pp 190–200 and 'An Organisational Interpretation of Evolution', *Evolution at a Crossroads: The New Biology and the New Philosophy of Science*, eds David J Depew and Bruce H Weber, MIT Press (Cambridge, MA), 1985, pp 133–68; see also the discussion of Depew and Weber, pp xiv, 248. The lonely pioneer in the study of 'transposons' was Barbara McClintock; see Evelyn Fox Keller, *A Feeling for the Organism: The Life and Work of Barbara McClintock*, Freeman (New York), 1983.

10 Ian Barbour, *Issues in Science and Religion*, Prentice-Hall, Englewood Cliffs, 1966, pp 295–9, 333.

11 Campbell, 'Organisational Interpretation of Evolution', pp 134–5.

12 JE Lovelock and Lynn Margulis, 'Atmospheric Homeostasis by and for the Biosphere: The Gaia Hypothesis', *Tellus* 26/2, 1973; JE Lovelock, *Gaia: A New Look at Life on Earth*, Oxford University Press, 1979; Lynn Margulis and Dorion Sagan, *Micro-Cosmos: Four Billion Years of Microbial Evolution*, Summit Books (New York), 1986. Neither Lovelock nor Margulis draws organismic conclusions from their hypothesis. Lovelock has distanced himself from the view that the planet as a whole is sentient and teleological, suggesting that all the phenomena can be interpreted cybernetically (*Gaia*, pp ix–x, 61–3), and Margulis has endorsed a fully mechanistic, reductionistic philosophy (*Micro-Cosmos*, pp 229, 256–75).

13 Bohm is reluctant to use the term *God* because of its supernaturalistic connotations. But he does think of the holomovement as holy, and as embodying intelligence and compassion; 'Hidden Variables, p 124, Renée Weber, 'The Enfolding-Unfolding Universe: A Conversation with David Bohm', *The Holographic Paradigm and Other Paradoxes*, ed Ken Wilber, Shambhala (Boulder, CO), 1982, pp 187–214, esp 60–70.

14 I have dealt with this issue in the 'Introduction', *Physics and the Ultimate Significance of Time*, pp 10–15.

15 See the essays by Swimme and Sheldrake in *The Reenchantment of Science*, ed David R Griffin.

16 See note 22 below.

17 An editorial in a British journal (*Nature* 293, 24 September 1981, pp 245–6) condemned Sheldrake's book, *A New Science as Life: The Hypothesis of Formative Causation*, Blond & Briggs (London), 1981, as an 'infuriating tract' and the best candidate for burning there has been for a long time'. The editorial complained that the book was being hailed as an answer to materialistic science and was becoming 'a point of reference for the motley crew of creationists,

anti-reductionists, neoLamarckians and the rest'. Calling the book 'pseudo-science', it dismissed Sheldrake's claim that the hypothesis is testable, adding that 'no self-respecting grantmaking agency will take the proposals seriously'. Of particular interest for the present discussion was the editor's statement that 'finding a place for magic within scientific discussion ... may have been part of the [author's] objective' and his apparent view that anti-reductionists and neo-Lamarckians are as far from the true faith as creationists. This editorial evoked a number of critical responses from scientists, including Nobel prize-winning physicist Brian Josephson (*Nature* 293, 29 October, p 594). In response to the editor's complaint that Sheldrake had not described the nature or origin of morphogenetic fields, Josephson said that the properties of heat, light, sound, electricity and magnetism were investigated long before their natures were understood. The editor's stipulation that *all* aspects of a theory must be testable if it is to be called scientific would, Josephson added, bar general relativity, black holes and many other concepts of modern science from the status of legitimate scientific ideas. Josephson closed by saying: 'The fundamental weakness is failure to admit even the possibility that genuine physical facts may exist which lie outside the scope of current scientific descriptions. Indeed, a new kind of understanding of nature is now emerging, with concepts like implicate order and subject-dependent reality (and now maybe formative causation). These developments have not yet penetrated to the leading journals. One can only hope that editors will soon cease to obstruct this avenue of progress. ...'

18 Jane Duran, 'Philosophical Difficulties with Paranormal Knowledge Claims', *Philosophy of Science and the Occult*, ed Patrick Grim, State University of New York Press (Albany), 1982, pp 196–206, esp 196. Paul Kurtz says that parapsychology's findings 'contradict the general conceptual framework of scientific knowledge' (*A Skeptic's Handbook of Parapsychology*, ed Paul Kurtz, Prometheus (Buffalo, NY), 1985, p 504). James Alcott, another critic, says that its constructs involve 'drastic violations of the currently accepted laws of nature' (ibid, p 540). On this ground they insist that the evidence for parapsychological interactions would have to be more repeatable and undeniable than the evidence demanded by some other sciences (pp 510, 540).

19 Duran, 'Philosophical Difficulties', p 196; these limiting principles are taken from 'The Relevance of Physical Research to Philosophy', CD Broad, *Religion, Philosophy and Psychical Research*, Humanities Press (New York), 1969, pp 7–26. Paul Kurtz, in referring to these principles, expresses the conventional, empiricist view that they 'have been built up from a mass of observations' (*A Skeptic's Handbook*, ed Kurtz, p 504). But we have learned that the denial of influence at a distance was based instead on a priori, originally theological, considerations. See Brian Easlea's book in note 22.

20 Duran, 'Philosophical Difficulties', p 202.

21 Broad, 'Relevance of Physical Research', p 9, cited by Duran, 'Philosophical Difficulties', p 197.

22 Mary Hesse points out that the rejection of action-at-a-distance in favour of action-by-contact explanations was based on the replacement of all organismic and psychological explanations by mechanical ones (*Forces and Fields: The Concept of Action at a Distance in the History of Physics*, Adams & Co (Littlefield), 1965, pp 98, 291). Richard Westfall makes clear how central was the change:

the mechanical philosophy also banished ... attractions of any kind. No scorn was too great to heap upon such a notion. From one end of the century to another, the idea of attractions, the action of one body upon another with which it is not in contact, was anathema ... An attraction was an occult virtue, and 'occult virtue' was the mechanical philosophy's term of opprobrium.

Westfall reports that Christiaan Huygens wrote that he did not care for whether Newton was a Cartesian 'as long as he doesn't serve us up conjectures such as attractions' ('The Influence of Alchemy on Newton', *Science, Pseudo-Science and Society*, eds Marsha P Hanen, Margaret J Osler and Robert G Weynant, Wilfrid Laurier University Press (Waterloo, Ontario), 1989, pp 145–70, esp 147, 150). Brian Easlea has provided convincing evidence that the desire to rule out the possibility of attraction at a distance was, in fact, the main motivation behind the mechanical philosophy and its denial of all hidden qualities within matter; see his *Witch Hunting, Magic and the New Philosophy: An Introduction to the Debates of the Scientific Revolution 1450–1750*, Humanities Press (Atlantic Highlands, NJ), 1980, esp pp 93–5, 108–15, 121, 132, 135, where he discusses the theological and sociological motives behind the rejection of action-at-a-distance. Another supporter of the view that the mechanistic worldview was adopted primarily for extra-scientific reasons is Jerome Ravetz, who says:

The 'scientific revolution' itself becomes comprehensible if we see it as a campaign for a reform of ideas *about* science, introduced quite suddenly, injected into a continuous process of technical progress *within* science ... [S]cientific revolution was primarily and essentially about metaphysics: and the various technical studies were largely conceived and received as corroborating statements of a challenging world-view. This consisted essentially of two Great Denials: the restriction of ordinary faculties such as sympathy and intelligence to humans and to a remote Deity; and the relegation of extra-ordinary faculties to the realms of the nonexistent or insignificant. ... The great historical myth of this philosophy is that it was the necessary and sufficient cause of the great scientific progress of the seventeeth century. This was a central point in its propaganda, for itself at the time and in histories ever since. Yet the results of historical enquiry, some old and some new, contradict this claim.

From 'The Varieties of Scientific Experience', *The Sciences and Theology in the Twentieth Century*, ed Arthur Peacocke, Notre Dame University Press (IN), 1981, pp 197–206 and 200–1.

23 Bohm. 'The Implicate Order', pp 87–93; Stapp, 'Whiteheadian Approach to Quantum Theory', Sheldrake, *A New Science of Life*, pp 93–6.

24 Bohm, 'Wholeness and the Implicate Order', pp 129, 186; Renée Weber, 'Conversations between Rupert Sheldrake, Renée Weber, David Bohm'. *ReVISION* 5/2, Fall 1982, esp pp 39, 44 (reprinted in *Dialogues with Scientists and Sages. The Search for Unity*, ed Reneé Weber, Routledge & Kegan Paul (London), 1986; Sheldrake, *A New Science of Life*, pp 95–6; Henry P Stapp, 'Bell's Theorem and the Foundations of Quantum Physics', *American Journal of Physics* 53, 1985, pp 306–17; Alfred North Whitehead, *Process and Reality*, corrected edition, eds David Ray Griffin and Donald W Sherburne, Free Press (New York), 1978, p 308, and *Adventures of Ideas*, Free Press (New York), 1978, p 248. For a comparison of Sheldrake and Whitehead on this point, see my review of Sheldrake's book in *Process Studies* 12/1, Spring 1982, pp 38–40.

25 Floyd W Matson, *The Broken Image: Man, Science and Society*, 1964; Doubleday & Co (Garden City, NY), 1966, p vi. In the light of Stephen Toulmin's crediting Frederick Ferré with having coined the term 'postmodern science' (*The Return to Cosmology: Postmodern Science and the Theology of Nature*, University of California Press (Berkeley), 1982, p 210), surely with reference to Ferré's 1976 book, *Shaping the Future: Resources for the Postmodern World*, it is of pedantic historical interest to note that Matson had, unbeknownst to Ferré and Toulmin, spoken of postmodern science in 1964.

26 The term *dualism* is perhaps the most ambiguous, multivalent term in our language. It can refer, among other things, to a distinction between any of the following: (1) a natural and a supernatural world; (2) an actual and an ideal world; (3) time anti eternity; (4) good and evil; (5) good and evil cosmic agents; (6) sentient and insentient things; (7) living and nonliving things; or (8) mind and body. Discussions about dualism often become unnecessarily charged because dualism in one sense is assumed to entail dualism in one or more of the other senses when it does not. In this discussion, dualism is always used, unless stated otherwise, to mean either (7) or (8) *in conjunction with* (6). The term *dualism* should not be used for (8) alone, ie, for the assertion that mind and body (or brain) are numerically distinct, rather than numerically identical, because this doctrine does not necessarily imply (6), ie, the assertion that the mind is sentient while the brain and its components are insentient. Because the term *dualism* in this context inevitably connotes *Cartesian* dualism, with its problem of interaction, the term should not be used unless meaning (6) is also involved.

27 Thomas Reid, *Essays on the Intellectual Powers of Man*, MIT Press (Cambridge, MA), 1969, pp 96–7, 99, 110, 118, 123, 220, 240, 318.

28 Whitehead, *Science and the Modern World*, Free Press (New York), 1967, p 156; *Process and Reality*, p 343.

29 Karl R Popper, *Of Clouds and Clocks*, Washington University Press (St Louis), 1966, p 15; emphasis his.

30 Karl R Popper and John C Eccles, *The Self and its Brain: An Argument for Interaction*, Springer-Verlag (Heidelberg), 1977, pp 16, 37, 105.

31 JCC Smart, 'Sensations and Brain Processes', *The Mind-Brain Identity Theory*, ed CV Borst, Macmillan (London), 1979, pp 52–66, esp 53–4.

32 JCC Smart, 'Materialism', ibid, pp 159–70, esp 165, 168–9.

33 Popper and Eccles, *The Self and its Brain*, pp 29–30.

34 Ibid, p 10.

35   Smart, 'Sensations and Brain Processes', pp 63, 56.

36   DM Armstrong, 'The Nature of Mind', *Mind-Brain Identity Theory*, ed Borst, pp 67–79, esp 75.

37   As Thomas Nagel says, 'much obscurity has been shed on the [mind-body] problem by faulty analogies between the mental-physical relation and relations between the physical and other objective aspects of reality' (*Mortal Questions*, Cambridge University Press, 1979, p 202). He argues that it is unintelligible to speak of the emergence of experience, which is something for itself, out of things that are purely physical: 'One cannot derive a *pour soi* from an *en soi*. ... This gap is logically unbridgeable. If a bodiless god wanted to create a conscious being, he could not expect to do it by combining together in organic form a lot of particles with none but physical properties' (p 189; see also pp 166, 172, 182, 188).

38   Herbert Feigl, 'Mind-Body, Not a Pseudoproblem', *Dimensions of Mind*, ed Sydney Hook, New York University Press (New York), 1960, pp 24–36, esp 32, 33.

39   Richard Rorty, 'Mind-Body Identity, Privacy and Categories', *Review of Metaphysics* 19, 1965, pp 25–54: *Philosophy and the Mirror of Nature*, Princeton University Press (Princeton, NJ), 1979, pp 70–127. Rorty claims in his later 'pragmatic' position no longer to espouse eliminative materialism, but it seems still to be presupposed.

40   DE Wooldridge, in *The Machinery of the Brain*, McGraw Hill (New York), 1963, p 240 says:
No useful purpose has yet been established for the sense of awareness that illumines a small fraction of the mental activities of a few species of higher animals. It is not clear that the behaviour of any individual or the course of world history would have been affected in any way if awareness were nonexistent.

41   See Charles Hartshorne, 'The Compound Individual', *Philosophical Essays for Alfred North Whitehead*, ed Otis H Lee, Longmans Green (New York), 1936, pp 193–220.

42   Of course, to understand a computer one must take into account final causation in the sense of the purpose for which it was made. But throughout this discussion the subject is internal, immanent final causation, not external, imposed final causation.

43   Sandra Harding supports this change, pointing out that physics, among other restrictions, 'looks at either simple systems or simple aspects of complex systems' so that it need not deal with the difficult question of intentional causality (*The Science Question in Feminism*, Cornell University Press (Ithaca, NY), 1986, pp 44, 46).

44   For a development of the ideas in these two sentences, see the writings of psychiatrist Jule Eisenbud, whom philosopher Stephen Braude has called 'parapsychology's premier living theoretician'. Many of Eisenbud's essays have been collected in *Parapsychology and the Unconscious*, North Atlantic Books (Berkeley, CA), 1983, the 'Preface' of which contains the accolade by Braude (p 7). For the various ideas, see pp 21, 22, 40, 72, 125, 167, 173, 183. On the resultant unlikelihood of obtaining repeatable experiments in the ordinary sense, see pp 156–61. These points are also supported in Braude's own *The Limits of Influence: Psychokinesis and the Philosophy of Science*, Routledge Kegan Paul (London), 1986, esp pp 7–10, 23, 70, 278.

45   Feyerabend's reputation as an extremist is due in large part to his advocacy of an 'anarchistic' theory of knowledge; but he clearly says that he intends his anarchism only as a medicine, not as an epistemology and philosophy of science (*Society in a Free Society*, NLB (London), 1978, p 127). What he has consistently opposed is the notion that the (modern) scientific method, as the successor to the One True Religion, gives us 'the one true method' (*Against Method: Outline of An Anarchist Theory of Knowledge*, Verso (London), 1975, pp 216–18).

46   My discussion in this and the following paragraph is dependent upon Grim, ed *Philosophy of Science and the Occult*, pp 314–15; Wilber, *Quantum Questions*, pp 13–14; and Nicholas Rescher, 'The Unpredictability of Future Science', *Physics, Philosophy and Psychoanalysis: Essays in Honor of Adolf Grünbaum*, eds Robert S Cohen and Larry Lauden, D Reidel (Dordrecht), 1983, pp 153–68.

47   It is often said that power and knowledge (or truth) have been the twin aims of modern science (eg Evelyn Fox Keller, *Reflections on Gender and Science*, Yale University Press (New Haven), 1985, p 71). Of these twin aims, traditional descriptions spoke mainly of the quest for truth, while recent appraisals, whether condemnatory or positivistic, have seen the drive for power as the central aim. My position is that, while much of modern science has sought those truths that would provide power over nature (and sometimes thereby over other humans), it is not the quest for power that makes modern science 'science' but the quest for truth (in the way specified in the second criterion), regardless of how limited these truths are and of the ulterior purposes for which they are sought.

48 Rescher ('The Unpredictability of Future Science', p 165) says: 'Domain limitations purport to put entire sectors of fact wholly outside the effective range of scientific explanation, maintaining that an entire range of phenomena in nature defies scientific rationalisation.' See also Wilber, *Quantum Questions*, p 14.

49 This is one topic on which I disagree with Rupert Sheldrake, who wishes to exclude the topic of the origin of laws from science, assigning it instead to theology or metaphysics; see the final chapter of his *A New Science of Life*.

50 Fox Keller, *Reflections on Gender and Science*, pp 131–6.

51 Grim, *Philosophy of Science and the Occult*, p 315.

52 Jule Eisenbud (*Psi and Psychoanalysis*, Grune & Stratton (New York), 1970, p 96) says that one particular kind of repeatability has given parts of physics such reliability that 'few people (strangely) question its right to provide a model of "reality"'. But, as he says, this kind of repeatability is only one of many considerations in authentication, not relevant for many questions in geology, meteorology, astronomy, biology and much of psychology. Both Kurtz and Alcott (see notes 18 and 19 above) have claimed that parapsychological experiments, to be acceptable, would have to exemplify 'strong' repeatability, meaning that, in Alcott's words, 'any competent researcher following the prescribed procedure can obtain the reported effect' p 540). But if the kind of phenomenon with which parapsychology is concerned is held to be an inherently elusive, not consciously controllable one, as Eisenbud and Stephen Braude hold (see note 44 above), this requirement for strong replicability amounts to a 'Catch-22': parapsychologists could only prove that it exists by proving that it does not!

53 Nicholas Rescher ('The Unpredictability of Future Science', p 163) says: 'The contention that this or that explanatory resource is inherently unscientific should always be met with instant scorn. For the unscientific can only lie on the side of process and not that of product – on the side of *modes* of explanation and not its *mechanism*; of arguments rather than phenomena.'

54 Rescher (ibid, p 166) says that 'there is no reason why, in human affairs any more than in quantum theory, the boundaries of science should be so drawn as to exclude the unpredictable'. Long ago, William James said: 'The spirit and principles of science are mere affairs of method; there is nothing in them that need hinder science from dealing successfully with a world in which personal forces are the starting-point of new effects.' (*William James on Psychical Research*, eds Gardner Murphy and Robert Ballou, Viking (New York), 1960, p 47.)

55 Rescher (ibid. p 169) says:

> Not only can we never claim with confidence that the science of tomorrow will not resolve the issues that the science of today sees as intractable, but one can never be sure that the science of tomorrow will not endorse what the science of today rejects. This is why it is infinitely risky to speak of this or that explanatory resource (action at a distance, stochastic processes, mesmerism, etc) as inherently unscientific. Even if X lies outside the range of science as we nowadays construe it, it by no means follows that X lies outside science as such.

56 If there are such common beliefs, their recognition by members of diverse linguistic communities is, while difficult, not impossible. Even though a given worldview will predispose its adherents to recognise some such beliefs while ignoring, distorting or even verbally denying other such beliefs that are noticed by adherents of other worldviews, it is possible, when the search for truth through public demonstration is sincere, to recognise such beliefs through conversation and self-observation.

57 In spite of my agreement, expressed in prior notes, with Nicholas Rescher's formal ideas, I cannot accept his substantive idea that actualities could have emerged out of a realm of mere possibility. I do not see how we can abandon the notion that agency requires actuality, and hence the 'hoary dogma', Rescher calls it, that *ex nihilo nihilfit*. I have reviewed Rescher's *The Riddle of Existence: An Essay in Idealistic Metaphysics*, University of America Press (Lanham, MD), 1985, in *Canadian Philosophical Reviews*, December 1986, pp 531–2.

58 Sandra Harding points out that one-sided attempts to explain science either from a purely externalist or a purely internalist approach led to paradox. The externalist approach, which understands the development of science in terms of external causes alone, leads to a self-refuting relativism. 'Why should changes in economic, technological, and political arrangements make the new ideas reflecting these arrangements better ideas? Why shouldn't we regard the externalist programme itself as simply an epiphenomenon of nineteenth- and twentieth-century social relations destined to be replaced as history moves along?' (*Science Question in Feminism*, p 215).

The internalist or intentionalist approach praises natural science for showing that all natural and social phenomena are to be explained in externalistic terms, then supports the truth of this idea by 'defending an intentionalist approach to explaining the development of science alone' (p 212). What we need is an approach that recognises the two-way causal influences between ideas and social relations, and which thereby allow us both to understand how 'social arrangements shape human consciousness' and 'to retain the internalist assumption that not all beliefs are equally good' (pp 209, 231, 214).

59 I have dealt with these issues in 'Introduction: Time and the Fallacy of Misplaced Concreteness', *Physics and the Ultimate Significance of Time*; there is a brief discussion of apparent precognition on pp 30–1. See also Eisenbud, *Parapsychology and the Unconscious*, p 45. Although Stephen Braude has not changed his earlier opinion that arguments against the very intelligibility of backward causation are unconvincing, perhaps because he has not developed a general theory of causation (*Limits of Influence*, p 261), he has concluded that the idea is very problematic, and that ostensible precognition can be explained without resort to this idea (pp 261–77). I have dealt much more extensively with this issue in 'Parapsychology and Philosophy: A Whiteheadian Postmodern Perspective', forthcoming in the *Journal of the American Society for Psychical Research*.

60 Frederick Suppe has pointed out that most discussions of the idea of knowledge as 'justified true belief' have assumed that 'knowing that X is true' entails 'knowing that one knows that X is true', ie having adequate evidence to defend the claim to know that it is true (*The Structure of Scientific Theories*, pp 717–28). This unjustified requirement, which leads to a vicious infinite regress, lies behind Hume's sceptical attacks on the possibility of knowledge and most recent rejections, by Kuhn, Feyerabend and others, of the relevance of the correspondence notion of truth to scientific beliefs (pp 718, 719, 723). Suppe argues rightly for 'a separation of the role of evidence in the rational evaluation and defense of knowledge claims from the role evidence plays in obtaining knowledge' (p 725). With that separation, we can maintain the traditional definitions of knowledge as justified true belief and of truth as correspondence of belief to reality. None of this entails, I would insist perhaps more strongly than Suppe, that the modern scientific worldview is true, or that any of the current scientific theories gives us anything approaching the whole truth about their referents. Indeed, it is only if we hold to these traditional definitions of truth and knowledge that we have a rational standard in terms of which to criticise the dominant contemporary knowledge-claims.

61 For the way in which panexperiential philosophy can make sense of a notion of correspondence, see my discussion in *Varieties of Postmodern Theology*, David Ray Griffin, William A Beardslee and Joe Holland, State University of New York Press (Albany), 1989, pp 133–41.

62 These principles, especially the latter four, have all, in fact, been denied by modern science-related thought. However, their explicit denial has been accompanied by implicit affirmation, producing massive incoherence. The reason for their explicit denial is *not* that they conflict with the implications of any other equally universal principles but that they conflict with the implications of contingent beliefs of modernity, which have been discussed above.

Postmodern Science and a Postmodern World

David Bohm

David Bohm explains that we have moved from a modern mechanistic physics where the world is reduced to its basic elements to a postmodern physics as new concepts of space, time and matter have been developed. After briefly explaining relativity theory ('the universe is one seamless, unbroken whole') and quantum theory ('all action or all motion is found in a discrete indivisible unit called a *quantum*'), Bohm proposes a view that he calls *unbroken wholeness*, in which the mechanistic picture is turned upside down and argues that everything is internally related to everything through mutual enfoldment. Discussing the new instrument, the holograph, he writes: 'The holograph hence suggests a new kind of knowledge and a new understanding of the universe in which information about the whole is enfolded in each part and in which the various objects of the world result from the unfolding of this information.' For Bohm, postmodern science will completely change the attitude towards knowledge.

American-born David Joseph Bohm (1917–92) was one of the foremost theoretical physicists of his generation and an influential theorist of the emerging holistic paradigm. He made a number of significant contributions to physics, particularly in the area of quantum mechanics and relativity theory. During the Second World War, he contributed to the Manhattan Project. *LCS*

Modern Physics and the Modern World

With the coming of the modern era, human beings' view of their world and themselves underwent a fundamental change. The earlier, basically religious approach to life was replaced by a secular approach. This approach has assumed that nature could be thoroughly understood and eventually brought under control by means of the systematic development of scientific knowledge through observation, experiment and rational thought. This idea became powerful in the 17th and 18th centuries. In fact, the great seal of the United States has as part of its motto 'the new secular order', showing the way the founders of the country were thinking. The main focus of attention was on discerning the order of the universe as it manifests itself in the laws of nature. The principal path to human happiness was to be in the discovery of these laws, in complying with them, in utilising them wherever possible for the benefit of humankind.

So great is the change in the whole context of thought thereby brought about that Huston Smith and some others have described it as the onset of the modern mind.[1] This mind is in contrast with the mind of the medieval period, in which it was generally supposed that the order of nature was beyond human comprehension and in which human happiness consisted of being aware of the revealed knowledge of God and carrying out the divine commandments. A total revolution occurred in the way people were aiming to live.

The modern mind went from one triumph to another for several centuries through science, technology, industry, and it seemed to be solidly based for all time. But in the early 20th century, it began to have its foundations questioned. The challenge coming from physics was especially serious because it was in this science that the modern mind was thought to have its firmest foundation. In particular, relativity theory, to a certain extent, and quantum theory, to a much greater extent, led to questioning the assumption of an intuitively imaginable and knowable order in the universe. The nature of the world began to fade out into something almost indescribable. For the most part, physicists began to give up the attempt to grasp the world as an intuitively comprehensible whole; they instead restricted their work mostly to developing a mathematical formalism with rules to apply in the laboratory and eventually in technology. Of course, a great deal of unity has emerged in this work, but it is almost entirely in the mathematical formalism. It has little or no imaginative or intuitive expression (whereas Newton's ideas were quite easily understandable by any reasonably educated person).

A similar current of thought has been developing at the same time in other fields. In philosophy, the trend has been to relinquish any notion that the general nature of reality could be known through some kind of metaphysics or worldview. Existentialists like Kierkegaard and Nietzsche and others following this line have emphasised instead what is personal and peculiar to each human being. Other philosophers have emphasised language as the main point, and positivists have said that the role of science is nothing more than a systematic and rationally ordered way of organising our observation data. In art, as in literature and other fields, universal values have also generally been dropped, replaced for the most part by a focus on personal reactions or on some kind of formal structure.

Clearly, during the 20th century the basis of the modern mind has been dissolving, even in the midst of its greatest technological triumphs. The whole foundation is dissolving while the thing is flowering, as it were. The dissolution is characterised by a general sense of loss of a common meaning of life as a whole. This loss of meaning is very serious, as meaning in the sense intended here is the basis of *value*. Without that, what is left to move people to work together towards great common aims sensed as having high value? Merely to operate at the level of solving problems in science and technology, or even of extending them into new domains, is a very narrow and limited goal which cannot really captivate the majority of the people. It cannot liberate humanity's highest and most comprehensive creative energies. Without such liberation, humanity is sinking into a vast mass of petty and transitory concerns. This leads, in the short run, to meaningless activity that is often counterproductive; in the long run, it is bringing humankind ever closer to the brink of self-destruction.

Needless to say, the development described above will have serious consequences for the individual human being, for society as a whole and for the overall quality of relationships among human beings and between human beings and the rest of nature.

Our entire world order has, in fact, been dissolving away for well over a century. This dissolution has tended further to erode all our basic values on which the stability of the world order must depend. Hence, we are now confronted with a worldwide breakdown which is self-evident not only at the political level but also in smaller groups and in the consciousness of the individual. The resort to mindless violence is growing and behind it all is the even more mindless threat of mutual annihilation, which is implicit in our current international situation and which could make everything we are doing quite pointless. I suggest that if we are to survive in a meaningful way in the face of this disintegration of the overall world order, a truly creative movement to a new kind of wholeness is needed, a movement that must ultimately give rise to a new order, in the consciousness of both the individual and society. This order will have to be as different from the modern order as was the modern from the medieval order. We cannot go back to a premodern order. A postmodern world must come into being before the modern world destroys itself so thoroughly that little can be done for a long time to come.

Even though physics is by now a rather specialised profession and even though the question of metaphysics or worldview is discussed seriously by only a few people within this profession, the worldview that physics provides is clearly still playing a crucial role as a foundation for the general mode of thinking which prevails throughout society. That is the worldview that physics provided from the 16th through the 19th centuries. It is therefore important to ask whether 20th-century physics actually implies a universe that is beyond intuitive and imaginative comprehension, as well as whether this universe is without any deep meaning, being only something to be computed mathematically and manipulated technically. For example, one of the leading physicists at this time, Steven Weinberg, has said that the more he looks at the universe the less it seems to have any meaning, that we have to invent our own meaning if any is to exist. But, if we find that that is the wrong conclusion to be drawn from recent physics, this discovery may help open the way to the truly original and creative step that is now required of humankind. We *cannot* go on as we are; we must have something really new and creative. This step cannot be merely a reaction to the breakdown of the modern world order, but it must arise out of a fresh insight that would make it possible to move out of this morass into which we have been sinking.

The possibility of a postmodern physics, extended also to postmodern science in general, may be of crucial significance for this sort of insight. A postmodern science should not separate matter and consciousness and should therefore not separate facts, meaning and value. Science would then be inseparable from a kind of intrinsic morality, and truth and virtue would not be kept apart as they currently are in science. This separation is part of the reason we are in our present desperate situation.

Of course, this proposal runs entirely contrary to the prevailing view of what science should be, which is a morally neutral way of manipulating nature, either for good or for evil, according to the choices of the people who apply it. I hope in this essay to indicate how a very different approach to science is possible, one that is consistent and plausible and that fits better the actual development of modern physics than does the current approach.

Mechanistic Physics

I begin by outlining briefly the mechanistic view in physics, which was characteristic of the modern view and which reached its highest point towards the end of the 19th century. This view remains the basis of the approach of most physicists and other scientists today. Although the more recent physics has dissolved the mechanistic view, not very many scientists and even fewer members of the general public are aware of this fact; therefore, the mechanistic view is still the dominant view as far as effectiveness is concerned. In discussing this mechanistic view, I start by listing the principal characteristics of mechanism in physics. To clarify this view, I contrast it with that of ancient times, which was organic rather than mechanistic.

The first point about mechanism is that the world is reduced as far as possible to a set of basic elements. Typically, these elements take the form of particles. They can be called atoms or sometimes these are broken into electrons, protons and neutrons; now the most elementary particles are called quarks, maybe there will be subquarks. Whatever they may be called, the assumption is that a basic element exists which we either have or hope to have. To these elementary particles, various continuous fields, such as electromagnetic and gravitational fields, must be added.

Second, these elements are basically external to each other; not only are they separate in space, but even more important, the fundamental nature of each is independent of that of the other. Each particle just has its own nature; it may be somewhat affected by being pushed around by the others, but that is all. The elements do not grow organically as parts of a whole, but are rather more like parts of a machine whose forms are determined externally to the structure of the machine in which they are working. By contrast, organic parts, the parts of an organism, all grow together with the organism.

Third, because the elements only interact mechanically by sort of pushing each other around, the forces of interaction do not affect their inner natures. In an organism or a society, by contrast, the very nature of each part is profoundly affected by changes in the other parts, so that the parts are internally related. If a man comes into a group, the consciousness of the whole group may change, depending on what he does. He does not push people's consciousnesses around as if they were parts of a machine. In the mechanistic view, this sort of organismic behaviour is admitted, but it is explained eventually by analysing everything into still smaller particles out of which the organs of the body are made, such as DNA molecules, ordinary molecules, atoms and so on. This view says that eventually everything is reducible to something mechanical.

The mechanistic programme has been very successful and is still successful in certain areas, for example, in genetic engineering to control heredity by treating the molecules on which heredity depends. Advocates do admit that the programme still has much to achieve, but this mechanistic reductionistic programme assumes that there is nothing that cannot eventually be treated in this way – that if we just keep on going this way we will deal with anything that may arise.

The adherence to this programme has been so successful as to threaten our very existence as well as to produce all sorts of other dangers, but, of course, such success does not prove its truth. To a certain extent the reductionistic picture is still an article of faith, and faith in the mechanistic reductionistic programme still provides the motivation of most of the scientific enterprise, the faith that this approach can deal with everything. This is a counterpart of the religious faith that people had earlier which allowed them to do great things.

How far can this faith in mechanism be justified? People try endlessly to justify faith in their religions through theology, and much similar work has gone into justifying faith in mechanism through the philosophy of science. Of course, that the mechanism works in a very important domain is given, thereby bringing about a revolution in our life.

During the 19th century, the Newtonian worldview seemed so certain and complete that no serious scientist was able to doubt it. In fact, we may refer to Lord Kelvin, one of the leading theoretical physicists at the time. He expressed the opinion that physics was more or less finished, advising young people not to go into the field because further work was only a matter of minor refinements. He did point, however, to two small clouds on the horizon. One was the negative results of the Michelson-Morley experiment and the other was the difficulty in understanding black-body radiation. Now he certainly chose his clouds well: the first one led to the theory of relativity and the second to quantum theory. Those little clouds became tremendous storms; but the sky is not even as clear today as it was then – plenty of clouds are still around. The fact that relativity and quantum together overturned the Newtonian physics shows the danger of complacency about worldview. It shows that we constantly must look at our worldviews as provisional, as exploratory, and to inquire. We must have a worldview but we must not make it an absolute thing that leaves no room for inquiry and change. We must avoid dogmatism.

The Beginning of Nonmechanistic Physics: Relativity Theory

Relativity theory was the first important step away from the mechanistic vision. It introduced new concepts of space, time and matter. Instead of having separate little particles as the constituents of matter, Einstein thought of a field spread through all space, which would have strong and weak regions. Some strong regions, which are stable, represent particles. If you watch a whirlpool or a vortex, you see the water going around and you see that the movement gets weaker the farther away it is from the centre, but it never ends. Now the vortex does not actually exist; there is only the moving water. The vortex is a pattern and a form your mind abstracts from the sensations you have of moving water. If two vortices are put together, they will affect each other; a changing pattern will exist where they modify each other, but it will still be only one pattern. You can say that two exist but this is only a convenient way of thinking. As they become even closer together, they may merge. When you have flowing water with patterns in them, none of those patterns actually has a separate existence. They are appearances or forms in the flowing movement, which the mind abstracts momentarily for the sake of convenience. The flowing pattern is the ultimate reality, at least at that level. Of course, all the 19th-century physicists knew this perfectly well, but they said that *really* water is made of little atoms that neither the vortices nor the water are the reality: the reality is the little atoms out of which it is all made. So the problem did not bother them.

But with the theory of relativity, Einstein gave arguments showing that thinking of these separate atoms as existent would not be consistent. His solution was to think of a field not so different from the flowing water, a field that spreads through all space and time and in which every particle is a stable form of movement, just as the vortex or whirlpool is a temporarily stable form that can be thought of as an entity which can be given a name. We speak of a whirlpool, but one does not exist. In the same way, we can speak of a *particle*, but one does not exist: particle is a name for a certain form in the field of movement. If you bring two particles together, they will gradually modify each other and eventually become one. Consequently, this approach contradicted the assumption of separate, elementary, mechanical constituents of the universe. In doing so, it brought in a view which I call *unbroken wholeness* or *flowing wholeness*: it has also been called *seamless wholeness*. The universe is one seamless, unbroken whole, and all the forms we see in it are abstracted by our way of looking and thinking, which is convenient at times, helping us with our technology, for example.

Nonetheless, relativity theory retains certain essential features of mechanism, in that the fields at different points in space were thought to exist separately and not to be internally related. The separate existence of these basic elements was emphasised by the idea that they were only locally connected, that the field at one point could affect a field only infinitesimally nearby. There was no direct effect of a field here on something far away. This notion is now being called *locality* by physicists; it is the notion of no long-distance connection. This notion is essential to the kind of mechanistic materialism developing throughout the science of the modern era, the notion of separate elements not internally related and not connected to things far away. The animistic view of earlier times was that spirits were behind everything and that these spirits were not located anywhere. Therefore, things far away would tend to be related. This view was taken to be most natural by astrologers and alchemists. But that view had been turned completely around in the modern period, and the modern view seemed so fruitful and so powerful that there arose the utter conviction of its truth.

More Fully Nonmechanistic Physics: Quantum Theory

With quantum theory, a much bigger change occurred. The main point is that all action or all motion is found in a discrete indivisible unit called a *quantum*. In the early form of the theory, electrons had to jump from one orbit to the other without passing in between. The whole idea of the continuous motion of particles, an idea at the heart of mechanism, was thereby being questioned. The ordinary visible movement, like my hand moving, was thought to comprise a vast number of quantum movements, just as, if enough fine grains of sand are in the hourglass, the flow seems continuous. All movements were said to comprise very tiny, discrete movements that do not, as it were, go from one place to another by passing through the space in between. This was a very mysterious idea.

Second, matter and energy had a dual nature; they manifest either like a wave or like a particle according to how they were treated in an experiment. An electron is ordinarily a particle, but it can also behave like waves, and light which ordinarily behaves like waves can also behave like particles; their behaviour depends on the context in which they are treated. That is, the quality of the thing depends on the context. This idea is utterly opposed to mechanism, because in mechanism the particle is just what it is no matter what the context. Of course, with complex things, this is a familiar fact; it is clear, for example, that organs depend very much on context, that the brain depends on the context, that the mind functions differently in a different context. The new suggestion of quantum theory is that this context-dependence is true of the ultimate units of nature. They hence begin to look more like something organic than like something mechanical.

A third point of quantum theory was the property of nonlocal connection. In certain areas, things could apparently be connected with other things any distance away without any apparent force to carry the connection. This 'nonlocality' was very opposed to what Einstein wanted and very opposed to mechanism.

A fourth new feature of quantum physics, which was against mechanism, was that the whole organises the parts, even in ordinary matter. One can see it doing so in living matter, in organisms, where the state of the whole organises the various parts in the organism. But something a bit similar happens in electrons, too, in various phenomena such as superconductivity. The whole of chemistry, in fact, depends on this idea.

In summary, according to quantum physics, ultimately no continuous motion exists; an internal relationship between the parts and the whole, among the various parts, and a context-dependence, which is very much a part of the same thing, all do exist. An indivisible connection between elements also exists which cannot be further analysed. All of that adds up to the notion that the world is one unbroken whole. Quantum physics thereby says what relativity theory said, but in a very different way.

These phenomena are evident only with highly refined modes of observation. At the ordinary order of refinement, which was available during the 19th century, there was no evidence that any of this was occurring. People formed the mechanistic philosophy on the basis of fairly crude observations, which demonstrates the danger of deciding a final philosophy on the basis of any particular observations; even our present observations may be too crude for something still deeper.

Now one may ask: if there has been such a disproof of mechanism why is it that most scientists are still mechanistic? The first reason is that this disproof takes place only in a very esoteric part of modern physics, called *quantum mechanical field theories*, which only a few people understand, and most of those only deal with it mathematically, being committed to the idea they could never understand it beyond that level. Second, most other physicists have only the vaguest idea of what quantum mechanical field theorists are doing, and scientists in other fields have still less knowledge about it. Science has become so specialised that people in one branch can apply another branch without really understanding what it means. In a way this is humorous, but it has some very serious consequences.

Unbroken Wholeness and Postmechanistic Physics
I propose a view that I have called *unbroken wholeness*. Relativity and quantum physics agree in suggesting unbroken wholeness, although they disagree on everything else. That

is, relativity requires strict continuity, strict determinism and strict locality, while quantum mechanics requires just the opposite – discontinuity, indeterminism and nonlocality. The two basic theories of physics have entirely contradictory concepts which have not been brought together; this is one of the problems that remains. They both agree, however, on the unbroken wholeness of the universe, although in different ways. So it has seemed to me that we could use this unbroken wholeness as our starting point for understanding the new situation.

The question is then, how to understand this wholeness. The entire language of physics is now analytic. If we use this language, we are committed to analysing into parts, even though our intention may be quite the opposite. Therefore, the task is quite difficult.

What I want to suggest is that one of the most important problems is that of *order*. Worldviews have always had views of order. The ancient Greeks had the view of the Earth as the centre of the universe and of various spheres in order of increasing perfection. In Newtonian physics, the order is that of the particles and the way they move. That is a mechanical order, and coordinates are used mathematically to express that order. What kind of order will enable us to consider unbroken wholeness?

What *is* order? That is a very deep question, because everything we say presupposes order. A few examples: there is the order of the numbers, the order of the words here, the order of the walls, the order in which the body works, the order in which thought works, the order in which language works, We cannot really define order, but we nevertheless understand order somewhat, because we cannot think, talk or do anything without beginning from some kind of order.

The order physics has been using is the order of separation. Here the lens is the basic idea. If one takes a photograph, one point on the object corresponds to one point on the image. This fact has affected us very greatly, suggesting that everything is made of points. The camera was thereby a very important instrument for helping to strengthen the mechanistic philosophy. It gives an experience that allows everybody to see what is meant by the idea that the universe is nothing but separate parts.

Another instrument, the *holograph*, can also illustrate this point. The Greek word *holo* means whole, and *graph* means to write; consequently, a holograph writes the whole. With the aid of a laser, which produces highly ordered light, the waves of light from everywhere can be brought to one spot, and just the waves, rather than the image of the object, can be photographed. What is remarkable is that in the resulting picture, each part of it can produce an image of the whole object. Unlike the picture produced by a camera, no point-to-point correspondence with the object obtains. Information about each object is enfolded in each part; an image is produced when this enfolded information is unfolded. The holograph hence suggests a new kind of knowledge and a new understanding of the universe in which information about the whole is enfolded in each part and in which the various objects of the world result from the unfolding of this information.

In my proposal of unbroken wholeness, I turn the mechanistic picture upside down. Whereas the mechanistic picture regarded discrete objects as the primary reality, and the enfolding and unfolding of organisms including minds, as secondary phenomena,

I suggest that the unbroken movements of enfolding and unfolding, which I call the *holomovement* is primary while the apparently discrete objects are secondary phenomena. They are related to the holomovement somewhat as the vortex, in the above example, is related to the unbroken flow of water. An essential part of this proposal is that the whole universe is *actively* enfolded to some degree in each of the parts. Because the whole is enfolded in each part, so are all other parts, in some way and to some degree. Hence, the mechanistic picture, according to which the parts are only externally related to each other is denied. That is, it is denied to be the primary truth; external relatedness is a secondary, derivative truth, applicable only to the secondary order of things, which I call the explicate or unfolded order. This is, of course, the order on which modern science has focused. The more fundamental truth is the truth of internal relatedness, because it is true of the more fundamental order, which I call the implicate order, because in this order the whole and hence all the other parts are enfolded in each part.

In my technical writings,[2] I have sought to show that the mathematical laws of quantum theory can be understood as describing the holomovement in which the whole is enfolded in each region, and the region is unfolded into the whole. Whereas modern physics has tried to understand the whole reductively by beginning with the most elementary parts, I am proposing a postmodern physics which begins with the whole.

Postmodern Science and Questions of Meaning and Value

We have seen that fragmentary thinking is giving rise to a reality that is constantly breaking up into disorderly, disharmonious and destructive partial activities. Therefore, seriously exploring a mode of thinking that starts from the most encompassing possible whole and goes down to the parts (sub-wholes) in a way appropriate to the actual nature of things seems reasonable. This approach tends to bring about a different reality, one that is orderly, harmonious and creative. For this actually to happen, however, a thoroughgoing end to fragmentation is necessary.

One source of fragmentation – perhaps the *major* one – is the belief that our thinking processes and what we are thinking about are fundamentally distinct. In this essay, I have stressed that everything is internally related to everything through mutual enfoldment. And evidently the whole world, both society and nature, is internally related to our thinking processes through enfoldment in our consciousness. For the content of our thought is just the world as we perceive it and know it (which includes ourselves). This content is not just a superficial part of us. Rather, in its totality, it provides us with the ground of all meaning in our lives, out of which arise our intentions, wishes, motivations and actions. Indeed, even imagining what life could mean to us without the world of nature and society enfolded within us is impossible.

The general way we think of this world will thus be a crucially important factor of our consciousness, and thus of our whole being. If we think of the world as separate from us, and constituted of disjointed parts to be manipulated with the aid of calculations, we will tend to try to become separate people, whose main motivation with regard to each other and to nature is also manipulation and calculation. But if we can obtain an intuitive and imaginative feeling of the whole world as constituting an implicate order that is also enfolded in us, we will sense ourselves to be one with this world. We will no longer be satisfied merely to manipulate it technically to our supposed advantage, but we will feel genuine love for it. We will want to care for it, as we would for anyone who is close to us and therefore enfolded in us as an inseparable part.

Vice versa, however, the idea of implicate order means that we are enfolded in the world – not only in other people, but in nature as a whole. We have already seen an indication of this fact in that, when we approach the world in a fragmentary way, its response is correspondingly fragmentary. Indeed, it can be said that, as we are not complete without the world which is enfolded in us, so the world is not complete without us who are enfolded in it. It is a mistake to think that the world has a totally defined existence separate from our own and that there is merely an external 'interaction' between us and the world. It follows that if we approach the world through enfolding its wholeness in our consciousness and thus act with love, the world, which enfolds our own being within itself, will respond in a corresponding way. This can obviously happen in the world of society. But even the world of nature will cease to respond with degeneration, due to pollution, destruction of forests and so on, and will begin to act in a more orderly and favourable way.

I want to emphasise this point. Because we are enfolded inseparably in the world, with no ultimate division between matter and consciousness, *meaning and value are as much integral aspects of the world as they are of us*. If science is carried out with an amoral attitude, the world will, ultimately respond to science in a destructive way. Postmodern science must therefore overcome the separation between truth and virtue, value and fact, ethics and practical necessity. To call for this nonseparation is, of course, to ask for a tremendous revolution in our whole attitude to knowledge. But such a change is now necessary and indeed long overdue. Can humanity meet in time the challenge of what is required? The coming years will be crucial in revealing the answer to this question.

Notes

1   See Huston Smith, *Beyond the Post-Modern Mind*, Crossroad (New York), 1982, esp chap 8, 'Beyond the Modern Western Mind-set'.

2   See David Bohm, *Wholeness and the Implicate Order*, Routledge & Kegan Paul (London), 1980 and other references given therein.

David Bohm, 'Postmodern Science and a Postmodern World' from David Ray Griffin (ed), *The Reenchantment of Science: Postmodern Proposals*, State University of New York Press (Albany), 1988. © 1988 The State University of New York Press.

The Postmodern Challenge to Biology

Charles Birch

According to Charles Birch, the 'postmodern challenge to biology is to recognise a second set of causes in addition to external relations', ie to admit that the human being is a subject that constitutes itself in response to the environment. This nonmechanistic view of biology, sometimes called the ecological model, explains evolution as a combination of chance and purpose. But, while in this text Birch discusses one of the alternatives to Cartesian mechanistic biology, he reminds us that other alternatives also need to be explored.

Louis Charles Birch (1918–) is an Australian geneticist who specialises in population ecology. He was Professor of Zoology and Biology at the University of Sydney and has written extensively on the interaction of science and religion and their influence in shaping our attitudes to the world around us. *LCS*

The dominant model of life in biology today is strictly mechanistic (substantialist) and reductionist. But it is not the model of life of the founders of modern biology in the 16th and 17th centuries. Vesalius, Harvey and others had a more organic view of life. What they discovered was later set in a mechanistic framework by their successors, particularly René Descartes. The methodology of mechanistic biology is to investigate the living organism as if it were a machine. Many biologists, probably most of them since Descartes, take the next step, a metaphysical one, and conclude that the living organism *is* a machine.

To be critical of the mechanistic model in biology is not to deny that it has been highly successful. The triumphs of molecular biology in describing and manipulating genes are triumphs of the mechanistic and reductionist approach. There are mechanical aspects of living entities. Limbs operate as levers. The heart operates as a pump. As Levins and Lewontin say:

> The great success of Cartesian method and the Cartesian view of nature is in part a result of a historical path of least resistance. Those problems that yield to the attack are pursued most vigorously, precisely because the method works there. Other problems and other phenomena are left behind, walled off from understanding by the commitment to Cartesianism.[1]

To be critical of the mechanistic model is not to deny a role to this way of thinking. It is to recognise that there are some problems in biology that have been singularly unresponsive to the mechanistic approach. These are developmental biology, the function of the central nervous system, aspects of animal behaviour and the evolution of mind and consciousness.

Contrast Between the Mechanistic and the Ecological Models

The mechanistic model of life recognises only one set of causes as operative in a living organism. These are external relations – those components of the organism's environment that push it or pull it. Descartes wanted to reduce the laws of biology to the laws of matter in motion. 'Give me matter and motion,' he said in effect, 'and I shall construct a universe.' Mind was recognised to exist only in human beings. The rest of the created things on our planet, including the human body, were understood in strictly mechanistic terms.

The postmodern challenge to biology is to recognise a second set of causes in addition to external relations. This second set is internal relations. We recognise internal relations in ourselves when our lives are profoundly influenced by a compelling purpose. Human lives are changed by such influences. I am what I am partly as a consequence of all the external relations that have impinged on me since conception. But I am also what I am by virtue of internal relations – the ways I have chosen to respond to those external conditions. An internal relation determines the nature of the entity, indeed even its very existence.

The notion of internal relation as causal strikes at the heart of the strictly mechanistic and reductionistic model. The ideal of this model is to divide the world into next to nothing as possible – call those entities 'atoms' [sic] or what you will – and then try to build the world up again from all those building blocks. When you do that, of course, you get a machine. In the mechanistic model the building blocks are substances. They have no internal relations. The definition of a substance is something that exists independently of anything else. In substance thinking, an atom of hydrogen is the same atom of hydrogen whether it be in the heart of the sun or in the molecules of my brain. It is what it is independently of its environment. That is the substance notion of a hydrogen atom. The idea of internal relations is that a human being, let us say, is not the same person independent of his or her environment. The human being is a subject and not simply an object pushed around by external relations. To be a subject is to be responsive, to constitute oneself purposefully in response to one's environment.

The postmodern view that makes most sense to me is the one that takes human experience as a high-level exemplification of entities in general, be they cells or atoms or electrons. All are subjects. All have internal relations. Consequently, in biology a distinction is made between a biology that is *compositional* (substantialist) and one that is *relational* (ecological).

As one moves up levels of organisation – electrons, atoms, molecules, cells, etc – the properties of each larger whole are given not merely by the units of which it is composed but also by the new relations between these units. It is not simply that the whole is more than the sum of its parts. The parts are themselves redefined and recreated in the process of evolution from one level to another. This means that the properties of matter relevant at, say, the atomic level do not begin to predict the properties of matter at the cellular level, let alone at the level of complex organisms. That is why, already 50 years ago, the Danish physicist Niels Bohr advised his students that the new laws of physics were most likely to be discovered in biology. This introduces a principle unrecognised by the mechanistic model, that as well as interpreting the higher levels in terms of the lower, we also interpret the lower levels in terms of the higher.

I have drawn a contrast between an organism or natural entity and a machine. The parts of a machine are subject only to the laws of mechanics, with its external forces acting on these parts. In some modern machines, such as computers, nuts and bolts are replaced by transistors and microchips. There is no evolution of computers in any real sense, but only change in design brought about by the designer outside the machine. There is of course also natural selection – in the marketplace! Likewise, in the mechanical model of life, no real evolution occurs, merely rearrangements of parts and natural selection among the different arrangements. Nuts and bolts cannot evolve! They can only be rearranged. This means that a completely mechanistic account of evolution is a gross abstraction from nature. Whitehead perceived this critical distinction when he wrote:

> A thoroughgoing evolutionary philosophy is inconsistent with materialism. The aboriginal stuff, or material, from which a materialistic philosophy starts, is incapable of evolution. This material is in itself the ultimate substance. Evolution, on the materialistic theory, is reduced to the role of being another word for the description of the changes of the external relations between portions of matter. There is nothing to evolve, because one set of external relations is as good as any other set of external relations. There can be merely change, purposeless and unprogressive ... The doctrine thus cries aloud for a conception of organism as fundamental to nature.[2]

Evolution, according to the ecological or organic model, is the evolution not of substances but of subjects. The critical thing that happens in evolution is change in internal relations of subjects.

Putting the Ecological Model into Practice

It is one thing, says Lewontin,[3] to call for a biology that is relational rather than compositional. It is quite another to put it into practice. Lewontin makes some attempt to do this in relation to this model of dialectical materialism. I want to do this in relation to the ecological model which I find more illuminating than dialectical materialism. What follows are some examples.

A mechanistic brain physiologist analyses my sitting at a word processor in terms of light waves impinging on my retina from the keyboard and the screen which set in train chemical processes in my nerves and brain. Messages from the brain to my muscles cause them to contract in ways that result in very complex movements of my fingers as I sit at the machine. This interpretation is fine as far as it goes – but it does not go very far. It does not account for the fact that I have some thoughts in mind that I purpose to put into writing. My thoughts initiate the complex sequence of events the physiologist studies. What the physiologist describes are external relations. The influence of my thoughts are internal relations. The distinction between these two sorts of causes in human behaviour was clearly made by Socrates as reported in Plato's dialogue the *Phaedo*. There are some, he tells us, who argue that the cause of his actions as he sits in prison awaiting death are the mechanical forces on his bones and muscles and sinews. But the real cause of his sitting in prison was that he made a *choice* to bow to the Athenians' sentence. In the mechanist analysis, an immense gap exists between what the scientist describes and what I experience. This is recognised by some brain physiologists, notably Sperry,[4] who considers that a thought itself can initiate chemical and electrical impulses in cells in the brain. His attempt to bring the mental and the physical together provides a richer understanding than the view that regards the physical account as exclusive and sufficient.

Some activities, such as the movement of fingers, appear to be represented in the brain in particular groups of cells. But in the case of visual memory, the brain does not seem to store information locally but widely. Karl Pribram and his colleagues[5] produced a holographic model of the brain in which the image is not represented in the brain as a point-to-point image from an object to a photographic plate. Rather, it is represented such that if some cells of the brain are removed, this removal does not destroy just one part of the image but reduces the clarity of the image as a whole. Dissecting the visual image down to particular cells is not possible. The image is a consequence of the interrelation of many cells as a whole. This is a far more ecological model of the brain than the strictly mechanistic model provided by most brain physiologists.

A mechanistic student of animal behaviour seeks to interpret all behaviour in terms of stimulus and response, analogously to the way in which a photoelectric cell receives a message from our approach to a door and responds with a message to a motor to open the door. These sorts of relationships can be made quite complex by incorporating negative feedback (cybernetic) mechanisms. We can then construct complex robots that perform quite complex activities. Such models add something to our understanding of animal behaviour. But the environment of these robots is extremely simple compared to the environment of any animal in the wild. The nonmechanistic student of animal behaviour tries to study animals in their complex relations with a complex world, as Jane Goodall has done with chimpanzees in Gombe Reserve.[6] Her success was dependent upon her establishing a rapport with the chimpanzee and, presumably, vice versa. She tried to think like a chimpanzee and to imagine what it was like to be one. She was, in fact, taking into account what she perceived to be critically important internal relations in their lives.

Hartshorne provided evidence that supports his view that birds have some musical feeling and that their song is not simply a matter of attracting the attention of mates.[7] In more general terms, Donald R Griffin argues that the needed step in research in animal behaviour is to attempt to understand the mind of the animal and he suggests ways to approach this.[8] I cannot really know what it is to be a chimpanzee, let alone a bee, unless I am one. Nor can I know that it is to be you instead of me. But in this latter case, we struggle imaginatively to enter one another's lives. Why should we not seek to do the same with other living organisms? Is not our neighbour all that participates in life? If so, the implication for ethics is revolutionary. If the needs of neighbours stretch beyond human need, so does the reach of love.

A mechanistic sociobiologist argues that the individual human limitations imposed by genes place constraints on society. The nonmechanistic student of societies argues that social organisations are able to negate individual limitations. Lewontin makes the analogy of human beings and flight.[9] Human beings cannot fly by flapping their arms and legs. Yet we do fly because of the existence of aircraft, pilots, fuel production, radios – all products of social organisation. Moreover, it is not society that flies, but the individuals who have acquired this property as a consequence of socialisation. The individual can be understood only in terms of the total environment. In different environments we have different properties. We are indeed different.

The naively mechanistic geneticist says that genes are particles located on chromosomes, that genes make proteins, proteins make us and that genes replicate themselves. The nonmechanistic geneticist says genes are not like particles at all. What a gene is depends upon neighbouring genes on the same and on different chromosomes and upon other aspects of its environment in the cell. The gene (DNA) makes nothing by itself. It does not even make more DNA. It depends on enzymes in the cell to do all these things. Geneticists no longer teach 'particulate genetics'. And molecular biology is properly called *molecular ecology*. We know that a particular DNA molecule can express itself in a great variety of ways – *which* way depends upon the environment of the cell and therefore of the molecule at the time.

The molecule and its chemical environment are in a state of perpetual dynamic equilibrium depending upon the magnitude of the physical forces and the concentrations of chemicals inside the cell. Which chemical pathway is *chosen* is a matter of probability rather than absolute determinism. The difference between 100 per cent determinism and even 99.99 per cent determinism is all the difference in the world. It is the difference between being completely determined by the environment and having a degree of self-determination. A thoroughgoing mechanist might argue that the difference between 100 per cent and 99.99 per cent may be due to defective functioning of a deterministic system, which is precisely the point. If accident can happen in the system, determinism by the environment is not complete. Self-determinism or choice is therefore possible. The substance or billiard-ball concept of the gene is no longer credible. The classical notion that genes were pellets of matter that remained in all respects self-identical, whatever the environment, has to be abandoned in the light of modern knowledge.

The challenge of postmodern thought to molecular biology is to pursue further this avenue of thought. I would claim that to exhibit self-determination is to exhibit mind. It is to have some degree of freedom, no doubt minute at the molecular level. I am not saying that, having investigated the life of the cell, biologists have found mind. I am saying that what they have found is *more consistent with* the proposition that the cells and their DNA molecules are mind-like in the sense of having internal relations than with the proposition that they are machine-like. They take account of their environment in the deep sense of taking account: they are constituted by their relations. Molecular genetics was the last into [sic] mechanistic biology. Maybe it will be the first out.

Mechanistic developmental biologists thought that an organism developed in complexity from a single fertilised egg into a complex living organism in the way a motor car is built up from individual bits and pieces. But we now know that if you cut out the limb bud of a developing frog embryo at a very early stage, shake the cells loose and put them back at random in a lump, a normal leg develops. It is not as though each cell in its particular place was initially destined to become a particular part. Each cell could become any part of the leg (but not of the eye) depending upon its total environment. Unlike a machine, which can be pulled to pieces and reassembled, the bits and pieces of the embryo seem to come into existence as a consequence of their spatial relationships at critical moments in the development of the embryo. Says Lewontin:

> If development is really, in an important sense, a consequence of the relations between things, how are we to reduce the incredible complexity of relationships to a manageable set of regularities? And how are we to do this using an experimental method that is itself so wedded to Cartesian analysis?[10]

An example of how developmental biology was misled along the Cartesian path was the hunt for the so-called organiser in development. For 60 years biochemists hunted for a single molecule or group of molecules that might be responsible for 'organising' the development of the parts of the embryo, such as a leg or an eye. But they found no 'organiser'. This reductionist programme was a colossal distraction.[11] Development evidently cannot be reduced to the action of single chemicals.

The mechanistic evolutionist seeks to interpret all in terms of chance and necessity. 'Chance alone,' said Monod, 'is at the source of every innovation, of all creation in the biosphere.'[12] He contrasts his position with those who sought to find in every detail of nature evidence of deterministic design. The choice he gives us is complete chance or complete determinism.

Darwinism was a shattering blow to those who conceived of nature as completely determined, be it by an outside designer or some inbuilt principle in nature. To take chance seriously is the first step in moving away from the concept of deterministic design. This was a problem for Darwin. It seems he could not admit the reality of chance, despite the role he attributed to it. In this respect, he was like Einstein who could not believe that God plays dice: 'I cannot think,' said Darwin, 'that the world … is the result of chance; yet I cannot look at each separate thing as the result of Design … I am, and shall ever remain, in a hopeless muddle.' So wrote Darwin in a letter to the Harvard botanist Asa Gray. Again and again Darwin's letters reiterate this refrain – is it all determined or is it all a result of chance? But are these the only possibilities?

Hartshorne hits the nail on the head when he says: 'Neither pure chance nor the pure absence of chance can explain the world.'[13] He goes on to say: 'There must be something positive limiting chance and something more than mere matter in matter, or Darwinism fails to explain life.'

The *something positive* that limits chance and the *something more* than mere matter in matter is the degree of self-determination exercised by natural entities in response to possibilities of their future. In other words, a causal role in evolution is played by internal relations as well as the external relation of natural selection about which Darwin wrote.

Chance (plus natural selection) alone cannot explain the evolution of life. Chance and purpose together provide a more substantial base for thinking about evolution.

This thought is not as revolutionary as it might at first appear. Evolutionary biologists have accepted an important role for purpose in human evolution in what is called *cultural evolution*. Cultural choices have determined the direction of genetical evolution. Cultural evolution and genetical evolution go hand in hand. But we can also recognise a role that choice and purpose play in the lives of other animals. For them, too, cultural evolution is a reality. How far down the line are we prepared to go with this argument? Logically there is no need to draw a line anywhere in the total evolutionary sequence from atoms to humans. This is a challenge of postmodern thought to evolutionary biology today – to propose a role for purpose together with chance in evolution all down the line. This is to propose that, in addition to external relations as causal, internal relations are causal also in determining the direction of evolution.

Evolution raises a profound question: Why did atoms evolve into cells and into plants and animals? Why didn't creativity stop with the first DNA molecule? Mechanism provides no answer. The ecological model opens up ways to explore it in terms of lure and response, or purposive influence and self-determination. Self-determination is minimal at the atomic level. It is greatest in the higher organisms. Because natural entities are always, with their own particular degree of freedom, in the process of relating to the lure to fulfilment, a constant tension between chaos and order occurs in nature.

Implicit in what I have said is that the scientists' methodology and the way in which they interpret the data depend upon their metaphysical stance. Scientists always take sides. I have given one alternative to Cartesian mechanistic biology. There are others and we need to see the parallels and differences between them.

In addition to the biologists I have already mentioned, others provide a challenge to mechanistic reductionistic biology, including Sewall Wright[14] in evolutionary biology, CH Waddington[15] in developmental biology, Ilya Prigogine and Isabelle Stengers[16] in molecular biology, and, in the broad field of all biology, JZ Young,[17] Rupert Sheldrake,[18] and John Cobb and me.[19]

The contrast between a bits-and-pieces view of nature and an holistic one is captured by Henry Reed in his poem 'Naming of Parts,' which begins:

Today we have naming of parts, Yesterday
we had daily cleaning. And tomorrow morning
we shall have what to do after firing. But today,
Today we have naming of parts. Japonica
Glistens like coral in all of the neighbouring gardens,
And today we have naming of parts.

Notes
1   Richard Levins and Richard Lewontin, *The Dialectical Biologist*, Harvard University Press, 1985, pp 2–3.
2   AN Whitehead, *Science and the Modern World*, Cambridge University Press, 1933, pp 134–5.
3   Richard Lewontin, 'The Corpse in the Elevator', *New York Review of Books* 30, 1983, pp 14–37, esp 36.

4   Roger Sperry, *Science and Moral Priority: Merging Mind, Brain and Human Values*, Blackwell (Oxford), 1983; 'Interview with Roger Sperry', *Omni* 5/ii, 1983, pp 69–100.

5   Karl H Pribram, 'Holonomy and Structure in the Organization of Perception', *Images, Perception and Knowledge*, ed John M Nicholas, Reidel (Dordrecht), 1977, pp 155–85; KH Pribram, M Nuwer, and R Baron, 'The Holographic Hypothesis of Memory Structure in Brain Function and Structure', *Contemporary Developments in Mathematical Psychology*, vol 2, eds R Atkinson, O Krantz, R Luce and P Suppes, Freeman (San Francisco), 1974, pp 416–57.

6   Jane van Lawick Goodall, *In the Shadow of Man*, Houghton Miflin Co (Boston), 1971; *The Chimpanzees of Gombe: Patterns of Behavior*, Harvard University Press, 1986.

7   Charles Hartshorne, *Born to Sing: An Interpretation and World Survey of Bird Song*, Indiana University Press (Bloomington), 1973; *Omnipotence and Other Theological Mistakes*, State University of New York Press (Albany), 1984.

8   Donald R Griffin, *The Question of Animal Awareness: Evolutionary Continuity of Mental Experience*, Rockefeller University Press (New York), 1976; *Animal Thinking*, Harvard University Press, 1984.

9   Lewontin, 'The Corpse in the Elevator', p 37.

10 Ibid, p 36.

11 Mae-Wah Ho and PT Saunders, *Beyond Neo-Darwinism: An Introduction to the New Evolutionary Paradigm*, Harcourt Brace Janovich (New York), 1984, pp 10, 267–90; Jam Witowski, 'The Hunting of the Organiser: An Episode in Biochemical Embryology', *Trends in Biochemical Science* 10, 1985, pp 379–81.

12 Jacques Monod, *Chance and Necessity: An Essay on the Natural Philosophy of Modern Biology*, Fontana/Collins (London), 1974, p 110.

13 Charles Hartshorne, *Omnipotence and Other Theological Mistakes*, p 69.

14 Sewall Wright, 'Biology and the Philosophy of Science', *Process and Divinity*, eds WL Reese and E Freeman, Open Court (La Salle, IL), 1964, pp 101–25.

15 CH Waddington (ed), *Toward a Theoretical Biology*, Vol 2, Sketches, Edinburgh University Press, 1969, pp 72–81.

16 Ilya Prigogine and Isabelle Stengers, *Order of Chaos, Man's New Dialogue with Nature*, Bantam Books (New York), 1984.

17 JZ Young, *Programmes of the Brain*, Oxford University Press, 1978.

18 Rupert Sheldrake, *A New Science of Life: The Hypothesis of Formative Causation*, Blond and Briggs (London), 1981.

19 Charles Birch and John B Cobb Jr, *The Liberation of Life: From the Cell to the Community*, Cambridge University Press, 1981.

Gaia and Evolution

Edward Goldsmith

In *Gaia and Evolution*, Edward Goldsmith questions the reigning neo-Darwinist paradigm, by suggesting 'cooperation is the true evolutionary strategy'. His main argument is that there is no such thing as true randomness, the essential element of the Darwinian theory, and that the principle of natural selection is a tautology. Instead a Gaian system operates – a system that is dynamic, goal-directed, cybernetic and cooperative, as well as highly coordinated.

Edward René David ('Teddy') Goldsmith (1928–2009) was an Anglo-French environmentalist and eco-philosopher. He was the founder and, for many years, the editor of *The Ecologist* magazine. LCS

The 'survival of the fittest' maxim of Darwinism is widely used to justify the disastrous process of unrestrained technological progress and economic development. However, if the world is seen as a single self-regulating system, then progress through competition becomes fundamentally anti-evolutionary. Cooperation is the true evolutionary strategy.

Neither Darwinism, nor the neo-Darwinism of Bateson and Weissman, nor its latest version, the Synthetic Theory, provides an evolutionary theory that is reconcilable with our knowledge of the structure and function of the world of living things. This is particularly so if the biosphere is seen as a single living system, whose constituent parts cooperate in achieving a specific strategy – the maintenance of its basic features or organisation in the face of internal or external challenges, that is to say its stability or homeostasis.

Little attempt has been made to provide any serious evidence for the Darwinist theory. This has been noted by a number of critics, for example Karl Popper, who considered that 'neither Darwin nor any Darwinian has so far given an actual causal explanation of the adaptive evolution of any single organism or any single organ. All that has been shown – and this is very much a hypothesis – is that such explanations might exist (that is to say, they are not logically impossible).' Popper does not, for that reason, consider Darwinism scientific theory – though he does not necessarily reject it.

Michael Polanyi accepts that though 'neo-Darwinism is firmly accredited and highly regarded by Science … there is little direct evidence for it.' Ludwig von Bertalanffy makes the same point. In the debate on evolution, he writes, there has been no more concern with proof 'than in the operation of a Tibetan prayer wheel'.

These criticisms apply equally to the role that random variations or random mutations, or indeed randomness itself, are supposed to play in the evolutionary process, and to the role which is supposed to be played in that process by natural selection.

Randomness

The notion that the biosphere is the product of random variations could not be stated more unequivocally – and indeed more dogmatically – than by Jacques Monod:

> Chance alone was the source of every innovation, of all creation in the biosphere. Pure chance, absolutely free but blind is at the very root of the stupendous edifices of evolution. This central concept of modern biology is no longer one among other conceivable hypotheses. It is the only conceivable hypothesis, the only one that squares with observed and tested fact. And nothing warrants the supposition – or the hope – that on this score our position is likely ever to be revised.

In the same way, nonhuman animals are seen as learning by random trial and error, and humans by 'induction', which involves making naive correlations between random observations. Human history is seen as composed of random events and historians such as HAL Fisher pour scorn upon historicists such as Arnold Toynbee and Spengler, who sought to introduce a pattern into our historical experience.

To tell us, as Monod does, that the thesis of randomness is the only conceivable thesis 'that squares with observed and tested fact' is untenable. There is no possible way of determining empirically whether an event is random. All that we can say of an event that appears to be random is that we do not know the circumstances that brought it about.

Lamarck noted this: 'Le mot hazard n'exprime que notre ignorance des causes.' Poincaré said the same thing in slightly different words: 'Le Hazard n'est que la mesure de notre ignorance.' Waddington also intimated that gene mutations may only appear to be random because of our present lack of knowledge. 'A gene mutation which consists of some alteration in the sequence of nucleotides in the DNA is from a chemical point of view presumably not wholly at random. There may well be quite considerable regularities in the processes by which the alterations come about: however, we know very little about them as yet.'

The important role attributed to random mutations appeared more credible in the days when the genome was seen as a random assortment of genes. It makes far less sense, however, now that the genome is known to be a highly sophisticated and elaborately regulated organisation, capable, among other things, as Lerner has shown, of maintaining its own homeostasis.

In response to such criticisms, neo-Darwinists have modified their position, cosmetically at least. Mutations may well be caused by factors that we ignore, they tell us, but as Julian Huxley wrote: 'in all cases they are random in relation to evolution. Their effects are not related to the needs of organism or to the condition in which it is placed. They occur without reference to their biological uses.' Dobzhansky and Waddington stated the same principle in slightly different words.

But this concession changes very little. Randomness necessarily means randomness vis-à-vis a specific process. An event cannot be random to all processes, as this would mean that it had occurred spontaneously, which would violate the principle of causality that is critical to the paradigm of reductionist science. Indeed, if an event is seen as the product of a 'cause', it cannot be random to the causal process of which it is the effect. The official position is thus still very close to Jacques Monod's and it is an untenable one – one that is in complete conflict with our knowledge of life processes in the world we live in.

Randomness: Fact or Fiction?

Indeed, even ordinary cultural phenomena with which we are all acquainted, and which, in terms of the paradigm of reductionist science, are interpreted as random, are not, in reality, random at all. For instance, art styles do not develop at random, but closely reflect the cultures in which they developed. The clothes people wear are indicative of the image of themselves they wish to communicate to others. The way people walk, eat, light cigarettes, blow their noses, do up their shoelaces, all convey some information as to the personality of the individuals concerned.

In fact, behaviour exhibits so little 'randomness' that it is questionable whether living things are in fact capable of behaving in a random way, even if they make a determined attempt to do so. This appears to be confirmed by various experiments such as those described by WR Ramsay and Anne Broadhurst, who experimented with a panel of 72 people by asking them to repeat in time to a metronome a series of numbers between 1 and 9, in as random a manner as possible. They found that '... in accordance with other studies on randomness and response in human subjects, the result of this experiment shows that even when subjects try to be random, there is a high degree of stereotype.'

In a world of living things, randomness is so rare that to achieve a state which even approximates it, it has to be 'manufactured' artificially. Stafford Beer points out the absurdity of such a situation:

> It really is ludicrous that we should have gone so far with Epicurus as to manufacture chaos where none exists, in order to provide ourselves with the properly certificated raw materials for system building. Take my own case. There are a random number of tables on my bookshelf; there are computer tapes for producing pseudo-random numbers next door; there is a large electronic machine for generating noise upstairs; down the road there is a room full of equipment designed to hurl thousands of little metal balls about in a random way; and I use ten-sided dice as paper-weights. The upkeep of this armoury is considerable. Think of all the time we spend trying to ensure that these artefacts produce results which are 'genuinely random' – whatever that may mean. This tremendous practical problem of guaranteeing disorderliness ought to be enough to satisfy any systems man that nothing is more unnatural than chaos.

Indeed, living things actively seek to eliminate randomness. We know, for instance, that mutant genes tend to be eliminated. Lerner has shown us how a genome tends to maintain its structure, thereby countering random changes. We know that random bodies within a biological organism are eliminated with the aid of the immune system; and that in all known vernacular societies, people whose behaviour is socially random, in that it diverts from the traditional norm, are ostracised or eliminated. We know too that the ability of natural systems to eliminate randomness increases as they develop or evolve, and that climax ecosystems are very much better at doing this than pioneer ecosystems. Natural systems are, in fact, committed to the elimination of randomness by virtue of the fact that they function cybernetically to maintain the basic features of their order – and hence their stability or homeostasis. Life, in fact, develops and indeed evolves at the expense of randomness.

Natural Selection: The Motor of Evolution?

Randomness is essential to the Darwinian notion of natural selection. Yet, it is hard enough to demonstrate that natural selection from random variations is even *one* of the mechanisms of evolution, as Darwin maintained, since the term 'natural selection' is a very vague one, indeed Darwin actually admitted that he used it metaphorically. To demonstrate that natural selection is the *only* mechanism of evolution, as is maintained by the neo-Darwinists, is still more difficult.

How do neo-Darwinists know that no other factors are involved? In particular, how do they know that no 'internal factors' are operative, that living things, in fact, do not evolve as a result of their own behavioural efforts and ontogenetic adaptations?

There is no epistemological justification for maintaining such a thesis. Neo-Darwinists simply assume that living things do not evolve in that way.

That natural selection is operated by the 'environment' is a further unjustified assumption. Why should the environment behave in that way? What motivates it to do so? How is it capable of displaying such highly discriminatory and indeed highly teleological behaviour? These questions have never been answered, nor can they be since the term 'environment' is never defined, it is simply taken to be that which is 'out there' – some strange mystical entity to which all the dynamic, creative and intelligent features of life have somehow been delegated.

Selection as God

If natural selection from random mutations is indeed the only mechanism of evolution, then the most sophisticated achievements must be attributed to it – and indeed they are. Thus, according to Ruse, natural selection can act not only to cause evolutionary change 'in the sense that it can cause change in gene ratios', it can also act 'as a conservative force preventing change, that is keeping gene ratios stable'.

Merrell tells us that natural selection 'will tend to operate in such a way as to minimise interspecific competition'. It is also capable of deciding, if we are to believe MacArthur and Wilson, whether to favour 'increased reproductive rates' (K selection) or 'greater efficiency of conversion of food and other resources into offspring' (R selection).

Selection can also decide, if we are to believe Lerner, whether it should be 'intensive' or 'less intensive'. It has the ability to eliminate deviants and thereby favour stability, hence Waddington's 'stabilising selection'. According to Dobzhansky, it is responsible 'for directedness of the general as well as for the grouping of particular evolution'.

Alistair Hardy notes too that 'moral and aesthetic qualities in man are not infrequently said to be explained by the operation of natural selection'. This is true of the sociobiologists who even see natural selection as giving rise to altruism (kinship selection). Similarly, Waddington, when it was suggested to him by Piaget, that it might be difficult for such a crude mechanistic device to create complexity, answered that Piaget greatly underestimated the capacity of natural selection.

Selection is thus invoked to explain everything (which indeed it must be, if we are to accept the neo-Darwinist thesis). Julian Huxley explicitly states:

> The hoary objection of the improbability of an eye or a hand or a brain being evolved by 'blind chance' has lost its force because natural selection, operating over stretches of geological time, explains *everything*.

Lewontin claims to have established this principle experimentally. 'There appears to be no character – morphogenetic, behavioural, physiological or cytological,' he writes, 'that cannot be selected in *Drosophila*.'

Selection, like God, is thus omnipotent. Neo-Darwinists may laugh at Lamarck's idea that if an animal needs some organ, that need will somehow call the organ into existence. Dawkins regards this notion as 'so obviously mystical to the modern mind that it is fairer to Lamarck for us to concentrate on those parts of his theory that at least seem to have some chance of explaining evolution'. But the neo-Darwinists entertain an almost identical notion, the only difference being that it is environment's 'need' that 'will call the organ into existence', which seems just as mystical.

The question that needs to be asked is how does 'natural selection' – supposedly a purely mechanical process, like a sorting machine in a post office, that does no more than sort the 'fit' from the 'unfit' – achieve this omnipotence? How can this mechanical sorting machine create complex living things?

One can understand that by selecting the most viable living things, and allowing them to reproduce themselves, their characteristics will be transmitted to the next generation, which will become correspondingly more viable, but this is only possible if living things can transmit such characteristics to the next generation. Billiard balls cannot, and it is difficult to see how they might be made to evolve by natural selection however much variability they might exhibit.

Whitehead noted this: 'A thoroughgoing evolutionary philosophy is inconsistent with materialism. The aboriginal stuff, or material, from which a materialistic philosophy starts, is *incapable of evolution*'.

Woodger made the same point. The Darwinian doctrine, he noted, 'is committed to ascribe to 'bits of matter' properties which they do not exhibit today, instead of searching for an adequate conception of organism'.

Popper also pointed out that 'only an organism which exhibits in its behaviour a strong tendency or disposition or propensity to struggle for its survival will in fact be likely to survive'. But to compete *is to exhibit goal-directedness*. Indeed, as Popper notes, goal-directedness is one of the conditions for evolution. But there are many other such conditions. Indeed, one can draw up a whole catalogue of conditions which must obtain before a sorting machine could conceivably be used to bring about constructive changes in the structure and function of living things, however great the diversity of random or nonrandom variations which it may have the privilege to select from. Von Bertalanffy notes this:

> Selection *presupposes* self-maintenance, adaptability, reproduction, etc of the living system. These therefore cannot be the effect of selection. This is the oft-discussed circularity of the selectionist argument. Proto-organisms would arise, and organisms further evolve by chance mutations and subsequent selection. But, in order to do so, *they must already have had the essential attributes to life*.

For Woodger, the neo-Darwinist thesis is unacceptable on this count alone: 'An explanation of this kind can only make out a case for itself by begging the fundamental question at issue – the essential characteristics of an organism *have to be surreptitiously introduced in vague general language*.'

They are so introduced largely by attributing to natural selection – the mechanical sorting machine – qualities which no machine can possibly display, and that are, in effect, little more than the very 'internal factors' whose role in determining the evolutionary process, neo-Darwinists are at such pains to deny.

The following passage makes clear how Darwin 'surreptitiously introduced' the highly sophisticated features of life processes into what he made out to be a purely mechanical process. In it, Darwin tries to explain how so phenomenally complex an organ as the eye could have been produced by natural selection:

> We must suppose that there is a power, represented by natural selection or the survival of the fittest, always intently watching each slight alteration in the transparent layers; and carefully preserving each which, under varied circumstances, in any way or in any degree, tends to produce a distincter image. We must suppose each new state of the instrument to be multiplied by the million; each to be preserved until a better one is produced, and then the old ones to be all destroyed. In living bodies, variation will cause the slight alterations, generation will multiply them almost infinitely, and natural selection will pick out with unerring skill each improvement. Let this process go on for millions of years; and during each year on millions of individuals of many kinds; and may we not believe that a living optical instrument might thus be formed as superior to one of glass, as the works of the creator are to those of man?

Note that selection is referred to as a 'power', that it is 'intently watching' each slight alteration, that it picks out each improvement 'with unerring skill'. Is Darwin really talking about a mechanical sorting machine? Indeed, it is difficult to avoid the feeling that there is some living being endowed with such nonmechanistic qualities as purpose, reason, knowledge and intelligence lurking in the background and secretly manipulating the sorting machine.

This is not altogether surprising, since a machine needs a living designer and operator. That is in itself sufficient reason why a mechanistic theory of evolution can only superficially replace a theistic, a vitalistic or an ecological theory.

Equating Selection with Adaptation

The subterfuge of disguising complex life processes as crude mechanistic processes by the use of the appropriate words and imagery is probably most discernible in the attempt by neo-Darwinists to prove how, in specific instances, natural selection has actually occurred.

The subterfuge consists in noting that adaptation has occurred and then *quite brazenly taking such adaptation as constituting evidence of natural selection at work*. Instead of demonstrating that natural selection leads to adaptive change, *it is simply assumed to do so by the expedient of equating natural selection with adaptation*. It thereby suffices to show that adaptation has occurred in order to prove, in the eyes of neo-Darwinists at least, that the corresponding adaptive characteristics have been elected.

Thus on the subject of the finches of the Galapagos that so impressed Darwin, Ruse writes, 'we find that all the different species show the effects of selection'. What are these effects, we might ask?

> Peculiar characteristic after peculiar characteristic *has some special adaptive function*. Some finches have evolved in such a way that they are ideally suited to the consumption of plant food; some mainly for the consumption of animal food; some solely for animal food. Then there are beaks for cactus eating, beaks for insect eating on the wing, beaks for general scavenging. One species has even developed the ability to probe with twigs for insects in hollow parts of trees.

In this passage, Ruse's identification of selection with adaptation is quite explicit. The fact that he is assuming what he set out to prove could not be more evident.

That evolution and natural selection are synonymous, so that to prove that the former has occurred provides proof of the effectiveness of the latter, is also assumed by Charlesworth:

> Probably the most general relevant prediction of the theory of natural selection is that episodes of rapid evolution should coincide with periods when the direction of selection is changing; this seems to be borne out at many different levels of evolution. Insecticide resistance evolves in populations exposed to a new insecticide. The molluscs of Lake Turkana changed when the level of the lake altered. The *drosophila* of Hawaii evolved an array of diverse species as they colonised an archipelago with numerous vacant ecological niches. And modern mammals underwent their period of most rapid evolution and diversification after the dominant land reptiles of the Cretaceous era went extinct.

But how do we know that these instances of rapid adaptation to new conditions are the result of natural selection? We do not, *unless that is we have already assumed, as does Charlesworth, that natural selection and adaptation are one and the same – unless in fact we start out by assuming what we set out to prove.* Von Bertalanffy was fully aware of this subterfuge:

> The principle of selection is a tautology in the sense that the selectionist explanation is always a construction *a posteriori*. Every surviving form, structure or behaviour – however bizarre, unnecessarily complex or outright crazy it may appear – must, *ipso facto* have been viable or of some selective advantage, for otherwise it would not have survived. *But this is no proof that it was a product of selection.*

Neo-Darwinism: The Dogma of Reductionist Science

Since there is absolutely no evidence for the neo-Darwinist thesis, and since it fits in so very poorly with our knowledge of the world of living things, the only reason why it should prove so durable seems to be that it fits in so well with the paradigm of reductionist science and hence with the worldview of modernism that the latter so faithfully reflects.

This was the view of Michael Polanyi. 'Neo-Darwinism', he wrote 'is firmly accredited and highly regarded by science though there is little direct evidence for it *because it fits in beautifully* with the mechanistic system of the universe and bears on the subject – the origin of man – which is of the utmost intrinsic interest.' This was also the view of Ludwig von Bertalanffy, who considered:

> that a theory so vague, so insufficiently verifiable and so far from the criteria otherwise applied in 'hard' science, has become a dogma, can only be explained *on sociological grounds*. Society and science have been so steeped in the ideas of mechanism, utilitarianism, and the economic concept of free competition that instead of God, selection was enthroned as ultimate reality.

Many biologists are now involved in developing a new post-Darwinian evolutionary theory. Such a theory, if it is to be a realistic one, is likely to clash with, rather than conform to, the paradigm of reductionist science, for which reason it is unlikely to be accepted until such time as that paradigm itself undergoes considerable change – and indeed itself becomes more realistic. This process is already under way. The paradigm of reductionist science is under assault across a broad front. Its transformation is indeed necessary because, among other things, it faithfully reflects the worldview of modernism, which serves above all to rationalise and hence to validate the Promethean enterprise to which modern society is committed, a path that is leading to the systematic annihilation of the world of living things.

Indeed, if humans are to survive for very long, one of the requirements of their survival will be the replacement of the paradigm of reductionist science by a new ecological paradigm. This new paradigm would also reflect a very different worldview, one that would serve to rationalise and hence validate a society committed to systematically reducing the impact of our economic activities on the ecosphere and, thereby, to the extent that this is still possible, of restoring the proper functioning of the Gaian process that can alone assure that our planet remains habitable.

A Post-Darwinian Evolutionary Theory

According to the Gaia thesis, the biosphere, together with its atmospheric environment, forms a single entity or natural system. This system is the product of organic forces that are highly coordinated by the system itself. Gaia has, in effect, created herself, not in a random manner but in a goal-directed manner since the system is highly stable and is capable of maintaining its stability in the face of internal and external challenges. It is, in fact, a cybernetic system, and for this to be possible, Gaia must display considerable order, indeed, she must be seen as a vast cooperative enterprise, very much as nature was seen by the Natural Theologists of the 19th century.

Such a view of the world of living things is, needless to say, totally incompatible with neo-Darwinism. Indeed, an evolutionary theory that would be consistent with this view of the world would be the very *negation of neo-Darwinism*. I shall suggest what some of its features might be:

Gaia as the Unit of Evolution: If Gaia is a single natural system that has created herself in a coordinated and goal-directed way, *then Gaia is clearly the unit of evolution*, not the individual living thing as neo-Darwinists insist.

Gaia is Evolution: Gaia is not just a contemporaneous organisation of living things. She is a *spatio-temporal system*. It is difficult for us to grasp the notion of a spatio-temporal system, as our language makes a clear distinction between things and processes and our thinking is clearly influenced by our language. It is nevertheless essential that we realise that all living things have a *temporal* as well as a *spatial* component. They exist in time just as much as in space. This means that Gaia is not only an entity but also a process, and what is that process *if it is not evolution*?

If this is so, *then the Gaian process – or evolution – must display the same fundamental structure as Gaia does when seen as a spatial entity*. If the latter is a biological, social and ecological structure, then the Gaian process cannot possibly be merely physical and mechanical as the neo-Darwinists tell us; *it must clearly also be seen in biological, social and ecological terms*.

Gaia as a Total Spatio-Temporal System: But what part of the temporal process must be seen as evolving? We assume that it must be the contemporaneous process, the one occurring before our eyes. But how do we justify this assumption? I suggest that the total process is involved, stretching back into the mists of time. The reason for suggesting this is that the information passed on from generation to generation of living things must reflect the experience of *the total spatio-temporal system involved and not just part of it*.

This information appears to be organised hierarchically, the most general information, that which reflects the longest experience, being particularly nonplastic, the more particular information, that which reflects the more recent experience, being very much more plastic and hence more easily adaptable to short-term environmental contingencies. This arrangement is clearly that which best assures the continuity or the stability of the total spatio-temporal Gaian system. If this is so, this means, among other things, *that evolution is a long-term strategy not just a set of ad hoc adaptations*.

Evolution as a Living Process: If Gaia creates herself, then the living world must be seen as dynamic and creative, not as passive and robot-like. The qualities that are tacitly attributed to the vague undefined 'environment' must be ascribed as well to the living things which it is seen as managing. Evolution is thereby no longer the mere product of natural selection from random variations or genetic mutations, but of living things exhibiting all those features whose involvement in the evolutionary process neo-Darwinists have been at such pains to deny.

Evolution as a Cybernetic Process: If Gaia is evolution, then evolution must also be a cybernetic process. Lovelock's 'Daisy World' model is a cybernetic process but a very rudimentary one. One must suppose that the cybernetic process that led to the development of a system as complex as Gaia herself must be very much more sophisticated.

Now we are beginning to understand how living cybernetic processes operate. Human behaviour, as Kenneth Craik was the first to show, is mediated on the basis of a mental model of an individual's relationship with his environment, in the light of which diversions from the appropriate pattern of behaviour are corrected.

Gerardo Reichel Dolmatoff and others have shown how the behaviour of tribal groups in Amazonia is controlled in similar fashion, the model of the tribe's relationship with its environment being formulated in the language of its mythology. I do not think that it is too outlandish to ask whether Gaia herself is not endowed with a similar model?

What is certain is that a cybernetic system must be capable of monitoring its responses otherwise it could not correct diversions from its optimum course, and hence maintain its *homeorhesos* and thereby its stability. How then is evolution monitored? There can only be one answer and that is ontogenetically and behaviourally. That such feedback must occur has been clear to serious students of evolution for a long time. Baldwin, Lloyd Morgan, Goldschmidt, Waddington and Schmallhausen have all proposed mechanisms that might achieve this. The case for such feedback is put very forcefully by Piaget in his excellent book, *Le Comportement Moteur de l 'Evolution*. The whole issue becomes much clearer, of course, once it is realised that the information that serves to mediate evolution is not just genetic but is formulated in different informational media including the cultural medium.

Evolution is a Goal-Directed Process: If evolution is a cybernetic process, then it must be goal-directed. The reason should be clear. To say that a process is under control means that it is maintaining itself on its optimum course or 'chreod' as Waddington referred to it, that which will enable it to achieve its optimum end-state or goal – a baby in the case of the embryological process, the climax ecosystem in the case of an ecological one. This implies that there is an optimum course and also that there is an end-state or goal. If there is not, then the very notion of control becomes meaningless.

Once a system has achieved its end-state, then to say that it is under control is to say that it is capable of maintaining itself at that end-state or thereabouts, that it is in fact homeostatic. Again this implies that there is an end-state. If there was not, then clearly it could not maintain itself there. It seems to me that one has to overcome the scientist's irrational attitude towards goal-directedness or purposiveness. Teleology is a fact of life, a fundamental feature of life processes, including evolution.

Stability is the Goal: To say that a cybernetic system maintains its homeostasis, and that its constituent parts cooperate with it in this enterprise, is to say that its goal is the maintenance of its homeostasis or stability – in effect the same thing. This implies that Gaia does not seek to evolve, and that the changes that it undergoes are simply those that it must undergo in order to avoid bigger and more disruptive changes. They are but part of a dynamic and creative strategy for maintaining the stability of the total spatio-temporal system that constitutes Gaia. Indeed, it is only by adapting the particularities of its structure to environmental contingencies that a dynamic system such as Gaia can best maintain the generalities of its structure and hence its stability or homeostasis.

Order and Cooperation: If Gaia is to be capable of acting as a cybernetic system and of maintaining its homeostasis, then it must display that specific structure that enables it to do so. It quite clearly cannot merely be but {a} random assortment of competitive individuals all frantically striving to achieve their own egotistic ends, as the neo-Darwinists maintain. Instead, Gaia must be seen, as Lovelock sees her, as a vast cooperative enterprise geared to the maintenance of its overall structure in the face of change. Clearly competition occurs: but it is not the most fundamental relationship between living things. It is a secondary relationship. So too, there is selection, but such selection is operated by the various natural systems that make up the Gaian hierarchy, acting their constituent parts, rather than by the vague, undefined 'environment' of neo-Darwinists. Its role, what is more, is not to assure the 'survival of the fittest' (in the sense of the most individualistic, and the most competitive), but on the contrary to eliminate such undesirable individuals, since they do not fit into Gaia's cooperative structure, assuring in this way the survival of those who do fit into Gaia and thereby contribute to the achievement of her strategy.

Evolution and Anti-Evolution: It must be noted that to attribute the above characteristics to the evolutionary process is simply to bring it into line with other life processes such as ontogeny, behaviour and indeed the Gaian life process itself as depicted by Lovelock. It is quite clear that these are living processes rather than mechanical ones, that they are dynamic rather than passive, orderly and goal-directed rather than random. It is equally clear that they are cybernetic processes – each subprocess being monitored so that diversions from its proper goal are corrected by the overall life process. For this to be possible each must be seen as cooperative and well coordinated, rather than competitive and individualistic. Why should evolution be different?

Finally, such life processes can go wrong. Nature is neither omniscient nor omnipotent. When life processes go wrong they are no longer under control. They cease to be properly coordinated, they become atomised and individualistic, order gives rise to disorder, and to further atomisation, coordination ceases, competition and aggression take over. This atomisation process gives rise to undifferentiated or random Gaian tissue that rapidly replaces Gaia's critical structure – that which she must display if she is to be capable of maintaining her homeostasis or stability.

When they occur at the level of the individual biological organism, these destructive processes are seen as pathological. For neo-Darwinists, however, they are the normal features of the evolutionary process. How can they be? Why should the overall life process behave in a diametrically opposite manner from that of all other life processes? Is it not apparent that they have got it completely wrong, that they have failed to distinguish between pathology and physiology, between the growth of a malignant tumour and the development of differentiated tissue – between anti-evolution and evolution?

References

Chaitanya, Krishna, *The Biology of Freedom*, Somaiya Publications, 1975.

Grasse, Pierre P, *L'Evolution du Vivant*, Albin Michel, 1973.

Julian Huxley, *Evolution, the Modern Synthesis*, George Allen and Unwin (London), third impression, 1942.

Jantsch, Erich and Conrad H Waddington (eds), *Evolution and Consciousness, Human Systems in Transition*, Addison Wesley Publishing Co (Reading, MA), 1976.

Koestler, Arthur and John R Smythies (eds), *Beyond Reductionism, The Alpbach Symposium*, Hutchinson, 1969.

Lerner, IM, *Genetic Homeostasis*, Oliver and Boyd (Edinburgh), 1954.

Medawar, Peter, *The Hope of Progress*, Wildwood House (London), 1974.

Medawar, Peter, *Pluto's Republic*, Oxford University Press (Oxford and New York), 1982.

Medawar, Peter and JS Medawar, *The Life Science, Current Ideas of Biology*, Wildwood House (London), 1977.

Piaget, Jean, *Le comportement moteur de l'évolution*, Gallimard (Paris), 1976.

Polanyi, Michael, *Personal Knowledge, Towards a Post-Critical Philosophy*, Routledge & Kegan Paul (London), 1958.

Popper, Karl R, *Objective Knowledge, An Evolutionary Approach*, Clarendon Press (Oxford), 1972.

Prigogine, Ilya and Isabelle Stengers, *La nouvelle alliance*, Editions Gallimard (Paris), 1979.

Ruse, Michael, *Darwinism Defended: A Guide to the Evolution Controversies*, Addison Wesley (Reading, MA), 1982.

Waddington, CH, *The Ethical Animal*, University of Chicago Press, George Allen & Unwin (London), 1960.

Woodger, JH, *Biological Principles*, Routledge & Kegan Paul (London), 1967.

Edward Goldsmith, 'Gaia and Evolution', this article first appeared in the 1989 issue of *The Ecologist*, vol 19, no 4, www.theecologist.org. © *The Ecologist*. Also published in *Ecology and Moral Choice*, the Centre for Human Ecology, University of Edinburgh.

Index